THE ECHOES OF MANY TEXTS

Program in Judaic Studies
Brown University
BROWN JUDAIC STUDIES

Edited by
Shaye J. D. Cohen and Calvin Goldscheider

Number 313

THE ECHOES OF MANY TEXTS
Reflections on Jewish and Christian Traditions
Essays in Honor of Lou H. Silberman

edited by
William G. Dever and J. Edward Wright

THE ECHOES OF MANY TEXTS
Reflections on Jewish and Christian Traditions
Essays in Honor of Lou H. Silberman

edited by
William G. Dever and J. Edward Wright

Scholars Press
Atlanta, Georgia

THE ECHOES OF MANY TEXTS
Reflections on Jewish and Christian Traditions
Essays in Honor of Lou H. Silberman

edited by
William G. Dever and J. Edward Wright

© 1997
Brown University

Library of Congress Cataloging-in-Publication Data
The echoes of many texts : reflections on Jewish and Christian
    traditions : essays in honor of Lou H. Silberman / edited by William
    G. Dever and J. Edward Wright.
        p.   cm. — (Brown Judaic studies ; 313)
    Includes 0-7885-0417-7 (alk. paper)
    1. Bible—Criticism, interpretation, etc. 2. Amidah.
I. Silberman, Lou H. II. Dever, William G. III. Wright, J. Edward.
IV. Series.
BS413.E24 1997
220.6—dc21   97-38267
                                                        CIP
ISBN 978-1-930675-72-8 (paper : alk. paper)

Printed in the United States of America
on acid-free paper

CONTENTS

A Scribe's Prayer, by James L. Crenshaw vii

Preface ix

List of Contributors xi

Abbreviations xiii

1. William G. Dever *On Listening to the Text – and the Artifacts* 1

2. David C. Hopkins *The First Stories of Genesis and the Rhythm of the Generations* 25

3. Ziony Zevit *Proclamations to the Fruitful Tree and the Spiritualization of Androgyny* 43

4. Susan Ackerman *The Prayer of Nabonidus, Elijah on Mount Carmel, and the Development of Monotheism in Israel* 51

5. Peter Machinist *Job's Daughters and Their Inheritance in the Testament of Job and Its Biblical Congeners* 67

6. James L. Crenshaw *The Restraint of Reason, the Humility of Prayer* 81

7. Shaye J. D. Cohen *Were Pharisees and Rabbis The Leaders of Communal Prayer and Torah Study in Antiquity? The Evidence of the New Testament, Josephus, and the Church Fathers* 99

8. Shemaryahu Talmon *The "Dead Sea Scrolls" or "The Community of the Renewed Covenant?"* 115

9. J. Edward Wright *Hebrews 11:37 and the Death of the Prophet Ezekiel* 147

10. James A. Sanders *Identity, Apocalyptic, and Dialogue* 159

11. Reuven Kimelman *The Literary Structure of the Amidah and the Rhetoric of Redemption* 171

12. Michael Fishbane *Justification through Living – Martin Buber's Third Alternative* 219

Addendum to the Bibliography of Lou H. Silberman 231

Index of Authors 237

Index of Places 243

Index of Passages 243

A Scribe's Prayer

IF
    I were the pen
    In your hand
    I would yield
    To your touch
    And pour myself out
    That you might
    Be manifest
    To others.

IF
    I were the ink
    In your pen
    I would take shape
    On the page
    As you breathe,
    Dancing
    Before your eyes
    For eternity.

IF
    I were a page
    In your diary
    I would drink
    From your pen,
    Absorb your thoughts,
    And mirror
    your soul.

IF
    I were the cover
    Of your diary
    I would shelter
    Your passion
    From prying eyes
    And surround you
    With tenderness.

James L. Crenshaw
23 December 1989

Preface

It is a special privilege for us to present this collection of essays to our esteemed friend and colleague, Professor Lou H. Silberman, in honor of his eightieth birthday. This is the second *Festschrift* that Professor Silberman has received. The first, *The Divine Helmsman*, edited by James L. Crenshaw and Samuel Sandmel (New York: KTAV, 1980), was given to him upon his retirement as Hillel Professor of Jewish Literature and Thought at Vanderbilt University.

We are proud to honor Lou's eightieth birthday with another *Festschrift*; and we would be confident of tendering a third volume upon his 120th birthday, except for the fact that while he may well still be active, we shall have been deceased long ago from attempting to keep up with him.

Lou Silberman and his wife had planned to move to Tucson upon his becoming *emeritus* at Vanderbilt, partly because their daughter and her physician husband and family were here. Unfortunately, his wife died in their final year at Vanderbilt. But in the end, Lou decided to move to Tucson alone, and that is how Peter Machinist (now at Harvard) and Dever came to meet him and invite him to share his long and rich experience with us at the University of Arizona.

That was in 1980, and Lou is still actively teaching part-time in our Judaic Studies program. We thought that Lou might want to teach a year or two for therapy, or simply to "keep his hand in," as it were. Perhaps neither Lou nor we anticipated that he would enjoy virtually a second career in his "retirement years" in Arizona. Yet his research and publication have continued, as the updated bibliography appended here will demonstrate. Moreover, he has taught a variety of subjects for us.

In 1982 Lou was further honored by being elected President of the Society of Biblical Literature. Lou entitled his Presidential Address in New York "Listening to the Text," and upon rereading that we have been struck again by the lifetime's distillation of wisdom reflected there. Most academics are knowledgeable about their field; some are scholars of distinction; only a few could be regarded as truly learned. Lou Silberman is among the latter. Lou's courtly manner, old-world charm, and wide-ranging erudition flourish in any company, reminding those fortunate enough to be in his presence of the almost-lost art of genteel conversation. In Lou's Presidential Address he ranges easily from Nietzsche's inaugural lecture, to obscure Classicists, to T. S. Eliot and Thomas Mann, to modern Russian and Czech literary theorists, to the latest deconstructionists – all of this in the service of "listening" to the Biblical text.

The range of Lou Silberman's lifetime interests has taken him into the First Temple period, Second Temple studies, Christian origins, Qumran, Rabbinics, medieval Jewish philosophy, modern Jewish history, and mainstream currents of 20th century Biblical scholarship. Not only has he been an original, productive scholar in all these disciplines, but he is the rare teacher who is able to communicate the excitement of new knowledge in all these fields. And Lou has not been confined to the academy he graces so well; for many years he has been active in ecumenical affairs, especially Jewish-Christian relations.

We would like to thank the following, whose contributions made possible the symposium honoring Lou Silberman in April 1993: Prof. Robert Burns and the Religious Studies Program at the University of Arizona; Rabbi Randall M. Falk and Congregation Ohabai Sholom (Nashville, TN); Prof. and Mrs. Walter Harrelson (Vanderbilt University); Wolli and Sarah Kaelter (Long Beach, CA); Bernadine and Jack Lerman (Tucson, AZ); Mrs. Dorothy May (Nashville, TN); and Dr. Howard and Betty Lee Rosen (Nashville, TN). The featured guest speakers at the symposium were Profs. James L. Crenshaw, Michael Fishbane, and James A. Sanders, whose papers, reprinted here, made for a joyous celebration.

These past 16 years we have come to know Lou Silberman the man, the scholar, and the colleague; and we have been blessed by the experience. These essays from us and a number of other colleagues are only a small token of our esteem, our affection, and our indebtedness. We wish him עד מאה ועשרים.

September 1995
William G. Dever
J. Edward Wright

We owe a special thanks to Leonard and Doris Weiner of Tucson whose generous gift made the publication of this volume possible.

List of Contributors

Susan Ackerman, Dartmouth College

Shaye J. D. Cohen, Brown University

James L Crenshaw, Duke University

William G. Dever, University of Arizona

Michael Fishbane, University of Chicago

David C. Hopkins, Wesley Theological Seminary

Reuven Kimelman, Brandeis University

Peter Machinist, Harvard University

James A. Sanders, Claremont Graduate School

Shemaryahu Talmon, The Hebrew University of Jerusalem

J. Edward Wright, University of Arizona

Ziony Zevit, University of Judaism

Abbreviations

AB	Anchor Bible
ABD	D. N. Freedman (ed.), *Anchor Bible Dictionary*
AfO	*Archiv für Orientforschung*
AJSL	*American Journal of Semitic Languages and Literature*
ANESTP	J. B. Pritchard (ed.), *Ancient Near Eastern Supplementary Texts and Pictures*
ANET	J. B. Pritchard (ed.), *Ancient Near Eastern Texts*
ANQ	*Andover Newton Quarterly*
ANRW	*Aufstieg und Niedergang der römischen Welt*
ATD	Das Alte Testament Deutsch
BA	*Biblical Archaeologist*
BASOR	*Bulletin of the American Schools of Oriental Research*
BBB	Bonner biblische Beiträge
BBSt	L. W. King, *Babylonian Boundary Stones*
BETL	Bibliotheca ephemeridum theologicarum lovaniensium
Bib	*Biblica*
BJRL	*Bulletin of the John Rylands University Library of Manchester*
BJS	Brown Judaic Studies

BZ	*Biblische Zeitschrift*
BZAW	Beihefte zur *ZAW*
CBC	Cambridge Bible Commentary
CBQ	*Catholic Biblical Quarterly*
CCSL	Corpus Christianorum. Series Latina
CII	*Corpus inscriptionum iudaicarum*
ConBOT	Coniectanea biblica, Old Testament
CSEL	Corpus scriptorum ecclesiasticorum latinorum
CTA	A. Herdner, *Corpus des tablettes en cunéiformes alphabétiques*
DJD	Discoveries in the Judaean Desert
EA	J. A. Knudtzon, *Die El-Amarna Tafeln*
ETL	*Ephemerides theologicae lovanienses*
FOTL	The Forms of the Old Testament Literature
GCS	*Griechischen christlichen Schriftsteller*
GKC	Gesenius' Hebrew Grammar, ed. E. Kautzsch, tr. A. E. Cowley
HAR	Hebrew Annual Review
HNT	Handbuch zum Neuen Testament
HTR	*Harvard Theological Review*
HUCA	*Hebrew Union College Annual*
ICC	International Critical Commentary
IDB	G. A. Buttrick (ed.), *Interpreter's Dictionary of the Bible*
IEJ	*Israel Exploration Journal*
IES	Israel Exploration Society
Int	*Interpretation*
ITQ	*Irish Theological Quarterly*
JAAR	*Journal of the American Academy of Religion*
JANES	*Journal of the Ancient Near Eastern Society*

Abbreviations

JAOS	*Journal of the American Oriental Society*
JBL	*Journal of Biblical Literature*
JCS	*Journal of Cuneiform Studies*
JJS	*Journal of Jewish Studies*
JPS	Jewish Publication Society
JQR	*Jewish Quarterly Review*
JSHRZ	Jüdische Schriften aus hellenistisch-römischer Zeit
JSNT	*Journal for the Study of the New Testament*
JSOT	*Journal for the Study of the Old Testament*
JSOTSup	Journal for the Study of the Old Testament – Supplement Series
JSS	*Journal of Semitic Studies*
JTS	*Journal of Theological Studies*
KTU	M. Dietrich, O. Loretz, and J. Sanmartín, *Die keilalphabetischen Texte aus Ugarit einschliesslich der keilalphabetischen Texte ausserhalb Ugarits 1: Transkription*
NCB	New Century Bible
NICNT	New International Commentary on the New Testament
NTS	*New Testament Studies*
PAAJR	*Proceedings of the American Academy of Jewish Research*
PEQ	*Palestine Exploration Quarterly*
PG	J. Migne, *Patrologia graeca*
PL	J. Migne, *Patrologia latina*
PVTG	Pseudepigrapha Veteris Testamenti graece
RA	*Revue d'assyriologie et d'archéologie orientale*
RB	*Revue biblique*
RevQ	*Revue de Qumran*

RSR	Recherches de science religieuse
SBLDS	SBL Dissertation Series
SBLMS	SBL Monograph Series
SBLTT	SBL Texts and Translations
SC	Sources chrétiennes
SNTSMS	Society for New Testament Studies Monograph Series
TDNT	G. Kittel and G. Friedrich (eds.), *Theological Dictionary of the New Testament*
TDOT	G. J. Botterweck and H. Ringgren (eds.), *Theological Dictionary of the Old Testament*
THKNT	Theologischer Handkommentar zum Neuen Testament
TLZ	*Theologische Literaturzeitung*
TU	Texte und Untersuchungen
TWAT	G. J. Botterweck and H. Ringgren (eds.), *Theologisches Wörterbuch zum Alten Testament*
TWNT	G. Kittel and G. Friedrich (eds.), *Theologisches Wörterbuch zum Neuen Testament*
TZ	*Theologische Zeitschrift*
VAB	*Vorderasiatische Bibliothek*
VT	*Vetus Testamentum*
VTSup	*Vetus Testamentum, Supplements*
WBC	Word Biblical Commentary
WMANT	Wissenschaftliche Monographien zum Alten und Neuen Testament
ZAW	*Zeitschrift für die alttestamentliche Wissenschaft*

1

"On Listening to the Text – and the Artifacts"

William G. Dever

In this tribute to an esteemed friend, colleague, and mentor, Professor Lou H. Silberman, I would like to respond as an archaeologist and historian to the theme of his 1984 SBL Presidential Address: "On Listening to the Text."[1] What I shall attempt to show in this essay is (1) that the textual and artifactual data now available concerning ancient Israel are remarkably similar in character; (2) that the history of scholarly interpretation of both classes of data runs surprisingly parallel; and (3) that these convergences point to an interdisciplinary dialogue that holds the best hope yet for writing an adequate history of ancient Israel. How, then, shall we listen to *both* texts and artifacts?

A. How the Textual Record and the Archaeological Record Compare

We may begin by noting that the *corpus* of individual texts and artifacts constitutes in each case what we may call a "record" of the past. That the texts of the Hebrew Bible are a record of sorts is obvious, although the nature of that record is disputed. On the other hand, archaeologists have also been seeking to define a phenomenon known as "the archaeological record" since the dawn of the "New Archaeology" some three decades ago. By general consensus today, the "archaeological record" may be said to consist of (1) all those physical remains that survive from past human actions, i.e., not only artifacts or objects strictly

---

[1] See L. H. Silberman "Listening to the Text," *JBL* 102:1 (1989) 3–26.

speaking; (2) any observable traces of human impact upon the external world and the natural environment, or "cultural deposits" of many kinds (including the burials of the humans themselves); (3) the above remains situated in their larger spatial and temporal context; and (4) the whole of the evidence seen in the light of the intellectual and social matrix that we moderns inevitably bring to the task of interpretation. Need it be stressed that Biblical texts must be seen as constituting a parallel and very similar kind of record of the past – indeed, with the same scope, complexity, and limitations?

Before proceeding, we may attempt in the interests of brevity to list some of the essential characteristics of both texts and artifacts – in a simplified chart–form, noting similarities and differences.

	Biblical Texts (as *preserved*)	*Archaeological Artifacts* (as *preserved*)
1.	Concretize thought and behavior	Concretize thought and behavior
2.	Symbolic, "encoded" messages of past	Symbolic, "encoded" messages of past
3.	Express deliberate intent, imagination	Express deliberate intent, imagination
4.	Selective, elitist by nature	Broadly representative, "populist"
5.	Heavily edited in transmission	Constitute random sample
6.	Reflect principally ideology	Reflect common practice
7.	Closed *corpus*	Dynamic, expanding source of data
8.	Continuous tradition	"Broken" tradition
9.	Only a residue of past	Only a residue of past
10.	"Curated artifact"	"Curated artifacts"
11.	Refract the past	Refract the past
12.	Literature	"Real" life

Of these 12 diagnostic characteristics, fully half are the same for both texts and artifacts, and a number of others are similar or overlap. And, as we shall argue, even those characteristics that differ share something, in the fact that the same *interpretive methods* are required of the historian who works with these two types of data. Specifically, both texts and artifacts are "objective," yet require "subjective" interpretation if the record is to be read correctly. Both contain valid information about the past, but only in the form of inferences we make that must be tested against some external criteria. These "facts," when established as such, come to constitute true *data* only when placed within an intellectual framework that gives them meaning in relation to specific questions that are appropriate to history–writing. Furthermore, the use of both classes of data requires an interpretive methodology that is fundamentally genetic, evolutionary, and comparative. Finally, if "reading" both the textual and archaeological record is the appropriate metaphor, then it is obvious that the interpreter must master the peculiar vocabulary, grammar, and syntax of each class of data. Otherwise, the text will remain as "mute" as some misguided Biblical scholars maintain that the artifacts are.

B. Parallel Schools of Interpretation Until Recently

We shall return shortly to this notion of a common hermeneutic that may be developing. First, however, we need to look at how texts and artifacts have in fact already been interpreted in various scholarly "schools" over the past century or so that have taken similar approaches, although not deliberately or explicitly so. Indeed, no one to my knowledge, writing on the history of either Biblical or archaeological scholarship, has ever pointed out these parallels.[2] Here we simply note some of the more obvious.

1. *Lower or textual criticism.* This earliest manifestation of modern Biblical criticism in the mid–late 19th century sought to establish, as nearly as possible, an *Urtext* (a *Hebraica Veritas*), so as to isolate the fundamental body of data with which the historian could then work. This approach had its counterpart in 19th and early 20th century Syro–Palestinian archaeology in the attempt of pioneers like Robinson, the explorers of the Survey of Western Palestine, and others to make the first modern site–maps and to clarifying the existence and nature of *tells* or stratified mounds – the raw source–materials of the archaeological record. Philology as the basic tool of textual studies was matched in archaeology by learning the "language" of the landscape. In both disciplines

---

[2] In the following discussion I shall give references only for more recent schools of Biblical interpretation, since earlier schools are well known. Recent histories of interpretation in general archaeology, with full bibliography, are *Archaeological Thought in America* (ed. C. C. Lamberg–Karlovsky; Cambridge: Cambridge University Press, 1989); and B. G. Trigger, *A History of Archaeological Thought* (Cambridge: Cambridge University Press, 1989). For the history of interpretation in Syro–Palestinian archaeology, see W. G. Dever "Syro–Palestinian Archaeology," *The Hebrew Bible and Its Modern Interpreters* (ed. D. A. Knight and G. M. Tucker; Chico, CA: Scholars Press, 1985) 31–74 and references there to earlier works. See also nn. 3, 10, 12, 39, 43, 45 below.

the foundations were thus laid for all subsequent research (although, of course, these efforts must still continue, even if with diminishing and less revolutionary results).

2. *Higher or literary criticism.* Building upon better manuscript traditions and a more secure text, higher or literary criticism of the Hebrew Bible was able to turn to the analysis of individual books and larger literary units, raising questions of composition, sources, authors/redactors, date, historical circumstances and intent, as well as the essential question of historicity. This effort was paralleled almost exactly in the "stratigraphic revolution" of Syro-Palestinian archaeology's second generation, following Petrie in the 1890's and extending through Kenyon's work in the 1950's–1960's. Here the questions addressed of the Palestinian *tell* were very much like those posed of the Biblical texts: how to understand, separate, and date the complex layers of a typical mound, and how to explain the origins and significance of these strata and their contents. In both disciplines, although they still operated mostly independently, the larger objective was to work out a chronological-cultural history, based upon a proper ordering and comprehension of the basic data in texts and artifacts.

It is not, I think, a coincidence that "typologies" of sorts played a prominent role in both disciplines – J, E, D, and P in Biblical studies, and soil-layers and ceramic and other artifact types in archaeology – or that a typologist like Albright could contribute simultaneously to both disciplines. More than anything else, it was a common methodology, although largely unacknowledged as such, that enabled "Biblical archaeology" in its heyday to relate to Protestant Old Testament Biblical studies during its *floruit* in the 1920's–1950's.[3]

3. *Form criticism.* Beginning early in the 20th century, form criticism (*Formgeschichte* or *Gattungsgeschichte*) began to focus on individual sub-units or pericopes of the text, attempting to classify literary forms. These smaller traditions, with their own history of transmission, were thought to derive largely from "folk literature" and to have been handed down orally for long

---

[3] On Albright's use of typology, see W. G. Dever, "What Remains of the House That Albright Built?" *BA* 56 (1993) 25–36 and references there. For the "Protestant bias" in Biblical and archaeological scholarship, see W. G. Dever "The Contribution of Archaeology to Canaanite and Early Israelite Religion," *Ancient Israelite Religion: Essays in Honor of Frank Moore Cross* (ed. P. D. Miller, P. D. Hanson, and S. D. McBride; Philadelphia: Fortress, 1987) 210–17.

periods in cultic circles or other social institutions. Thus following Gunkel there were efforts to place such literary forms as myth, sagas, cult-legends, legal material, and other genres in their original setting – or *Sitz im Leben* – so as to understand them better. Unfortunately, as I shall show, an incipient historical thrust was usually blunted by the literary bias of form critics, who settled for what was in fact merely a *Sitz im Literatur*, and who indeed were often poorly informed by a knowledge of *actual* socio-economic conditions in ancient Palestine, such as archaeology might have provided. This deficiency of form criticism has finally been acknowledged by a few current Biblical scholars, with at least lip-service paid to archaeology.[4]

The archaeological parallel to form criticism of the early-mid 20th century was the further development of typology as an *explicit* method. This aimed not simply at classifying artifacts, but included the beginning attempts to explain recurrent patterns (either individual traits or larger "assemblages") in the light of cultural and technological factors (and, later, environmental factors). Thus the discussion in the 1940's–1960's focused more and more on typical archaeological genres in their overall context. It could be argued that this approach in both disciplines was fundamentally a further attempt to get at the "prehistory" of the basic record as we now have it, either textual or artifactual. Yet there was a tendency to beg the question of any *actual* history to be derived from either source.

4. *Tradition and redaction criticism.* These approaches, often combined (as *Überlieferungsgeschichte*), moved further in order to study the nature and development of the individual genres that form criticism had sought to isolate. The questions were "How did these genres grow from oral to written traditions?" "How were they combined into larger literary units?" "How did they grow by stages into *the* tradition?" Finally, "How was this larger tradition transmitted and finally transformed into the Hebrew Bible as we have it?" In short, "How did oral and literary genres/traditions become 'text' (or in this case, Scripture)?" Here, we are dealing not simply with the prehistory of the Biblical text, but with the development of the final (or, shortly,

---

[4] For tacit acknowledgments of the limitations of traditional searches for a *Sitz im Leben* in Biblical scholarship, see R. Knierim, "Criticism of Literary Features, Form, Tradition, and Redaction," *The Hebrew Bible and Its Modern Interpreters*, 144; T. L. Thompson, *Early History of the Israelite People from the Written and Archaeological Sources* (Leiden: Brill, 1992) 391, 392.

Canonical) form of the text itself. Again, however, establishing the history of the formation of the *text* as "record" did not necessarily lead to grappling with the issue of how one might derive any history *per se* from that record. That omission would lead ultimately to the present crisis in Biblical historiography, to which we return below.

An uncannily exact parallel to the *Überlieferungsgeschichte* of the 1960's–1970's came in Syro–Palestinian archaeology in the 1960's–1980's in what was often called "formation processes" of the archaeological record."[5] At first, this approach was mainly an outgrowth of the stratigraphic revolution of the 1950's. This had been spearheaded by Kenyon at Jericho, then followed up by American excavations at Shechem, Gezer, and other sites in the 1960's. Prompted initially by the pragmatic question of how best to excavate and record a stratified Palestinian mound, excavators soon realized that they had first to grasp the complex natural and cultural factors that make up the depositional history of a typical mound. In short, how did a *tell*, like a text or textual tradition, take shape? Neither the textual nor the archaeological record can be read properly until we possess an adequate understanding of the process of its original formation, *plus* its long transformation over time until it comes into our hands today.

5. *Religionsgeschichte.* Overlapping and closely related to the above schools of Biblical criticism was a school of historical and comparative religion (*Religionsgeschichte,* or religio–historical criticism) that was influential up until the 1940's and still has some proponents. Here the focus was upon what seemed to be the dominant role of religion and cult in ancient Israel on the shaping of the literary traditions of the Hebrew Bible. This school extended the critical, historical, and comparative methods already in vogue specifically to Israelite religion, often with the positivist presuppositions of that period. Occasionally, ethnographic and folkloric parallels from other religions were employed, and even some archaeological evidence as it was understood at the time.

---

[5] For general orientation, see M. B. Schiffer, *Formation Processes of the Archaeological Record* (Albuquerque: University of New Mexico Press, 1987). Only scant literature exists with specific reference to Palestinian archaeology, although there is considerable experience with *tell*–formation and a kind of common "oral tradition."

It is instructive to note parallels to *Religionsgeschichte* in archaeology of the same era. Indeed, the interest in ancient Israelite religion and cult had prevailed from the very beginning of Syro–Palestinian, and especially "Biblical," archaeology, to the extent that the early literature abounds in attempts to explain nearly everything that seemed "exotic" as evidence of religious belief and practice. The one effort, however, to completely rewrite the history of Israel's religion in the light of archaeological discoveries was in W. C. Graham and H. C. May, *Culture and Conscience: An Archaeological Study of the New Religious Past in Ancient Palestine*.[6] It is no accident that H. G. May, a distinguished Biblical scholar, was also a member of the Staff of the Oriental Institute of Chicago excavations at Megiddo and co-authored with Graham another work entitled *Material Remains of the Megiddo Cult*.[7] The positive and lasting contribution of the "cultic school" in archaeology was limited, however, by the fact that the field was then dominated by Biblical scholars. Thus it was dependent upon the naïveté of conservatives on the one hand, and upon the equally naïve evolutionary optimism of liberal scholars on the other hand. The result was that all these early reconstructions of Israelite religion have been overturned by modern scholarship, both Biblical and archaeological, which in the last decade has returned to the subject of religion and cult with a wealth of new data and vastly superior models, much of the evidence drawn from archaeology. It is no exaggeration to say that this fledgling dialogue implies that we are currently in the process of rewriting the entire history of ancient Israelite religion.[8]

6. *The ethnographic approach.* Closely related to *Religionsgeschichte* with its commitment to empirical method and comparative religion was a school of Biblical studies that was never perhaps formalized, but which utilized universal folklore and ethnographic data from primitive societies past and present to illuminate the cultural and religious background of the Hebrew Bible. This approach, often called the "anthropological school," goes all the way back to W. Robertson Smith's *Lectures on the Religion of the Semites* (1909)[9] and continues in the well known

---

[6] (Chicago: University of Chicago Press, 1936). See further Dever, "Contribution of Archaeology," 210–22.
[7] (University of Chicago Oriental Institute Publications 26; Chicago: University of Chicago Press, 1935).
[8] See further Dever, "Contribution of Archaeology"; J. S. Holladay, "Religion in Israel and Judah under the Monarchy: An Explicitly Archaeological Approach," *Ancient Israelite Religion: Essays in Honor of Frank Moore Cross*, 249–99.
[9] (3d ed.; London: A & C Black, 1927).

works of J. G. Frazer in the early 20th century. Part of this approach's momentum continued in later *Religionsgeschichte*, particularly in the Scandinavian and British "Myth and Ritual" schools; and it was felt later still in modern socio-anthropological approaches (below).

The parallel to this early school of Biblical studies in archaeology was obviously ethnoarchaeology. This, however, did not break upon the scene in Near Eastern archaeology until the 1970's, as a strong component of the "New archaeology," and even today ethnoarchaeology has made little impact upon Syro-Palestinian archaeology.[10] That is partly because few practitioners of our discipline have been trained in anthropology, much less ethnography; and in any case, the rapid modernization of pastoral nomads and other marginal groups in the Middle East and the politicization of the whole area have made productive ethnographic fieldwork virtually impossible.

7. *Old Testament Theology.* Old Testament theology has had a venerable tradition within Biblical studies since the 18th century, and despite frequent obituaries it remains vigorous in some circles even today.[11] Its primary objective, whether in its dogmatic or its supposedly "descriptive-historical" guise, has been to describe the normative religion of the Old Testament (*sic*) and to systematize this theologically in terms of binding religious beliefs and practices for the modern Christian community. We may specify "Christian," since Biblical theology has never had any appeal for Jewish scholars of the Hebrew Bible. Indeed, Old Testament theology may best be described not as a historical (or even exegetical) discipline at all, but as a branch of Christian apologetics. As I have recently shown,[12] it is scarcely interested in the history of ancient Israel *per se*; unable to

---

[10] For convenient orientation, see *Ethnoarchaeology: Implications of Ethnography for Archaeology* (ed. C. Kramer; New York: Columbia University Press, 1979); I. Hodder, *Symbols in Action: Ethnoarchaeological Studies of Material Culture* (Cambridge: Cambridge University Press, 1982). The literature on pastoral nomadism is vast, but references will be found in *Pastoralism in the Levant: Archaeological Materials in Anthropological Perspectives* (ed. O. Bar-Yosef and A. Khazanov; Madison, WI: Prehistory Press, 1992).

[11] See G. F. Hasel, *Old Testament Theology: Basic Issues in the Current Debate* (4th ed.; Grand Rapids: Eerdmans, 1992).

[12] On the implications for archaeology and the history of Israelite religion, see my forthcoming paper "Philology, Theology, Archaeology, and the Pursuit of Israelite Religion" (SBL/ASOR Annual Meeting, 1993); and, provisionally, "Biblical Theology and Biblical Archaeology," *HTR* 73 (1980) 1-16; and "Contribution of Archaeology."

grasp the actual vitality and diversity of Israelite religion, especially the "popular cults"; and of little interest to comparative religionists or Syro–Palestinian archaeologists today.

Nevertheless, Old Testament Theology had its direct counterpart in previous generations in the classic school of "Biblical archaeology." Though now defunct as a serious intellectual enterprise, much less an academic discipline, "Biblical archaeology" dominated much of the history of American Syro–Palestinian and even broader Near Eastern archaeology from its beginnings in the 19th century up until the 1970's. Since I have discussed this movement in detail elsewhere,[13] here I shall only point out briefly the similarities between Biblical theology and Biblical archaeology, which not by chance ran their courses concurrently. Again, at the risk of over–simplifying, we may chart the convergences, which in every case are direct.

Biblical Theology	*Biblical Archaeology*
The Bible text taken as starting–point	The Bible text taken as starting–point
"Historical" agenda actually drawn from theological issues	"Historical" agenda actually drawn from theological issues
Conservative, tendentious throughout in basic method	Conservative, tendentious throughout in basic method
Drew heavily on popular religious mentality in America	Drew heavily on popular religious mentality in America
Operated with positivist presuppositions	Operated with positivist presuppositions
Actually begged the broader historical questions	Actually begged the broader historical questions
Resisted newer inter–disciplinary methods	Resisted newer inter–disciplinary methods
Could not accommodate "secular" approaches	Could not accommodate "secular" approaches
Gradually became parochial or obsolete	Gradually became parochial or obsolete

Even though there were factors other than these that were operative in the demise of "Biblical archaeology" in the 1970's – such as competition from foreign "national schools" and a crisis in funding – two

---

[13] See Dever, "Pursuit of Israelite Religion."

facts remain clear. (1) As Albright and Wright, with their peculiar *combination* of Biblical studies and archaeological research, passed from the scene in the early 1970's, so did "Biblical archaeology," which had in many ways always been uniquely Protestant and American.[14] (2) At the very same time, Brevard S. Childs could write an obituary of the Biblical *theology* movement, *Biblical Theology in Crisis*.[15] Both movements had construed the history of ancient Palestine and of Israel as a sort of "religio–political history" that was thought to yield a universal, self-evident cultural meaning. The effort was perhaps noble, but doomed to failure.

8. *Socio–anthropological approaches*. Partly continuing but expanding the older *Religionsgeschichte* and ethnographic approaches, several newer ways of looking at the Hebrew Bible and ancient Israel have drawn upon modern sociological studies and various anthropological models and case–studies ("social scientific" criticism). From Max Weber in the 1920's–1930's to current studies by Gottwald, Frick, Flannagan, Coote, Lemche, Wilson, and many others, the value of the socio–anthropological approach, while never dominant, has been clear – never moreso than today, I would argue.

Not only does this approach produce many exciting new insights, it also draws Biblical studies closer methodologically to Syro–Palestinian archaeology, which has been moving in similar directions because of its own *rapprochement* with general and especially with New World archaeology. For the latter discipline, at least as practiced by Americans, nearly all the underlying theory, the working hypotheses, and the analytical methods are drawn not from history (certainly not theology), but from anthropology in one fashion or another. And the recent volume *The Archaeology of Society in the Holy Land*, edited by T. E. Levy, will mark the beginnings of a more self–conscious archaeology of society in our discipline.[16]

---

[14] See references in nn. 2, 12 above. See further Dever, "Syro–Palestinian and Biblical Archaeology," 31–74; *idem*, "Archaeology, Syro–Palestinian and Biblical," *Anchor Bible Dictionary* (6 vols.; ed. D. N. Freedman; New York: Doubleday, 1992) 1.354–64.
[15] (Philadelphia: Westminster, 1970); cf. Dever, "Biblical Theology."
[16] (London: Leicester University Press, 1995). For socio–anthropological approaches to the Hebrew Bible, see J. W. Rogerson, *Anthropology and the Old Testament* (Oxford: Blackwell, 1978); N. W. Gottwald, "Sociological Method in the Study of Ancient Israel," *Encounter with the Text: Form and History in the Hebrew Bible* (ed. M. J. Buss; Philadelphia: Fortress, 1979) 69–81; R. R. Wilson, *Sociological Approaches to the Old Testament* (Philadelphia: Fortress, 1984); R. C. Culley,

C. Recent Interpretive Approaches: Toward a New Hermeneutic?

The foregoing sketch of parallel schools of interpretation in Biblical and archaeological studies up until some 20 years ago is suggestive. I would argue, however, that more recent trends in both disciplines pave the way for the first dialogue *between* texts and artifacts, with unique possibilities for illuminating the past in general, and the phenomenon of ancient Israel in particular.

1. *Structuralism.* Structuralism as a putative method, much less a school, is nearly impossible to define. But the approach as applied sporadically in recent Biblical studies has sought to penetrate behind the texts to comprehend the underlying mental construct as a whole, as a closed system yet one capable of transformation (the "deep structure"). Often the analysis focuses on bipolar opposites that constitute universal themes in the myths, and often function as symbols or "signs": male/female; life/death; good/bad; nature/culture; immanence/transcendence; etc. Structuralism originated not, of course, in Biblical studies, but in cultural anthropology, and especially in linguistics. Because of its interest in the structure of society, Structuralism is sometimes allied with Marxist notions of the social relations of production, and the relation of these to ideology, as they shape society (Marx was not simply a "vulgar materialist").

Structuralism has had little if any impact on Syro–Palestinian archaeology, although it has had its advocates in the general field of archaeology. Yet if there *is* a discernible "deep structure" in texts, then it is reasonable to suppose that some such structure exists in artifactual remains as well; and, furthermore, it is evident that artifacts, like texts, are "signs" and have symbolic meaning.

2. *Structuralism, Semiotics, and New Literary Criticism.* Similar in many ways to Structuralism is Semiotics – a "science of how language works as a set of symbols" – and several related approaches that sometimes go under the banner of New Literary

---

"Exploring New Directions," *The Hebrew Bible and Its Modern Interpreters*, 184–89; J. W. Flanagan, "New Constructions in Social World Studies," *The Bible and the Politics of Exegesis* (ed. P. Jobling, P. L. Day, and G. T. Sheppard; Cleveland: Pilgrim Press, 1991) 209–23. For socio–anthropological approaches in Syro–Palestinian archaeology, see Ø. S. La Bianca, "Sociocultural Anthropology and Syro–Palestinian Archaeology," *Benchmarks in Time and Culture. An Introduction to Palestinian Archaeology* (ed. J. F. Drinkard, G. L. Mattingly, and J. M. Miller; Atlanta: Scholars Press, 1988) 369–87.

Criticism.[17] The effort of the latter is directed toward a formal description of the fundamental structure of a text as "discourse." Obviously this discourse is associated with some meaning; but the question is not primarily what texts "mean," but rather "what makes meaning possible?" In short, how is the text *able* to say what it says; how does it "signify," and to whom? The basic tool of the newer literary approaches is often "metalanguage," a special language of description that focuses on the play among "signifying elements" in the text – mostly opposites/contrasts that are said to make "meaning" possible.

At the heart of these varied approaches is the notion of *symbol*, understood as a primary language that emerges directly and simultaneously out of experience. In a secondary stage, this symbolic language comes to be arranged in narrative form as "myth," but this is not, however, yet at the stage of reflective thought. These symbolized myths, in turn, must be analyzed by the interpreter in terms of a double structure, as: (1) conveying obvious, literal meaning; and (2) as analogies. Texts, then – Biblical or other – do refer to a "reality," but in different and special ways. They do say something to somebody; they offer at least the possibility of recreating the world that was real to their authors and/or editors, if not an "objective" reality.

New Literary Criticism, with its emphasis on narrative history and the intent of the text, is clearly related to older approaches, as well as more recent schools like rhetorical and canonical criticism, and therefore it seems accessible to many Biblical scholars (at least in its less extreme forms). Unfortunately, New Literary Criticism falls easily into a deconstructionist mode: the text itself means nothing, and *we* must supply whatever meaning we choose, largely in terms of our own contemporary needs. There are no "truths" about the past to be learned; our supposed knowledge of the past is conditioned entirely by the modern context of the quest, mostly political. Ultimately, there is no history, only propaganda – theirs and ours. Thus the extremes of New Literary Criticism – often in the guise of the radical New Critical Theory of the "Frankfurt school" (below) – may tend to discredit it. In that case, few Biblical historians or historical archaeologists will find this approach congenial or productive.

---

[17] On various aspects of New Literary Criticism, including semiotics, see R. Alter, *The Art of Biblical Narrative* (New York: Basic Books, 1981); Culley, "Exploring New Directions," 175–80; P. Ricoeur, *Essays on Biblical Interpretation* (Philadelphia: L. S. Modge, 1980).

Despite these caveats, a few Syro–Palestinian archaeologists (this writer and one or two others!) are beginning to show an interest in semiotics, structuralism, and New Literary Criticism – if for no other reason than the fact that it is instructive to view the textual record and the archaeological record as parallel "texts to be read." Indeed, one of the emergent trends in today's "post–processualist" archaeology, after the long reign of the "New Archaeology," is epitomized in Ian Hodder's recent book, *Reading the Past: Current Approaches to Interpretation in Archaeology*.[18]

The main title is significant. Moving substantially beyond the "New Archaeology," with its largely functionalist notion of culture as ecological/technological adaptation, as well as his own previous structuralist models, Hodder advocates a more idealist and historical approach that he calls "contextual" – literally artifacts "with texts." But he goes even further in defining the archaeological record itself as a "text," and conversely written texts as "artifacts." Thus both can and must be "read" – indeed in similar ways, if a common "generative grammar" can be developed. Hodder says that such a notion "has long been tacitly assumed in archaeology." But he gives few examples; and he does not expand much on this fecund idea, beyond saying that artifacts are not necessarily "mute," if we can work out suitable principles of interpretation. At the Second International Congress on Biblical Archaeology in Jerusalem in 1990, I called attention to the work of Hodder and other current "post–processualist" archaeologists as possibly heralding a return to the concept of history in Syro–Palestinian archaeology – with wide–ranging implications for a "new Biblical archaeology" (although I prefer another name).[19] Yet it is now possible to go much further.

3. *Toward a "New Hermeneutic."* The foregoing list of parallels between interpretive schools in Biblical studies and Syro–Palestinian archaeology, while already impressive, could be expanded. For instance, canonical criticism (noted above) addresses the Hebrew Bible as a complete witness, a literary *corpus* closed for good reasons at a given point in time, as though

---

[18] (Cambridge: Cambridge University Press, 1986); for critical assessment of Hodder and other "post–processual" archaeologists, see W. G. Dever "Archaeology and the Current Crisis in Israelite Historiography" (forthcoming in *Eretz–Israel* 25 [1996], the Y. Aviram volume) and many references there.

[19] W. G. Dever, "Biblical Archaeology: Death and Rebirth," *Biblical Archaeology Today, 1990. Proceedings of the Second International Congress on Biblical Archaeology* (ed. A. Biran, J. Aviram; Jerusalem: Israel Exploration Society, 1993) 706–22.

religious authorities then "knew best."[20] Studies of the formation processes of the archaeological record (above) seek similarly to address the question of why a *tell* is the way we confront it today, and whether it is possible to penetrate behind human and cultural transformations over time to reveal an alternative or more comprehensive view of past realities, no longer easily visible in the mound itself. Or again, in current Biblical studies several marginal movements such as Radical Feminism, Liberation Theology, New Critical Theory, and New Hermeneutics have had some impact, even on mainstream scholarship.[21] Parallels to all these approaches to Biblical texts can be found in world archaeology,[22] although only sporadically in Syro–Palestinian archaeology. Some women's issues, however, have been raised in the call for a shift of attention from the prevailing "political history" to a new family or "domestic archaeology," which would include the study of popular and women's cults in the light of archaeological evidence.[23] Also significant is the willingness of a few Syro–Palestinian archaeologists to confront the role of modern ideology in shaping archaeological research, including not only religion and politics, but elitism, economic considerations, nationalism, and even racism.[24] Such protests are, however, little more than murmurs compared to the bold views of writers like M. Shanks and C. Tilley, whose work *Re-constructing Archaeology: Theory and Practice*[25] regards archaeology as a powerful tool for "cultural

---

[20] On canonical criticism, see J. A. Sanders, *Canon and Community: A Guide to Canonical Criticism* (Philadelphia: Fortress Press, 1984); G. T. Sheppard, "Canonical Criticism," *Anchor Bible Dictionary*, 1.861–66.

[21] On some of the most recent trends in Biblical criticism, see Culley, "Exploring New Directions"; N. K. Gottwald, *The Bible and Liberation: Political and Social Hermeneutics* (rev. ed.; Mary Knoll, NY: Orbis Books, 1993); and several of the essays in Jobling, Day, and Sheppard, eds., *Politics of Exegesis*.

[22] See, for instance, M. Shanks and C. Tilley, *Re-constructing Archaeology: Theory and Practice* (Cambridge: Cambridge University Press, 1987); G. Marcus and M. M. J. Fisher, *Anthropology as Cultural Critique* (Chicago: University of Chicago Press, 1987); and other references in Dever, "Crisis in Israelite Historiography." The latest and best introductions are *Critical Traditions in Contemporary Archaeology* (ed. V. Pinski and A. Wylie; Cambridge: Cambridge University Press, 1989); and *Processual and Post–Processual Archaeologies* (ed. R. W. Preucel; Carbondale, IL: University of Southern Illinois Press, 1991).

[23] See C. Meyers, *Discovering Eve: Ancient Israelite Women in Context* (New York: Oxford University Press, 1988).

[24] See, for instance, M. Broshi, "Religion, Ideology, and Politics and Their Impact on Palestinian Archaeology," *Israel Museum Journal* (1987) 13-32.

[25] See n. 22 above.

critique." A considerable radical, post-positivist, post-modern, literature of this sort is now appearing, especially in Britain, in both archaeology and anthropology, some of it Neo-Marxist, all of it controversial. Yet the hubbub surrounding the "new nihilism" could serve as a timely reminder of the value and relevance of archaeological investigation – of "the uses of the past" – one that might be heartening to Syro-Palestinian and "Biblical" archaeologists who have always thought of themselves as being in the humanist tradition. The continuing dilemma, however, is simply: "What, if anything, *can* we know with certainty of the past?"

4. *Back to epistemology.* Most encouraging of all recent parallel developments in both Biblical and archaeological studies is the growing concern with epistemological and historiographical issues, what might be called the "new hermeneutics."[26] The maturation of both disciplines, and particularly the interdisciplinary thrust, has brought us to the point where we *must* ask basic methodological questions. In particular, the question of how to write an adequate history of ancient Israel and her religion – of *sources* – is one that both Biblical scholars and archaeologists (at last) are beginning to confront. Indeed, it is not too much to speak of a crisis in current scholarship that is fundamentally hermeneutical. As Rolf Rendtorff recently put it: "The question is rather whether the texts are Pre-Exilic or post-Exilic ... We will have to redesign our image of Israel's history and the history of its religion."[27]

Above I noted some of the problems and possibilities of semiotics, structuralism, and New Literary Criticism for developing a common hermeneutic. It may be useful to expand that discussion at this point. These and related newer approaches, which in anthropology may simply be called "interpretive anthropology," may be congenial to archaeologists because they tend to use the metaphor of "culture as a text to be read," a notion popularized by Clifford Geertz.[28] It is obviously only one step further to extend the notion of "text" to that which is

---

[26] See Culley, "Exploring New Directions"; Knierim, "Literary Features"; and several essays in Jobling, Day, and Sheppard, eds., *Politics of Exegesis*.
[27] R. Rendtorff, "The Paradigm is Changing: Hopes – and Fears," *Biblical Interpretation* 1:1 (1992). See further my forthcoming "Crisis in Israelite Historiography."
[28] See, for example, C. Geertz, "Thick Description: Toward an Interpretive View of Culture," in Geertz, *The Interpretation of Cultures* (New York: Basic Books, 1973).

enmeshed with culture and gives it concrete expression, namely *material culture*. Furthermore, despite the unfortunate anti–historical bias of some of its practitioners, Structuralism is attractive because focusing on "structure" means looking critically at society and culture, which are the basic phenomena that the archaeologist seeks ultimately to comprehend, as well as being the "context" (Hodder's phrase) within which all material culture remains must be understood. Finally, both Structuralist and archaeological (as well as Biblical/textual) studies today must grapple with the fundamental problem of the "meaning" of symbols and symbolic actions – that is, not merely with materialist but with idealist explanations of culture and culture change (including religion). Here Hodder's "cognitive" archaeology, or "archaeology of mind" – which to many New Archaeologists signals a return to the pre–scientific and subjective *Kulturgeschichte*, or historical particularism, of the past – is actually a positive sign of anthropology and archaeology's coming of age.[29] Partly as a reaction to the reductionist paradigms of the previous generation, it is now being recognized once again, and with a new sophistication, that *ideology* is not a mere "epiphenomenon," but instead is a basic component of all cultures. Thus we may speak of archaeological (and historical) data as consisting of (1) "artifacts"; (2) "ecofacts"; (3) "textual facts"; and (4) "ideofacts." All these facts, and the culture they make up, are indeed "texts to be read."

Yet as Hodder has observed, somewhat ruefully, "there are no grammars and dictionaries of material culture language." What is offered in the following is a first, tentative outline of a "grammar of artifacts," based on the parallels that we are presupposing here with texts, where such grammars exist in abundance. Since we presented the similarities between texts and artifacts above in chart–form, we use that device again, to list what we must know in order to "read" or interpret texts and artifacts, both as "objects" and as "signs."

---

[29] On "archaeology of mind," see especially I. Hodder, *Reading the Past, passim*; and cf. the reaction in L. R. Binford, "The 'New Archaeology,' Then and Now," in Lamberg–Karlovsky, ed., *Archaeological Thought*, 50-62; cf. also the works cited in n. 22 above. For a positive reaction, see my paper cited in n. 18 above. On the new respectability of ideology as a factor in cultural change, however, see the essays of A. Gilman, A. A. Demarest, and M. W. Conkey, in Lamberg–Karlovsky, ed., *Archaeological Thought*; also Trigger, *History of Archaeological Thought*, 329-69.

Texts	Artifacts
Writing system	"Language" of material culture
Vocabulary	Artifacts of all types
Grammar	Formation processes
Syntax	Ecological, socio-cultural context
Author, composition, date	Date, technology
Cultural context (*Sitz im Leben*)	Overall historical setting
Intent	"Mental template" of makers
Later transmission, interpretation	Natural-cultural transformations
What the text "symbolizes"	What the artifact "symbolizes"
How its "meaning" is relevant today	How its "meaning" is relevant today

Once again, the parallels in reading the two types of texts are striking. Although we are sanguine about the possibilities for eventually reading the archaeological record as effectively as the textual record in the Hebrew Bible has been read in the past century of critical scholarship, examples of such readings – what have been called "formalist-structuralist" interpretations – are still relatively rare. One thinks, however, of New World examples such as Deetz' analysis of early New England houses and their furnishings; Glassie's similar study of folk-housing in Georgia; Muller's study of the American Southwest; Washburn's of ceramic design; Hall's interpretation of Indian peace-pipes; and even of the revealing studies of modern discard patterns by my colleague William Rathje and his fellow "garbologists." All these are studies in "reading" material culture texts.[30]

In Old World prehistory, Leroi-Gourhan has elucidated what appear to be underlying structural principles that can be useful in understanding Paleolithic cave-art. This is a sort of "vocabulary, grammar, and syntax" for reading the "statements" made by the various representations and arrangements of animal drawings – what Leroi-Gourhan considers a "cave-as-text," or "mythogram." Here is a striking example of the potential of post-Structuralist "archaeology of mind" for doing prehistory, if not history itself. It is from such challenges to "realism" and "naturalism" that the reader of cultural texts – such as literary myths, visual images, and archaeological artifacts – can profit. But as T. Hawkes points out, the textual-artifactual record is not simply a static one-to-one representation of an underlying "reality" in the natural world, but is dynamic in nature, subject interacting with object.

---

[30] Hodder, *Reading the Past*, 123.

Thus, he says, all art (and, we would add, texts and artifacts) "acts as a mediating, molding force in society rather than an agency which merely reflects or records."[31] The conclusion might be that in the Structuralist view, as opposed to the empiricist/rationalist view, "reality" is not expressed by culture (or language) but *produced* by it. Yet I think we need not go that far. There is a real, tangible world "out there"; but intervening between us and our perceptions (*sic*) of it are always ideas, beliefs, and meanings, both individual and cultural.[32] Nevertheless, as George Cowgill, a leading formalist, puts it: "I believe it is possible to construct models of the world that increasingly approximate how it really is, even if we never get beyond approximations."[33] On this positivist note, I cannot help remarking how ironic I find it that at the very time when Biblical historians, basing themselves on texts, are rejecting von Rankian notions of *wie es eigentlich gewesen war* – despairing of writing a genuinely historical picture of ancient Israel – some archaeologists are about to take up the challenge.[34] How is that possible?

D. "History from Things": Why Neither Texts nor Artifacts are "Mute" for the Sensitive Historian

One of the enduring canards regarding archaeology, perpetuated by certain schools of Biblical historians (beginning apparently with Martin Noth), is that "archaeological data without texts are mute."[35] But is that true? If so, the dialogue between texts and artifacts as equals envisioned here is obviously impossible; archaeology would be merely a silent partner. The charge, however, is patently false, as every archaeologist knows – and not just prehistorians who have no texts and yet espouse legitimately to write history. After all, in Palestine the whole of the

---

[31] Cited in M. W. Conkey "The Structural Analysis of Paleolithic Art," *Archaeological Thought in America* (ed. C. L. Lamberg–Karlovsky; Cambridge: Cambridge University Press, 1989) 139.

[32] For fuller discussion and references, see Conkey, "Paleolithic Art," 135-54; Hodder, *Reading the Past*, 34-54, 118-34. On the University of Arizona Garbage Project, see W. J. Rathje "The Garbage Project: A New Way of Looking at the Problems of Archaeology," *Archaeology* 27 (1974) 236-41.

[33] This summary is based on the stimulating discussion of Leroi–Gourhan in Conkey, "Paleolithic Art," 134–54, with references.

[34] G. L. Cowgill, "Formal Approaches in Archaeology," in Lamberg–Karlovsky, ed., *Archaeological Thought*, 79.

[35] Cf. M. Noth, *The History of Israel* (New York: Harper & Row, 1960) 47, 48. The term "mute" (German *dumm*) is perpetuated in the works of R. Rendtorff, A. Soggin, G. W. Ahlström, and several others; see, most recently, J. M. Miller, "Is it Possible to Write a History of Israel Without Relying on the Hebrew Bible?" *The Fabric of History: Text, Artifact and Israel's Past* (ed. D. V. Edelman; Sheffield: JSOT Press, 1991) 93–102.

remains of the Paleolithic, Neolithic, Chalcolithic, and Early–Middle Bronze ages are anepigraphic. Does that mean that we cannot give a connected account of cultural and historical (*sic*) developments throughout these eras? Certainly not! As we shall see, the controversy revolves around what we *mean* by "history," although the issue is rarely posed as such. As for archaeological data being "mute," Ernst Axel Knauf has pointed out that both sources of data for history-writing are similar; for the scholar who does not know Hebrew, the Hebrew Bible is "mute."[36]

Part of the failure of communication lies in the fact that most Biblical scholars who address the issues are *not* historians broadly trained, but philologians, and secondarily theologians. And they tend by temperament, training, and profession to over-value *texts*, while at the same time they are woefully ignorant of the nature and potential of parallel material culture remains. (Texts, like artifacts, are "metaphors," not objective reports on the way it really was in the past.) It must also be admitted that few Syro-Palestinian archaeologists today, highly specialized as they must be, are conversant enough with Ancient Near Eastern and Biblical texts to be able to use the textual data critically.[37] Thus there is little true dialogue, only the monologues of scholars in each discipline, talking to each other rather than daring to cross disciplinary boundaries.

T. L. Thompson's recent *Early History of the Israelite People from the Written and Archaeological Sources*[38] and G. W. Ahlström's *The History of Ancient Palestine from the Paleolithic Period to Alexander's Conquest*[39] both purport to be syntheses of the archaeological and cultural history of ancient Palestine, by *Biblical* scholars who have no training or experience in archaeology. Meanwhile, few American, European, or Israeli Palestinian archaeologists (especially the latter) are even aware of the current crisis in Israelite historiography, or see their research as contributing to a solution.[40] If ever a dialogue between texts and artifacts

---

[36] E. A. Knauf, "From History to Interpretation," in Edelman, ed., *The Fabric of History*, 41.

[37] Dever, "Biblical Archaeology: Death and Rebirth," and references there to earlier published remarks going back twenty years. Others in both disciplines (most recently Ahlström and Thompson) seem to assume that some sort of dialogue may be beneficial or even essential; but one sees very few specific calls for it in print among Biblical specialists.

[38] (Leiden: Brill, 1992).

[39] (Sheffield: JSOT Press, 1992). On Ahlström's *Ancient Palestine*, see my forthcoming review in *JBL* (1996).

[40] The literature is vast, but for orientation see W. G. Dever, "Archaeological Data on the Israelite Settlement: A Review of Two Recent Works," *BASOR* 284 (1991) 77–90; idem, "Unresolved Issues in the Early History of Israel: Toward a Synthesis

were needed, it is now – not just for the sake of the promising results, but in order to keep *both* disciplines healthy. Precisely because the two classes of data with which we both work as historians (*sic*) are so similar, we depend upon each other methodologically. Yet this raises the issue of whether or not either source of data is indeed properly "historical."

Biblical scholars have wrestled with this question from the beginning, with renewed vigor in the last decade or so, as seen in the works of Van Seters, Halpern and others, and now in the fierce debate over the origins of Israel – the latter involving archaeologists as well, since it is they who have produced the compelling new data.[41] Yet there is no consensus. The Hebrew Bible is "theocratic history" (Miller and Hayes); "historicized myth" or "mythologized history" (many scholars); "rationalized myth" (Garbini); simply "myth" (Oden); texts possessed only of a certain "historicality" (Knierim); "history–like" (Frei); "tradition" (Knight); the "final form of narrative history" (Childs); *kerygma* or *Heilsgeschichte* (von Rad, Wright, many others); "story" (Barr and others); "prose fiction" (Alter); or simply "fiction" (Davies).[42] No wonder there is currently a crisis in Israelite historiography! Of late, the rather desperate question is being raised: "Is it possible to write a history of ancient Israel *without* the Bible?" The answer usually given by Biblical scholars, textually biased as they are, is "No." But it *is* possible, and even desirable to write such a history; it all depends upon what *kind* of history one wants. *Heilsgeschichte?* "Political history?" Socio–economic history? T. L. Thompson has seen this point in several programmatic statements, but his own recent attempt at such a history (above) must be judged a

---

of Archaeological and Textual Reconstructions," in Jobling, Day, and Sheppard, eds., *Politics of Exegesis*, 195–207; *idem*," Cultural Continuity, Ethnicity in the Archaeological Record and the Question of Israelite Origins," *Eretz–Israel* 24 (1993) 23*–33* (Malamat volume). The standard work is I. Finkelstein, *The Archaeology of the Israelite Settlement* (Jerusalem: Israel Exploration Society, 1988). On current historiographical issues in Syro–Palestinian archaeology, see several of my treatments cited in nn. 12, 18, 27; and add "Archaeology, Material Culture and the Early Monarchical Period in Israel," in Edelman, ed., *The Fabric of History*, 103–15; "Archaeology, Texts, and History-writing: Toward an Epistemology," *Uncovering Ancient Stones: Essays in Memory of H. Neil Richardson* (ed. L. M. Hopf; Winona Lake, IN: Eisenbrauns, 1994) 105–17.

[41] The literature is too cumbersome to cite, but it will of course be well known to Biblical scholars. For orientation, see Knierim, "Literary Features"; Rendtorff, "Paradigm is Changing." See also n. 42 below.

[42] P. R. Davies, *In Search of Ancient Israel* (Sheffield: JSOT Press, 1993). Davies position, however, is too extreme for most American Biblical scholars, as reviews have indicated.

failure – in my judgment precisely because he is unable, despite his efforts, to utilize critically the rich archaeological data now available.[43]

Archaeological evidence, I would maintain, constitutes *primary* data, and indeed such evidence is often more useful than the textual data in the Hebrew Bible for purposes of historical reconstruction. For example, Syro–Palestinian archaeology at its present stage of refinement as an autonomous, professional and academic discipline[44] can comment, often extensively, on the following cultural–historical categories.

1. Environmental setting
2. Settlement types and patterns
3. Subsistence
4. Technology
5. Demography
6. Socio–economic structure
7. Political organization
8. Architecture, ceramics, and other aspects of material culture
9. "Daily life"
10. Art, ideology, and cult
11. Trade and International relations
12. Chronology

These categories, or "sub-systems" in a General Systems Theory approach, taken together actually *constitute* culture in its manifold expressions; and what is history–writing if not the analysis of culture-change? Yet a moment's reflection will reinforce the point that most of the information we now have concerning the above categories has to do with matters not described explicitly anywhere in the Hebrew Bible, nor capable of being derived from the texts as they now stand except by

---

[43] See Miller, "History of Israel Without Relying on the Hebrew Bible," 93–102; and cf. the responses in the same volume by Knauf, "From History to Interpretation," and Dever, "Early Monarchical Period." Further on the possibilities of a parallel "secular history" of ancient Israel, see my remarks in the works cited in nn. 12, 18, 27, 38 above. T. L. Thompson has expressed similar views in his *Early History*, 108–16, 158–70, 316; and already remarks in *The Origin Tradition of Ancient Israel I: The Literary Formation of Genesis and Exodus 1–23* (Sheffield: JSOT Press, 1987) 25–28. See my reaction to his recent *Early History*, however, in "Pursuit of Israelite Religion."

[44] This assessment of the current status of Syro–Palestinian archaeology is by now too well known – to both Biblical scholars and archaeologists – to need further defense. For earlier characterizations, see my "Syro Palestinian and Biblical Archaeology" and works cited there.

"reading between the lines."[45] The omissions should not be surprising. The Biblical writers and editors could be competent historians when they chose; but their steadfastly fixed view *sub specie aeternitatis* did not usually concede much importance to such mundane matters as the daily life of the masses. Yet Braudel and historians of the *Annales* school have shown forcefully that this is the *real* "stuff of history." Such an approach, over *la longue durée*, is only belatedly making an impact on archaeologists; but it seems to have been neglected almost entirely by Biblical historians.[46] Is the latter fault because the parochial, elitist, theocratic biases of the writers and final editors of the Hebrew Bible have been (unconsciously?) adopted by most modern Biblical scholars?[47]

Since there is no such thing as an "objective" history of ancient Israel (or anything else), it may be necessary to cultivate a certain empathy with the Biblical text and the world of its writers; but it is not admissible for the modern historian to blur the boundaries between confessional history and critical historical *scholarship*. Unfortunately, we get the kind of history we deserve, and most histories of Israel are hopelessly inadequate. They are either little more than "paraphrases of the Biblical story," or else so minimalist (like Thompson's) that they are no histories at all.

---

[45] See, for example, W. G. Dever, "Ancient Israelite Religion: How to Reconcile the Differing Textual and Artifactual Portraits?" *Ein Gott allein? JHWH–Verehrung und biblischer Monotheismus im Kontext der Israelitischen und altorientalischen Religionsgeschichte* (ed. W. Dietrich and M. A. Klopfenstein; Freiburg: Universitäts Freiburg, 1994) 105–25. Cf. also W. G. Dever, "The Silence of the Text: An Archaeological Commentary on 2 Kings 23," *Scripture and Other Artifacts: Essays in Honor of Philip J. King* (ed. M. D. Coogan, C. Exum, and L. E. Stager; Louisville: Westminster/John Knox, 1994), 143-68.

[46] On *annales* approaches in general archaeology, see J. Bintliff, *The Annales School and Archaeology* (Leicester: Leicester University Press, 1991); *Archaeology, Annales, and Ethnohistory* (ed. A. B. Knapp; Cambridge: Cambridge University Press, 1992). Specifically in Syro–Palestinian archaeology, see W. G. Dever, "Impact of the 'New Archaeology'," *Benchmarks in Time and Culture: Introduction to Palestinian Archaeology* (ed. G. L. Mattingly and J. M. Miller; Atlanta: Scholars Press, 1988) 337–52 and references there. Few references to Braudel and the *annales* school can be found among Biblical scholars – perhaps because of their turning away recently from history to literature – but note Coote and Whitelam, *The Emergence of Early Israel in Historical Perspective* (Sheffield: Almond Press, 1987); Knauf, "From History to Interpretation," 42, 43 and references there; Thompson, *Early History*, 149–170; 377–394; and Ahlström, *History*, 20–24.

[47] See the scathing, but not entirely undeserved, critique of most Biblical "historians" in G. Garbini, *History and Ideology in Ancient Israel* (New York: Crossroads, 1988) 10–20, 170–78; cf. also Knauf, "From History to Interpretation," *passim;* and N. P. Lemche, *Early Israel: Anthropological and Historical Studies on the Israelite Society Before the Monarchy* (Leiden: Brill, 1985) *passim*.

It is my contention that it is *only* in the dialogue between texts and artifacts – pursued rigorously by scholars committed to interdisciplinary inquiry – that we can hope for more comprehensive, better balanced, ultimately more satisfying histories of ancient Israel in all her variety and vitality. The fixed textual data, although of somewhat restricted value historically, can yield an outline of political and theocratic history, of ethnic and religious ideology, together with numerous details of real life embedded in the older materials now incorporated into the literary traditions of the Hebrew Bible – an "internal history." The archaeological data – theoretically almost unlimited in extent and variety, more flexible, and less deliberately biased – can yield a broader environmental and socio–economic history, an "external, secular" history that is parallel, complementary in many ways, and often corrective. *Both* histories of ancient Israel are now essential, and possible – if scholars in several disciplines are willing to set aside conventional approaches and cooperate in a true dialogue between texts and artifacts.[48]

Conclusion

Let us return to the point at which we began, attempting to heed Professor Silberman's sage advice to "listen." That means that as historians, when we have been able to read both texts and artifacts as accurately as possible with all means at our disposal, assessing all the data as disinterestedly as possible, we must then be content to sit back and listen – intently, patiently, with a disciplined but sympathetic imagination, and above all with humility. As Hodder reminds us, in the quest for meaning in history there are always these subjective elements. The role of history is "to understand human action, rather than events ... To get at action is to get at subjective meanings, at the *inside* of events."[49] By listening perceptively to the human past as it speaks to us today we may appropriate that past, and thus we gain the only insights that we shall ever have into the future.

---

[48] There are only a few articles on theory and method by Israeli archaeologists, and none betrays any significant interest in a *critical* dialogue between archaeology and Biblical studies. See my critique in "Yigael Yadin: Prototypical Biblical Archaeologist," *Eretz–Israel* 20 (1989) 44*–51* (Yadin volume) and references there; add now T. Shay, "Israeli Archaeology – Ideology and Practice," *Antiquity* 63 (1989) 768–72. For prospects in the archaeology of Judaism and early Christianity, see C. and E. Meyers, "Expanding the Frontiers of Biblical Archaeology," *Eretz–Israel* 20 (1989) 140*–47* (Yadin volume). Among the very few pioneering attempts by archaeologists at dialogue for the period of ancient Israel, one might cite my "Silence of the Text"; and L. E. Stager, "The Archaeology of the Family in Ancient Israel," *BASOR* 260 (1985) 1–35.

[49] N. K. Gottwald, *The Tribes of Yahweh: A Sociology of the Religion of Liberated Israel, 1250–1050 B.C.E.* (Maryknoll, NY: Orbis Books, 1979) XXV.

2

The First Stories of Genesis and the Rhythm of the Generations*

David C. Hopkins

The first stories of Genesis embody a striking reflection on the dynamic of rhythm. Genesis 1-12 offers the reader a coherent and artful arrangement of genealogical metronome and narrative departure from its cadence. The dynamic of rhythm holds the key for solving the puzzle of the interrelation of the genealogies and stories of chapters 1-12.[1] What is the relationship between the taut rhythmic framework of genealogies and the rubato slackening of the circumscribed narrative plots?

It is no news that the opening chapters of Genesis are composed of a sequence in which the stories alternate with genealogical material.

NARRATIVE AND *GENEALOGY* IN GENESIS 1-12

1-2:3	Seven-Day Creation
2:4a	*Generations of the Heavens and the Earth*
2:4b-3:24	Man and Woman in the Garden

---

* This paper is offered in homage to Lou H. Silberman, whom I am honored to call "teacher."
[1] R. B. Robinson, "Literary Functions of the Genealogies of Genesis," *CBQ* 48 (1986) 595-608, also reflects on the rhythm of the Genesis genealogies and their "measured pace" (595), likening their presence to that of "a *basso continuo* below the narrative, marking the linear progression of the promise in solid block chords" (606). Robinson masterfully sketches the interplay of genealogy and narrative throughout Genesis as the tension between order and contingency and offers numerous observations which parallel and bolster those arrived at independently here.

4:1-2a	*Eve's Children*
4:2b-16	Cain and Adonai
4:18-26	*Cain's Children, their Descendants, and Seth*
5:1-32	*Generations of Adam through Noah*
6:1-9:29	Noah and the Flood: The Storm in God's Heart
10:1-32	*Noah's Children and their Descendants*
11:1-9	The Fortified City
11:10-26	*The Generations of Shem through Terah*
11:27-32	*Terah's Children especially Abram and Sarah*
12:1-9	Abram, Sarah , and Lot Journey to Canaan

This broad structure has long been observed.[2] The functional linkage between the two types of material has been little noticed. Scholarly attention has focused primarily on the diachronic question (which came first the story or the genealogy?).[3] An exception to this myopic preoccupation, Naomi Steinberg has argued that in the Genesis presentation of ancestor stories (12-50) "genealogy allows for narrative to explore the problem of generational continuity; only within the context of

---

[2] See C. Westermann, *Genesis 1-11: A Commentary* (trans. J. J. Scullion; Minneapolis: Augsburg, 1984) 6-18; B. S. Childs, *Introduction to the Old Testament as Scripture* (Philadelphia: Fortress, 1979) 145-47; M. Fishbane, *Text and Texture: Close Readings of Selected Biblical Texts* (New York: Schocken, 1979) 27-29; D. J. A. Clines, *The Theme of the Pentateuch* (JSOTSup 10; Sheffield: JSOT, 1978) 66-69; T. L. Thompson, *The Origin Tradition of Ancient Israel, 1: The Literary Formation of Genesis And Exodus 1-23* (JSOTSup 55; Sheffield: Sheffield Academic, 1987) 64-65; J. van Seters, "The Primeval Histories of Greece and Israel Compared," *ZAW* 100 (1988) 10; and B. Renaud, "Les généalogies et la structure de l'histoire sacerdotale dans le Livre de la Genèse," *RB* 97 (1990) 5-30.

[3] D. Damrosch, *The Narrative Covenant: Transformations of Genre in the Growth of Biblical Literature* (San Francisco: Harper & Row, 1987) 126, 135, has offered a sophisticated genetic explanation for the mixture of genealogies and narratives in Genesis 2-11: the genealogies represent a first step in the historization of the poetic epic genres carried out by Israelite culture. These "historicizing multigenerational sequences unite the ordinary genealogical material of king lists and chronicles with the thematic concerns of poetic epic now cast into prose." Attention to genealogies *per se* has burgeoned in the past two decades, beginning with M. D. Johnson, *The Purpose of the Biblical Geneaologies with Special Reference to the Setting of the Geneaologies of Jesus* (SNTSMS 8; Cambridge: Cambridge University Press, 1969) and R. R. Wilson, *Genealogy and History in the Biblical World* (Yale Near Eastern Researches 7; New Haven: Yale University Press, 1977). Other recent studies include: D. T. Bryan, "A Reevaluation of Gen 4 and 5 in Light of Recent Studies in Genealogical Fluidity," *ZAW* 99 (1987) 180-88; R. S. Hess, "The Genealogies of Genesis 1-11 and Comparative Literature," *Bib* 70 (1989) 241-54; G. A. Rendsburg, "The Internal Consistency and Historical Reliability of the Biblical Geneaologies," *VT* 40 (1989) 185-206; and T. J. Prewitt, *The Elusive Covenant: A Structured-Semiotic Reading of Genesis* (Advances in Semiotics; Bloomington and Indianapolis: Indiana University Press, 1990).

genealogical structure do the narratives take on meaning."[4] This principle serves for Genesis 1-12 as well: the genealogies create inheritance ambiguities that the narratives resolve. As soon as Eve gives birth to two sons, ambiguity and the potential for rivalry arise: who will inherit a place on the genealogical tree? The story of Cain and *Adonai* takes both contenders out of the picture. The question of Adam's successor waits for a resolution in the announcement of Seth's birth. Next, the genealogy of Adam through Noah breaks off the moment the birth of Noah's three, named children is made public. The genealogical ambiguity provides the occasion for the flood narrative, which, in concluding with the story of Ham's "incest," ratifies Shem's place in the succession. For ten generations from Shem to Terah, the genealogy of Genesis 11 spills effortlessly until the report of Terah's three offspring, and story begins once more.[5] The entire account of Abraham and Sarah holds in suspense the genealogical place following Terah until a voice from heaven halts Abraham's sacrifice of his designated heir, and the succession is finally secured.[6] Whatever else they may do, the narratives in the first stories of Genesis resolve genealogical ambiguities by determining which son's name will follow that of his father.[7]

The genealogical structure of the first chapters of Genesis is more than just a principle of organization or loose redactional device. Indeed, the basic plot of these chapters is genealogical, pursuing the actuality as

---

[4] "The Genealogical Framework of the Family Stories in Genesis," *Semeia* 46 (1989) 47.
[5] S. Tengström, *Die Toledotformel und die literarische Strucktur der priesterlichen Erweiterungsschicht im Pentateuch* (ConBOT 17; Uppsala: CWK Gleerup, 1981) 39-43, shows the analogous structure and function of the *toledot* of Noah and Terah and how they create the point of departure for subsequent narration. Tengström also draws attention to the similar function of Noah's (9:5-27) and Jacob's (4:2-27) blessings.
[6] I owe this realization to Silberman, who explored the Genesis plot of "The True Heir" in his SBL presidential address, "Listening to the Text," *JBL* 102:1 (1983) 3-26.
[7] The exceptions to this pattern occur when the genealogies are horizontal rather than vertical and thus provoke no inter-generational interest. These expansive, horizontal genealogies still serve importantly. The first set, The Generations of the Heavens and the Earth, bridges the cosmologically and terrestrially focused aspects of the double creation account. Positioned at the other end of the primeval history, the Descendants of Noah's Children itself provides the positive counterpart to the text into which it leads, the Babel story of the forced populating of the world. These horizontal genealogies flesh out the setting for the action rather than instigate it. See also Tengström's observations on the functions of the two types of genealogies, *Die Toledotformel*, 25-26.

well as the identity of the next named successor.⁸ The genealogies create a rhythm in which stories emerge, first to deal with the succession of the second generation, i.e., where Seth succeeds Adam, and again to deal with the succession of the tenth generation both before the flood, i.e., where Shem succeeds Noah, and after, i.e., where Abram succeeds Terah. These stories participate in the first chapters of Genesis by showing how human and divine actions figure in the process of discrimination and determine the named successor.

The effect of narrative digression to resolve genealogical ambiguity can be gauged by scanning the results of recent literary-critical interest in the stories themselves. The impressive results achieved, for example, by Trible's and Walsh's renderings of "Eve and Adam," Wenham's demonstration of "The Coherence of the Flood Narrative," and Fokkelman's exploration of the *Narrative Art* of the Babel story, demonstrate the presence of very definite structural, formal patterning to the stories of these chapters.⁹

Basic to the story of the Man and Woman in the Garden is a tripartite division into creation – disobedience – disintegration. While the narrative density of this story permits the mapping of several different intricate structures, the central focus rests on the disobedience scene in which conversation that distances the creator is the turning point. Both serpent and woman speak about אלהים (*elohim*) rather than to יהוה אלהים (*adonai elohim*, 3:1-7). The story is bordered by an *inclusio* marked out by repetition of key vocabulary.¹⁰

After an introduction (4:2b), the story of Cain and *Adonai* takes the shape of two panels (4:3-7, 8-15) in which description of events leads to encounters between Cain and *Adonai*, both of which are initiated by

---

⁸ Focusing on the ancestor stories, N. Steinberg, "The Genealogical Framework of the Family Stories in Genesis," *Semeia* 46 (1989) 40, asserts: "Genesis is a book whose plot is genealogy."
⁹ See P. Trible, *God and the Rhetoric of Sexuality* (Philadelphia: Fortress, 1978) 75-162; J. T. Walsh, "Genesis 2:4b-3:24: A Synchronic Approach," *JBL* 96 (1977) 161-77; G. Wenham, "The Coherence of the Flood Narrative," *VT* 28 (1977) 336-48; and Fokkelman, *Narrative Art in Genesis* (Assen/Amsterdam: Van Gorcum, 1975). For a discussion of method in analyzing narrative structures, see S. Bar-Efrat, "Some Observations of the Analysis of Structure in biblical Narrative," *VT* 30 (1980) 154-74.
¹⁰ In addition to Trible, *God and the Rhetoric of Sexuality*, and Walsh, "Genesis 2:4b-3:24," see also A. J. Hauser, "Genesis 2-3: The Theme of Intimacy and Alienation," *Art and Meaning: Rhetoric in Biblical Literature* (ed. D. Clines, D. Gunn and, A. Hauser; JSOTSup 19; Sheffield: JSOT, 1982) 20-32; D. Jobling, "Myth and Its Limits in Gen 2:4b-3:24," *The Sense of Biblical Narrative: Structural Analyses in the Hebrew Bible II* (JSOTSup 39; Sheffield: JSOT, 1986); and H. N. Wallace, *The Eden Narrative* (HSM 32; Atlanta: Scholars Press, 1985).

Adonai. The first panel presents the failure of dialogue of the main actors followed by murder, while the second panel presents the success of dialogue that leads to Cain's protective mark and his expulsion.[11]

The flood story displays a symmetrical structure encased in the genealogy of Noah (5:32, 9:28-29) and bounded on either end by stories of prohibited sexual relations (6:1-4, 9:20-27). This symmetrical arrangement focuses on God whose remembering stands at the very center of the account (8:1).[12] The concluding story of Babel (11:1-9) possesses a very tight symmetrical pattern that balances scenes and vocabulary. A manifestation of the distance between *Adonai* and the human world stands at absolute center (11:5). The rounded completeness of the text leaves the impression of a period at the end of a sentence. The "fortified city" is the premier example of the sharply delineated nature of all of the narrative units in the first stories of Genesis.[13]

The contrast between the dramatic and clearly bordered plots of individual narratives and the relentless rhythm of genealogy could not be more sharp. The generational flow – "the ideal stable succession"[14] – gives way to highly dramatic narrative, but the drama starts and stops in brief compass. "Each generation spotlighted is allotted just one episode" writes Cohn, "and then time marches on to the next generation."[15] The individual stories of Genesis 1-12 have limited horizons: some background, but minimal foreground. They create no more than islands of interest in a genealogical flow that is but held in abeyance. They are

---

[11] The parallel panel construction of this story has received little comment. An introduction (v. 2b) follows the genealogical announcement of story (vv. 1-2a) and opens up the way for action (sacrifice and rejection, vv. 3-5) followed by a failed dialogue in which *Adonai* addresses Cain but receives no response (vv. 6-7). In the second panel, action (murder, v. 8) leads to a consummated dialogue (interrogation, evasion, confession, assurance), again initiated by *Adonai* (vv. 9-15). A conclusion follows (v.16). This panel structure gives scant attention to any conflict between Cain and Abel, but places all its emphasis on appraising the relationship between Cain and *Adonai*. Compare the treatment of this story by R. Culley, *Studies in the Structure of Hebrew Narrative* (Semeia Supplements; Philadelphia: Fortress and Missoula: Scholars Press, 1976) 106-8.

[12] In addition to Wenham's study, "Coherence of the Flood Narrative," see also B. Anderson, "From Analysis to Synthesis: The Interpretation of Genesis 1-11," *JBL* 97 (1978) 23-39, and I. M. Kikawada and A. Quinn, *Before Abraham Was: The Unity of Genesis 1-11* (Nashville: Abingdon, 1985) 83-106.

[13] Alongside Fokkelman's exhaustive analysis in *Narrative Art*, set Fishbane, *Text and Texture*, 34-38, and I. M. Kikawada, "The Shape of Genesis 11:1-9," *Rhetorical Criticism: Essays in Honor of J. Muilenburg* (ed. J. Jackson and M. Kessler; Pittsburgh: Pickwick, 1974).

[14] Steinberg, "Genealogical Framework," 43.

[15] R. L. Cohn, "Narrative Structure and Canonical Perspective in Genesis," *JSOT* 25 (1983) 4.

stories that fail to develop and are quickly swept back into the onward rush of the generations. They are seeds of generational history, in a sense, that fail to germinate.

Genesis 1-12 is formally a disjunctive account of the way divine and human interacted in shaping the world as Israel knew it. The contrast between the smoothly flowing genealogies and the circumscribed narrative units represents a formal reflection of a failure in the relationship that is the subject matter of the each narrative segment, the relationship between creator and creature. The disjunctiveness itself serves as an element of the plot and a crucial thematic contributor. Genesis 1-12 is a stalemated story, a story of fits and starts.[16]

As an aside, it is worth noting at this point that none of the other sub-sections of Genesis share the formal characteristics of Genesis 1-12, either at the level of the overall narratives or the individual story units that comprise them.[17] Comparing the overall structures of the Genesis subsections suggests a formal reflection of the movement from the story of fits and starts of first chapters dominated by a stalemated relationship between creature and creator, to family story of the patriarchs and matriarchs dominated by the question of inheritance, to "national history" of the twelve sons of Israel dominated by the increasingly complex question of political leadership. Cohn has clearly perceived this movement in the theological discourse of Genesis that "depicts the evolution of the divine-human relationship from the never-never land of Eden to the real world of exile."[18] At the level of the individual stories, few of those found in Genesis 12-50 come anywhere close to matching the rigid, circumscribed structures of the first story narrative units. Indeed, narratives in Genesis 12-50 are more fluid and open because they are leading somewhere. The first stories are closed cul-de-sacs in comparison.

The stalemate between creator and creature that cuts short the first stories of each highlighted generation is no surprise given what we know of the ancient Near Eastern creation-flood epic genre and its

---

[16] Compare L. Thompson's treatment of Genesis 1-11 as depicting life as a "series of recurring stalemates," in *Introducing Biblical Literature: A More Fantastic Country* (Englewood Cliffs: Prentice-Hall, 1978) 80.

[17] Noted also by T. Thompson, *Origin Tradition*, 80, who offers a genetic explanation for this phenomenon: "From the genealogy of Shem onwards, we are no longer dealing simply with narratives with self-enclosed plots which have at a later date been secondarily linked together by an external formal structure. The unities we find are rather much more complex." Y. T. Radday, H. Shore, et al., *Genesis: An Authorship Study in Computer-Assisted Statistical Linguistics* (Rome: Biblical Institute, 1985) 184, speak of Genesis 2-11 as being "quasi-mythical," 12-36 "semi-heroic' and 37-50 "fully human" based upon content and presentation.

[18] "Narrative Structure," 14-15.

transformations in various cultures.[19] In Israel's rendition of this Mesopotamian literary tradition, the way is prepared for exposing the problematic creator-creature relationship in the initial account of creation. Genesis 1:1-2:3 embodies the rhythm of genealogy, yet not fully.[20] Despite its balanced, complete rendering of a world made "very good," the opening creation account breaks from its own rhythm and leaves two dimensions in suspension. On the structurally highlighted sixth day of creation, the human family is commissioned (1:28).[21] Three of the commissions are shared with all other living creatures: be fruitful and multiply and fill the earth (cf. 1:22). Two are special: subdue the earth, and have dominion. Will the human family carry out its commissions? These are not mere definitions of the nature of human life, matter-of-factly located by the text in the beginning. Neither are they farcical: "Have dominion!!" Rather success or failure in carrying out these commissions determines the progress and retreat of story in Genesis.

The second matter left in suspension by Gen 1:1-2:3 is the future role of the creator. The divine rest of the seventh day is the climax of the whole account (2:1-3). The verses are elaborately interwoven into a very tight structure that signals the close of divine involvement in creating. The concluding rest of the creator matches and stills the opening rush of the wind of God (1:2). Is that it for God? The widespread notion of the leisure of the creator god in the ancient Near East cautions against too quickly dismissing the potential force of this conclusion to the account of

---

[19] Compare the point made by Damrosch, *Narrative Covenant*, 139-40 concerning human parity as source of the conflict in Israel's rendition of the creation account. J. D. Levenson, *Creation and the Persistence of Evil: The Jewish Drama of Divine Omnipotence* (San Francisco: Harper & Row, 1988) 132-35, 140-41, proceeds differently to a similar notion concerning humans as a worthy challenge for divine governance, replacing the lesser gods of the Enuma Elish. See also R. A. Oden, Jr., "Divine Aspirations in Atrahasis and in Genesis 1-11," *ZAW* 93 (1981) 197-216.

[20] Literary-critical studies of Gen 1:1-2:3 include B. Anderson, "A Study of the Priestly Creation Story," *Canon and Authority* (ed. G. Coats and B. Long; Philadelphia: Fortress, 1977); Fishbane, *Text and Texture*, 3-16; and Trible, "Ancient Priests and Modern Polluters," *ANQ* 12 (1971) 74-79. See also A. Scult, M. C. McGee, and J. K. Kuntz, "Genesis and Power: An Analysis of the Biblical Story of Creation," *Quarterly Journal of Speech* 72 (1986) 113-31. Levenson, *Creation and Persistence*, 58, notes the repetitiveness and regularity of Genesis 1 as well at its "austere self-control."

[21] Robinson, "Literary Functions," 600, also calls attention to the commissions as the sole dynamic elements of the seven-day creation story. J. Cohen, *Be Fertile and Increase, Fill the Earth and Master It: The Ancient and Medieval Career of a Biblical Text* (Ithaca, NY: Cornell University Press, 1989) offers a detailed summary of the discussion of these commissions in the context of the Hebrew Bible.

creation.[22] Of course, the text presents an etiology of the Sabbath which undercuts any foreboding that God's repose might conjure.[23] But it is a peculiar Sabbath, deprived of the standard concluding formula that has brought each previous day to a close. The issue raised is: will God, the creator, relate to creation?

These two unresolved dimensions of the creation story bring to literary expression the creator-creature relationship highlighted as problematic by the formal structure of Genesis 1-12's disjunctive interplay of genealogy and story. The human commissions focus the reader's attention on human agency in the created world. The seventh-day rest focuses attention on theology, on the chapters' portrait of God.

The unresolved divine portrait receives the text's first attention. The suspense created by the divine rest about God's future involvement in creation is immediately dispelled. *Elohim*, the resting transcendent creator, awakens in Gen 2:4b-3:24 as *Adonai Elohim* whose intimate involvement with creation and creature is portrayed by a piling up of the most astonishing and arresting anthropomorphic portraits. *Adonai Elohim* is potter (2:7), gardener (2:8), judge (3:11ff), and seamstress (3:21). Alongside this multiple divine portraiture stands the obvious focus on human failure to carry out the commissions. If the initial creation account portrays creation as "without opposition," as Levenson would have it,[24] then the continuing creation saga presents the opposite. But note how the story raises subtle questions about the involvement of *Adonai Elohim* in this failure. The prohibition against eating from "the tree of the knowledge of good and evil" is announced by a lawgiver who thereby places explicit limits on human dominion. This prohibition is a confusing contradiction. Had not the human family previously been granted eating privileges from every tree with seed in its fruit (Gen 1:29)? Why now this afterthought? It is clear from this unforeseen development that the quick

---

[22] J. T. E. Renner, "The Rest of God in the Creation Account of Genesis," *Lutheran Theology Journal* 5 (1981) 19-21, argues that the divine rest on day seven bears no resemblance to the *otiositas* since God appears active (blessing, sanctifying) even in rest. He interprets the fact of divine rest on a certain day as demonstrating that God enters into time – a signal of intimacy with the creatures created in time rather than aloofness. On the motif of the *deus otiosus*, see Westermann, *Genesis 1-11*, 167-68, and more recently Levenson, *Creation and Persistence*, 100-111, who argues that Gen 2:1-3 is intended to supplant the widespread notion of God's rest as retirement with a sabbatical notion of rest as "limited in its duration and positive in its effect" (110).

[23] For a creative interpretation of the rest of God on the seventh day as a sabbatical rest adumbrating God's will to liberate the powerless, see Levenson, *Creation and Persistence*, 100-120. T. Thompson, *Origin Tradition*, 171, also observes the way in which the sabbatical rest points ahead to the Exodus story.

[24] *Creation and Persistence*, 122.

The First Stories of Genesis and the Rhythm of the Generations 33

and disappointing end to life in the garden has its ironic roots in the acts of the commissioner as well as the commissioned.[25] The irony is heightened by the fact that the disobedience of the humans in the garden issues from their likeness to God. As is made plain by her choice of vocabulary as she surveys the tree (3:6 compared with 2:9), the woman "is tempted not through rebellion against God, but through a slightly skewed exercise of the very traits she shares with God."[26] Thus surfaces the appropriateness of describing the relationship as stalemated. Uncertainty about the relationship between God and the human family comes from both sides. God's aspiration for an earthly "image bearer" and God's responsibility for contradiction join human inability to exercise dominion within the limits imposed to extinguish the garden episode.

The genealogy that follows the expulsion from the garden presents the deity in the role of blesser.[27] God's active involvement in blessing is made explicit by the statement of Eve: "I have gotten a man with the help of *Adonai*." All of the subsequent genealogies reinforce this portrait of the God who blesses through the gifts of fertility and fecundity even as they depict the success of the human family in carrying out this one of the shared commissions.

Following upon the garden story, with its almost mundane portraits of *Adonai Elohim*, the theological contribution of the story of Cain and *Adonai* is to recloak the divine in mystery. Appropriately using the name *Adonai* exclusively, the Lord is portrayed as the chooser of one rather than the other, no explanation offered (4:4-5; compare Exodus 33:19). This surprising deity also appears as a solicitous counselor, pursuing a dialogue with Cain that is somehow out of reach (4:6-7).[28] As with the dénouement of the Garden story, *Adonai's* final act before expulsion casts God in the role of sustainer, equipping the human beings with some form of external protection. The description of Cain's murder and the subsequent interrogation scene use language from the garden story to make explicit the impropriety of dominion's extending to human domination of fellow humans. Prominent are the motifs of "keeping" (שמר; 4:9) and "hand" (יד; 4:11) drawn from the final garden expulsion scene (3:22-23).

The flood story makes the most radical contribution to the developing divine portrait and the definition of the human commissions.

---

[25] T. Thompson, *Origin Tradition*, 79.
[26] Damrosch, *Narrative Covenant*, 140.
[27] See Westermann, *Genesis 1-11*, 360-62.
[28] The questions posed by *Adonai* to Cain in the first panel of this story are read by A. Waskow, *Godwrestling* (New York: Schocken, 1978) 15-17, as real rather than rhetorical questions, probing Cain's depression and anger.

By following the story's structural focus on God, it is apparent that the text posits nothing short of a change in the nature of deity: the destroyer becomes a sustainer accommodating the nature of the human creature, evil from its youth.[29] From the internal monologue that signals *Adonai's* entry into the story (6:5-7) to the post-deluvian divine assessment of the recalcitrant human predisposition toward evil (8:21), the story's decisive action all takes place "off-stage" in the mystery of the divine being. This new portrait of God represents a breakthrough visible as well in the introduction of three new divine activities: God covenants with Noah (6:18: והקמתי את־בריתי אתך); God calls Noah to participate in the divine plan to preserve life (6:19: להחית); and God remembers, the quintessential act of covenant fidelity (8:1: ויזכר).

The flood also occasions a restructuring of the human commission to exercise dominion. The recommissioned Noahide family hears a repeat of shared commissions, "Be fruitful and multiply and fill the earth" (9:1), but the special commissions are recast. Over the non-human creatures of the earth, more human power is now given: "into your hand they are delivered" (9:2: בידכם נתנו). But there are also more explicit limits and requirements and a concrete saying about intra-human violence (9:4-6). The reappearance of the legal genres now has a covenantal context (9:8-17); they do not contradict or confuse dominion (as in Genesis 2:4b-3:24), but define it. It cannot escape notice that this recasting of the commissions to subdue and have dominion is accomplished through an explicit use of the "hand" motif drawn from the earlier narratives. The vocabulary of the Genesis 1 commissions of "subdue" and "have dominion" is brought into direct relationship with the chief motif from the Garden and *Adonai* and Cain stories relating to the exercise of human power.[30]

Have the flood story transformations provided an end to the divine-human stalemate and perhaps the basis for a sustained plot? Part of the answer comes in acts – Noah's drunkenness and Ham's sexual violation (9:20-23) – intended to manifest the truthfulness of God's conclusion about the inherent evil of humanity. Moreover, Noah's first speaking part offers the first human curse (9:25-27).

It is the account of the fortified city of Babel, however, that counts as the narrator's most definitive response to the potential for an on-going story. Narrative progress is stymied by human resistance to the

---

[29] See W. Brueggemann, *Genesis* (Interpretation; Atlanta: Knox, 1982) 75-81.
[30] In the Garden disobedience scene itself, the "hand" is present in the taking and eating without being mentioned explicitly (3:6). Its presence is first called to attention in the woman's rephrasing of the divine prohibition, adding "nether may you *touch* it" (compare 2:16-17 with 3:3).

commission to fill the world. Settling down into a language and lifestyle homogeneity behind fortified city walls, the human beings scorn the task of populating all the earth. *Adonai* undermines the linguistic basis of unity and scatters the city's populace, more for the sake of the earth than as punishment for human overreaching. The commission is thus fulfilled by divine fiat. Communication between humans and *Adonai*, a motif in the garden story and central to the *Adonai* and Cain account, is never attempted. The parting of the story's actors – humans to the far corners of the earth, *Adonai* to the divine abode in heaven – leaves one wondering if the possibility of a divine-human relationship has not vanished entirely.

But the paradoxical nature of both these responses to the post-diluvian renewal is equally clear. Noah's curse is an acting out of renewed human dominion and announces the genealogical succession which leads to Abram. Similarly, the climatic dispersion of the fortified city sows the seeds of the narrative soon to be opened.

Almost as a consequence of the abruptness of the period-like Babel story, the following genealogy hurries, not pausing even once, to reach the tenth-generation birth of Terah's three sons (Gen 11:27).[31] The structural annunciation of story to determine genealogical succession indicates the essential connectedness of the first chapters of Genesis with the ancestor stories. This connection has been increasingly recognized over and against a long-tenured emphasis on disparity between the so-called "primeval history" and "patriarchical history." Van Seters has argued in like fashion that the genealogical framework of the patriarchical stories militates against their possessing a so very distinct compositional history.[32] Thompson joins van Seters in dismissing any radical break between Genesis 1-11 and 12ff, noting that on formal grounds the ancestor stories are an expansion of material within the

---

[31] The genealogy of Genesis 5 hesitates momentarily on the first rung of the ladder (Adam 5:3), again on the seventh (Enoch 5:24), and finally on the ninth rung to announce Noah's special future.

[32] *Primeval Histories*, 15. On the distinctiveness of Genesis 2-11 from the standpoint of vocabulary habits, see the discussion by Wenham, *Genesis 1-15* (WBC 1; Waco, TX: Word Books, 1988) 12-13, based upon the work of Radday and Shore, *Genesis*. The traditio-historical explanation of this distinctiveness – the deep roots of the narrative material of Genesis 1-12 in the ancient Near Eastern primeval epic tradition (cf. Atrahasis) does not necessitate the conclusion that this material was linked secondarily to the more exclusively Israelite ancestor stories, except under the dubious assumption that Israel was an outsider to ancient Near Eastern culture in general (see R. Gnuse, *Heilsgeschichte as a Model for Biblical Theology: The Debate Concerning the Uniqueness and Significance of Israel's Worldview* (College Theology Society Studies in Religion 4; Lanham, MD: University Press of America, 1989) 97-120.

toledot structure.³³ For Coats, "the primeval history is not to be considered for itself but only in relationship to the patriarchs."³⁴ To reiterate an earlier observation, readers wait through nearly the entire story of Abraham, Sarah and Hagar, Lot, and Ishmael and Isaac before it is certain that Abraham's name will follow that of his father Terah in the genealogy.

Yet clearly a transition is underway at this juncture. The inability of commentators to arrive at a consensus on boundary divisions – with vv. 11:27, 29, and 30 each having numerous adherents – demonstrates the ambiguity in the text as well as distinctions imposed upon the text from later tradition and the modern world.³⁵ In any case, the juncture between first stories and ancestral stories cannot be explained as the result of a haphazard combination of generically different materials with different relationships to Israel's historic memory.³⁶ Rather, the transition represents the subtle overcoming of the stalemate that has heretofore precluded the blossoming of generational histories in the pre-Abrahamic world.

The major signs of this demarcation become clear in relationship to the commissions of Genesis 1 that here take on new life.³⁷ First in view, the twice-intoned commission to be fruitful and multiply runs headlong into Abram and Sarah's barren childlessness (11:30, repeated for emphasis). The couple's dilemma shocks after the reproductive success of previous generations. Truly, the real world is upon us. The commission to be fruitful and multiply narrows to the pursuit of a single

---

³³ *Origin Tradition*, 10.

³⁴ G. W. Coats, *Genesis with and Introduction to Narrative Literature* (FOTL 1; Grand Rapids: Eerdmans, 1983) 105.

³⁵ See Steinberg, "Genealogical Framework," 47-48. Among those who have begun to explore the unity of the "primeval history" and the "patriarchal history" are T. Thompson, *Origin Tradition*, 61-80; van Seters, "Primeval Histories;" Clines, *Theme of the Pentateuch*, 77-79; and Coats, *Genesis*, 27-34. The indistinctness of the boundary between Genesis 1-11 and 12-50 is manifest in the verse divisions adopted by recent commentators: 1:1-11:26 (Westermann, *Genesis 1-11*, 559); 1:1-11:27 (Wenham, *Genesis 1-15*, xxii); 1:1-11:29 (Brueggemann, *Genesis*, 11); and 1:1-11:30 (Kikawada and Quinn, *Before Abraham*, 96). Coats, *Genesis*, 14-38, demonstrates how the choice of framework (e.g., Pentateuch versus Hexateuch) determines the divisions between units. Coats settles on a primeval saga encompassing 1:1-11:9 following the guidance of the *toledot* structure. He treats 11:10-12:9 as the first unit of the Abrahamic saga (103-109).

³⁶ The movement of scholarship toward fuller inclusion of the first stories has been engendered by the willingness of scholarship to abandon speculation about the genesis of Genesis and concentrate on exploring its coherence. As Silberman, "Listening," 11, puts the first rule of renewed literary-critical investigations: "suspend explanations; describe."

³⁷ L. Thompson, *Introducing Biblical Literature*, 80-81.

heir. Next, Terah moves to Haran (11:31), a journey that is wholly integrated into the spreading of families, languages, lands, and nations of the horizontal genealogy of chapter 10 as well as the scattering of the fortified city. Terah and Abraham's journey is not a response to the situation of disunity created by Babel, but is a part of it. Continuing Terah's venture, Abram and Sarah, like all the earth's families, set out for a particular place, their "ancestral" home. Their journey brings the commission to fill the world down to size. Noteworthy is the fact that the specific direction of this family's journey geographically reverses the previous eastward movement of Genesis 1-11, away from a place. Abram, Sarah, and Lot wend westward, back toward the center. The sacral character of their journey is thus indicated.

We have already witnessed the transformation of the special commissions to more covenantal form with Noah. Here, too, Abram receives both call and promises, but the latter now eventuate in accented purpose clauses (12:2-3).[38] Noah was an agent in the preservation of life, Abram is called in order to bring about its blessing. Here we find in full form an attribution of purposefulness to creation. Previously, the unity of creation and redemption (God's gracious will to liberate the oppressed) was only adumbrated in the portrait of the seventh-day rest of God.[39] In the narrative that follows Abram's call, it is this sense of futurity that will control the action.[40] Slowly at first – the initial endangering of the matriarch (12:10-13:1) represents another circumscribed panel story creating no forward movement – the self-contained story of stalemate will give way. More complex verisimilar plots appear in which action and narrative tension more completely efface the genealogical rhythm in portraying multigenerational conflict and reconciliation.[41] Now the story begins, the stalemate is overcome, and the divine-human relationship is productive of full-blown generational history.

---

[38] On the translation of the final clauses of vv. 2-3 as purpose clauses, see Westermann, *Genesis 12-36: A Commentary* (trans. J. J. Scullion; Minneapolis: Augsburg, 1985) 144, 150-52.
[39] Levenson, *Persistence of Evil*, 100-111.
[40] Cohn, "Narrative Structure," 6.
[41] Damrosch, *Narrative Covenant*, 126, suggests that the genealogical element in Genesis 1-11 evinces the narrator's interest in and preparation for the historicizing multigenerational sequences seen in the patriarchal narratives and the complex dynastic struggles of Saul and David. The tentativeness of this movement is communicated by the first complete narrative unit of the Abraham and Sarah stories (Gen 12:10-13:1) and its panel-shaped, closed depiction of the descent to Egypt which ends up precisely where it started (Gen 12:10 = 13:1).

What did this artful combination of genealogy and narrative that constitutes Gen 1-12 contribute as social discourse in ancient Israel?[42] The basic genealogical rhythm of the text appears as a form of special pleading. The genealogies relativize historical time. Their smooth rap-tap of generational succession relativizes the travail of any generation, even the generation of the flood, and pushes on inexorably toward the future. Interpretation has long demonstrated greater acuity in hearing the narrative deviation from this rhythm. One interpreter labels the narrative plots "flashes of light illuminating the dark passage of time,"[43] but this is not the perspective of the text nor presumably of its ancient audience.

Does the essence of rhythm consist in predictable, emphatic regularity or in nonrecurrent configurations of movement? Contemporary novelist Milan Kundera's reflection on rhythm displays a negative bias about the value of rhythmic regularity: "I hate to hear the beat of my heart; it is a relentless reminder that the minutes of my life are numbered. So I have always seen something macabre in the bar lines that measure out a musical score. But the greatest masters of rhythm know how to silence that monotonous and predictable regularity, and transform their music into a little enclave of 'time outside time.'"[44] Seen from this perspective, the narratives of Genesis 1-12 may serve formally to weaken the measure bars of the genealogical progression. In the midst of genealogical rhythm, story rises and falls in incalculable ways. The arrangement of story and genealogy raises a challenge to the dominance of the repetitive regularity of generational progression. Valuing the thematic contributions of both the genealogical and narrative genres, Robinson's commentary is instructive. The interplay between narrative and genealogy, he notes, "prevents the tendency toward determinism of the genealogies from negating the narrative events' contingency or the characters' freedom."[45] Yet a society threatened with dissolution might reverse the order of this statement, asserting that the contingency of the narrative will not imperil the certainty of the genealogy.[46] The

---

[42] W. Wuellner, "Where is Rhetorical Criticism Taking Us?" *CBQ* 49 (1987) 449, employs the language of C. Perelman and L. Olbrechts-Tyteca, *The New Rhetoric: A Tentative Argumentation* (Notre Dame, IN: University of Notre Dame Press, 1969) 513, to urge rhetorical criticism toward "the social aspect of language which is an instrument of communication and influence on others," i.e., social discourse.

[43] Cohn, "Narrative Structure," 4.

[44] *New York Times Book Review*, March 6, 1986.

[45] Robinson, "Literary Functions," 606.

[46] The genealogical material that forms the story line of Genesis 1-12 belongs to the traditional source P. The rhetorical need of the exilic situation that engendered P continues to assert itself in the use made of the genealogies in the final form of the first stories. For a discerning recent treatment of Pentateuchal origins, see Blenkinsopp, *The Pentateuch*.

genealogical metronome of Genesis 1-12 sounds its regular beat: the continuity of the generations is sure.

Damrosch has recently suggested that the Deuteronomistic historian portrayed Israel as an extra-young and a fundamentally contingent cultural identity.[47] For this historian, Israel's distance from its cultural break was very short, and Israel was always threatened with non-existence, slipping back into Canaanite culture, by the abandonment of Torah. An analogous theme animates the narrative digressions of Genesis 1-12. The life of each generation is highly precarious: disobedience, violence, resistance to the divine imperative can result in its speedy demise. But these failed generations are swept up into a purposeful flow of divine blessing. Since the demise of the first-story generations primarily takes the form of land loss (expulsion from the garden and from the face of the earth and dispersion from the central city); the genealogy also makes a response to the necessity, even the urgency of preserving the line. The cascade of heirs suggests that there will be a future generation to reclaim the lost land.[48] In its present form, Genesis 1-12 answers the precariousness of Israel's contingent reality. Israel is portrayed as an ancient, eternal, and deeply-rooted entity.[49] By tracing the line of named ancestors back to creation itself, Genesis actualizes the perdurability of Israel, not just in general, but over and against the narrative cul-de-sacs.

It is not just Israel's existence, but its chosenness that is rooted in the very processes of creation. Indeed, this phenomenon of choosing, of discrimination, of separation has been a startling part of the story from the beginning, demanding some manner of justification. Detailed by the opening six-day creation account, the process of creation posits the paradigm of separation, ordering, and hierarchical structuring as inherent in the acts of the creator and intrinsic to the process of creation

---

[47] *Narrative Covenant*, 44.
[48] Blenkinsopp, *The Pentateuch*, 109-111, argues that land is the central element of the ancestral stories, the foundation upon which all else depends. He notes, however, that the fact that the fulfillment of the land promise can be postponed "gives urgency to the continuation of the line."
[49] T. Thompson, *Origin Tradition*, 195, has noted that the self-understanding evinced by the Pentateuch arose out of Israel's "view of the fragility of history and the transitoriness of all that gives meaning to being a nation" except for being called into and maintained in existence by God. Similarly, B. G. Webb's recent interpretation of Judges has assayed its theme as "Yahweh is angry at Israel's apostasy but cares too much for it to let it disintegrate or be destroyed;" see *The Book of Judges: An Integrated Reading* (JSOTSup 46; Sheffield: Sheffield Academic, 1987) 209.

whose dominant verb is the Hifil of בדל.⁵⁰ The seventh-day rest itself extrudes from its surroundings and focuses on acts of sacral separation. In the more roundly structured garden story, conflict crops up between life in the isolated enclave (Eden) and the larger earth that needs the human tiller (Gen 2:5).⁵¹ Acts of the creator stand out in the very first story with inter-generational interest (Gen 4:1-16), where the whole enterprise of choosing is attached unabashedly to *Adonai* who has regard for one but not the other (4:4b-5).

The genealogies are the means by which the process of separation and hierarchical ordering most fully expresses itself. They focus attention on the single named bearer of genealogical prominence, the product of a primordial differentiation of the human family which elevates one heir. The "other sons and daughters" (Gen 5:4 et passim and Gen 11:11 et passim), of which the genealogies never lose sight, serve as nameless reminders of the ineluctable process of discrimination under way. The affirmation of this process lays at the heart of Genesis 1-12 and its dominating rhythmic cadence. As ancient Israel followed this interplay of genealogies and stories, it affirmed the emphatic genealogical progression that was leading toward Abram. Then, in the purposeful call of Abram, Israel tells, as Thompson puts it, "the very specific value which it has in the context of the origins of the world and its nations."⁵² Israel justifies the place of genealogical concentration on a single heir within the context of cosmological creation. In this way Israel asserted its identity and pointed to boundaries and separation as means of social survival and maintenance. In this ideology of genealogical discrimination, Israel created a mechanism of survival by which it, often a displaced and refugee minority, always on the periphery of imperial power, defended itself in confrontation with a larger world it could do little to control or command.⁵³ Israel puzzled as well at the roots of the

---

⁵⁰ Vv. 5, 6, 7, 14, and 18. See also the use of בדל in Lev 20: 22-26. D. Smith, *The Religion of the Landless: The Social Context of the Babylonian Exile* (Bloomington, IN: Meyer-Stone, 1989) 146-48, offers an analysis of all the occurrences of בדל, recognizing it as "a key term in the post-exilic concept of a separated and pure people." On the fundamental position of categorization (separation), hierarchy, and boundary maintenance in Israelite cosmology, see T. Freymer-Kensky, "Biblical Cosmology," *Backgrounds for the Bible* (ed. M. P. O'Connor and D. N. Freedman; Winona Lake, IN: Eisenbrauns, 1987) 235-38.
⁵¹ See, Jobling, *Myth and Its Limits*, 22-26.
⁵² *Origin Tradition*, 84.
⁵³ Smith's *Religion of the Landless* provides a survey of contemporary experience of exile and ethnic identity preservation as an invaluable guide to the study of the biblical literature of exile and its origin in creative response to the conditions of minorities amidst a culture of power. See especially his discussion of the

failure of the these pre-Abrahamic generations to achieve a durable and productive (covenantal) divine-human relationship. Influenced by a sense of the perfection of God's *creatio ex nihilo*, modern readers may well be predisposed to see only the human roots of these failures, but Israel observed a divine role as well.[54]

The basic story of Genesis 1-12 is genealogical. The undeniably fascinating narratives of these chapters serve dependently to resolve genealogical ambiguity and are quickly swept up into the dominating generational rhythm. This genealogical rhythm parallels the essential inherence of separation and hierarchy in the processes of creation. It fastens the Abrahamic line to the creative process and anchors the social and religious identity of Israel to these deep-running roots. The formal witness of the combination of genealogy and story has another side as well: the stories' unrealized challenge of the genealogical cadence creates an account of fits and starts in which the rise and fall of drama is determined by the roles both of the commissioned creatures and the commissioning creator. The overcoming of this situation of stalemate is signaled by the transition to the ancestor stories of Abraham and Sarah, which are told on the basis of recast human commissions and a covenantal theology of purposive will. These first stories probe the divine and human roots of the failures of individual, pre-Abrahamic generations that momentarily efface, but are ultimately transcended by, the genealogical rhythm. It pushes on, with predictable, emphatic regularity, toward the announcement of Abraham's journey to the national home. The sustained narrative experience of Abraham and Sarah is the hopeful destiny of those who undertake to enter the Genesis account of how the world Israel knew came into being.

---

elaboration of purity legislation as a Priestly social survival and maintenance mechanism (139-51).

[54] E.g., Cohn, "Narrative Structure," 5, who views the divine role in the narrative as reacting to human errors, and D. A. Knight, "Cosmogony and Order in the Hebrew Tradition," *Cosmogony and Ethical Order* (ed. R. W. Lovin and F. E. Reynolds; Chicago: University of Chicago Press, 1985) 142, who brands human evil as "radically intrusive." For a full discussion of the theme of the vulnerability of the created order, see Levenson *Creation and Persistence*, 3-50. Blenkinsopp, *The Pentateuch*, 93, emphasizes the sapiental tenor of the narrative portions of Genesis 1-12 (associated with source hypothesis's Yahwist).

3

Proclamations to the Fruitful Tree and the Spiritualization of Androgyny*

Ziony Zevit

I

In Jer 2:26-27, Israelites, along with their kings, administrators, priests and prophets are accused of proclaiming to the tree אבי אתה, "you are my father" and to the stone, את ילדתני, "you gave birth to me."[1] This statement, an oral public declaration, was obviously not to be taken literally; rather, in some way, with these words each speaker acknowledged that his or her existence was owing to divine powers in or associated with these two objects. In contemporary discourse, we recognize that the statements did not deal with physical but with metaphysical realities, and that the language of proclamation was not philosophic but mythic.

What is strange about this verse is that the *yin* image, the feminine one, appears to be assigned to the stone. Investigations of the tree motif and its function in the ancient Near East indicate that it was a

---

* Although this study is concerned with an ancestral form of the Judaism with which the honoree of this volume usually deals, it is a pleasure to present it in a volume dedicated to Lou H. Silberman.
[1] The phrase את ילדתני (with the Ketib) is confusing, employing a feminine pronoun with a seemingly masculine verb. Some manuscripts support the reading את ילדתיני with correct agreement (cf. BHS). However, the MT actually preserves a second person, feminine, singular verb which lacks a vowel between it and the suffix, cf. Josh 2:17, 20 and Song of Songs 5:9 and GKC § 59h.

conventional symbol of fertility and nurturing almost always associated with a goddess.² This leads us to question why, in this verse, the *yang* image, the masculine one, was assigned to the tree. The discordant strangeness of Jeremiah's utterance dissipates when we realize that Jer 2:27 contains a metathetic parallelism. This parallelism is defined as one in which "an object or predicate that logically or grammatically or formulaically belongs to one stich may be interchanged at times with that of a corresponding stich resulting, chiastically, in a strangely striking synonymous parallelism."³

Two examples of metathetic parallelism are the following:

והכה הבית הגדול רסיסים והבית הקטן בקעים (Am 6:11) "and he smote/smashed the large house into tiny bits and the small one into large splinters."⁴ Logically, the smaller structure is the one that should have been smashed into small pieces and not have been merely breached and cleft.

וצרתי עליך מצב והקימתי עליך מצרת (Isa 29:3) "I will besiege you with a tower and raise against you siege works." Logically, מצב, "tower," is the object of והקימתי "I will raise up," and not of וצרתי, "I will besiege."

All told, twenty-eight examples of metathetic parallelism have been recognized in Biblical literature, five in Akkadian, and two in Ugaritic.⁵ Although not all examples adduced may be equally convincing, this type of parallelism is real, even though it is rare. Recognizing it can spare exegetes from unfounded emendations and from the grammatical contortions used to wrest sense from apparently difficult verses.⁶

Such parallelism may have arisen initially because in many synonymous parallelisms, the metathesizing of many synonymous vocables has no effect on the meaning, e.g. Ps 92:3, להגיד בבקר חסדך ואמונתך בלילות "to declare your saving acts in the morning

---

² P. Beck, "The Taanach Cult Stands: Iconographic Traditions in the Iron I Cult Vessels," *From Nomadism to Monarchy: Archaeological and Historical Aspects of Early Israel* (ed. N. Na'aman and I. Finkelstein; Jerusalem: Izhak Ben-Zvi, 1990) 429 (Hebrew); O. Keel, *The Symbolism of the Biblical World* (New York: Seabury, 1978) 186-87.
³ N. M. Bronznick, "'Metathetic Parallelism' – An Unrecognized Subtype of Synonymous Parallelism," *HAR* 3 (1979) 25.
⁴ The translation of רסיסים and בקעים follows Bronznick, "Metathetic," 29-30.
⁵ Bronznick presents twenty-six biblical examples, while W. G. E. Watson presents all the others ("More on Metathetic Parallelism," *Welt des Orients* 19 [1988] 40-44).
⁶ Critical research has long recognized the incongruity of the image, so it can hardly be considered a contemporary discovery. Cf. W. L. Holladay, *Jeremiah I* (Hermeneia; Philadelphia: Fortress, 1986) 103-4 for a summary of earlier attempts to resolve the difficulty.

and your faithful acts in the nights," or Isa 1:3, ידע שור קנהו וחמור אבוס בעליו, "an ox knows its owner and a donkey the trough of his master." In the first example, the psalmist's point would be made no matter if the חסדים were declared in the evening and not in the morning; and in the second, Isaiah's point would remain the same if it were the donkey who was mentioned first as recognizing its owner followed by the ox who knew his master's trough. In other words, these could be reversed with no discernible affect on the meaning of the lines.

But such random transpositions are not possible in all lines of poetry. In many lines, they would create confusing metaphors or dissonant images that could affect and even subvert meaning. However, if manipulated consciously by the poet, as in the examples above from Amos and Isaiah, metathetic parallelism could involve (1) a foreshadowing element delaying the semantic parse of a poetic line until all necessary words were delivered; and (2) the creation of complicated semanto-syntactic units of larger than average length.[7] The effect of such a structure within a (written or oral) text would be to delay comprehension by forcing the audience to think about what it perceived until it understood the images. Thus, metathetic parallelism is revealed to be a rhetorical ploy used to force an audience to focus on an idea. It stopped the linear comprehension of a poem or speech until the information, delivered in an unconventional order, was parsed, until the audience "got it." Simultaneously, it self-consciously attracted attention to itself as the linguistic "medium" while highlighting itself as a significant element of the "message."

Recognizing metathetic parallelism in Jer 2:27 enables us to untangle the verse. Judahites were accused of confessing to the stone, "You are my father," and to the tree, "You gave birth to me." They were not accused of addressing these words to trees and to stones in general, i.e. לאבנים ... לעצים, but to a specific tree and to a specific stone.[8] Furthermore, since Jeremiah chose the word אבן, stone, and not מצבה, a hewn stele, a manufactured cult object, there is no *a priori* reason to think that עץ does

---

[7] Bronznick, 37-38; Z. Zevit, "Cognitive Theory and the Memorability of Biblical Poetry," *Let Your Colleagues Praise You: Studies in Memory of Stanley Gevirtz, Part II* (*Maarav* 8 [1992]; ed. R. Ratner, *et. al.*) 199-212.

[8] עץ and אבן form a common pair in Biblical Hebrew, most likely referring to building material or to inanimate "things," i.e. vegetation and mineral matter, cf. Exod 7:19; Deut 4:28; 28:36, 64; 2 Kgs 19:18; Ezek 20:32. It is also attested in Ugaritic, *KTU* 1:3 III:22 and *KTU* 1:23 RS 66. The latter verse may be relevant: *šu'db tk mdbr qdš tmtgrgr labnm wl'ṣm*, "Raise an offering (?) in the wilderness of Qadesh. There speak/murmur to stones and trees." *'db*, however, might mean "depart" and *tgrgr* "dwell," in which case the relevance of this line disappears.

not refer to a natural object, a tree, rather than to one manufactured from wood.

Finally, Jeremiah's citation of the proclamation was not intended to make Israelites look silly. Jeremiah did not use it to mock them – as if they did not know their own liturgy – and he did not treat it sarcastically as nonsense. In its literary context, the only way that we encounter it, it is presented as what Jeremiah, book or prophet, considered incriminating evidence. It is part of the case against those who participated in certain cultic rites, illuminating their intentions and their comprehension of what they were doing. The reconstituted proclamation, then, bears additional consideration.

II

אבן, "stone," in the name אבן ישראל (Gen 49:24), *may* refer to a stone of some status. In this notoriously difficult verse in the Blessing of Jacob, the deity, אביר יעקב, appears to be referred to as the shepherd of the stone of Israel, perhaps the stone used by Jacob at Bethel.[9] אבן ישראל could also be taken as a divine name in parallelism with אביר יעקב.[10] Better grounded in the mythic metaphors of Israel is the use of צור, "large rock/boulder," as a divine epithet: Ps 18:3 (along with סלע, another lithic metaphor), 28:1; Isa 26:4. In Deut 32:3, the poet says that he will call on YHWH's name, and then in the following verse, he states, הצור, "the boulder, his deeds are perfect." In addition, צור is used along with the divine name as a metaphor for protection (e.g., Ps 31:3; 95:1; 144:1). A recent study calculates that metaphoric uses of צור associated with deity slightly outnumber those in which the word refers to a natural object comprised of minerals.[11]

The same lithic terminology is applied also to non-Israelite deities: Deut 32:31, כי לא כצורנו צורם, "not like our צור, "boulder," is their צור" (cf. 32:30, 37). This indicates that the term was generalized within the mythic language and not considered particularly Yahwistic.[12]

YHWH, invoked as הצור in Deut 32:4, is said to have children in v. 5; thus the אבן, to whom fatherhood was ascribed in the unscrambled form

---

[9] A. Rofe, *The Belief in Angels in the Bible* (Jerusalem: Makor, 1979) 219-32 (Hebrew).

[10] Cf. also אל סלעי, "god of my rock" (Ps 42:10), which if taken literally refers to the deity who is associated with a boulder. Had אלי סלעי, "my god, my rock," been written, a stronger case could be made for the metaphorical nature of the image. For סלע as a metaphor, cf. Ps 18:2; 31:4.

[11] M. P. Knowles, "'The Rock, His Work is Perfect': Unusual Imagery for God in Deut xxxii," *VT* 39 (1989) 307.

[12] The semantic development appears to have been as follows: rock/boulder > *protection > *protector > divine protector.

of Jer 2:27 could conceivably refer either to YHWH or to a YHWH symbol. However, within the extended context of the verse in Jeremiah, especially the last half of v. 27, "because they turned their backs to me, not their faces," this interpretation is unlikely. The half-verse should be taken literally. It accused the Judahites of a significant cultic impropriety vis-à-vis YHWH. During their ritual prostrations, they were not facing the direction that Yahwistic convention determined, perhaps to the west, towards the *adytum* of the temple; they were bowing in such a way that their backside was where their faces ought to have been.

References in proximate passages to the prophets who prophesy by the Baal (Jer 2:8), to the בעלים, Baals (Jer 2:23), and to "gods" (Jer 2:28), indicates that the אבן of v. 27 is a Baal symbol.[13] The tree addressed as a birthing figure stands in some relationship to the stone addressed as "father." It could be wife, consort, or daughter; but it was obviously "mother" to the confessing Judahite. It was most likely either a place of indwelling for, or dedicated to, or a symbol of a fertility goddess.[14] An evaluation of the iconographic and inscriptional data from Lachish, Kuntillet ᶜAjrud, and perhaps Kh. El-Qom, in addition to Biblical and Tannaitic sources suggest minimally that "the tree" of Jer 2:27 was called an אשרה, "asherah," and that it marked or bore the (potential) presence of the goddess Asherah.[15]

III

The sacred tree and its associated goddess were already a problem to some Yahwists at least 125 years before Jeremiah. In Hos 14:9, the prophet creatively usurped the fruitful tree image as a YHWH

---

[13] S. Olyan concludes that it represents YHWH. Olyan, however, isolates the verse in Jeremiah from its literary context, preferring to evaluate it within the context of the pithoi inscriptions found at Kuntillet ᶜAjrud that are dated more than a century earlier ("The Cultic Confession of Jer 2, 27a," *ZAW* 99 [1987] 256-58). Jeremiah's concern with Baal worship is reflected also outside of this chapter in Jer 7:9; 9:13; and 12:16.

This verse has one additional implication: אבן, like צור, was not a uniquely Yahwistic metaphor. Of course, it is theoretically possible that Israelite Yahwists used אבן in a particular way for YHWH alone, but we lack sufficient data to determine this. But if so, then the same vocable may have enjoyed the same status with Israelite Baalists.

[14] I. Cornelius, "Paradise Motifs in the 'Eschatology' of the Minor Prophets and the Iconography of the Ancient Near East: The Concepts of Fertility, Water, Trees, and 'Tierfrieden' and Gen 2-3," *Journal of Northwest Semitic Languages* 14 (1988) 58.

[15] R. Hestrin, "The Lachish Ewer and the 'Asherah'," *IEJ* 37 (1987) 220-23; B. Margalit, "Some Observations on the Inscriptions and Drawing from Khirbet El-Qom," *VT* 39 (1989) 371-78. I am skeptical about Margalit's interpretation of the scratches as a sketch of a tree.

metaphor:[16] "Ephraim, what do I still have to do with idols? אני עניתי ואשורנו. I am like a leafy fir tree.[17] From me your fruit is found."

The Bible is replete with plant imagery, but throughout, YHWH is the gardener, and human beings, Israel or foreign nations, are equated with the vegetation. Only in Hos 14:9 is the pattern broken.[18] Later Yahwistic polemicists did not pick up this metaphor, perhaps because it smacked of what they perceived of as idolatrous language and/or perhaps because it was part of a recognizable text from an idolatrous ritual appropriated by Hosea for his own ends.[19]

The words left untranslated above in the rendering of Hos 14:9 are translated variously:

> RSV: It is I who answer and look after you;
>
> NEB: I have spoken and I affirm it;
>
> NJPS: when I respond and look to him.

All of these translations involve various types of emendations or revocalizations because the phrase, if not textually corrupt, is quite difficult. אני עניתי, "I answer(ed)," simply makes no sense both in the immediate and in the general context.[20] In the defective Hebrew orthography of the 8th century, the sentence may have appeared as follows: אני ענתי ואשרנה.[21] In view of this orthography, J. Wellhausen's emendation, אני ענתו ואשרתו, "I am his Anat and his Asherah," seems less radical now than when he first suggested it in 1893.[22] If the original was intended to mean what Wellhausen suggested, it would have been spelled originally אני ענתה ואשרתה which would have been retranscribed as

---

[16] Cornelius, "Paradise," 58.
[17] For this translation of ברוש, cf. K. A. Tanberg, "I am Like An Evergreen Fir; From Me Comes Your Fruit," *SJOT* 2 (1989) 84-85.
[18] T. Frymer-Kensky, "The Planting of Man: A Study of Biblical Imagery," *Love and Death in the Ancient Near East: Essays in Honor of Marvin H. Pope* (ed. J. H. Marks and R. M. Good; Guilford, CT: , 1987) 129-36.
[19] Tanberg, "I am Like An Evergreen," cites numerous examples of deities associated with trees: *Nin-gis-zi-da*, "the Lord who is the tree" (p. 86). A letter sent to Esarhaddon (?) states " a pine [*burašu*] is the Lord, my king, who gives life to numerous people" (p. 87). Tanberg notes that according to Philo of Byblos, the Phoenicians had a goddess named "Berouth" (> *beroṯ* = ברוש) (90).
[20] A newly discovered sense of עי, "to submit" does not appear applicable to this verse. Cf. A. Frisch, "ועניתם (I Reg 12,7): An Ambiguity and its Function in Context," *ZAW* 103 (1991) 415.
[21] Z. Zevit, *Matres Lectionis in Ancient Hebrew Epigraphs* (Cambridge, MA: ASOR, 1980) 14-15.
[22] J. Wellhausen, *Die Kleinen Propheten ubersetzt, mit Noten* (Skizzen und Vorarbeiten 5; Berlin: Reimer, 1893) 21, 131: "ich bin seine Anath und seine Aschera ...."

אני ענתו ואשרתו some time after the 6th century.²³ The extant, nonsensical text may have emerged due to scribal error: ענתו > ענתי (in the Aramaic square script where word final *waw* and *yod* could be confused) > עניתי (post-exilic *plene* spelling); אשרתו > אשרנו (in the Aramaic square script where a poorly formed *taw* might be misread as a *nun*) > אשורנו (*plene* spelling). Another possibility is that it was subverted and is an unrecorded *tiqqun soferim*, a pious change in the text, made by teachers of the early Second Temple period to guard the honor of YHWH by neutralizing offensive material. Unfortunately, this emendation must still be classified as clever but conjectural, and thus it will not be factored into my discussion.²⁴

Despite the difficulties, the implication of Hos 14:9 is that people in his audience claimed that a deity identified or associated with a leafy tree, not YHWH, was the source of their "fruit." I assume that "fruit" in this utterance referred to human progeny and agricultural produce as well as to the natural increase of flocks and herds.²⁵

Liturgical pronouncements of the type cited in Jeremiah were appropriated by Jerusalem Temple Yahwism, although in a less daring formulation than the one used by Hosea, long before Jeremiah. Psalm 2, most likely from the 8th century or even earlier, that reflects a self-confident Judahite monarchy, contains an important example. If the adoption formula placed into YHWH's mouth in Ps 2:7 is adjusted so that the anointed king could recite it, he would have said, אבי אתה היום ילדתני, "You are my father. Today, you gave me birth." This combined the two confessional statements into a single one, since it

---

²³ Zevit, *Matres*, 33.
²⁴ O. Loretz supports a version of the Wellhausian emendation, אני ענתך ואשרתך. He cites the use of the divine name with a possessive suffix in Hebrew from inscriptions on pithoi found at Kuntillet 'Ajrud in Sinai, אשרתה, and in Ugaritic, '*Anth*, "his Anat" (KTU 1. 43:13) and *atrty*, "my Atiratu" (KTU 2.31:41). Loretz considers "his Asherah" at 'Ajrud a reference to a deity and not a symbol, a "thou" and not an "it" to employ Buberian terms ("'Anat-Aschera [Hos 14,9] Und Die Inschriften Von Kuntillet 'Ajrud," *Studi Epigrafici e Linguistici* 6 (1989) 59-61; M. Dietrich and O. Loretz, "Jahwe und seine Aschera": *Anthropomorphes Kultbild in Mesopotamien, Ugarit und Israel* [Münster: Ugarit-Verlag, 1992] 110-12; 173-89).
²⁵ M. S. Smith's discussions of the punning on the word אשרה and the evolution of the tree image associated with it in Israelite wisdom demonstrate the hold that these had in the sophisticated high culture of Jerusalem (*The Early History of God* [San Francisco: Harper & Row, 1990] 94-97, where Jer 2:27 and Hos 14:9 are also discussed). Granting his conclusions, and those on which his work is based, it is clear that both Hosea and Jeremiah, just to name prophets cited in this study, were not confronting low, unofficial, peasant, or rural culture. Quite the contrary, those who followed these cults included people from sophisticated, elite urban classes.

was now addressed to YHWH.[26] In other words, in this Yahwistic formulation, YHWH was both father and mother. In this statement, *yin* and *yang* were united into a single principle and fused into each other; androgyny was spiritualized, and divine gender transformed into amorphous life giving power.

Ps 2:7 and Hos 14:9 indicate that the proclamation metathesized in Jer 2:27 and the religion in which it was used had a long and venerable history in pre-exilic Israel. The two prophets, however, were not referring to exactly the same cult; there is a distinction between the two. Hosea either quoted or paraphrased a group that attributed all fertility to a female tree; Jeremiah cited a group that attributed fertility both to Baal, comprehended as a stone, and to Asherah, comprehended as a living tree.[27] The transformation of myth attested in Ps 2:7 seems to have been a subtlety that was either unappreciated or rejected by many Judahites in the time of Jeremiah.

---

[26] Attested adoption formulae in the Tanakh do not involve the birthing motif: 2 Sam 7:14: "I will become a father for him, and he will become a son for me," the reverse of which would be, "I will become a son for you and you will become a father for me;" and Ps 89:27: "You are my father."

[27] Holladay's interpretation of Jer 2:27 which dovetails mine differs from it in that he considers the passage part of a general mocking condemnation of paganism whereas I maintain that it is a very specific indictment that provides an oblique glimpse into a particular cult (104-5). Only if viewed within the broader context of the book as whole, and within the even broader context of the Deuteronomic tradition, may it be considered part of a general condemnation.

4

The Prayer of Nabonidus, Elijah on Mount Carmel, and the Development of Monotheism in Israel

Susan Ackerman

I spent 1989–90 as a member of the faculties of Near Eastern Studies and Judaic Studies at the University of Arizona and thus became, for that one year, a colleague of Lou Silberman's. Because my tenure in Tucson was short, however, there were not many opportunities to talk with Lou about his work or mine. Still, Lou was able to attend a lecture I gave based on a much earlier version of the paper presented below. The revised paper, moreover, is one that has benefited greatly from the methodological principles I learned from my occasional conversations with Lou, from his writings, and from working with his students at Arizona. This paper, then, is one that I very much associate with my time in Tucson and with my colleague there, Lou Silberman, and it is a privilege and pleasure to present it to him on the occasion of his second retirement.

I

In 1956 J. T. Milik published four small leather fragments from Qumran Cave 4, part of a first–century (75–50 B.C.E.) Aramaic text.[1] Three of these four fragments, plus another small piece that came to Milik's attention after his article was completed, make up the first eight

---

[1] J. T. Milik, "'Prière de Nabonide' et autres écrits d'un cycle Daniel: Fragments araméen de Qumrân 4," *RB* 63 (1956) 407-11, with an Addendum on p. 415.

lines of the first column of what was called by Milik the "Prayer of Nabonidus" (4Q Or[atio] Nab).[2] Although a perfect understanding of this text has proven to be impossible due to the medial and final lacunae found in each line, Milik and all subsequent commentators[3] have agreed concerning the Prayer's broad outlines. In the first line there is an introduction in the third person identifying the Prayer as the words prayed by the Babylonian king Nabonidus (*nbny*)[4] when he was stricken with grievous boils (*šḥn' b'yš'*) by the word of God Most High (*bptgm '[lhy 'ly']*)[5] while in Teima (*btymn*) in the north Arabian peninsula. The

---

[2] The fourth of the four initial fragments published by Milik comes from another column of the work (it is written on different leather) and is very broken. Although a few words can be made out, the lack of context renders any speculation about this orphan pure guesswork.
[3] The bibliography is extensive, strikingly so considering the limited amount of text available and its fragmentary nature. Studies include (in chronological order) E. Vogt, "Precatio Regis Nabonid in pia narratione Iudaica," *Bib* 37 (1956) 532-34; H. M. I. Gevaryahu, "The Prayer of Nabonidus from the Scrolls of the Wilderness of Judah," *Studies in the Dead Sea Scrolls: Lectures Delivered at the Third Annual Conference (1957) in Memory of E.L. Sukenik* (Jerusalem: Kiryat Sepher, 1957) 12-23 (Hebrew); D. N. Freedman, "The Prayer of Nabonidus," *BASOR* 145 (1957) 31-32; A. Dupont-Sommer, *Les écrits esseniens découvertes près de la Mer Morte* (Paris: Bibliothèque historique, 1959); A. Dupont-Sommer, "Remarques linguistiques sur un fragment araméen de Qoumrân ('Prière de Nabonide')," *Comptes Rendus du Groupe Linguistique d'Études Chamito-Semitiques* 8 (1957-1960) 48-50; R. Meyer, "Das Qumranfragment 'Gebet des Nabonid,'" *TLZ* 85 (1960) 831-34; idem, *Das Gebet des Nabonid: Eine in den Qumran-Handschriften wiederentdeckte Weisheitserzählung* (Sitzungsberichte der sächsischen Akademie der Wissenschaften zu Leipzig, Philologisch-historische Klasse, Band 107, Heft 3; Berlin: Akademie Verlag, 1962); G. Fohrer, "4 Q Or Nab, 11 Q Tg Job und die Hioblegende," *ZAW* 75 (1963) 93-97; M. Delcor, "Le testament de Job, la prière de Nabonide et les traditions targoumiques," *Bibel und Qumran: Beiträge zur Erforschung der Beziehungen zwischen Bibel-und-Qumranwissenschaft* (Hans Bardke zum 22.9.66; ed. S. Wagner; Berlin: Evangelische Haupt-Bibelgesellschaft, 1968) 57-74; P. Grelot, "La prière de Nabonide (4Q Or Nab): nouvel essai de restauration," *RevQ* 9 (1978) 483-95; A. S. van der Woude, "Bemerkungen zum Gebet des Nabonid," *Qumrân, sa piéte, sa théologie, et son milieu* (ed. M. Delcor; BETL 46; Paris et Gembloux: Ducurot; Louvain: Louvain University Press, 1978) 121-29; F. Garcia, "4Q Or Nab. Nueva sintesis," *Seferad* 40 (1980) 5-25; F. M. Cross, "Fragments of the Prayer of Nabonidus," *IEJ* 34 (1984) 260-64.
[4] Aramaic *nbny* is a hypocoristicon for Akkadian *Nabû-na'id*, Nabonidus. The *-ay* hypocoristicon is well-known on Aramaic personal names (Milik cites M. Lidzbarski, *Ephemeris für semitische Epigraphik* 2 [Giessen: Alfred Töpelmann, 1908] 13-17).
[5] Although only the *'alep* of *'lhy 'ly'* is present on the leather in line 2, a divine title following *bptgm* is required. While *'lhy 'ly'*, originally proposed by Milik, 408, and *'lhy šmy'*, preferred by I. D. Amusin, "The Qumran Fragment of the 'Prayer' of the King of Babylon, Nabonidus," *Vestnik drevnej istorii* (Moskow) 66/4 (1958) 104 (Russian; summarized in I. M. Diakonoff, "The Ancient Near East in Soviet

Prayer then shifts, presumably already in the lacuna at the end of line 2 and definitely by the beginning of line 3, to a first-person speech by Nabonidus, who begins by reporting in his own voice what the narrator has already told us – that he was stricken with grievous boils – and then adds that his affliction lasted seven years until his sin was forgiven. At that point, a Jewish seer commanded[6] the king to write an account of his experience in order to glorify the name of God Most High (šm '[lhy 'ly']).[7] In lines 6–8, Nabonidus' written account begins, telling the story once more: that the king was stricken with grievous boils in Teima for seven years. We are further told that Nabonidus, seeking divine succor during this seven years, prayed to gods of silver and gold, bronze, iron,[8] wood, stone, and clay. Then the text breaks off, but as all commentators have noted, the conclusion is obvious: Nabonidus' prayers to the gods of silver and gold, bronze, iron, wood, stone, and clay were of no avail, but only through devotion to God Most High was Nabonidus able to be healed of his skin afflictions.

It was also obvious to Milik in the *editio princeps* and it has been clear to scholars ever since that the story told in the Prayer of Nabonidus has close literary affinities to the book of Daniel, especially Dan 3:31–4:34. Indeed, long before the Qumran text had been discovered, biblicists had posited that Dan 3:31– 4:34, the story of Nebuchadnezzar's madness and his exile from Babylon, was a story originally told about one of Nebuchadnezzar's successors, Nabonidus. The reasons for suspecting such literary confusion were multiple. First, the lack of material anywhere else in the Bible about the insanity of such a major figure as Nebuchadnezzar had been perceived as problematic since the time of Jerome.[9] Second, the Daniel tradition describing a royal exile from Babylon was not in accord with what Mesopotamian archaeology of the nineteenth and early twentieth centuries had revealed about Nebuchadnezzar but was consistent with Babylonian materials

---

Research," *Archiv Orientalni* 27 [1959] 148, and by A. H. Haberman, "From the Scrolls of the Dead Sea," *Had-Do'ar* 37/12 [16 Shevat, 1957] 215 [Hebrew]), are equally possible, I have opted for '*lhy 'ly*' based on its occurrence in Dan 3:32. Dan 3:31–4:34, the story of Nebuchadnezzar's madness, has, as will be discussed below, close affinities with 4Q Or Nab.

[6] To read *ḥḥwy* and *wktb* as imperatives at the beginning of line 5 was first proposed by Dupont-Sommer, *Les écrits esseniens*, 338.

[7] On the reconstruction of '*lhy 'ly*', see above, n. 5.

[8] The words "bronze" and "iron" (*nḥš·* and *przl·*) occur in the lacuna at the end of line 7 but have been restored with confidence by all commentators based on Dan 5:4 and 5:23. On the affinities between 4Q Or Nab and the Daniel material, see above, n. 5, and the discussion below.

[9] Pointed out by M. McNamara, "Nabonidus and the Book of Daniel," *ITQ* 37 (1970) 132.

pertaining to Nabonidus. Finally, the genealogical notice claiming Nebuchadnezzar as the father of Belshazzar in Dan 5:2, 11, 13, 18–23 was contradicted by cuneiform records concerning Bel–shar–usur, son of Nabonidus.[10] Given these data, previous generations[11] had determined that Dan 3:31–4:34 was originally told about King Nabonidus, who ruled after Nebuchadnezzar and who fathered Belshazzar. The discovery of the Prayer of Nabonidus has provided striking confirmation of this thesis. Indeed, a comparison of Dan 3:31–4:34 with the Prayer provides an excellent example of the phenomenon common in folk literature, whereby a less common name, in this case, Nabonidus, is replaced by a more famous one, Nebuchadnezzar.

A comparison of Dan 3:31–4:34 and the Prayer of Nabonidus also illustrates a second behavior characteristic of folk literature, in which the broad outlines of a story remain constant while particular details are allowed to change. The most striking example of this in Dan 3:31–4:34 and the Prayer is the two stories' depictions of the king's illness. According to Dan 3:31–4:34, Nabonidus goes mad: "He was driven from among men, and ate grass like an ox, and his body was wet with the dew of heaven till his hair grew as long as eagles' feathers, and his nails were like birds' claws" (Dan 4:33). Finally, at the end of seven years the insanity is ended; the king proclaims, "My reason returned to me" (Dan 4:34). But according to the Prayer, Nabonidus is afflicted with *šiḥnā bîšā*, which has been translated here fairly literally as grievous boils. These boils are the same kind of inflammation (*šĕḥîn rāʿ*) with which the Egyptians were afflicted in the sixth plague (Exod 9:8–12), which Job scraped away as he sat among ashes (Job 2:7–8), and from which Hezekiah is healed because of his devotion and piety (2 Kgs 20: 1–11 [Isa 38:1–22]). As Lev 13:18–23 implies, they are festering sores akin to *ṣāraʿat*. *ṣāraʿat*, moreover, although usually translated as "leprosy," based on the Greek *lepra*, is in fact better analyzed as some kind of eruptive skin

---

[10] Particularly significant here are four inscribed cylinders from the corners of the temple of Sin at Ur discovered in 1854 and translated by H. C. Rawlinson. See G. Rawlinson, *Egypt and Babylon from Scripture and Profane Sources* (London: Hodder and Stoughton, 1885) 151.

[11] See, e.g., F. Hommel, "Die Abfassungszeit des Buches Daniel und der Wahnsinn Nabonids," *Theologisches Literaturblatt* 23 (1902) 145–50, with a reply by F. Buhl and further comments by Hommel on 204–7; P. Riessler, *Das Buch Daniel erklärt* (Vienna: von Meyer & Co., 1902) 43; P. Dhorme, "Cyrus le Grand," *RB* 9 (1912) 37–38; S. Smith, *Babylonian Historical Texts* (London: Methuen, 1924) 36, 46, 50, 78; W. von Soden, "Eine babylonische Volksüberlieferung von Nabonid in den Danielerzahlungen," *ZAW* 53 (1935) 81–89.

disease, since true leprosy, Hansen's disease, was unknown in the ancient Near East.[12]

In the literature on 4Q Or Nab and Dan 3:31–4:34, there has been little discussion about this discrepancy in the two sources concerning Nabonidus' malady.[13] To be sure, there has been some commentary on the Daniel tradition of madness, generated in particular by the ever-increasing body of relevant cuneiform material. This material, as mentioned above, confirms that Nabonidus did exile himself to Teima for a number of years (as Dan 3:31–4:34, obliquely, and 4Q Or Nab, directly, claim). In addition, it provides hints, at least, about what the reasons behind the exile might have been. One reason hinted at is that, as in Dan 3:31–4:34, Nabonidus was thought by the authors of the cuneiform texts to be mad. The Cyrus Cylinder, published in 1890,[14] details bizarre behaviors characteristic of Nabonidus, as does the Persian Verse Account of Nabonidus, published in 1924.[15] According to these documents, Nabonidus engaged in inappropriate religious rituals and blabbered incorrect prayers,[16] in addition to inexplicably exiling himself to Teima for a number of years.[17]

From our point of view, however, this kind of behavior, while possibly eccentric, is by no means insane. Moreover, historians should remember that the Cyrus Cylinder and the Persian Verse Account are polemical in nature, propagandistic pieces that attempt to vilify Nabonidus in order to give greater glory to the Persian conqueror, Cyrus. Still, while neither can be taken as wholly reliable, the Cyrus Cylinder and the Persian Verse Account do have underlying them some trustworthy traditions concerning Nabonidus' self-imposed exile to Teima. Their notices concerning Nabonidus' inappropriate religious rituals and incorrect prayers, for example, suggest that Nabonidus, while not mad, was in his devotions at odds with the cult of at least some of the

---

[12] See Y. Feldman, "Dermatology in the Hebrew Bible," *Cutis* 2 (1966) 987–88, 1027; E. V. Hulse, "The Nature of Biblical 'Leprosy' and the Use of Alternative Medical Terms in Modern Translations of the Bible," *PEQ* 107 (1975) 87–105; J. Zias, "Lust and Leprosy: Confusion or Correlation?" *BASOR* 275 (1989) 27–31.

[13] See only the brief comments of L. Hartman, "The Great Tree and Nebuchodnosor's Madness," *The Bible in Current Catholic Thought* (ed. J. L. McKenzie; St. Mary's Theological Studies 1; New York: Herder and Herder, 1962) 81.

[14] See E. Schrader, *Keilinschriftliche Bibliothek* 3.2 (Berlin: H. Reuther's Verlagsbuchhandlung, 1890) 120–27; easily accessible in *ANET* (3d ed.) 315b–316b.

[15] See Smith, 27–97; easily accessible in *ANET*, 312b–315a.

[16] Cyrus Cylinder, lines 1–9 (*ANET*, 315b); Persian Verse Account, Cols. 1, 2, and 5 (*ANET*, 313a–b, 314b).

[17] Persian Verse Account, Col. 2, 18–29 (*ANET*, 313b).

religious leadership. To anyone at all familiar with Nabonidus, this should come as no surprise, for in addition to the Cyrus Cylinder and the Persian Verse Account, almost every other cuneiform text concerning Nabonidus reports in one way or another that Nabonidus in his personal religion strayed from the orthodoxies of the state cult of Marduk by fervently devoting himself to the worship of the moon god, Sin.[18]

Whether Nabonidus began his reign as a committed Sin worshiper or whether his allegiance to the moon god developed over time, as H. Tadmor has forcefully argued,[19] need not concern us here, for certainly for the bulk of his reign, that is, throughout his time in Teima and during the years that followed, Nabonidus' pro–Sin tendencies are undeniable. For example, Nabonidus' own account of his sojourn in Teima, namely a Harran inscription (Harran 2 A/B), which has been described as "une véritable explosion de louanges fanatiques,"[20] claims that the king went to Teima, a center of the moon god's cult, and stayed there ten years by the command of Sin himself.[21] A second and contemporary Harran inscription (Harran 1 A/B) is the story of Nabonidus' mother, who was similarly devoted to Sin's cult, particularly as it was practiced in Harran.[22] The mother in all likelihood exerted a strong influence on the son, and it is probably no coincidence that a third text, usually called

---

[18] See especially J. Lewy, "The Late Assyro–Babylonian Cult of the Moon and its Culmination at the Time of Nabonidus," *HUCA* 19 (1945–46) 405–18, 434–41; W. G. Lambert, "Nabonidus in Arabia," *Proceedings of the Fifth Seminar for Anatolian Studies* (London: Seminar for Arabian Studies, 1972) 58–63; less recently, R. P. Dougherty, *Nabonidus and Belshazzar* (Yale Oriental Series, Researches 15; New Haven: Yale University Press, 1929) 154–57.

[19] H. Tadmor, "The Inscriptions of Nabunaid: Historical Arrangement," *Studies in Honor of Benno Landsberger on his Seventy–Fifth Birthday, April 21, 1965* (Assyriological Studies 16; Chicago: University of Chicago Press, 1965) 351–63, especially 358–63. Tadmor's argument is based on a chronological arrangement of the major Nabonidus inscriptions. His dating system is followed here. See further P.–A. Beaulieu, *The Reign of Nabonidus King of Babylon 556–539 B.C.* (New Haven and London: Yale University Press, 1989) 1–65.

[20] P. Garelli, as quoted by W. L. Moran, "Review of L. Pirot, A. Robert, H. Cazelles, *Dictionaire de la Bible*," *Bib* 41 (1960) 296.

[21] Col. 1, lines 11–24; see C. J. Gadd, "The Ḫarran Inscriptions of Nabonidus," *Anatolian Studies* 8 (1958) 56–59, but note the important correction to line 23 by W. L. Moran ("Notes on the New Nabonidus Inscriptions," *Or* 28 [1959] 138), who reads, *ultu ālīya babili^{ki} useriqannimma uruh ^{alu}te-ma-a*, "from my city, Babylon, he [Sin] caused me to flee (on the) road to Teima." See also *ANESTP*, 562a–563b.

[22] Harran 1 A, the so–called "Family of Nabonidus," was published by H. Pognon, *Inscriptions sémitiques de la Syrie, de la Mésopotamie, et de la région de Mossoul* (Paris: Imprimerie Nationale, 1907) 1–14; an easily accessible translation is in *ANET*, 311b–312b, with a revised translation, based on Harran 1 B, in *ANESTP*, 560b–562a. For Harran 1 B, see Gadd, "Ḫarran Inscriptions," 46–53.

"Nabonidus' Rise to Power,"[23] claims that one of Nabonidus' first official acts as king was to restore the Sin temple of Éḫulḫul at Harran.[24] The same text also notes that Nabonidus established a place for Sin to give oracles in Ésagila, the state temple of Marduk in Babylon.[25]

Nabonidus claims in this early text (from his second regnal year) that Marduk ordered him to introduce Sin worship in Babylon, thus acknowledging, it seems, the sovereignty of Marduk as the head of the Babylonian pantheon. But this early confession and paeans like it may be forays into religious diplomacy, attempts to pay lip service to the state cult as the political reality of sixth-century Babylon demanded. Certainly this is true for later texts, where Nabonidus only reluctantly acknowledges the Marduk cult. W. L. Moran has argued convincingly, for example, that the Nabonidus Sippar Cylinder[26] shared a *Vorlage* with the very pro–Sin Harran inscription of Nabonidus' mother but was then "reworked ... in order to minimize Sin's importance" and to elevate Marduk's.[27] Yet even the reworked Sippar Cylinder in places puts Sin on a par with Marduk: thus in a well-known passage from Col. 1 (lines 18–19), Nabonidus says, "Marduk, the great Lord, and Sin, the light of heaven and earth, were standing on both sides." Moreover, Nabonidus, unlike every other Neo–Babylonian king, elsewhere uses Marduk's epithets to refer to Sin.[28] Building inscriptions from Sippar, Larsa, and Agade even claim the Marduk temples of Ésagila and Ézida as abodes of Sin's great divinity.[29] Similar sentiments can be found in inscriptions from Ur, which describe how Nabonidus rebuilt Égišnugal, the Sin temple there,[30] as well as how he appointed his own daughter as Sin priestess.[31] Other major building projects went on in Teima: the Persian

---

[23] First published by V. Schiel, "Inscription de Nabonide," *Recueil des Travaux Relatifs à la Philologie et à l'Archéologie egyptiennes et assyriennes* 18 (1896) 15–29; easily accessible in *ANET*, 308b–311b. See in particular Col. 10 on the restoration of Éḫulḫul (*ANET*, 311a).
[24] Although whether this temple was really restored early in Nabonidus' reign is dubious; see Tadmor, "The Inscriptions of Nabunaid," 355–56.
[25] Col. 10 (*ANET*, 311a–b).
[26] S. Langdon, *Die neubabylonische Königsinschriften* (VAB 4; Leipzig: J. C. Heinrichs, 1912) 218–29 (Nab. 1).
[27] Moran, "Notes," 132.
[28] W. Dommershausen, *Nabonid im Buche Daniel* (Mainz: M. Grunewald Verlag, 1964) 52.
[29] S. Langdon, "New Inscriptions of Nabuna'id," *AJSL* 32 (1915) 102–17.
[30] Langdon, *Neubabylonische Königsinschriften*, 250–53 (Nab. 5).
[31] As attested in duplicate inscriptions usually entitled "The Priestess of Sin." The *editio princeps* of the first was P. Dhorme, "La fille de Nabonide," *RA* 11 (1914) 105–17; for the second, see A. Clay, *Miscellaneous Inscriptions in the Yale Babylonian Collection* (Yale Oriental Studies; New Haven: Yale University Press, 1915) #45 (pp. 66–75, pl. 33–35, 54).

Verse Account, at least, reports that Nabonidus made that city as beautiful as Babylon.³² The construction surely included a Sin temple.

In Babylonian religion the god of the moon, like the god of the sun who similarly sees all that goes on both in this world and in the world below, is a god of justice. But Sin has another significant attribute: he is the god who causes "leprosy" (again to be taken in the generic sense as an eruptive type of skin disease). That is, Sin is the god who inflicts festering sores and the like on those who displease him, and the god who cures those who are devoted to him of these inflammatory skin ailments.

Numerous examples of Sin's association with skin diseases could be adduced from the Old Babylonian period well into the first millennium. Among the Ur excavation texts, in a petition to the moon god concerning an unrepaid debt, the frustrated creditor reminds Sin that the debtor swore an oath before the moon god to repay and, having failed to do so, he should be "filled with leprosy" (*e-ip-qa-am i-ma-al-la*) by Sin.³³ The use of *malûm*, "to fill," is frequent in this context; Sin is also said to "clothe" (*labāšum*) or "cover" (*ḫalāpum, katāmum*) the "body" (*zumrum, pagrum, gimir lānīšu*) with "leprosy" (*epqum, išrubum, saḫaršubbum*)³⁴ like a "garment" (*ṣubātum, lubārum, naḫlapti*). Thus, in the eighth–century treaty between Assurnirari V of Assyria and Mati'ilu of Bit-Agusi, Assurnirari asks of Sin that if Mati'ilu should break the treaty, the god might "clothe him, his sons, his nobles, and the peoples of his land with leprosy like a garment" (*iš-ru-ba-a kīma na-ḫa-lap-ti li-l[ab-bi-is-su-nu]*).³⁵ Similarly, in the seventh–century vassal treaties of Esarhaddon, among the curse formulae in lines 414–493, we read, "May Sin, the brightness of heaven and earth, clothe you with leprosy" (*saḫar-šub-ba-e li-ḫal-lip-ku-nu*).³⁶ Another commonly occurring idiom concerning Sin's afflicting with "leprosy" or a like inflammation is *erretum rabītum*, "the great curse," or similarly *šēritum rabītum*, "the great penalty."³⁷ So, for example, when we read in the list of curses found in the Epilogue to the

---

³² Persian Verse Account, Col. 2, 28–30 (*ANET*, 313b–314a); see Lambert, "Nabonidus in Arabia," 61.

³³ G. J. Gadd and S. N. Kramer, *Ur Excavation Texts* 6/2 (London: The Trustees of the British Museum, 1963) 402, line 37.

³⁴ On *išrubum* and *saḫaršubbum*, in addition to the standard lexica, see A. L. Oppenheim, *The Interpretation of Dreams in the Ancient Near East, with a Translation of an Assyrian Dream-Book* (Transactions of the American Philosophical Society 46/3; Philadelphia: American Philosophical Society, 1956) 273, n. 54.

³⁵ E. Weidner, "Der Staatsvertrag Assurniraris VI von Assyrien mit Mati'ilu von Bit Agusi," *AfO* 8 (1932) 20–21 (Rs. IV, 4–5).

³⁶ D. Wiseman, "The Vassal-Treaties of Esarhaddon," *Iraq* 20 (1958) 59–60 (lines 419–21); see also the comments of R. Borger, "Zu den Asarhadden-Verträgen aus Nimrud," *ZA* 54 (1961) 187.

³⁷ J. Nougayrol, "*Sirrimu* (non *purîmu*) 'âne sauvage,'" *JCS* 2 (1948) 207, n. 12.

Code of Hammurapi that Sin is asked to curse anyone who disregards the stele with "his great penalty which will not depart from his body" (*še-re-sú ra-bi-tam ša i-na zu-um-ri-šu la i-ḫal-li-qú;* Col. 50 [Rs. 37], 48–50), we are again encountering evidence of the association of Sin with skin diseases.

References to skin inflammations as a curse of Sin are especially common on Babylonian boundary stones (*kudurru*), and examples are attested from the Kassite period through the fall of Babylon. From late fourteenth-century Larsa, for example, comes the *kudurru* of Nazimaruttas, which reads ^d*Sin EN GAL sa-ḫar-šup-pa-a li-mi-li-šu-ma,* "may Sin, the great lord, fill him with leprosy."[38] Another Larsa *kudurru* from a quarter-century later gives voice to the same sentiment: ^d*Sin EN É.GIŠ.NU.GAL sa-ḫar-šup-pa-a li-ŠÚ-ma,* "may Sin, the lord of Égišnugal, cover him with leprosy."[39] In 1970, R. Borger published two twelfth-century examples from the reign of Merodach-baladan I.[40] Borger has also commented on a parallel formulation in a third Merodach-baladan *kudurru* (SB 26, Col. VI, 14).[41] Three additional examples of Sin's curse of "leprosy" from twelfth-century *kudurru* can be found in L. W. King's 1912 collection, *Babylonian boundary-stones*. King also cites another *kudurru* from a later period.[42] J. Nougayrol has collected an even more extensive collection of *kudurru* references to skin diseases as a curse of Sin.[43] Nougayrol cites all of King's examples, one of

---

[38] D. Arnaud, "Deux *kudurru* de Larsa: II. Etude épigraphique," *RA* 66 (1972) 166 (line 38).
[39] Arnaud, "Deux *kudurru* de Larsa," 173 (line 74).
[40] R. Borger, "Vier Grenzsteinurkunden Merodachbaladans I. von Babylonien," *AfO* 23 (1970) 1–26. The texts read: ^d*XXX na-an-na-ru ša AN-e saḫar-šub-ba-a pa-gar-šu ki-ma ṣu-ba-ti lik-tu-um,* "May Sin, the brightness of heaven, cover his body with leprosy like a garment" (Teheran *kudurru,* Col. III, 1–3); [^d*Sin*] *nanna-ru pa-ri-is EŠ.BAR saḫar-šu]b-ba-a li-ma-li-šu,* "May Sin, the bright one, the one who renders judgment, fill him with leprosy" (SB 33, Col. III, 9–10).
[41] Found in W. J. Hinke, *Selected Babylonian kudurru Inscriptions* (Leiden: Brill, 1911) No. 3.
[42] L. W. King, *Babylonian boundary-stones and Memorial Tablets* (London: Oxford University Press, 1912). The texts read: ^d*Sin na-a-nar šamê ellûti iš-ru-ba-a la te-ba-a gi-mir la-ni-šu li-lab-biš-ma,* "May Sin, the light of the bright heavens, clothe his whole body with leprosy which never departs" (*BBSt* VII.ii.16–17); ^d*Sin a-šib šamê el-lu-ti išrubâ ki-ma lu-ba-ri li-li-bi-ša zu-mu-ur-šu,* "May Sin, who dwells in the bright heavens, clothe his body with leprosy like a garment" (*BBSt* VIII.iv.7–9); ^d*Sin bêlu rabû iš-ru-ba-a zu-mur-šu ki-ma ṣu-ba-ti li-la-bi-iš-su-ma,* "May Sin, the great lord, clothe his body with leprosy like a garment" (*BBSt* XI.iii.2–4); ^d*Sin ên šamê u erṣetim iš-ru-ba-a ki-i lu-ba-ri li-li-bi-ša zu-mur-šu,* "May Sin, the eye of heaven and earth, clothe his body with leprosy like a garment" (*BBSt* IX.i.46–47).
[43] Nougayrol, "*Sirrimu* (non **purîmu*) 'âne sauvage,'" 203–8.

Borger's, and adds another eleven of his own. To be sure, one of these eleven examples summons Šamaš and Ištar along with Sin to inflict the curse of "leprosy," and another invokes the entire pantheon.⁴⁴ But overwhelmingly, "leprosy" is shown to be the "arme redoutée du dieu-lune." It will be sufficient to quote only a fragmentary *kudurru* of c. 1150 of which Nougayrol provides the *editio princeps*: ᵈ*Sin bēlu rabû iš–ru–[b]a-a zu–mur–šu ki–ma ṣubāti li–lab–biš–ma*, "May Sin, the great lord, clothe his body with leprosy like a garment." In a study entitled, significantly, "Leprosy in Ancient Mesopotamia," J. Kinnier–Wilson concludes that "true leprosy appears to have been taken as peculiarly the result of affliction from the moon–god, Sin."⁴⁵

This ability of Sin to curse his enemies with and, simultaneously, to protect his adherents from "leprosy" and other forms of skin inflammation is, I propose, critical for our understanding of 4Q Or Nab. For is it not ironic that in the Prayer of Nabonidus, Nabonidus, the fervent devotee of this moon god Sin, is inflicted with and then healed of grievous boils through the agency of God Most High, the Israelite God? Or, to put it another way, God Most High causes Nabonidus to contract an eruptive type of skin disease and then cures him of it, even though these kinds of skin inflammations are the very thing over which Sin, Nabonidus' patron god, should have power. What this suggests is that the focus on the grievous boils in the Prayer of Nabonidus is anything but chance. Our author, rather, has purposely chosen the motif of skin disease in order to create a remarkable piece of religious propaganda. The text becomes not only an obvious polemic against "gods of silver and gold, bronze, iron, wood, stone, clay," but also includes a much more subtle, even sly, demonstration of the ineffectiveness of one particular idol from among these gods: Sin, although patron god of skin diseases, cannot shield his worshipers, even Nabonidus, his most loyal worshiper, from grievous boils. Nor can Sin heal Nabonidus once the king is afflicted. Yet while Sin may be powerless to affect Nabonidus' skin disease, the God of Israel is not: God Most High, according to the Prayer, causes the odious inflammation, and God Most High heals it. The God of Israel has thus usurped from Sin the ability to inflict and cure skin ailments. Israel's God, the Prayer of Nabonidus intimates, has laid claim to the heart of the Babylonian moon god's might.⁴⁶

---

⁴⁴ See similarly R. C. Thompson and M. E. L. Mallowan, "The British Museum Excavations of Nineveh, 1931–1932," *Annals of Archaeology and Anthropology* 20 (1933) 113–15 ("Decree of Adad–nirari III, Conferring the Rule of the Province of Hidnana on Nergal–eresh," Rev., lines 28–30, 33–34).

⁴⁵ J. V. Kinnier–Wilson, "Leprosy in Ancient Mesopotamia," *RA* 60 (1966) 57.

⁴⁶ J. Tigay has evidently advanced, independently, a similar (although not identical) analysis of 4Q Or Nab. According to M. Weinfeld (*Deuteronomy and the*

II

This motif, in which the God of Israel usurps from some other ancient Near Eastern deity his primary attribute, is not unknown elsewhere in ancient Israelite religion. The same theme occurs in 1 Kings 18.[47] The story is a familiar one. As it opens, there has been a drought in the land of Israel, inflicted by Yahweh because of his anger over the Ba'al worship promoted by King Ahab and Queen Jezebel (1 Kgs 17:1; 18:2–6). But Yahweh is now prepared to end the drought, and he informs Elijah of his intention (18:1). Before the drought is to end, however, there must be a contest on Mount Carmel between the four hundred and fifty prophets of Ba'al and Elijah, the prophet of Yahweh. The outcome of the contest is, of course, that Yahweh and Elijah win: all Israel falls to the ground and repents of Ba'al worship (18:39); the prophets of Ba'al are seized and killed (18:40). But the story is not yet over; Elijah next says to Ahab, "there is a sound of the rushing of rain" (18:41). This rain is not immediately audible or visible to anyone except Elijah, but after looking out to sea six times, Elijah's servant, on his seventh reconnaissance, finally reports: "Behold, a little cloud like a human hand is rising up out of the sea" (18:44). Then, "in a little while the heavens blackened with clouds and wind, and there was a great rain" (18:45). Yahweh, as he had promised, ends the drought.[48]

Deuteronomic School [Oxford: Clarendon, 1972] 121, n. 2), "J. Tigay from the University of Pennsylvania (an unpublished study) suggests that behind the tradition of Nabonidus' "leprosy" is hidden a polemic to the effect that even Sin, his own beloved god, turned against him." But while Tigay and I would agree (apparently) that the skin disease of 4Q Or Nab is an allusion to Nabonidus' devotion to Sin, I would argue that the skin disease points not to Sin's desertion of Nabonidus but to Sin's powerlessness in comparison to the might of Israel's God Most High.

[47] Does the motif occur even in the book of Daniel itself? Many of the Babylonian texts detailing Sin's curse of skin disease describe how the one inflicted with eruptions will be forced to "lie down like a wild ass outside the walls of the city." Is this what stands behind the tradition of Nebuchadnezzar's madness in Dan 3:31–4:34, where the king becomes like a wild beast? That is, does the Daniel material, like the related 4Q Or Nab, put forward, albeit with more subtlety, the idea that the Israelite God, by driving the royal figure mad, has usurped from Sin his primary attribute? See Weinfeld, *Deuteronomy*, 121, n. 2.

[48] The unity of 1 Kings 18 has been questioned, especially by A. Alt, "Das Gottesurteil auf dem Karmel," *Kleine Schriften zur Geschichte des Volkes Israel*, 2 (Munchen: C. H. Beck'sche, 1953) 135–49. According to Alt, 1 Kings 18 contains two independent traditions, a story of drought and deluge (18:1–16, 41–46) and a story of a contest on Carmel (18:17–40). While I would instead regard the chapter as a unity (see J. Gray, *I and II Kings* [Old Testament Library; London: SCM, 1964] 343), the issue is not one of overwhelming concern to my thesis. Whether the association of drought and rain with the contest between Ba·al and Yahweh is

There has been some debate in the literature about the identity of the Ba'al who is Yahweh's enemy in the contest on Mount Carmel. The bulk of the evidence, however, suggests that the Ba'al with whose prophets Elijah contends should be identified with Ba'al Haddu (Hadad). Certainly the fact that the patron of the Ba'al of Carmel, Jezebel, carries one of Haddu's primary Ugaritic epithets, *zebul*, "prince," in her name suggests this. A statue found on Carmel, dating from the second or third century C.E., is of even more significance. It is inscribed *dii hēliopoleitē karmēlō*, "Heliopolitan Zeus, god of Carmel."[49] As his name makes obvious, this "Heliopolitan Zeus, god of Carmel" is solar in character; we also know from other sources that Heliopolitan Zeus is a storm god. He shares these characteristics, moreover, with Nabatean Zeus Helios, who in Nabatean sources is regularly identified with *Ba'al Šāmêm*. All this suggests that the Ba'al of Carmel is *Ba'al Šāmêm*.[50] Furthermore, *Ba'al Šāmêm*, several scholars feel, should be identified with Ba'al Haddu,[51] given that *Ba'al Šāmêm*'s cult symbols at Heliopolis include an ear of corn, indicating that he is a fertility god, and a thunderbolt, a weapon of the storm god. Also *Ba'al Šāmêm* is, according to Sakkunyaton, a storm god (*PE* 1.10.7).

Ba'al Haddu is in Canaanite religion the storm god *par excellence*. His chariot is the storm cloud (*CTA* 19.1.43–44); he travels with an entourage

---

primitive or is the creative work of some editor, the fact remains that someone in ancient Israel saw 18:1–16, 41–46 and 18:17–40 as causally linked. The analysis proposed below should thus hold.

[49] M. Avi-Yonah, "Mount Carmel and the God of Baalbek," *IEJ* 2 (1952) 118–124.

[50] O. Eissfeldt, *Der Gott Karmel* (Sitzungsberichte der deutschen Akademie der Wissenschaft zu Berlin, Klasse für Sprachen, Literatur und Kunst 1953, No. 1; Berlin: Akademie Verlag, 1953) 5, 22–23; idem, "Ba'alšāmēm und Yahwe," *ZAW* 57 (1939) 1–31; S. M. Olyan, *Asherah and the Cult of Yahweh in Israel* (SBLMS 34; Atlanta: Scholars Press, 1988) 62–64; and Avi-Yonah, "Mount Carmel," 118–24, are among those who identify the Ba'al of Carmel with Ba'al Šāmêm. But R. de Vaux, "The Prophets of Baal on Mount Carmel," *The Bible and the Ancient Near East* (London: Dartman, Longman, and Todd, 1972), 238–51; H. H. Rowley, "Elijah on Mount Carmel," *BJRL* 43 (1960–61) 190–219; Alt, "Gottesurteil auf dem Karmel," 135–49; and A. S. Peake, "Elijah and Jezebel: The Conflict with the Tyrian Baal," *BJRL* 11 (1927) 297, propose that the Ba'al of Carmel is Tyrian Melqart. Others, for example, K. Galling, "Die Gott Karmel und die Achtung der fremden Götter," *Geschichte und Altes Testament, Festschrift A. Alt* (ed. G. Ebeling; Beitrage zur historischen Theologie 16; Tübingen: J. C. B. Mohr, 1953) 105–25, and D. R. Ap-Thomas, "Elijah on Mount Carmel," *PEQ* 92 (1960) 146–55, doubt that any possible identification of the Ba'al of Carmel is possible. For further bibliography on this debate, see Rowley, "Elijah on Mount Carmel," 194, nn. 1 and 2. In my opinion, however, the statue published by Avi-Yonah is decisive, not just for the Roman period from which it comes, but for the Iron Age as well. Religious traditions, we note, are notoriously conservative.

[51] Note, however, R. A. Oden, "Ba'al Šāmêm and 'El," *CBQ* 39 (1977) 457–73.

of wind, thunder, and rain (*CTA* 5.5.7–8). His iconography characteristically shows him holding aloft a bolt of lightning as a spear; descriptions of Haddu also depict him brandishing lightning as his weapon (*Ugaritica* 5, 3.3–4). His voice is the roar of thunder (*CTA* 4.5.68–71; 4.7.29–35; *Ugaritica* 5, 3.3–4; cf. *EA* 147:13–15). His female attendants are Misty One, daughter of Light, Dewey One, daughter of Showers, and Muddy One, daughter of Floods (*CTA* 4.1.17–19).

As the storm god, it is Ba'al who in Canaanite myth sends rain, and, conversely, it is Ba'al who causes drought. *CTA* 4.5.68–71, for example, relates that Ba'al, upon being granted the right to build his own temple, will rejoice by sending rain. Alternatively, when displeased, Ba'al's rains fail (e.g., *CTA* 19.1.42–46). But in 1 Kings 18, Yahweh is the god who controls the rains. When he is displeased with Ahab, Jezebel, and their followers, he sends drought; when all Israel repents and acknowledges Yahweh as God, he sends rain. After the contest on Carmel, the prophets of Ba'al are rejected and killed; the story implies that a similar event occurs in heaven. Yahweh strips from Ba'al Haddu his primary attribute, his ability to withhold or bring the rains. The motif is the same as in the Prayer of Nabonidus. Indeed, the irony of the Prayer, where the very aspect of nature over which Sin should have power, skin disease, is inflicted on Sin's devotee, is found also in 1 Kings 18: rain, which should be plentifully abundant to Ahab and to Jezebel as followers of Ba'al is, as the story begins, denied to Israel. Then, when the rains do come, they are sent because the people choose to reject Ba'al and instead worship the God of Israel. Thus, as God Most High in the Prayer of Nabonidus usurped from Sin the power to inflict and heal inflammatory skin diseases, God also usurps from Ba'al in 1 Kings 18 the power to bring rains or cause drought.

III

The historical origins of Israelite monotheism are still a matter of some debate among scholars.[52] But almost all would now suggest that what we know today as self-conscious, philosophical, or radical monotheism[53] was a fairly late development in Israel, and a date during the exile is commonly cited. Yet this does not imply that the Israel of the

---

[52] The position of Y. Kaufmann, on the one hand, and the more prevailing views espoused by continental scholars, on the other, are well summarized in B. Halpern, "'Brisker Pipes than Poetry': The Development of Israelite Monotheism," *Judaic Perspectives on Ancient Israel* (ed. J. Neusner, B. A. Levine, and E. S. Frerichs; Philadelphia: Fortress, 1987) 79–82.
[53] The terminology is that of Halpern, "'Brisker Pipes than Poetry,'" especially p. 81.

pre-exilic period was radically polytheistic. Scholars tend instead to describe the nation as monolatrous or henotheistic. That is, while Israel does not deny the existence of other gods, she does reject the idea that these other gods play a significant role in her national cult.[54] For the Israel of the first half of the first millennium, then, while Yahweh is not the only god, Yahweh is the only god who matters.

1 Kings 18, which purports to describe an event of the mid-ninth century B.C.E., tells its story in a way fully consistent with this henotheistic stance of pre-exilic Israel. Of special significance are the national identifies of those whom the contest of Carmel seeks to convince of the superiority of Yahweh over Ba'al Haddu. They are Israelite, led by the Israelite king, Ahab. But curiously missing from those present at the contest is Jezebel, Ahab's Phoenician queen. Moreover, when Jezebel is told about the outcome of the contests, she scoffs and refuses to assign to the results theological significance. In fact, she threatens the life of Carmel's human hero and Yahweh's spokesperson, Elijah (1 Kgs 19:1–2). Since the Bible particularly blames Jezebel for the popularity of the Haddu cult on Carmel, we might have supposed that her refusal to repudiate Ba'al worship would lead the biblical writers to evaluate Elijah's victory as hollow or, at best, a limited success. But the text gives no evidence of such reservations. The reason is henotheism: Yahweh is the only god who matters for Israel. It is crucial, then, that the Israelites at the contest, Ahab and his subjects, acknowledge Yahweh's claims of pre-eminence. But the religious beliefs of a foreigner, Jezebel, are not, in the henotheism of pre-exilic Israel, a matter for concern.

However, the religious beliefs of a foreigner, the Babylonian king Nabonidus, are a Yahwistic concern in 4 Q Or Nab; in fact, Nabonidus' beliefs and his recognition of the sovereignty of God Most High are the *sole* concern of the Prayer. Issues of date are crucial in explaining this change. The Prayer of Nabonidus and the related Dan 3:31–4:34 purport to describe an event that occurred during the last days of the Babylonian exile. Furthermore, the stories themselves are post-exilic in date. Not coincidentally, it is the exilic period that is generally acknowledged to be the birthdate of self-conscious, philosophical, or radical monotheism in Israel. Also not coincidentally, the post-exilic period is considered to be the time when this new monotheism became normative within Judaism.

The new monotheism differed from the preceding henotheism by claiming that Yahweh was the only god who mattered, not just for Israel,

---

[54] Although these other gods may have a role in Israel's international affairs, as is suggested by Solomon's building shrines for the gods of his foreign wives in Jerusalem and by Jezebel's promotion of her native cult of Ba'al in Samaria.

but for all the nations. This is nowhere made more clear than in a sixth-century speech attributed to Yahweh (Isa 45:22–23):[55]

> Turn to me and be delivered, all the ends of the earth.
> For I am God, there is no other...
> To me every knee will bend, every tongue will swear.

The exilic satire against idolatry in Isa 44:6–20, which claims that idols and all who make them are nothing, is also a classic presentation of this new ideology. Equally descriptive are the post–exilic perorations in Daniel 5 and in the Prayer of Nabonidus against "gods of silver and gold, bronze, iron, wood, stone, clay." In the henotheism of the pre–exilic period, these gods were deemed unsuitable for worship in Israel. In the radical monotheism of the exile and the centuries that followed, they were deemed unsuitable for all. Hence, while 1 Kings 18 need require only that the Israelites, and not the Phoenician Jezebel, acknowledge Yahweh's superiority over other gods, the Prayer of Nabonidus belies an understanding that Yahweh's pre–eminence must be celebrated by Israelite and foreigner alike.

1 Kings 18 and the Prayer of Nabonidus, then, while both exploring the motif of Yahweh's supremacy over a rival god, ultimately differ significantly in their conception of who needs to be persuaded of Yahweh's superiority. By so doing, the two texts are able to shed some literary light on the complex theological process that led ultimately to the development of monotheism in Israel.

---

[55] On which see J. Blenkinsopp, "Yahweh and Other Deities: Conflict and Accommodation in the Religion of Israel," *Int* 40 (1986) 362–64.

5

Job's Daughters and Their Inheritance in the Testament of Job and Its Biblical Congeners

Peter Machinist

I

As a quick reading makes clear, the pseudepigraphical Testament of Job is much interested in the restoration of Job's fortunes after his trials.[1] To it almost a quarter of the book is devoted – the last twelve of fifty-three chapters – describing the reconciliation with the friends, the doubling of Job's property, the division of his estate among his new brood of seven sons and three daughters, and his beatific death, as recorded by his brother, Nereus. Prominent in this recital is what happens to Job's daughters. Their complaint to Job, when he gives all his property to their brothers, brings the response that they will receive an even greater inheritance. And Job, we learn, is as good as his word. To each daughter he presents one of three multicolored cords or girdles, which, as he emphasizes, he had gotten from God Himself, and which

---

[1] The Greek text of the Testament is available in two recent editions: Robert A. Kraft, *The Testament of Job* (SBLTT 5; Missoula: Scholars Press, 1974) and, with a much fuller Greek apparatus, S. P. Brock, *Testamentum Iobi* (PVTG 2; Leiden: E.J. Brill, 1967). Recent translations, with commentary, include, in English, Kraft, *loc. cit.*, and R. P. Spittler, "Testament of Job," *The Old Testament Pseudepigrapha* (2 vols.; ed. James H. Charlesworth; Garden City, New York: Doubleday, 1983, 1985) 1.829-68; in French, Marc Philonenko, "Le Testament de Job," *Semitica* 18 (1968); and in German, Berndt Schaller, *Das Testament Hiobs* (JSHRZ III/3; Gütersloh: Gütersloher Verlagshaus Gerd Mohn, 1979).

purged his body of all the diseases and worms in it once he put them on. Now the daughters bind or wrap these cords around themselves covering their breasts, and in each case, they are transformed by the divine force within, breaking out in the language of angelic hymns, which, Nereus tells us, he wrote down in a book. Three days later, as Job falls into his final illness, he gives additional gifts to his daughters; and they, in turn, greet the divine chariot, come to take his soul away, and then the burial of his body by singing more hymns.

How to deal with this elaborate description of Job's restoration and final days, and, more particularly, the prominence in them of his daughters? Several approaches have been taken. There has been, inevitably, a redactional concern: do chapters 42-53, more particularly 46-53 where the inheritance of the daughters and Job's death actually are narrated, fit with the preceding part of the Testament as one composition, or are they secondary?[2] Alternatively, the daughters have been considered in the context of the other women in the Testament – Job's two wives, especially the first, Sitis or Sitidos; and his doorkeeper, who unwittingly becomes the mediator of his first encounter with the Satan – all in a discussion about the attitude toward women in this Testament and, by extension, in the Second Temple world from which the Testament comes.[3] There has also been a concern with the otherworldly focus of the three daughters at the end of the text: specifically, the apparently mystical connotations of the three cords given to the daughters, and the connection of these to other indications of a heaven-earth dichotomy in the Testament which helps to define the problem and solution of Job's situation.[4] Finally, some have focused, here with more attention to the Biblical book of Job and other sources than to the Testament, on the underlying history of inheritance practices in Israel and early Judaism and the place of women in them.[5]

---

[2] See M. R. James, *Apocrypha Anecdota* II (Texts and Studies 5/1; Cambridge: Cambridge University Press, 1897), xciv-xcvi; John J. Collins, "Structure and Meaning in the Testament of Job," *Society of Biblical Literature 1974 Seminar Papers* 1 (Cambridge: Society of Biblical Literature, 1974) 47-49; Pieter W. van der Horst, "Images of Women in the Testament of Job," *Studies on the Testament of Job* (ed. Michael A. Knibb and Pieter W. van der Horst; SNTSMS 66; Cambridge: Cambridge University Press, 1989) 101-14.
[3] See especially van der Horst, "Images of Women," 93-116; and Susan R. Garrett, "The 'Weaker Sex' in the *Testament of Job*," *JBL* 112 (1993) 55-70.
[4] E.g., Spittler, "Testament of Job," 834-35, 864-66 *ad loc.* (However, his theory that the Testament, including chaps. 48-50, underwent a Christian Montanist revision, has not won support); Philonenko, "Le Testament de Job," 17-18; Collins, "Structure and Meaning," 48-49; van der Horst, "Images of Women," 107-114.
[5] Zafrira Ben-Barak, "Inheritance by Daughters in the Ancient Near East," *JSS* 25 (1980) 22-33; *idem*, "Parašat Benot 'Iyyov," *Eretz-Israel* 24 (1993) 41-48; Ze'ev

Job's Daughters and Their Inheritance

These four approaches all highlight legitimate and important issues – a number of them, in fact, overlapping – which emerge from the narrative of Job's restoration at the end of the Testament. But there is another issue, another way into the Testament and its final narrative, that is no less important: the issue of midrash. The Testament, after all, is not an independently conceived composition; it clearly presumes and is built on the Biblical book of Job. But how to place the Testament, and specifically, the treatment of the daughters' inheritance, in its underlying Biblical context has only briefly, if at all, been considered.[6]

I propose, therefore, to look at these Biblical connections more leisurely and fully, mindful of what Lou Silberman was able to achieve in his own work on the Qumran Biblical commentaries. It was indeed Silberman, in his still fundamental analysis of the Qumran Pesher on Habakkuk,[7] who taught us how this and related Qumran texts functioned as interpretations of their Biblical counterparts: that they were not crude, heavy-handed impositions of contemporary events and theology on the ancient Biblical books, willy nilly, but subtle efforts, undertaken, to be sure, in the light of the interpreters' own concerns, to wrestle with the words and problems that the Biblical books pose.

II

So let us begin with the Biblical texts which form the background to the Testament of Job. Our first text, of course, is the epilogue to Job, where the restoration of his daughters is recounted (42:13-15). Three details appear. The daughters, as against the restored sons, are all mentioned as being given names by Job – names apparently expressive of their beauty.[8] This beauty is then commented on explicitly as

---

Feliks, "Yerušat Habbat weha'almana bammiqra' ubattalmud," *Tarbiz* 23 (1951) 9-15; Pinhas Ne'eman, "Yerušat Habbat battorah ubahalaka," *Beth Mikra* 47 (1971) 476-89; Jacob Milgrom, *Numbers* (The JPS Torah Commentary; Philadelphia: Jewish Publication Society, 1990) 230-33, 296-98, 482-84; Schaller, *Das Testament Hiobs*, 366 ad XLVI 2a; Tal Ilan, *Jewish Women in Greco-Roman Palestine* (Texte und Studien zum Antiken Judentum 44; Tübingen: J. C. B. Mohr [Paul Siebeck], 1995) 167-72; Menachem Elon, *Jewish Law. History, Sources, Principles* II (Philadelphia: Jewish Publication Society, 1994) 573-80, 828-29, 835-46; Ephraim E. Urbach, *The Halakhah. Its Sources and Development* (Jerusalem: Yad la-Talmud, 1986) 121, 222-23.

[6] E.g., Spittler, "Testament of Job," 864 ad 46c; van der Horst, "Images of Women," 101, 107, 113.

[7] Lou H. Silberman, "Unriddling the Riddle: A Study in the Structure and Language of the Habakkuk Pesher (1 Q p Hab.)," *RevQ* Tome 3/3/No. 11 (1961) 323-64.

[8] See, e.g., Marvin H. Pope, *Job*³ (AB 15; Garden City, New York: Doubleday, 1973) 352-53.

unsurpassed in the land. Finally, Job assigns to the daughters "an inheritance in the midst of their brothers" (נחלה בתוך אחיהם, 42:15). It is this last detail that invites particular attention, for it stands out against the otherwise pronounced Biblical emphasis on male inheritance. To be sure, there is no law in the Bible explicitly stating that inheritance passes to the males in the family, but that is the sense behind any number of passages. One example, of course, is the narratives in Genesis dealing with the problem of the heir to Abraham's estate and, more important, to the blessing given him by God; in these the matter is always one of a male, never a female heir. Or one may consider the law in Deuteronomy 21:15-17,[9] concerning a man who has two wives, one of whom he prefers to the other (the text uses the terms "loved" and "hated"). Here the problem is how the man shall divide his inheritance among the sons of his wives, more specifically, who shall be his primary heir when the oldest son (בכור) is the issue of the "hated" wife. Once more the matter of daughters is never raised; the assumption is that inheritance is a concern only where sons are involved.

There is one Biblical text, however, that comes close to adumbrating a rule about male inheritance, although at first sight, it appears to state the opposite. This is the story of the family of Zelophahad, an Israelite of the Manasseh tribe who had for children five daughters, but no sons (Num 27:1-11 and 36; Joshua 17:3-4; note also Num 26:33; 1 Chr 7:15). At his death, as reported in the longest version of the story, Num 27 and 36, the daughters appeal to Moses, Eleazar, and the community to be allowed to inherit his estate, else "the name of our father be withdrawn from his clan" (Num 27:4). Moses takes the case to God, and a divine oracle is given granting the daughters' request and extending it to a broader set of provisions for inheritance when a man dies without a son. The oracle is then supplemented, after a complaint from the other tribes of Joseph (Num 36), to the effect that the daughters may not marry outside of the clan (משפחה) of the tribe (מטה) of their father, thus preventing the father's estate from passing to husbands of other tribes. What is important in this whole story, clearly, is the controlling interest of the males and the male line. It is not simply that inheritance by daughters can come into play only when there are no sons; the very purpose of daughter inheritance is to safeguard the patrimonial clan property.

Seen in the light of this case of Zelophahad's daughters, the restoration at the end of the book of Job looks familiar. On the one hand,

---

[9] Brought to my attention in conjunction with the daughters' inheritance in Job by Georg Fohrer, *Das Buch Hiob*[3] (KAT XVI; Gütersloh: Gütersloher Verlagshaus Gerd Mohn, 1989) 544.

Job's Daughters and Their Inheritance

both stories represent a deliberate intervention by an authority in behalf of daughter inheritance, which, explicitly, in the case of Zelophahad, or implicitly, in the case of Job, amends the reigning rule of inheritance by sons.[10] Yet against Zelophahad's daughters, Job's are to inherit even when there are also sons, and further, even when the sons are alive. Indeed, the prominence of Job's daughters is signaled by the fact that they, not their brothers, are named[11] and described, and that in that description it is the inheritance of the brothers that forms the backdrop for highlighting what is now being given to the daughters (42:15).

What Job's daughters receive, however, is barely described: as we have seen, it is an "inheritance" (נחלה) "in the midst of (בתוך) their brothers." What can this mean? Crucial here is the preposition בתוך, which occurs frequently in the Bible. Among these occurrences are a number that, like our Job passage, involve matters of inheritance. And of the latter, six are particularly illuminating, including one drawn from the Zelophahad story:[12]

> Num 27:4, 7 - "... (Daughters of Zelophahad speaking) Give us a possession in the midst of the brothers of our father (בתוך אחי אבינו) [13](אחזה) ... (God answering) You shall without conditions give them (= the daughters) a possession of inheritance in the midst of the brothers of their father and so transfer the inheritance of their father to them" (נתן תתן להם[14] אחזת נחלה בתוך אחי אביהם והעברת את־נחלת אביהן להן). The version in Josh 17:4 reads: "'Yahweh commanded Moses to give us (= the daughters) an inheritance in the midst of our brothers (נחלה בתוך אחינו),' and so he gave them (להם, the daughters), according to the mouth of Yahweh, an inheritance in the midst of the brothers of their father" (נחלה בתוך אחי אביהן).
>
> Josh 19:1, 9 - "The second lot went out for Simeon, (that is,) the tribe of the sons of Simeon according to their clans; and their inheritance (נחלתם) was in the midst of the inheritance of the sons of Judah

---

[10] Cf. Ben-Barak, "Parašat Benot 'Iyyov," 42b.

[11] The legal importance of naming here is signaled by Baruch Levine, *apud* Michael David Coogan, "Job's Children," *Lingering Over Words. Studies in Ancient Near Eastern Literature in Honor of William L. Moran* (ed. Tzvi Abusch, John Huehnergard, and Piotr Steinkeller; HSS 37; Atlanta: Scholars Press, 1990) 145, n. 44.

[12] For other occurrences, see Gen 23:9; Lev 25:33; Num 18:20,23; 26:62; 32:30; Josh 14:3; 21:39 (Heb); 22:19; Jer 37:12.

[13] The Samaritan has here *'aḥuzzat naḥalâ*, conforming to the phrase in vs. 7.

[14] Note here and elsewhere in these citations the occasional use of masculine plural suffixes for feminine. This gender switching, or better, use of the unmarked form for the marked, is frequent enough in Biblical Hebrew to make emendation to grammatically "correct" forms unnecessary. See recently John Huehnergard, "Review of Jaakov Levi, *Die Incongruenz im biblischen Hebräisch*," HS 35 (1994) 179.

(בתוך נחלת בני־יהודה) ... The inheritance (נחלת) of the sons of Simeon (was) from the portion (מחבל) of the sons of Judah, because the allotment (חלק) of the sons of Judah was too large for them; so the sons of Simeon inherited (וינחלו) in the midst of their (= Judah's) inheritance (בתוך נחלתם)."

Josh 19:49 - "When they completed assigning inheritances in the land according to its territories (ויכלו לנחל־את־הארץ לגבולתיה), the sons of Israel gave an inheritance (נחלה) to Joshua, son of Nun, in their midst (בתוכם)."

Judg 18:1 - "... in those days the Danite tribe was seeking for itself an inheritance (נחלה) in which to live, for there had not fallen to it until that time in inheritance in the midst of the tribes of Israel (כי לא־נפלה לו עד־היום ההוא בתוך־שבטי ישראל בנחלה).[15]

Ezek 47:22-23 - "And when you assign it (= the land) as an inheritance by lot (והיה תפלו אותה בנחלה) for yourselves and for the aliens, viz., those who reside in your midst (בתוככם) who have begotten sons in your midst (בתוככם), then they will be to you as natives among the sons of Israel; with you they shall have an inheritance by lot in the midst of the tribes of Israel (אתכם יפלו בנחלה בתוך שבטי ישראל). And in whatever tribe in which the alien resides, there you shall give (him) his inheritance (נחלתו)."

Prov 17:2 - "A servant who shows insight will dominate a son who causes shame, and in the midst of the brothers he will get an inheritance as a share (בתוך אחים יחלק נחלה)."

Common to the above six passages is the statement, in some variations, that X receives "an inheritance in the midst of Y" (Y נחלה בתוך). As the passages show, Y is clearly the frame or group within which the inheritance of X is a member or element. X, then, becomes a member, or more precisely has an inheritance like all the other members, in group Y. In this, there is some ambiguity about whether בתוך is an indicator of geography or status or both. Thus, in Josh 19:1, 9, בתוך would seem, first and foremost, to indicate geography, describing where the plot of land that the tribe of Simeon receives as its inheritance is physically located, namely, within the boundaries of the land allotted as inheritance to the "sons," i.e., "clans" of Judah. One need not assume that Simeon thereby was somehow subordinated in status to the tribe of Judah, on the level of

---

[15] The construction here is grammatically difficult. For related examples, see Num 26:53; 34:2; Josh 13:6; 23:4; Ezek 45:1; 47:22. Considering these examples, G. F. Moore, *A Critical and Exegetical Commentary on Judges* (ICC; New York: Scribner's, 1895) 388, and C. F. Burney, *The Book of Judges* (New York: KTAV, 1970 [reprint of 1918]) 424, follow G. L. Studer and suppose that the subject of the verb נפלה in Judg 18:1 is ארץ, which has dropped out. Alternatively, one could read, with some manuscripts of the LXX and the Peshitta, נחלה instead of בנחלה, and make that the subject of נפלה.

Job's Daughters and Their Inheritance

one of its clans; Simeon was just given some of the surplus land originally assigned to Judah, thus allowing the tribal leaders to deal with a limited supply of land for the community as a whole. On the other hand, a text like Judg 18:1 appears to emphasize status in its use of בתוך. Here the tribe of Dan is in a sense not a full tribe within the community of Israel until it can acquire an inheritance of land "in the midst of the tribes of Israel," i.e., just like all the other tribes. Finally, with Ezek 47:22, בתוך may describe both geography and status. That is, the alien is to be given a land inheritance which is physically within the boundaries of the land allotted to the tribes of Israel, but that assignment, the text suggests, signifies that the alien has become "as" (whether the preposition כ means "like" or "identical with" is ambiguous) a native Israelite.

How to apply these observations to the phrase נחלה בתוך אחיהם in Job 42:15? It is frankly difficult in this case to consider geography, since the text provides no indication that נחלה must be a plot of land and otherwise does not describe its physical location. Rather, the focus would appear to be on status, the daughters receiving inheritances from Job as heirs alongside their brothers - we might even add, as though they too were brothers. In other words, male inheritance continues to define the perspective here, and that is confirmed in the next verse (42:16), as Ben-Barak has noted,[16] where descent from Job is still reckoned through the sons. But, it should be emphasized, the בתוך phrase gives no indication that the daughters' inheritances are different from the sons'; structurally, in fact, it suggests that they are both on the same level in their capacity as their father's heirs, although it could well allow that the inheritance for each might be in different items and amounts.

This understanding of Job 42:15 is strengthened if we go back to one of the six passages listed above, from the story of Zelophahad's daughters. What these daughters want, and what is granted by God echoing the language of their petition, is "a possession of inheritance in the midst of the brothers of their father" (Num 27:7). From the context this must mean that the daughters are now considered on the same level as their uncles, in the sense that they hold as heirs to their father his share of the patrimonial estate, just as the uncles hold their shares. As the Zelophahad daughters are to their uncles, thus, so the Job daughters are to their brothers.

But can we go beyond this? Is it possible that the relationship between the Zelophahad and Job stories is deliberate? That is, could the Job author have known of the Zelophahad story and be intentionally reacting to it as he details the restoration of Job's daughters? On the positive side, we may recall that Zelophahad and Job are the only two

---

[16] Ben-Barak, "Parašat Benot 'Iyyov," 43a.

texts in the Hebrew Bible which lay down rules for female inheritance, and then only as a result of active intervention by an authority. Further, we have observed, where Zelophahad's daughters ground their appeal in the fact that their father had no sons for heirs, Job takes what appears to be the logically next step by granting his daughters inheritances even when there are sons who are alive. Yet the key clause in each story, X receives *naḥălâ bĕtôk* Y, is, as we have seen, not exclusive to these two texts. Even the more specific form of it, נחלה בתוך אחיהם, which appears in the Job story, is found also in Prov 17:2 (where אחים occurs instead of אחיהם). But here is an interesting matter. While the Numbers version of Zelophahad (Num 27:7) does not have בתוך אחים, it does have the related בתוך אחי אביהם; even more, in the Joshua version (17:4), the daughters of Zelophahad do once talk about their inheritance as בתוך אחינו, by which they must mean that, in their kinship system, "their father's brothers" can qualify as their "brothers." When we observe, additionally, that Prov 17:2 does not use בתוך אחים in reference to daughter inheritance, as do Zelophahad and Job, but to the normal inheritance by sons, then it looks as if our key clause, X receives *naḥălâ bĕtôk* Y, does have a specific resonance in the Zelophahad and Job texts that it does not have in its other Biblical occurrences.

What, then, to make of the relationship between the Zelophahad and Job texts? It may be that the Job author is, in fact, reacting to the Zelophahad story, in its Numbers and Joshua versions, in liberalizing the definition of female inheritance, and doing so by playing on the phrasing- בתוך אביהם / אחיהם / אחינו. On the other hand, perhaps it is better to be more cautious about how exclusive the connections between the two texts are, especially because it is not clear that on other criteria we can date Zelophahad, in either its Numbers or its Joshua form, earlier than Job.[17] In other words, perhaps we should remain content with saying that, at the least, the restoration of Job comes out of the same orbit of discussion in which the Zelophahad story is also involved, with the same issues and terms, and that in comparison, Job broadens the possibilities for a daughter to inherit.

---

[17] The Numbers version of the Zelophahad story is normally credited to P, although some, like Martin Noth (*Das vierte Buch Mose. Numeri* [ATD 7; Göttingen: Vandenhoeck & Ruprecht, 1966] 12, 183, 222), see it as a later addition to P. The Joshua version of Zelophahad belongs, obviously, to the Deuteronomistic History. Dates for these literary sources vary roughly over a period of two centuries, the seventh and the sixth B.C., that is, the late pre-Exilic and Exilic eras. The book of Job has been dated somewhere within this same range, but some have gone even later (see, e.g., Pope, *Job*, xxxii-xl). All of this, however, remains too uncertain to fix a relative chronological relationship between Job and the P and Deuteronomistic sources.

However close Job is to Zelophahad, why the Job author should have wanted to broaden female inheritance as he has is not made clear in his text. Some medieval Jewish commentators thought that the daughters were rewarded because of "their importance/worth" (חשיבתן) and "their beauty" (יפין), in the latter case, apparently reasoning from the fact that in the Biblical text the statement of the daughters' inheritance follows upon, and is connected by the conjunction "and" (ו) with, the statement of their beauty.[18] Alternatively, one could speculate that the award of inheritance was to underscore the horrendous adventure Job had just been through, of losing his first family and being himself subjected to further trials, all of which put his now restored life, with a restored but different family, on a different level, thus with some new and different conventions, from his former situation. Or, with N. M. Sarna and M. D. Coogan, one could argue that the inheritance of the daughters, and their general prominence vis-à-vis their brothers, represent a survival of an old West Semitic "epic" motif in the Job story, taking its place alongside other such motifs that scholars have identified there.[19]

The above explanations are not exhaustive, nor must they be mutually exclusive. But whatever the explanation for this new conception of female inheritance at the end of the book of Job, the important point, it may be suggested, is that an explanation is not, in fact, given, over against the case of the Zelophahad daughters. If we return now to the Testament of Job, we will see why this point is important. With the Testament, of course, there is no doubt about its dependence on the Biblical text of Job (in the LXX version),[20] unlike that of Job on Zelophahad. And given this dependence, the author of the Testament was left in the present instance with an exegetical, and legal-religious problem: how to make sense of the unexplained broadening of female inheritance at the end of the Biblical Job in the light of the dominant Biblical tradition of male inheritance.

Our Testament author begins his attack on the problem with an acknowledgment of the male tradition, for he has Job first offer inheritances only to his sons, disregarding his daughters (45:1-46:2). The daughters, one will recall, immediately protest, saying that they too are

---

[18] See Rashi, followed by Meṣudat David, *ad* Job 42:15.
[19] N. M. Sarna, "Epic Substratum in the Prose of Job," *JBL* 76 (1957) 24, and Coogan, "Job's Children," especially 146-47. For other "epic" motifs and features in Job, see, e.g., the rest of Sarna, 13-15, which focuses, as its title indicates, on the prose framework of Job.
[20] For the connections between the Testament and the LXX version of Job, see James, *Apocrypha Anecdota*, lxxiii-lxxix; Collins, "Structure and Meaning," 35-37; and, most elaborately, B. Schaller, "Das Testament Hiobs und die Septuaginta-Übersetzung des Buches Hiob," *Bib* 61 (1980) 377-406.

Job's children, and deserve "a part of your property" (ἐκ τῶν ὄντων σοι, 46:3b). Can one hear in this protest an echo of the words of Zelophahad's daughters, who too press their claim for their father's possession when it appears that they would be ignored by the relevant authority (Num 27:3-4)?[21] Job then answers, in the Testament, in an unusual way. He says that he has not forgotten his daughters, indeed has already designated for them "an inheritance better than that for your seven brothers" (κληρονομίαν κρείττονα τῆς τῶν ἑπτὰ ἀδελφῶν ὑμῶν, 46:5). The inheritance is now brought out from golden boxes fetched by one of the daughters: "three multicolored cords" (τρεῖς χορδὰς τὰς ποικίλας) that "are not from earth, but from heaven" (ἐπεὶ μὴ εἶναι ἐκ τῆς γῆς ἀλλὰ τοῦ οὐρανοῦ εἰσιν, 46:8), which Job proceeds to give one to each daughter. In this whole episode, the distinction that Job is made to draw between his sons and his daughters provides, I suggest, the answer of the Testament author to the conflict of Biblical traditions on inheritance. For in Job's distribution, his sons get his *worldly* goods (τὰ ὄντα; τὰ χρήματα, 46:1-2), thus satisfying the dominant Biblical rule for male inheritance of the father's estate. The multicolored cords, in turn, satisfy the text of the Biblical book of Job that the daughters get an inheritance, but since these cords are of *heavenly* origin, they do not interfere with the worldly distribution. Note that in working out the details of Job's inheritance, the Testament author is at pains to show that the heavenly cords are no invention of his own, but are alluded to in the Biblical text of Job itself. Thus, he informs us, it was the three cords which God meant when He said to Job in the whirlwind speeches, "Arise, gird your loins like a man! I shall question you, and you then shall reply to me" (47:5-6, quoting Job 38:3/40:7). And, as the Testament author understands that moment in the speeches, Job then "girded" on the cords and was immediately relieved of the diseases and worms with which he had been suffering so terribly at the hands of God and the Satan (47:7-10).

What about the description, in the Biblical Job, of the daughters' "inheritance" (נחלה) as בתוך אחיהם? Tentatively, I would propose, this is what the author of the Testament of Job is referring to and interpreting when he has Job describe their inheritance as "better than that for your seven brothers." To be sure, "better" (κρείττονα) is not obviously a translation of "in the midst of" (בתוך), nor does it fit the meaning of נחלה בתוך אחיהם suggested above. But the connection becomes clearer once we suppose that the Testament is understanding the Biblical phrase

---

[21] This similarity, I should hasten to add, is in asking a similar question under similar, though not identical, circumstances; it does not extend to the actual language used, if one compares the Greek of Testament 46:3a-b with the Greek, or Hebrew, of Num 27:3-4.

נחלה בתוך אחיהם (or its equivalent in the LXX, κληρονομίαν ἐν τοῖς ἀδελφοῖς) as "inheritance (standing out prominently) in the midst of (those assigned to) their brothers," rather like, and perhaps influenced by, such other Biblical occurrences of בתוך as Gen 23:6 "A pre-eminent prince (נשיא אלהים) you are in our midst (בתוכנו)", or Gen 40:20 "and he (Pharaoh) lifted up the head (וישא את־ראש) of the chief of the cupbearers and the head of the chief of the bakers in the midst of (בתוך) his servants."[22]

We should consider one other problem in the Biblical version of Job's restoration that the Testament of Job appears to try to resolve. It is the fact that after Job awards "inheritances" (נחלה) to his daughters "in the midst of" those awarded to the sons, he lives another 140 years (so the MT; the LXX has 170, and then offers the total years of Job's life as 248), allowing him to see four generations of descendants (42:16). If the awards are made, thus, so much before Job's death, can they really qualify as inheritances? Milgrom thinks not, understanding them simply as gifts made during the father's lifetime, for which he adduces several other Biblical and apocryphal examples: Gen 25:6; 2 Chr 21:3; Ben Sira 33:20-24.[23] But these examples either do involve inheritance at death (2 Chr 21:3; Ben Sira 33:24, which uses נחל / κληρονομία) or else refer to gifts possibly made during the donor's lifetime, but which do not then use the term נחל / κληρονομία (Gen 25:6, which uses מתנת [MT]/δόματα [LXX]; perhaps Ben Sira 33:20, which uses שלך or τὰ χρήματα). The point is that the use of נחלה would appear to signal an inheritance, and it may be possible to understand Job's action, in the light of his death many years later, as a declaration of intent, to be realized on his death (assuming, then, that his sons and daughters outlasted him), or as a grant made in his lifetime which serves as a part of or as a substitute for an inheritance.[24]

Whatever explanation we choose, the range of our choices and uncertainty about which is best only underscore the tension remaining in the Biblical text between the moment when Job awards נחלה to his children and the many years he has still to live. It is just at this juncture, I suggest, that the Testament of Job comes to the rescue. For it has Job

---

[22] It will be noticed, of course, that the indication of prominence in these two examples is not actually supplied by the preposition בתוך, but by other words, namely, the נשיא אלהים in Gen 23:6 and נשא ראש in Gen 40:20. But that would not have stopped the effort to use such texts as these midrashically to interpret the Biblical book of Job.
[23] Milgrom, *Numbers*, 483.
[24] For these forms of grant, to be described, on the basis of Roman law, as dismission and compensation, respectively, see briefly in Reuven Yaron, *Gifts in Contemplation of Death in Jewish and Roman Law* (Oxford: Clarendon Press, 1960) 2.

make unequivocally clear, before he begins to assign the inheritance, that he is doing so because he is dying (45:1). And then it concludes the episode by describing Job's end and death three days later, after a short period of activity involving his daughters and brother Nereus, connected with the three heavenly cords (48:1-52:6, especially 52:1-2). The new scheme, thus, safeguards the understanding of Job's grant as an inheritance by resolving the problem between the time of the grant and the time of Job's death. But it does so at the cost of an outright emendation of the Biblical version, since to avoid contradiction it has to give up now any notice of Job's surviving another 140 or 170 years. In short, the resolution of one problem has produced another. This break with the Biblical version, as one might expect, did not go without response. For in three manuscript traditions of the Testament, we find the notice of Job's survival, using the LXX figures, restored in subscripts at the end – even while keeping the preceding narrative, of Job granting the inheritance as he was dying.[25] Evidently, in these manuscripts, the contradiction in chronology was judged less important than the failure to account for all the Biblical evidence.[26]

III

The preceding discussion has been one of texts and their relationships, all having to do with the issue of daughter inheritance. The suggestion has been that we have a kind of ongoing conversation on the issue, as the Biblical Job relates and reacts to the story of the Zelophahad daughters, or at least to the common problems and terms at stake, and then, more certainly and precisely, the Testament of Job reacts to the Biblical Job, perhaps with an echo of Zelophahad. Of course, none of this conversation, if it has been reconstructed properly, took place in an

---

[25] The manuscripts are the Messina, Sicily (S) and Vatican (V), both in Greek, and the version in Old Church Slavonic (Slav). See discussions in the works listed above, n. 1, particularly Kraft and Brock for the text and apparatus of variants. A full translation of the subscript of the Slavonic version is given by J. Kolsti, *apud* Spittler, "Testament of Job," 868, n. 53f. The other two Greek manuscripts of the Testament, both from Paris (P and its copy, P_2), do not have these subscripts. As for the earliest manuscript, in Coptic (Cop), no edition of it has yet appeared, and the published information on it, so far as I am aware, does not deal with the present issue.

[26] This kind of all-inclusiveness, purchased even at the risk of inconsistencies, is well known in the history of the Biblical text and of commentaries on it. Indeed, the recognition of it lay at the heart of the development of the Documentary Hypothesis. Note, for example, the present form of the Flood story in Gen 6-8, which preserves side by side two different, and contradictory traditions, labeled as P and J, about such matters as the numbers and kinds of animals taken on the Ark (Gen 6:19-20 and 7:2-3).

Job's Daughters and Their Inheritance

exclusive vacuum. There were additional influences at work besides the effect of each text on the other. One such instance brings us back to the heavenly cords in the Testament of Job. Despite the effort on the part of the Testament author to locate these cords in the Biblical text of Job through the mention of the verb "gird," the connection, as various modern commentators have pointed out,[27] is a loose one at best. For while "gird" in Job 38:3/40:7 may suggest the concrete act of putting on a piece of clothing or an object, especially for some kind of combat, it may rather be used there, as elsewhere in the Bible, only figuratively to indicate preparation for a strenuous challenge.[28] And even if "gird" is intended in the Biblical Job concretely, it is not obvious, to say the least, that what the Biblical text is referring to are three divine cords that cure diseases and allow, mystically, the gift of heavenly song. The point is that our Testament author must have depended on other sources, beyond the Biblical text, for these cords and their mystical connotations, even if he was driven to find a Biblical hook on which to hang them.[29] In a similar way, we can imagine that the Testament's concern for the issue of female inheritance grew out not simply of literary interest, to make sense of the contradictory indications in the Biblical corpus on this matter. It must also have been motivated by the actual problems of male and female inheritance in the Second Temple period in which the Testament was composed – problems that are attested to by a variety of other texts.[30]

And yet given these other, non-Biblical influences in the Testament, what is noteworthy is that they were mediated through a concern for the Biblical text. We may call this process midrashic, and if we can connect the Biblical Job with the Zelophahad story, then in our instance the process can be said to have begun already within the Biblical period, as, indeed, a number of recent studies, on other parts of the Biblical corpus,

---

[27] See Spittler, "Testament of Job," 864, n. 47e; 865, n. 47i, commenting on the "Midrashic style" evident here. Schaller, *Das Testament Hiobs*, 368, n. 5a, and van der Horst, "Images of Women," 102, n. 24 are more particular, singling out the latter part of the text from Job that the Testament quotes, "I shall question you, and you then shall reply to me," as irrelevant to the context in the Testament and so as a secondary addition to it.

[28] Adapting the formulation of Pope, *Job*, 291 *ad* 3a.

[29] For discussion of some possible sources, see van der Horst, "Images of Women," 101-105, who also remarks on the variety of terms used in the Testament for these cords; Schaller, *Das Testament Hiobs*, 367, n. 7a, 9a; 368, n. 11a; Spittler, "Testament of Job," 865, n. 47i.

[30] For examples and discussion of these texts, see the works listed above in n. 5, especially the recent volume of Ilan.

have made clear.³¹ At the core of this process was the emergence of an authoritative community tradition, oral and written, commuted gradually into a written Scriptural corpus, which acted increasingly as a magnet for all the other traditions and problems of community life. Dealing with these traditions and problems, thus, involved more and more the task of interrogating Scripture for what it might say about them; in fact, the very act of interrogating it, one could argue, is what made Scripture Scripture. In this development, what was often laconic and unsystematic in the beginning became more elaborate and explicit later, as there emerged a more defined Scriptural corpus to respond to. And that seems to be reflected in the particular case we have been examining, where within the Bible daughter inheritance is treated rather reticently and Job exhibits at the most only indirect allusions to Zelophahad, but in the Second Temple and later rabbinic periods, the Testament of Job and other texts make direct reference to the Biblical corpus on inheritance which now stands behind them, clarifying its deficiencies and extending and supplementing it to meet the demands of changing social preferences.³² The Testament of Job, in sum, is simply one example of the Scripturalization³³ of society that came to characterize Jews and Judaism; and however else we may approach it, we misunderstand its nature and significance if we do not also take seriously its midrashic grappling with its Biblical antecedents.

---

[31] The *locus classicus* of contemporary discussion is Michael Fishbane, *Biblical Interpretation in Ancient Israel* (Oxford: Clarendon Press, 1985).
[32] See the discussions listed above in n. 5.
[33] I borrow this term from Gary Anderson, who uses it in a somewhat different sense to characterize the treatment of the cult in the Second Temple period; see his "Sacrifice and Sacrificial Offerings: Old Testament," *Anchor Bible Dictionary* (6 vols.; ed. David Noel Freedman; New York: Doubleday, 1992) 5.882-86.

6

The Restraint of Reason, the Humility of Prayer

James L. Crenshaw

A fundamental assumption of proverbial wisdom was that an individual could act in such manner as to bring about desirable consequences. This effective use of the intellect was facilitated by the nature of the universe itself, ultimately deriving from the generosity of its creator who guaranteed its general dependability. By studying human conduct and the behavior of animals, as well as observing the phenomena of the heavens, one could in large measure discover how to control destiny. Thus the responsibility for the course of one's life fell directly on human shoulders; so did any praise for successfully avoiding pitfalls along the way.[1]

Such a world view had an intrinsic flaw: radical egocentrism leading to pride based on significant achievement. In addition, this understanding of reality often encouraged intolerance toward persons of less personal ambition and accomplishment, who sport such tags as "fools" and "lazy bums" in proverbial sayings.[2] Furthermore, this

---

[1] Note the qualifying prepositional phrase, "in large measure." The sages understood that exceptions to the rule took place, for not everyone enjoyed the fruit of his or her labors. Moreover, divine freedom and inscrutability imposed limits on human knowledge, forcing individuals to take chance into account. Despite all this, the sages' aphorisms sound remarkably life–affirming, and their message confidently urges hearers to walk in the path that leads to life.

[2] At least seven types of "fools" enliven the sapiential literature, ranging from simple naiveté to cruel mocker. I have translated עצל by "lazy bum," because "sluggard" does not quite carry the force of the Hebrew noun.

emphasis on self-empowerment stood out because an alternative world view downplayed the importance of human deeds and emphasized divine providence.[3] Proverbial wisdom resisted this religious emphasis and substituted a remarkably "secular" approach to existence, although the adjective "secular" fails to capture the thoroughly religious basis for such stress on human possibilities.[4] Hence the non–moralistic maxims that Hermann Gunkel and Otto Eissfeldt laid claim to in discussing secular wisdom[5] must be interpreted in the light of an assumption that the creator instituted order and also set definite limits on the intellect. The same applies to the political sentences that William McKane used in distinguishing between counselors who could not afford the luxury of theological convictions and prophets for whom such beliefs dictated their counsel to trust in the Lord.[6] None has seen that fact more clearly than Gerhard von Rad, whose discussion of the limits of knowledge highlights the unpredictable factor that most individuals come up against sooner or later.[7]

Such proverbial wisdom therefore cannot be expected to preserve elements of piety, particularly prayers. An elevated view of human potential negates any need for emphasis on divine compassion, for individuals shaped their own future. The situation is analogous with nineteenth and twentieth century liberal theology's agonizing debate over petitionary prayer, which seemed to contradict the nature of God

---

[3] Because the understanding of the world as reflected in wisdom literature differs radically from the dominant view in Torah and Prophecy, some modern scholars have designated wisdom "an alien body" within the Bible and have ignored its teachings in theological discussion. Franz-Josef Steiert, *Die Weisheit Israels–ein Fremdkörper im Alten Testament?* (Freiburger Theologische Studien; Freiburg: Herder, 1990) responds to the question with an emphatic "no."

[4] Modern distinctions such as sacred and secular ultimately distort the picture of ancient Israelite society, for even the principle of cause and effect was subject to a higher authority. Moreover, adherence to the divinely ordained order was both an ethical and a religious act, one in their view that maintained the structure of the universe.

[5] Eissfeldt's conclusions derive from study of isolated proverbial sayings outside the wisdom corpus; these traditional sayings have been examined in a broader phenomenological context by Carole R. Fontaine (*Traditional Sayings in the Old Testament* [Sheffield: The Almond Press], 1982).

[6] Few interpreters have accepted McKane's thesis in *Prophets and Wise Men* (London: SCM, 1965). His book illustrates the difficulty in trying to grasp the essence of contrasting sapiential traditions, for instructional wisdom is thoroughly religious, as opposed to proverbial sayings.

[7] *Wisdom in Israel* (Nashville and New York: Abingdon, 1972). Although widely praised, this book has significant flaws, which I have noted in "Wisdom in Israel by Gerhard von Rad," *RSR* 6:2 (1976) 6–12.

and the scientific understanding of the universe.[8] Like the modern debate, the sapiential struggle against opposing viewpoints encountered immense resistance from champions of popular religion. In both instances, too, historical circumstances placed huge question marks over an optimistic reading of daily existence. We do not know whether or not instructional wisdom represents a response to Judah's changed circumstances after the fall of Jerusalem to the Babylonians, but theological directives unquestionably incorporate a religious piety into the subject matter.[9]

A comparable shift took place in Egyptian wisdom literature, as Miriam Lichtheim has observed: "It is no longer assumed that righteous living guarantees a successful life. Success and happiness are now thought to depend entirely on the grace of the gods. The individual can achieve nothing without their help; but the will of the gods is inscrutable."[10] In Israel both the book of Job and Qoheleth bear witness to a loss of confidence in the power of the intellect to ensure well-being, but this sense of powerlessness does not give way to devout prayer, except in a comparable text preserved in Prov 30:1–14 and attributed to a foreign sage. Here the restraint of reason issues in the humility of prayer. Gone forever is pride of achievement, as this sage focuses only on modest reward and faithful relationship with God.

The origin of prayer in general remains obscure, although individual prayers have survived throughout the ancient Near East.[11] Their close

---

[8] Perry LeFevre, *Understandings of Prayer* (Philadelphia: Westminster, 1981) has examined this intense debate in the thought of Karl Barth, Henry Nelson Wieman, Paul Tillich, Dietrich Bonhoffer, C. S. Lewis, Thomas Merton, Karl Rahner, and Abraham J. Heschel. The stage was set for this controversy much earlier, particularly in the work of Immanuel Kant, Friedrich Schleiermacher, Ludwig Feuerbach, and Albrecht Ritschl.

[9] Most scholars today distinguish between sentence literature and instructions; the latter contain overt religious teachings, whereas the former rarely enter this realm of discourse. The difference may derive to some extent from the formal characteristics of each, imperatives functioning best in theological settings, but the issue is more complex than this answer suggests.

[10] *Ancient Egyptian Literature* (3 vols.; Berkeley: University of California, 1980) 3.5. Lichtheim goes on to say that life was still prized and that piety demanded that life should be enjoyed.

[11] The importance of prayer to Mesopotamian sages can be gathered from texts that complain of its failure in some instances, for example "Ludlul" ("I called to my god, but he did not show his face, I prayed to my goddess, but she did not raise her head... For myself, I gave attention to supplication and prayer: To me prayer was discretion, sacrifice my rule... The king's prayer—that was my joy, and the accompanying music became a delight for me... But I know...Sun-god will have mercy... [After he had] received my prayers." W. G. Lambert, *Babylonian Wisdom Literature* [Oxford: Clarendon, 1960] 39, 41, 46, 51). "The

relationship to magical incantations cannot be refuted, but wherever emphasis falls on a deity's freedom, a quite different kind of supplication exists, one characterized by pure praise. Friedrich Heiler's thesis that free prayer by individuals represents the original form and that fixed collective prayers indicate a later, less spiritual, manner of addressing the deity[12] corresponded to the nineteenth century emphasis on great individuals. Likewise, the shift to emphasizing collective prayer as original in the studies by Sigmund Mowinckel, Erhard Gerstenberger, and Menahem Haran coincided with changed attitudes toward the community as formative in shaping tradition.[13] Perhaps Moshe Greenberg's mediating position describes the situation best, spontaneous prayer having existed contemporaneously with fixed prayer for communal use.[14] A similar controversy has surrounded such issues as individual freedom versus traditional constraints in form critical studies, a debate best illustrated by the individual and the community in the psalms.[15]

The subject of prayer in wisdom literature has not generated a single article thus far, except for specific studies of two prayers in Sirach.[16]

Babylonian Theodicy" complains that "Those who neglect the god go the way of prosperity, while those who pray to the goddess are impoverished and dispossessed." It adds: "In my mouth I sought the will of my god; with prostration and prayer I followed my goddess. But I was bearing a profitless corvée as a yoke. My god decreed instead of wealth destitution" (Lambert, *Babylonian Wisdom Literature*, 5, 77). Nevertheless, "Counsels of Wisdom" dares to commend prayer: "Prayer, supplication, and prostration offer him daily, and you will get your reward...and prayer atones for guilt" (Lambert, *Babylonian Wisdom Literature*, 105).

[12] *Das Gebet* (München: Ernst Reinhardt, 1919).
[13] Mowinckel, *The Psalms in Israel's Worship* (2 vols.; Nashville & New York: Abingdon, 1962); Gerstenberger, *Der bittende Mensch* (WMANT 51; Neukirchen-Vulyn: Neukirchener, 1980); and Haran, "Priest, Temple, and Worship," *Tarbiz* 48 (1978) 184.
[14] *Biblical Prose Prayer* (Berkeley: University of California, 1983) 43. Greenberg argues that biblical prayers are patterned after daily speech and therefore should not be viewed as purely fictional. The most comprehensive analysis of spontaneous prayer remains that of Adolf Wendel, *Das freie Laiengebet im vorexilischen Israel* (Leipzig: Eduard Pfeiffer, 1932).
[15] Hans-Joachim Kraus, *Theology of the Psalms* (Minneapolis: Fortress, 1992).
[16] P. C. Beentjes, "Sirach 22:27-23:6 in zijn Context," *Bijdragen* 39 (1978) 144-51; Heinrich Germann, "Jesus ben Siras Dankgebet und die Hodajoth," *TZ* 19 (1963) 81-87; and Johannes Marböck, "Das Gebet um die Rettung Zions Sir 36,1-22 (G:33,1-13a; 36,16b-22) im Zusammenhang der Geschichtsschau Ben Siras," *Memoria Jerusalem* (ed. J. B. Bauer; Jerusalem/Graz: Akademische Druck und Verlagsanstalt, 1977) 93-116.

Claus Westermann's recent history of research from 1950–1990,[17] which updates my own earlier analysis,[18] isolates two fundamental problems: popular versus professional origins of the literature, oral teachings or written texts. His separate treatment of wisdom literature, *Wurzeln der Weisheit*, fails to bring prayer to the fore even when discussing popular piety.[19] In this respect, Johannes Fichtner's synthesis of ancient Near Eastern wisdom remains instructive, although never really attending to prayer as such.[20] Even Ronald Clements' *Wisdom in Theology* makes no advance here, despite his demonstrated interest in biblical prayer.[21] My efforts to introduce the topic of prayer into the literature about ancient wisdom grow out of suspicion that such a discussion is long overdue. They also belong to a broader theme, that of human achievement and the necessity for divine assistance, which I have treated at length in an essay entitled "The Concept of God in Old Testament Wisdom."[22]

The relative silence of Israel's sages with regard to the cult, if not actual antipathy toward it, has led to varying interpretation among modern scholars. Leo G. Perdue's comprehensive examination, *Wisdom and Cult*,[23] attributes considerable interest in cultic matters to ancient sages, a claim much enhanced by the changes introduced by Ben Sira in the early second century. Like silence about schools in wisdom literature, which also gives way in Ben Sira's day,[24] the reluctance to speak about the cult has been interpreted in two contradictory ways. Some scholars assume that the cult was simply presupposed, while others insist that the sages' silence amounts to intentional rejection of established religion in favor of inner piety or human works.

One thing appears certain, as Clements has recognized. The exile brought about a thorough reconsideration of the cultic apparatus,

---

[17] *Forschungsgeschichte zur Weisheitsliteratur 1950–1990* (Arbeiten zur Theologie 71; Stuttgart: Calwer, 1991).
[18] *Studies in Ancient Israelite Wisdom* (New York: KTAV, 1976) 1–60 and "The Wisdom Literature," *The Hebrew Bible and its Modern Interpreters* (ed. Douglas A. Knight and Gene M. Tucker; Chico, CA: Scholars, 1985) 369–407.
[19] (Göttingen: Vandenhoeck und Ruprecht, 1990).
[20] *Die altorientalische Weisheit in ihrer israelitisch–Judischen Ausprägung* (BZAW 62; Giessen: A. Töpelmann, 1933) 35–59.
[21] (Grand Rapids: Eerdmans, 1992); *In Spirit and in Truth* (Atlanta: John Knox, 1985).
[22] *In Search of Wisdom: Essays in Memory of John G. Gammie* (eds. Leo G. Perdue, Bernard Brandon Scott and William Johnston Wiseman; Louisville: Westminster/John Knox, 1993) 1-18.
[23] (Missoula: Scholars, 1977).
[24] Evidence for schools in Israel is meager (James L. Crenshaw, "Education in Ancient Israel," *JBL* 104 [1985] 601-15). Even in classical Greece, literacy was less than ten percent, according to William V. Harris, *Ancient Literacy* (Cambridge: Harvard University, 1989).

inasmuch as new circumstances necessitated a different world view.[25] The existence of the altar had made sacrifice the sole means of atoning for sin,[26] but now another way of achieving that goal had to be devised. External confirmation of inner conviction was visibly removed, and the people were forced to place more emphasis on the sacrifice of the heart and its external expression in praise. Coinciding with an emphasis on prayer and praise was a chastened conscience arising from subjection to foreigners and the religious consequences of such bondage. Those who once viewed themselves as the norm and resident aliens as foreigners now understood themselves as outsiders in an unfamiliar world. Moreover, the family became a refuge replacing the temple, and "neighbors" took on more importance than an extended family, i.e., "brothers," in a different setting. Such far-reaching alterations in world view accompanied a growing emphasis on God as universal judge rather than champion of an elect people. What Judah Goldin has called demanding prayer[27] could find little support in such a rigorous concept of deity, one that eventually led to Qoheleth's view of a distant despot, the heavenly record-keeper with pen poised to jot down every mistake one makes. In such circumstances the sages' earlier optimism inevitably gave way to a sense of inadequacy in the face of overwhelming temptations. Restraints on human knowledge produced more than humility; they brought forth a feeling that life had become too much of a burden. Suddenly, a different kind of deity was urgently needed, one who graciously bestows mercy on sinful subjects. The universal Judge is somehow balanced by understanding God as father, and people relate to deity as sovereign and parent, the last two of the three metaphors characterizing ancient Mesopotamian religion according to Thorkild Jacobsen.[28] These two concepts of God co-exist in tension, for, in

---

[25] *Wisdom in Theology*, especially 26–31.
[26] Elias J. Bickerman, *The Jews in the Greek Age* (Cambridge: Harvard University, 1988) writes that "In the covenanted system of daily oblations a prayer would have been superfluous; the priests only supplicated the Deity to accept the gifts of the chosen people. So long as the temple stood, the altar atoned for Israel" (136). Bickerman suggested that a sense of unworthiness led Jews in Ben Sira's time "to supplement the daily sacrifice with a special prayer for the protection of the chosen people" (137).
[27] *Studies in Midrash and Related Literature* (ed. Barry L. Eichler and Jeffrey H. Tigay; Philadelphia: Jewish Publication Society, 1988) 331-35.
[28] *The Treasures of Darkness* (New Haven & London: Yale University, 1976). The fourth millennium metaphor, that of gods as providers, emphasized the fertility of dying and rising deities. The emergence of powerful cities in the third millennium shifted the emphasis to gods as rulers, and the rise of personal religion in the second millennium brought about still another shift, this time to lift up the parental relationship with the gods as central.

Clements' words, "If god is the ultimate Ruler and Master of Life, and has established the principles of wisdom which govern all human actions, then what place is left for prayer and a personal relationship with him?"[29]

One could even argue that the sages' elevation of a principle of retribution tilted the scales in the direction of an exacting judge from the very beginning. Clements is undoubtedly wrong in seeing a change in sapiential thought from paternal imagery to that of harsh schoolmaster, but he recognizes the contradiction between a retributive concept of deity and affectionate language. He writes: "The warm personalism of the descriptions of God as 'Father' to human children – presenting a portrait to one who is 'loving and gracious' – yields place to the image of the heavenly Schoolmaster, whose eye misses nothing and who has made the rules and expects everyone of his creatures to abide by them."[30] Actually, reference to deity as "father" rarely occurs in the Hebrew Bible, except to designate YHWH as creator (cf. Deut 32:6; Jer 3:4,19; Isa 63:16; 64:8[7]; Mal 1:6; 2:10; Ps 68:5[6]; 2 Sam 7:14; Ps 89:27[26]). The expression occurs twice in a prayer by Ben Sira (23:1,4) and once in Tobit (13:4). The ancient credal statement in Exod 34:6–7 never once finds expression in canonical wisdom literature, despite the appropriateness of describing God as demanding Judge.[31] Not until Ben Sira does the other half of the confessional formula appear, the affirmation that the Lord is gracious and merciful. This part of the creed was frequently quoted in prophetic and liturgical texts.[32] Martin Hengel has argued that the book of Job led to excessive reliance on divine mercy and that Ben Sira resisted this trend.[33] If Hengel is correct, this situation constitutes one more instance of religious polemic in which the viewpoint under attack actually dominates the discussion, for Ben Sira mentions divine mercy again and again.

---

[29] *Wisdom in Theology*, 167.
[30] *Ibid.*, 160.
[31] R. C. Dentan, "The Literary Affinities of Exod. xxxiv 6f.," *VT* 13 (1963) 34–51 claimed that this text represents sapiential teaching, but the idea that a compassionate deity also punishes the wicked occurs throughout the Old Testament.
[32] I have discussed this formula in "Who Knows What YHWH Will Do? The Character of God in the Book of Joel," *Fortunate the Eyes That See: Essays in Honor of David Noel Freedman in Celebration of his Seventieth Birthday* (ed. Astrid B. Beck, Andrew H. Bartlett, Paul R. Raabe, Chris A. Franke; Grand Rapids: William B. Eerdmans Publishing Company, 1995) 185-96. See also Michael Fishbane, *Biblical Interpretation in Ancient Israel* (Oxford: Clarendon, 1985) 335–50, and Thomas B. Dozeman, "Inner–Biblical Interpretation of Yahweh's Gracious and Compassionate Character," *JBL* 108 (1989) 207–23.
[33] *Judaism and Hellenism* (Philadelphia: Fortress, 1974) 143.

The distancing of God that characterizes the books of Job and Qoheleth eventually led to the introduction of a mediating figure, חכמה (Wisdom). Affectionate language, indeed open expression of passion for a lover,[34] surrounds this fascinating figure who boasts about heavenly origins and who embodies divine instruction. A comparable distancing of God in apocalyptic literature occurred, with angels receiving prayers uttered by men and women in distress. The intertestamental literature witnesses a proliferation of prayers, and that trend continues in the texts from Qumran as well. Our attention will be restricted to the three prayers within wisdom literature.

The only prayer in the book of Proverbs occurs in an astonishing context – within the sayings of the skeptic Agur preserved in Prov 30:1–14. However one reads this unusual text, whether as a dialogue between a skeptic and a believer,[35] or as the cry of an exhausted pious one,[36] the brief prayer in vv. 7–9 comes entirely without warning. Furthermore, the prayer does not specify the addressee and surprisingly refers to God in the third person after having begun with second person pronominal suffixes and an implicit transcendent referent. The translation is reasonably straightforward, and the only significant textual variant is the Greek τίς με ὁρᾷ ("who can see me?").

> Two things I ask of you; do not withhold them from me before I die. Empty, lying words keep far from me; give me neither poverty nor riches; tear off for me my allotted bread. Lest I be full and lie, saying "who is the Lord?" or lest being destitute I steal, sullying the name of my God.

Formally, the initial request resembles Job's desperate plea in 13:20–21, where the verb הרחק (keep far away) is also used with reference to the deity.

> Only do not do two things to me; then I will not hide from your face. Keep your anger far away from me, and let not dread of you terrify me.

This precedent and the absence of versional support for reading a numerical saying in either instance rules out Georg Sauer's emendation,

---

[34] The erotic features of the description of Wisdom in Prov 8:22–31 and beyond have been explored by Samuel Terrien, *Till the Heart Sings* (Philadelphia: Fortress, 1985) 87–120.
[35] James L. Crenshaw, "Clanging Symbols," *Justice and the Holy* (ed. Douglas A. Knight and Peter J. Paris; Atlanta: Scholars Press, 1989) 51–64.
[36] Paul Franklyn, "The Sayings of Agur in Proverbs 30: Piety or Scepticism?" *ZAW* 95 (1983) 238–52; compare Rick D. Moore, "A Home for the Alien: Worldly Wisdom and Covenantal Confession in Proverbs 30:1–9," *ZAW* 106 (1994) 96–107.

"Two things I ask of you, indeed three...."[37] The presence of three requests in Prov 30:7-9 invites such speculation, however, for the prayer asks for protection from uttering, or uttered, falsehoods and from a life style at either extreme of riches or poverty, but it also seeks a proper portion of food each day.[38] The third petition actually relates to the second, specifying the bare minimum that would prevent one from resorting to theft. If the author of Prov 30:1-14 found inspiration in Job's death-defying determination to be heard and thereby to obtain vindication from the God he addresses directly, the absence of a vocative in 7-9 makes sense.

One need not, therefore, assume that the requests look to parents or teachers rather than to God for fulfillment, although this view has much to commend it. Either group could supply these needs, if the first petition is taken to mean the character of the teachings conveyed to students. The lying or empty words in this instance would be someone else's prattle rather than the petitioner's, although one might expect something like "Do not make me hear lying words" if this were its meaning. The reference to God in the third person fits more naturally in requests directed to parents or teachers. Nevertheless, no precedent exists for a student's response in biblical wisdom, although a unique instance of a dialogue between father and son, teacher and student, occurs in the Egyptian Instruction of Ani.[39] For Israel's students, however, Carol Newsom's perceptive assessment stands that their voice is not heard.[40] Instead an uninterrupted, authoritative voice fills instructional wisdom in the Bible.

The larger context of the prayer emphasizes the restraint of reason, the acknowledgment that the human intellect knocks at a closed door where ultimate mystery is concerned. Grasping the meaning of Agur's initial remark resembles such an assault on a closed door, as A. H. J. Gunneweg's recent essay demonstrates.[41] His emendation of the twice

---

[37] *Die Sprüche Agurs* (Stuttgart: Kohlhammer, 1963) 101.
[38] Compare this Prayer to Thoth in P. Sallier I.8,2-7, which reads: "Supply my needs of bread and beer, and guard my mouth (in) speaking" (Lichtheim, *Ancient Egyptian Literature*, 2.149).
[39] Khonshotep protests that the life of a sage demands too much rigor, but Ani responds that even animals can be taught to conduct themselves differently. Nowhere does the son object to the character of his father's teachings; his complaint is limited to their difficulty.
[40] "Woman and the Discourse of Patriarchal Wisdom: A Study of Proverbs 1-9," *Gender and Difference in Ancient Israel* (ed. Peggy L. Day; Minneapolis: Fortress, 1989) 142-60.
[41] "Weisheit, Prophetie und Kanonformel: Erwägungen zu Proverbia 30,1-9," *Alttestamentlicher Glaube und Biblische Theologie* (ed. Jutta Hausmann und Hans-Jürgen Zobel; Stuttgart: Kohlhammer, 1992) 253-60.

recurring לאיתיאל to לאה את אל yields "who has concerned himself with God" and ואכל, which he understands as a verbal form of כול, כלה or יכל, enables him to translate "that I could grasp it." This rendering has no advantage over my own or those of Paul Franklyn and Rick Moore. Whereas I emphasize Agur's ironical dismissal of some sages' optimistic claims about the deity's existence or activity, Franklyn and Moore think of a humble Agur at the hour of death or simply faced with his own limits. Given such consensus with regard to the confession of human ignorance about divine mystery, one expects any prayer in this context to link up with that theme. This one does not. Instead, it concentrates on more mundane things such as deceit and temptations specific to riches and poverty. That fact strengthens my hypothesis that Agur's skeptical opening assault has provoked a devout response, with considerable give and take. Placing opposing viewpoints in direct juxtaposition is an effective rhetorical strategy. One looks in vain for a clearer example of reason's restraint and the humility of prayer.[42]

Elsewhere in the book of Proverbs the sages seldom mention prayer, and the author of the deeply religious opening collection in chs 1–9 never does. A single chapter, fifteen, contains two thirds of these occurrences – a total of two.

> The sacrifice of the wicked is an abomination to YHWH, but the prayer of the just is his delight (15:8). YHWH is far from the wicked, but he hears the prayer of the righteous (15:29). Whoever turns his ear from receiving instruction, even his prayer is an abomination.

The same Hebrew word for prayer, תפלה, occurs in all three places. References to sacrifice in the book of Proverbs exceed those to prayer by only two, and one of these, 7:14, attests to the worship of a goddess of fertility. The other four allude to contentious offerings (17:1) and those brought by unworthy persons (15:8; 21:27) or exalt ethical deeds over sacrificial ritual (21:3). The denial that sacrifice works automatically is balanced by a similar rejection of prayer issuing from the lips of unrepentant sinners. Both assessments indicate the extent to which Israel's sages internalized religion (cf. Ps 50:14).

Arguably technical terms, תועבת יהוה (abomination of the Lord) and תורה (instruction), occur in these negative evaluations of sacrifice (15:8) and prayer (28:9), although the former concept appears in Egyptian wisdom literature and the latter may mean no more here than parental teaching. The verb שמע (to hear, משמע) may also have a technical sense in Prov 28:9 as its equivalent in the concluding section of the Egyptian

---

[42] I have borrowed this language from Miriam Lichtheim, *Ancient Egyptian Literature*, 1.131.

The Restraint of Reason, the Humility of Prayer

Instruction of Ptahhotep undoubtedly does. The hearer is one who accepts instruction and internalizes it so that the teaching produces character and deeds commensurate with the four cardinal virtues of integrity, restraint, eloquence, and timeliness.

The sages who wrote the books of Job and Qoheleth also spoke sparingly of prayer. Within the poetic dialogue between Job and his three friends, the subject comes up three times. In 16:16–17 Job describes his miserable state despite an admirable relation toward God.

> My face is red from weeping, and on my eyelids – deep darkness, although no violence is in my hands and my prayer (תפלתי) is pure.

The essential nuance of this defense accords with the broader forensic context, here reinforced by the intensive form of the verb פלל (to pray) and the root זכך (to be pure). Job makes a legitimate claim of innocence that seems to be contradicted by his suffering. In 21:15 he rejects the theological argument of evildoers who question the value of being religious.

> They ask Who is Shaddai that we should serve him, and what do we gain that we pray to him (נפגע־בו)?

The verb פגע with reference to deity has the sense of "entreat, intercede" as in Jer 7:16, where a combination of terms for intercession occurs.

> But as for you, do not pray (אל תתפלל) on behalf of this people and do not lift up (ואל־תשא) a cry (רנה) or prayer (ותפלה) for them, and do not entreat me (ואל־תפגע־בי), for I will not listen to you.

Job's friend Eliphaz urges him to return to God and make peace so that he may eventually offer up a successful prayer.

> You will entreat (תעתיר) him and he will hear you, then you will complete your vows (22:27).

Within the speeches by Elihu a similar sentiment unfolds.

> A person will entreat (יעתר) Eloah and he will accept him;
> he will look on his face with joyous shout,
> restoring to man his vindicating deeds (33:26).

One additional text in the poetic dialogue alludes to meditation (שיחה).

> But you are making fear ineffectual (תפר) and diminishing (ותגרע) meditation before El (15:4).

The framing narrative to the book of Job refers to prayer twice in the epilogue – when YHWH rebukes the three friends and then when he recommends his servant Job as a competent intercessor. Both in the initial divine observation and in the narrative report of Job's intercession, the verb פלל occurs (42:8,10).

And Job my servant will pray for you (יתפלל). Then YHWH turned
the captivity of Job when he prayed for his friends (בהתפללו).

The unusual expression in the Qere, ויהוה שב את־שבות, occurs only here with relationship to a single individual. Normally it signifies a reversal of national circumstances, specifically the return of exiled peoples to Judah.

A single reference to discourse with a distant deity occurs in Qoh 5:1 [E 5:2].

> Do not be quick to speak and do not think hastily to cause a word
> to go forth before God, for God is in heaven and you are on earth,
> so let your words be few.

The context suggests that vows rather than prayer occupy Qoheleth's thinking here. Gerhard von Rad correctly perceived that Qoheleth had given up on trying to enter into dialogue with God.[43]

The situation differs notably when one turns from the books of Proverbs, Job, and Qoheleth to consider the teachings of Ben Sira. In the words of H. Ludin Jansen, "Thoughts cross over from prayer to instruction. Prayer and instruction go hand in hand. For Sirach that is entirely natural."[44] Josef Haspecker has observed that prayer is mentioned in Sirach as frequently as law,[45] and although this emphasis on prayer supports Haspecker's thesis that fear of YHWH, not Torah, occupies center stage, the point stands that Ben Sira talks freely about the importance of prayer. In addition, he incorporates a personal and a national prayer in his teachings, along with a thanksgiving psalm.

According to Ben Sira the occasion for prayer is not restricted to personal distress, although he recognizes that individuals will turn to God in such times. That includes personal distress brought on as a result of sickness (38:9) as well as economic deprivation (4:6; 21:5; 35:13–18). In Ben Sira's view, the impartial judge will execute justice, listening attentively to deserving persons. Prayers by the traditional representatives of this special divine solicitude – widows, orphans, and the poor – pierce the clouds and mount up to heaven. An earlier correlation in the book of Proverbs between laziness and poverty does not deter Ben Sira from sheltering these unfortunate people under divine wings. His discussion of illness has not freed itself entirely from the concept of act and consequence,[46] and this uneasiness manifests itself

---

[43] *Wisdom in Israel*, 233.
[44] *Die spätjüdische Psalmendichtung: Ihr Entstehungskreis und ihr Sitz im Leben* (Oslo, 1937).
[45] *Gottesfurcht bei Jesus Sirach* (Analecta Bib 30; Rome: Päpstliches Bibelinstitut, 1967) 339.
[46] Clements, *Wisdom in Theology*, 65–93, has studied the sapiential notion of sickness and health more thoroughly than anyone else, to my knowledge, with

when Ben Sira attempts to justify the vocation of physicians. Although he argues that the creator put roots on earth that possess medicinal properties, Ben Sira rests his case on the fact that physicians pray for guidance in diagnosing diseases (38:14). Nevertheless, Ben Sira's surrender to the ancient view evokes an incongruous final remark: "Whoever sins before the maker, may he fall into the power of a doctor" (38:15). Just as physicians seek instruction from the Lord, ordinary citizens are urged to pray for guidance in planning their future (37:15), while at the same time paying strict attention to their inner voice.

Where forgiveness is concerned, Ben Sira has more confidence in prayer than in the sacrificial system.[47] Even a host of gifts in the temple does not receive automatic acceptance unless accompanied by prayer and alms (7:10). Repentance reinforces a sinner's plea for acceptance (17:25–26; 21:1; 39:5), provided that the individual abandons all sinful practices (34:26). Anyone who harbors hatred within but prays for forgiveness has no success; in order to obtain forgiveness from God, one must first extend forgiveness to one's fellows (28:2–4). Because human nature embraces both good and evil, God must listen to curses and prayers, responding in an appropriate manner (34:24–26).

Ben Sira places prayer and praise at the very center of the intellectual endeavor. Students try to gain mastery of the torah, prophecy, and wisdom so that they may make an impact on the ruling hierarchy, but above all they rise early to cultivate a spiritual life. They do not stop with petition but move beyond personal need to hymnic praise of the Most High (39:1–6). Such praise in prayer is the fundamental meaning of existence for all people (17:10) and the special calling of sages (15:9–10; 39:6). Ben Sira the teacher offers a fine example for students in this regard (42:15–43:33). Within the praise of famous men in 44:1–50:24, Ben Sira specifically mentions prayers by Joshua, Samuel, David, and Israel.[48] It is perfectly natural, therefore, that he includes two prayers in the book, one in each half. To them I now turn.

The Hebrew text of 22:27–23:6 has not survived; scholars therefore rely on Greek manuscripts for its content. The prayer belongs to the

---

the possible exception of Johann Marböck, *Weisheit im Wandel* (BBB 37; Bonn: Peter Hanstein, 1971) 154–60.
[47] Nevertheless, Saul M. Olyan, "Ben Sira's Relationship to the Priesthood," *HTR* 80 (1987) 261–86, argues forcefully that Ben Sira belonged to the priestly order.
[48] Thomas R. Lee, *Studies in the Form of Sirach 44–50* (SBLDS 75; Atlanta: Scholars Press, 1986) labels the praise of famous men an encomium. Burton L. Mack, *Wisdom and the Hebrew Epic* (Chicago: University of Chicago Press, 1985) cautiously accepts Lee's hypothesis, but it is vigorously denied by Chris A. Rollston, "The Non-Encomiastic Features of Ben Sira 44–50," M.A. Thesis, Emmanuel School of Religion, 1992.

larger context beginning at 18:15 and extending through 23:27, which is immediately followed by the well-known praise of wisdom and its identification with the Mosaic legislation. As early as 18:30–31 a topos of the prayer is introduced, namely the restraint of sensual appetites. According to P. C. Beentjes[49] the prayer itself divides naturally into two parts, 22:27–23:1 and 23:2–6. The first half of the prayer is then elaborated upon in 23:7–15 and the second half is elucidated in 23:16–27. The prayer begins with a wish, τίς δώσει, that was undoubtedly expressed in Hebrew by מי יתן, a rhetorical question. Two formulas, each containing three vocatives, follow this initial petition in each half of the prayer (23:1; 23:4). The first reads κύριε πάτερ καὶ δέσποτα ζωῆς μου (Lord, father, and ruler of my life), and the second varies it slightly to κύριε πάτερ καὶ θεὲ ζωῆς μου (Lord, father, and God of my life). Beentjes has discerned remarkable consistency in the structure of the two halves.[50]

	A	B
τίς	22:27a	23:2a
καὶ	22:27b	23:2b
ἵνα μὴ	22:27c–d	23:2c–3
κύριε πάτερ	23:1a	23:4a
μὴ	23:1b–c	23:4b–6

He has also recognized chiasm in subject and verb usage within 23:2c–d and 23:3a–b.[51]

ἀγνοήμασιν – φείσωνται

παρῇ – ἁμαρτήματα

πληθύνωσιν – ἄγνοιαι

ἁμαρτίαι – πλεονάσωσι

Two topics occupy Ben Sira in this prayer: speech and sexual lust. The image of setting a guard over one's mouth occurs also in Ps 141:3.

> YHWH, set a guard over my mouth, a sentry over the door of my lips.

Ben Sira opens with a similar request without identifying at first precisely who is being addressed. He desires a sentry, perhaps even a seal that would prevent his lips from parting unless properly attended. Such a guard would save his life from a dangerous tongue (cf. Ahiqar 14b,15). Having stated the peril in which he finds himself, Ben Sira then

---

[49] "Sirach 22:27–23:6 in zijn Context," 145.
[50] Ibid.
[51] Ibid.

names the one from whom he seeks assistance, "YHWH, father, and ruler of my life." In this context he mentions adversaries for whom nothing thus far has paved the way, leading W. O. E. Oesterley to rearrange the prayer so that the pronominal suffix makes sense.[52] One thing is clear: Ben Sira does not want the Lord to abandon him to his enemies, whether his tendency to speak too hastily or others who slander him mercilessly.

The other topic occupies vv. 2–6 and thus moves within the human mind to the source of actions. Those at issue here are arrogance and lust of the flesh. Ben Sira asks for whips that will control his thoughts; he also desires a disciplined and informed mind. Such active chastening, an image that realistically draws on familiarity with conditions in ancient classrooms, will alert him to danger and enable him to escape harsher critics, those unspecified adversaries who delight in his discomfiture. He asks to be delivered from self-serving pride and excessive sexual appetite, the characteristics of someone who has lost the capacity to blush. Together, the two halves of the prayer cover sin's source and its external expressions. The prayer's motivation arises from fear of being abandoned to merciless foes or to one's own base inclination.

The section immediately following the prayer calls attention to the dangers of unguarded speech (23:7–15), and this valuable advice then gives way to a discussion of sexually loose behavior, first by men and then by women. A familiar aphorism, "To a fornicator all bread tastes sweet," is supplemented by a traditional description of sinners who deny that anyone can observe their clandestine affairs. Ben Sira uses hyperbole to emphasize YHWH's clear gaze: "...he does not realize that the eyes of the Lord are ten thousand times brighter than the sun; they look upon all the ways of men and perceive even the hidden places" (23:19). Women, too, who break their marriage vows will suffer for their actions, which bear powerful negative testimony to the sweetness of religious devotion and adherence to the law of Moses. In this final verse (23:27) Ben Sira sums up the two fundamental themes of the entire book, the fear of YHWH and the Torah.

The other prayer in Sirach addresses national interests, in doing so resembling ancient laments. Th. Middendorp has questioned the authenticity of 36:1–22 on two grounds,[53] its use of language that does not occur elsewhere in the book and its emphasis on themes that seem out of place, specifically hope in divine intervention, the gathering of Israel, high esteem for the prophetic message, polemic, and focus on the

---

[52] *Ecclesiasticus* (Cambridge: Cambridge University Press, 1912) 150–51.
[53] *Die Stellung Jesu Ben Siras zwischen Judentum und Hellenismus* (Leiden: Brill, 1973) 125–36.

nation's discomfiture. Johann Marböck defends the prayer and negates some of Middendorp's arguments, concluding that its authenticity strengthens Ben Sira's stress on historical continuity and that no conflict exists between wisdom and a priestly theocracy, so that the natural place for divine activity and revelation is Israel, hence Zion and the sanctuary.[54]

This prayer has four stanzas, vv. 1–5, 6–12, 13–19, 20–22.[55] The first and last verses have a sort of chiastic structure consisting of הכל : כל : אל : אלהי. The initial strophe has an *inclusio* in vv. 1 and 5 where the general name for God, אלהים, occurs. The epithets for deity throughout the prayer indicate considerable foreign influence, although the state of the text makes it difficult to determine the exact form of the Hebrew. The first verse addresses the deity as "God of all," presumably אדן הכל or אלה הכל, an expression also occurring in Ugaritic literature with respect to Ba'al the *ba'alu 'arṣi* and in the Bible as אדן כל הארץ. The final verse designates the deity as the eternal God, אל עולם. The first two stanzas conclude with the variants of the familiar statement of recognition that Ezekiel uses so often, "Thus they will know ... that there is no God but you."

The occasion for the nationalistic sentiment was probably the Seleucid victory over the Ptolemaic army at Panium in 198 B.C.E., which changed the balance of power in Palestine and subjected Judah to the Seleucids. The arrogance of the new rulers provoked the emphasis on the uniqueness of Ben Sira's deity. Rapid deterioration of the political situation revived ancient messianic hopes and prompted fervent prayer for renewed signs and wonders, indeed for the end-time. The prayer opens with a plea for deliverance and closes with a recapitulation of the essential argument that Judah's God will be known as אל עולם, the eternal God. The precarious political situation requires the author of the prayer to resort to a cipher for the Antiochenes, who are identified in the Hebrew as Moab's chiefs, recalling Balaam's oracle in Num 24:17. Similarly, the Hebrew text of v. 8 cites Isa 45:9, "who can say, 'what are you doing?'" Ben Sira asks for fresh indication of divine intervention on behalf of Israel, YHWH's firstborn (vv. 6,17), and he concludes with a confession that the Lord is always gracious to Israel.[56] This last remark localizes the setting for the prayer, which falls directly after an impassioned declaration that the judge of all nations will punish them and defend the cause of those who keep the law.

---

[54] "Das Gebet um die Rettung Zions."
[55] Patrick W. Skehan and Alexander A. DiLella, *The Wisdom of Ben Sira* (AB 39; New York: Doubleday, 1987) 420–23.
[56] For the development and form of prayer in the time of Ben Sira and later, see Heinemann, *Prayer in the Talmud: Forms and Patterns* (Studia Judaica 9; Berlin/New York: Walter de Gruyter, 1977).

Elias Bickerman has perceived the signal importance of prayer to Ben Sira. He observes that "If Ben Sira's sage prays to God in order to obtain sapience, the Stoic does the same: the gift of grace is required before either can attain right knowledge."[57] In a word, for Ben Sira prayer is the means to the acquisition of knowledge. We have thus come a long way from the first prayer in wisdom literature, which follows Agur's confession that he could not attain knowledge. Ben Sira has discovered an effective way of overcoming skepticism; he pours out his heart to a merciful ruler and father.

---

[57] Bickerman, *The Jews in the Greek Age*, 173.

7

Were Pharisees and Rabbis the Leaders of Communal Prayer and Torah Study in Antiquity?

The Evidence of the New Testament, Josephus, and the Church Fathers[*]

Shaye J. D. Cohen

Were the Pharisees before 70 CE and the rabbis after 70 CE the leaders of Jewish communal prayer and Torah study? Since "the synagogue" was home to Jewish communal prayer and Torah study, the question can also be formulated as follows: were the Pharisees before 70 CE and the rabbis after 70 CE the leaders of the synagogue? Until recently most scholars had no doubt, and many scholars still have no doubt, that the Pharisees and their rabbinic continuators were in charge of synagogues,[1] but, as far as I know, no one has yet collected and

---

[*] I am grateful to Steve Mason (York University), Catherine Hezser (King's College, Cambridge), and Saul Olyan (Brown University) for their comments and suggestions. I have also benefited from the discussions that ensued after I presented this paper at the World Congress for Jewish Studies in Jerusalem (June 1993) and at a Brandeis Seminar (May 1994).

[1] George F. Moore, *Judaism in the First Centuries of the Christian Era* (2 vols.; Cambridge, MA: Harvard University Press, 1927, 1930) 1.287, "... it is certain that they [the Pharisees] took possession of it [the synagogue] and made most effective use of it. Through it, more perhaps than by any other means, they

evaluated the evidence that supports this view. In my conclusion, I will briefly touch upon negative evidence, that is, evidence that the Pharisees and rabbis were not the leaders of Jewish communal prayer and Torah study, but in the body of my presentation I will cite and discuss only positive evidence, or that which might be thought to be positive evidence.

This essay stands at the intersection of three difficult and complicated questions – the origins and history of the synagogue, the origins and history of the Pharisees, and the origins and history of the rabbis – and I cannot even attempt to treat these topics here.[2] In order to keep the essay to reasonable length, I am excluding rabbinic and archaeological evidence, since each requires sustained treatment in its own right.[3] Even if I cannot discuss the history of the synagogue, I must comment briefly on the range of meanings of the word "synagogue."

The basic meaning of the Greek συναγωγή is "a gathering, a collection," and can refer to either people or things (for example, water, utensils). In Jewish contexts the word may designate either the Jewish community of a certain place, or a gathering of Jews, or the place where Jews are gathered or habitually gather. The English "synagogue" is narrower than Greek συναγωγή in three respects: the English word does

---

gained the hold upon the mass of the people which enabled them ... to establish such power as Josephus ascribes to them ... The synagogue in the hands of the Pharisees was doubtless the chief instrument in the Judaizing of Galilee." Martin Hengel writes, "... das Synagogeninstitut ... sich im Mutterland vor allem aufgrund pharisaischer Initiative verbreitete"; see his "Der vorchristliche Paulus," *Paulus und das antike Judentum* (ed. Martin Hengel and Ulrich Heckel; Tübingen: Mohr-Siebeck, 1991) 177-291, at 260 (I owe this reference to Günther Stemberger). "They [the Pharisees] thus fostered the synagogue as a place of worship, study, and prayer, and raised it to a central and important place in the life of the people," writes M. Mansoor, *Encyclopaedia Judaica*, 13.363-366, s.v. Pharisees, at 366. Even Howard Kee, "The Transformation of the Synagogue after 70 CE: Its Import for Early Christianity," *NTS* 36 (1990) 1-24, assumes that the development of the synagogue should somehow mirror the development of Pharisaism (as outlined by Jacob Neusner). See the doubts of Lester Grabbe, "Synagogues in pre-70 Palestine: A Re-assessment," *JTS* 39 (1988) 401-410, at 408, "There is nothing particularly Pharisaic about the institution of the synagogue ... The early sources on the Pharisees mention nothing in particular about them in relationship to synagogues."

[2] Thus I do not discuss here such questions as: when did communal prayer and Torah study become localized in synagogues? where did communal prayer and Torah study take place before being localized in synagogues? what other activities took place in the synagogues of antiquity? what is the relationship between communal leadership and synagogal leadership?

[3] Thus this essay is a companion piece to my "Pagan and Christian Evidence on the Ancient Synagogue," *The Synagogue in Late Antiquity* (ed. Lee Levine; Philadelphia: American Schools of Oriental Research, 1987) 159-181.

not mean "community," while the Greek often does; the English word implies the existence of a building, while the Greek does not;[4] the English word designates a gathering of Jews (or a place where Jews gather) for the sake of communal prayer and/or Torah study, while the Greek can refer to a gathering of various sorts. This last point is important; as I shall discuss below, the Greek word συναγωγή sometimes is used to designate a gathering of Jews for judicial or communal or political purposes, but if in these passages the word is translated "synagogue," this point is lost. Not every (Greek) συναγωγή is necessarily a (English) synagogue, because not every gathering or assembly is necessarily for the sake of prayer and Torah study.[5] It is likely that when Jews gathered for judicial or communal or political purposes, they gathered in the same places in which they would gather for the sake of communal prayer or Torah study,[6] but we must recognize the range of social activities that can be said to be taking place in a συναγωγή. Perhaps to resolve at least some of this ambiguity, Diaspora Jews in antiquity coined the word προσευχή to designate a place (usually a building) of prayer, and used συναγωγή to refer to the community (or the meeting of the community).[7] In recognition of this ambiguity in my discussions of the evidence, I shall first leave συναγωγή untranslated and then discuss whether the intent of the word is "assembly" in general or specifically an assembly for the sake of communal prayer and Torah study (that is, a "synagogue"). I am attempting to locate evidence that specifically and unambiguously states that Pharisees/Rabbis lead communal prayer and/or Torah study,

---

[4] In the Synoptics it is not always clear whether συναγωγή necessarily means a building; only Luke 7:5 clearly refers to a building. Kee, "Transformation," makes much of this ambiguity and of Luke's exceptional usage, but many of his arguments are effectively dismissed by Richard Oster, "Supposed Anachronism in Luke-Acts' Use of συναγωγή," NTS 39 (1993) 178-208, esp. 182-191.

[5] Similarly, the rabbis can speak of a כנסיה (equivalent to συναγωγή) "not for the sake of heaven," m. Avot 4:11.

[6] Thus Josephus, Life 277, 280, 290-303, describes a meeting in the "prayer house" in Tiberias to discuss the war; in general see Sidney B. Hoenig, "The Ancient City-Square: The Forerunner of the Synagogue," ANRW II.19.1 (1979) 448-476.

[7] The best discussion of these terms remains the classic article of Martin Hengel, "Proseuche und Synagoge," Tradition und Glaube ... Festgabe für Karl Georg Kuhn (ed. G. Jeremias et al.; Göttingen: Vandenhoeck & Ruprecht, 1971) 157-183, reprinted in The Synagogue: Studies in Origins, Archaeology and Architecture (ed. J. Gutmann; New York: Ktav, 1975) 27-54. See too Schrage, "συναγωγή," Theological Dictionary of the New Testament (10 vols.; ed. G. Kittel, G. Friedrich, and G. W. Bromiley; Grand Rapids, MI: W. B. Eerdmans, 1964-1976) 7.798-841, and Emil Schürer, The History of the Jewish People in the Age of Jesus Christ (4 vols.; rev. by G. Vermes et al.; Edinburgh: T. & T. Clark, 1973-1987) 2.429-431 and 439-441.

activities that in both common and scholarly parlance are associated with (English) synagogues.[8]

I have found eight passages that indicate (or might be thought to indicate) Pharisaic or rabbinic leadership of communal prayer and/or Torah study. They are: (1) Matthew 12:9-14 (and parallels); (2) Matthew 23:2; (3) Matthew 23:6-7 (and parallels); (4) Matthew 23:34; (5) Josephus, *Jewish Antiquities* 18.15; (6) John 12:42; (7) Justin Martyr, *Dialogue with Trypho* 137.2; and (8) various passages in Jerome. I shall treat each of these in turn.

1. Matthew 12:9-14: "And he [Jesus] went from there and entered their συναγωγή." The meaning of συναγωγή here is fairly clear: the assembly is meeting on the Sabbath (12:10-11), presumably for communal Torah study; the Lucan parallel even adds "he went to the assembly and taught" (Luke 6:6). Thus the assembly is clearly a "synagogue." The problem is the referent of "their" (αὐτῶν). The nearest previous masculine plural noun, the Pharisees of 12:2, is seven verses away; thus it is possible, even if syntactically unlikely, that the Pharisees of 12:2 are the "they" of 12:9-14. It is more likely, however, that "they" are the Jews generally. The phrase συναγωγή/αἱ αὐτῶν recurs four other times in Matthew (4:23, 9:35, 10:17, 13:54) and in all four the referent of "their" is not the Pharisees but – even if the syntax is not always clear – the Jews generally.[9] (Similarly 11:1 refers to "their cities.") In three of these passages (4:23, 9:35, 13:54) συναγωγή clearly means, as it does here, a synagogue. The fourth passage (10:17), and a passage with a related expression (23:34), will be discussed below. If, then, αὐτῶν refers to the Jews generally, the passage is no evidence for Pharisaic leadership of communal Torah study. If αὐτῶν refers to the Pharisees specifically, it is only Matthew which implies that the synagogue was theirs, the

---

[8] Scholars have long recognized the diversity of functions that were filled by "the synagogue," but it is the merit of Kee, "Transformation," to insist that not every New Testament συναγωγή is equivalent to a "synagogue" in its fullest sense. The relationship between communal prayer and communal Torah study, and the relationship between בתי כנסת and בתי מדרשות, cannot be pursued here; for a recent discussion see D. Urman, "The House of Assembly and the House of Study," *JJS* 44 (1993) 236-257.

[9] Douglas R. A. Hare, *The Theme of Jewish Persecution of Christians in the Gospel according to St. Matthew* (SNTSMS 6; Cambridge: Cambridge University Press, 1967) 104-105; W. D. Davies and Dale Allison, *A Critical and Exegetical Commentary on the Gospel according to St. Matthew* (2 vols.; ICC; Edinburgh: T. & T. Clark, 1988) 1.413 on 4:23, "The fixed nature of the expression is shown by 4.23; 12.9; and 13.54, where 'their' has no proper grammatical antecedent."

Pharisees'; the parallels in Mark and Luke omit αὐτῶν (Mark 3:1 and Luke 6:6).[10]

2. Matthew 23:2: "The Pharisees and the Scribes sit [or: sat] on the seat of Moses." This verse, unique to Matthew, opens a long polemic against the Pharisees. The theme of the polemic is that the Pharisees are powerful and influential, but hypocritical and wrong.[11] This verse can be used as direct evidence for our subject by means of the following chain of argumentation: (a) "the seat of Moses" is not a metaphor but a real chair or seat; (b) the reality of this seat is confirmed by a reference to it in *Pesiqta deRav Kahana*; (c) this seat was located in the synagogue, a place of honor in front of the congregation; (d) such seats have actually been found in the archaeological excavations of various synagogues; (e) therefore Matthew 23:2 is evidence for Pharisaic (and rabbinic) leadership of synagogues: the Pharisees sit on seats of honor in the synagogue and there exercise their authority. Each link in this chain is weak.

(a) Is "the seat of Moses" real or metaphoric? In all likelihood the latter.[12] Most commentators on the passage, ancient (including Origen, Cyril of Jerusalem, and Jerome), medieval, and modern, understand "seat of Moses" as a metaphor or symbol: the Pharisees have inherited, or claim to have inherited, the authority of Moses to teach law to the people. To "sit on the seat of Moses" means to teach like Moses, since teachers sit when they teach.[13] The phrase says nothing about the actual seats of real Pharisees.

---

[10] Συναγωγή/αἱ αὐτῶν is typically Matthean; the phrase occurs only twice in Mark (1:23 [note the variants] and 1:39 ∥ Matthew 4:23) and only once in Luke (4:15 [note the variants]).

[11] For the social setting of this polemic see David Garland, *The Intention of Matthew 23* (NTSup 52; Leiden: Brill, 1979); Anthony Saldarini, "Delegitimation of Leaders in Matthew 23," *CBQ* 54 (1992) 659-680.

[12] The singular καθέδρα might suggest that the metaphorical interpretation is preferable, for how can the Pharisees and the Scribes (!!) sit on a single seat? Contrast the plural πρωτοκαθεδρίαι in verse six. This argument is at best suggestive, since verse six also has the singular πρωτοκλισία (but see the variants!).

[13] So Origen, *Matthauserklarung: Series Commentariorum* (GCS 38, ed. E. Benz and E. Klostermann; Leipzig: Hirzel, 1933) 16-17; Cyril of Jerusalem, *Catechesis* 12:23 (a reference I owe to Oded Ir-Say); Jerome, *Commentary on Matthew*, 23:1-3 (Corpus Christianorum, Series Latina 77, p. 210), "*per cathedram doctrinam legis ostendit.*" Reflecting the consensus of patristic and medieval interpretation, Cornelius à Lapide writes, "*Per cathedram metonymice intelligit honorem, gradum, dignitatem, auctoritatem docendi et iubendi, quam apud Iudaeos habuit Moyses quam scribae post Moysen acceperant*"; see *Commentarius in quattuor Evangelia* (1639) 422, commentary on Matthew 23:2. For a list of modern commentators who interpret the phrase metaphorically see I. Renov, "The Seat of Moses," *IEJ* 5 (1955) 262-267

(b) In 1897 Wilhelm Bacher observed that the term "seat of Moses" occurs in *Pesiqta deRav Kahana*.[14] In a discussion of the throne of the kings of Israel, the midrash quotes 1 Kings 10:19, *and the throne had a back with a rounded top*. R. Aha comments, "like the seat of Moses" (כהדא קתדרא דמשה) (*Pesiq. Rav. Kah*. 1:7 7b Buber = 12 Mandelbaum). The manuscripts provide several variants, and the parallel passage in Esther Rabbah 1:12 provides yet further variants. It is not impossible that the text is corrupt; but, on the assumption that קתדרא דמשה is the correct reading, what does it mean? Numerous rabbinic texts have rabbis sitting on קתדראות,[15] and the rabbis may well have imagined Moses "our rabbi" doing likewise when he taught.[16] In *Exod. Rab.* 43:4, R. Drosai says, "He [God] made for him [Moses] a קתדרא like the קתדרא of *scholastikoi*."[17] Thus the Pesiqta passage confirms the reality of the קתדרא as a piece of contemporary rabbinic furniture, but says nothing about the reality of a קתדרא דמשה as a piece of contemporary rabbinic furniture.

(c) No matter how "the seat of Moses" is construed in Matthew and the Pesiqta, neither text locates the seat in the synagogue. Indeed, to the best of my knowledge no ancient text places a קתדרא in a synagogue.[18]

(reprinted in *The Synagogue* [ed. Joseph Gutmann; New York: Ktav, 1975] 233-238), at 264 n. 13. See too Frank W. Beare, *The Gospel According to Matthew* (Oxford: Blackwell, 1981) 448, "Moses' seat – the post of teaching authority. This is hardly to be taken as a reference to a special chair in the synagogue for the chief elder. It is simply a metaphor." A similar view is articulated in *Anchor Bible Dictionary* (6 vols.; ed. D. N. Freedman; New York: Doubleday, 1992) 4.919.
[14] Wilhelm Bacher, "Le siège de Moise," *Revue des études juives* 34 (1897) 299-301.
[15] Renov, "Seat of Moses," 266, drawing on M. Ginsburger, "La 'chaire de Moise'," *Revue des études juives* 90 (1931) 161-165; Hans-Jürgen Becker, *Auf der Kathedra des Mose. Rabbinisch-theologisches Denken und antirabbinische Polemik in Matthaus 23:1-12* (Arbeiten zur neutestamentlichen Theologie und Zeitgeschichte 4; Berlin: Institut Kirche und Judentum, 1990) 31-49; and Meir Bar-Ilan, "The Rock, the Seat, and the *qatedra* on which Moses sat," *Sidra* 2 (1986) 15-23 (Hebrew). I am grateful to Samuel Byrskog of Lund University for bringing Becker's book to my attention.
[16] According to *Sifre Numbers* 140 (Horovitz 186), Moses sat on a bench (ספסל) when he taught. Cf. *Assumption of Moses* 12:2. Some scholars connect these passages with rabbinic ordination; see E. Lohse, *Die Ordination im Spätjudentum und im Neuen Testament* (Göttingen: Vandenhoeck & Ruprecht, 1951) 25 and 30. I owe these references to Dr. Catherine Hezser.
[17] Avigdor Shinan, who is preparing a critical edition of *Exodus Rabbah*, informs me that there are serious variants here too; for an alternative to the transcription *scholastikoi* see D. Sperber, *A Dictionary of Greek and Latin Legal Terms in Rabbinic Literature* (Ramat Gan: Bar-Ilan University Press, 1984) 22.
[18] The text that comes closest is *t. Sukk.* 4:6 (Lieberman 273 [and parallels]), a description of the διπλόστωον of Alexandria. For an ἐξέδρα at the προσευχή of Athribis, see *CII* 1444 (=William Horbury and David Noy, *Jewish Inscriptions of*

(d) In the synagogues of Chorazin, En Gedi, Hammath Tiberias, Delos, and Dura Europus, archaeologists discovered ornate stone objects resembling chairs; they were identified as "seats of Moses" and juxtaposed to Matthew 23:2 by Eleazar Sukenik in an influential article published in 1930.[19] Sukenik's conjecture is attractive, but is not without its problems. The function of these objects is not clear; some archaeologists have suggested that they were not chairs but stands (or tables or platforms).[20] Furthermore, the synagogues of Chorazin, En Gedi, Hammath Tiberias, and Dura Europus postdate Jesus and the gospel of Matthew by at least 150 or 200 years, and these later buildings cannot readily be cited as evidence to elucidate the realities of a much earlier time. The synagogues of Delos (perhaps first century BCE) and Dura Europus are diaspora synagogues, and they cannot readily be cited as evidence to elucidate the realities of a much different place. It is also worth noting that only five "seats of Moses" have been discovered – a tiny percentage of the dozens and dozens of synagogues that have been excavated. If the archaeological remains really were to confirm the Matthean statement, "seats of Moses" should have been discovered in large numbers.

(e) I conclude that Matthew 23:2 clearly regards the Pharisees as a powerful and influential group, but whether or not this power and influence extended to the "synagogue," the text says not a word. Perhaps we should conclude that a group that sits "on the seat of Moses," in other words, that claims Mosaic authority, will, like Moses, teach the community and lead communal Torah study, but this conclusion is not necessary, for Mosaic authority might express itself more in judicial verdicts than in synagogal study. In any case, the archaeologically attested "seats of Moses" are irrelevant to the question.

3. In its indictment of the Pharisees and Scribes, Matthew 23 continues (23:6-7): "They love (a) the first couch at feasts (b) and the first seats in the συναγωγαί, (c) and salutations in the market places, (d) and being called 'rabbi' by men." The parallels in Mark (12:38-39) and Luke (11:43 and 20:46) offer minor variants but nothing significant for our

---

Graeco-Roman Egypt [Cambridge University Press, 1992] #28 [with full discussion of the meaning of ἐξέδρα]).

[19] E. L. Sukenik, "The Seat of Moses in Ancient Synagogues," *Tarbiz* 1 (1930) 145-151. For recent discussion and bibliography see R. Hachlili, *Ancient Jewish Art and Archaeology* (Handbuch der Orientalistik 7; Leiden: Brill, 1988) 193-194; L. Y. Rahmani, "Stone Synagogue Chairs: Their Identification, Use, and Significance," *IEJ* 40 (1990) 192-214; Lee Levine, "From Community Center to 'Lesser Sanctuary': The Furnishings and Interior of the Ancient Synagogue," *Cathedra* 60 (1991) 36-84, at 60-63 (Hebrew).

[20] See Renov, "Seat of Moses," and Rahmani, "Stone Synagogue Chairs."

purposes (except that in Mark and in the second Lucan parallel the polemic is directed against Scribes, while in the first Lucan parallel it is directed against the Pharisees; only Matthew combines the Pharisees and Scribes here).[21] Συναγωγαί here is parallel to feasts and market-places and therefore seems to mean "assemblies" (just as it does in Matthew 6:2 where it is parallel to "streets"). The verse is concerned not with leadership of communal prayer and Torah study, but with social prominence.[22] This interpretation receives some support from Josephus, *Ant.* 15.21 (a parallel duly noted by several commentators). Herod greets Hyrcanus "with every honor, assigned him the first place in assemblies (συλλόγοι), gave him the first couch at banquets, and called him father." The only thing Herod could have done to make the parallel with Matthew complete would have been to salute Hyrcanus in the market-place. Josephus' συλλόγοι corresponds to Matthew's συναγωγαί, and clearly means "assemblies."

Even if this explanation is incorrect, and συναγωγαί here means synagogues (that is, assemblies for the sake of communal prayer and/or Torah study), Matthew 23:6-7 and its parallels would merely demonstrate that when Pharisees attend synagogues they are given (they take?) prominent seats befitting their social prominence. The verse does not claim that Pharisees lead the prayer or the study.[23] Similarly, Matthew 6:2 and 5 decry the prominence which "the hypocrites" arrogate to themselves when giving alms and praying in the συναγωγαί

---

[21] Parallels: Mk 12:38-39, different order (c, b, a; om. d); Lk 20:46 (c, b, a; om. d); Lk 11:43 (b, c; om. a and d). I cannot discuss here the much debated question of the relationship of the Scribes to the Pharisees.

[22] For what it may be worth, I note that the rabbinic expression לשב בראש, as far as I have been able to determine, is not used in synagogal contexts. Prominent seating in the synagogue is described in other terms; see *t. Meg.* 3:21 (Lieberman 360). B. Brooten appositely cites *CII* 738 = B. Lifshitz, *Donateurs et fondateurs* 13, an inscription from Phocaea (3rd century CE?) which honors a woman named Tation. She donated "to the Jews" a building and an enclosure around a courtyard, and in return was honored by the συναγωγή with a golden crown and the right to sit in front (προεδρία). See Brooten, *Women Leaders in the Ancient Synagogue* (Brown Judaic Studies 36; Atlanta: Scholars Press, 1982) 143-144. Brooten assumes that the προεδρία is to be exercised in the synagogue (that is, assemblies for the sake of prayer and Torah study), but the point is not clear; the word συναγωγή in the inscription means "community," not "synagogue" (it is correctly translated by Lifshitz, but incorrectly translated by Brooten, 157), and the προεδρία might have been exercised at non-religious meetings. Brooten assumes that both Matthew and the inscription are referring to synagogues; I am suggesting that both are referring to assemblies.

[23] I owe this observation to Dr. Catherine Hezser. Similarly, even in Brooten's reading, the Tation inscription does not state that she is a leader of the synagogue (see previous note).

and the streets (or street corners); even if here too συναγωγαί means "synagogues," these verses attribute prominence, not leadership, to "the hypocrites," a Matthean synonym for Pharisees. Indeed, Matthew 6:5 strongly implies that "the hypocrites" are not communal prayer leaders; the accusation that they do what they do "in order that they may be seen by men," makes far more sense if "the hypocrites" are private individuals eager to flaunt their piety rather than communal leaders performing a legitimate communal function.

4. In its indictment of the Pharisees and Scribes, Matthew 23 continues (23:34), "Therefore I send you prophets and wise men and scribes, some of whom you will kill and crucify, and some you will flog in your συναγωγαί and persecute from town to town." The motif of persecution in the συναγωγαί recurs several times in the synoptics, although Matthew 23:34 is the only passage to link this motif with the Pharisees.[24] Note Matthew 10:17, "Beware of men; for they will deliver you up to councils (συνέδρια), and flog (μαστιγώσουσιν) you in their συναγωγαί," paralleled by Mark 13:9, "But take heed to yourselves: for they will deliver you up to councils (συνέδρια); and you will be beaten (δαρήσεσθε) in συναγωγαί," and Luke 21:12, "... they will lay their hands on you and persecute you, delivering you up to the συναγωγαί and prisons." Compare also Luke 12:11, "And when they bring you before the συναγωγαί ..." All of these parallel passages continue with reference to how the disciples should behave when brought before kings and governors. In these passages, συναγωγαί, parallel to συνεδρία and prisons (and kings and governors), seems to refer to assemblies with a judicial function, rather than assemblies for prayer and study.[25]

5. In his description of the Pharisees, Josephus writes the following (*Ant.* 18.15): "On account of these (views) they happen to be most persuasive to the people; of prayers and sacred rites, whatever is considered divine happens to be conducted according to their interpretation" (trans. S. Mason).[26] The Greek is very difficult, but the basic meaning seems clear.[27] The only real ambiguity is the word εὐχαί,

---

[24] Persecution in the συναγωγαί is missing from the parallel in Luke 11:49, and may have been an addition to Q by Matthew; see Hare, *Jewish Persecution*, 92.

[25] Wellhausen correctly translates συνέδρια "judicial assemblies," "courts"; see Schrage, "συναγωγή," *TDNT*, 7.834 n. 230. Συναγωγαί probably has the same meaning in Acts 22:19. Similarly, כנסת in *m. Mak.* 3:12 (flogging is administered by בית הכנסת) means either "community" (so Rashi) or "court" (so R. Ovadya Bartenora).

[26] Steve Mason, *Flavius Josephus on the Pharisees* (Leiden: Brill, 1991) 305.

[27] The crucial clause is καὶ ὁπόσα θεῖα εὐχῶν τε ἔχεται καὶ ἱερῶν ποιήσεως ἐξηγήσει τῇ ἐκείνων τυγχάνουσιν πρασσόμενα. Feldman's translation in the Loeb is a bit freer, "Because of these views they are, as a matter of fact, extremely influential among the townsfolk; and all prayers and sacred rites of divine

which can mean either "prayers" (as translated here) or, as Feldman correctly notes in his translation in the Loeb edition, "vows." Given the Pharisees' reputed expertise in matters connected with vows (Matthew 23:16-22),[28] the latter translation cannot be ruled out. Certain kinds of vows, especially Nazirite vows, involved a sacrifice in the temple (cf. Acts 21:23-26; Josephus, J.W. 2.313), and these sacrifices, if not the vows themselves, certainly could be considered "sacred rites" and "divine." The pairing of εὐχαί with ἱερῶν ποίησις ("sacred rites") gives a slight edge to the translation "prayers," because this pair of nouns seems to be the equivalent of εὐχαί και θυσίαι (or ἱερουργίαι), a common Josephan pair which means "prayers and sacrifices."[29] However εὐχαί is understood, this passage is unique in the Josephan corpus. In many places Josephus emphasizes that the Pharisees are powerful and influential, whereas the Sadducees are powerless and ineffective (Ant. 18.17),[30] but this is the only passage which highlights the Pharisees' power in religious matters, specifically prayers/vows and sacred rites. The passage refers to Pharisaic power not just in the temple (no matter what εὐχαί means, surely all temple rituals would be considered "sacred rites" and "divine") but also among "the people" (δῆμοι) and "the cities" (πόλεις). If, then, εὐχαί means "prayers," this passage is important evidence for our subject: the passage claims that public prayers are conducted according to the instruction of the Pharisees. If, however, εὐχαί means "vows," this passage remains important evidence – but not for our subject.

6. John 12:42, "Nevertheless many even of the authorities believed in him, but because of the Pharisees they did not confess it, lest they should be put out of the συναγωγή" (literally, lest they should become out-of-the-συναγωγή). As many commentators have noted, the term ἀποσυνάγωγοι is

---

worship are performed according to their exposition." Schürer-Vermes, *The History of the Jewish People*, 2.402 takes the Greek as referring to three categories, "They held the greatest authority over the congregations, so that everything to do with worship, prayer, and sacrifice took place according to their instructions." This translation misses the mark.

[28] See too m. *Nazir* 3:6.

[29] εὐχαί καὶ θυσίαι: J.W. 7.155; Ant. 6.19, 6.24 (note εὐχαί, θυσίαι, ὅρκοι), 6.102, 14.260, 20.112; εὐχαί καὶ ἱερουργίαι: Ant. 1.231. In Ant. 11.9 εὐχαί καὶ θυσίαι appears to mean "vows and sacrifices," but there each noun is the object of a separate verb (τὰς εὐχὰς ἀπεδίδοσαν τῷ θεῷ means, as translated in the Loeb edition, "they made the offerings vowed to God"; cf. 11.77). It is not clear whether εὐχῶν in 18.15 is dependent on ποιήσεως (parallel to ἱερῶν) or not; in either case, the meaning is ambiguous, because Josephus uses the phrase εὐχήν/εὐχάς ποιεῖν/ποιεῖσθαι to mean either "to pray" (J.W. 7.128; Ant. 3.191, 6.128, 11.134-135, 12.55) or "to vow" (Ant. 1.284, 11.77).

[30] For references and discussion, see note 46 below.

unique to John in the New Testament. It recurs in 9:22, in the story of the healing of the blind man, in a passage closely resembling this one, "His parents [i.e. the parents of the blind man healed by Jesus] ... feared the Jews, for the Jews had already agreed that if any one should confess him to be Christ, he was to be put out of the συναγωγή" (literally, he was to become out-of-the-συναγωγή). In 16:2 Jesus tells his disciples "they shall make you out-of-the-συναγωγή." Who is the "they" who have the power to put people out of the συναγωγή? In 12:42 it is the Pharisees. In 9:22, it is "the Jews," who are probably to be identified with the Pharisees of 9:13-17. For John, as for Matthew 23, the distinction between "the Jews" and "the Pharisees," has all but disappeared.[31] John 12:42 distinguishes between the rulers (ἄρχοντες) and the Pharisees: but for fear of the Pharisees many of the archons would have confessed Christ.[32] This statement closely resembles the view of Josephus that the Sadducees are unable to accomplish anything because they must perforce obey the dictates of the Pharisees.

What is the meaning of "out-of-the-συναγωγή"? Many recent scholars have taken it to refer to exclusion from the synagogue (that is, assemblies for the sake of prayer) and have connected the exclusion with the rabbinic institution of the "benediction against heretics" (*birkat ha-minim*). But, as I shall discuss below in connection with Justin Martyr, in all likelihood these Johannine passages have nothing to do with the *birkat ha-minim*. If this is correct, the simplest way to take συναγωγή here would be in the sense "community." Those who confess Christ will be excluded from the Jewish community. I presume that exclusion from the community would manifest itself most immediately in exclusion from assemblies for the sake of prayer and Torah study, but the synagogue per se is not the focus of the statements. According to John the Pharisees have great power over the community.

7. In his dialogue with Trypho, Justin Martyr (c. 140-150 CE) writes as follows (137.2), "Agree with us, therefore, and do not revile the Son of God, nor, obeying Pharisaic teachers (φαρισαῖοι διδάσκαλοι), ever mock the King of Israel, as the rulers of your synagogues (ἀρχισυνάγωγοι) teach you after the prayer (μετὰ τὴν προσευχήν)." Two groups demand of Trypho and the Jews that they revile and mock Christ: Pharisaic teachers and rulers of synagogues. In response, Justin asks of Trypho and the Jews to ignore their leaders and never to mock Christ.

---

[31] "Pharisees" and "the Jews" are parallel also in John 1:19 // 1:24 and 7:32 // 7:35 (perhaps).
[32] Archons and Pharisees form a contrasting pair also at 7:48 (although Nicodemus is both a Pharisee and an archon, 3:1).

What is the relationship between the Pharisees, teachers, and the rulers of synagogues? Justin mentions the Pharisees seven times in his Dialogue; five of these seven refer unambiguously to the Pharisees (and Scribes) of Jesus' time.[33] The sixth reference occurs in a list of seven Jewish sects (αἱρέσεις), among them the Pharisees (80.4); this list has caused great difficulties for interpreters and requires separate discussion.[34] The seventh reference is our passage. In the light of the five unambiguous references, surely it is best to understand the reference in our passage as a reference to a group of the second temple period. The same conclusion emerges from a study of Justin's references to teachers (διδάσκαλοι). The rulers of the synagogues (ἀρχισυνάγωγοι) are mentioned only here in the Dialogue, but teachers (διδάσκαλοι) are mentioned frequently. They were and are the leaders of the Jews; they teach and interpret Scripture, cite tradition, and establish law. The Jews in turn seek to understand and perform the dictates of these teachers.[35] Insofar as the teachers were the leaders of the Jews in the time of Jesus, Justin can identify or associate them with Pharisees, Scribes, and priests.[36] Insofar as the teachers are the leaders of contemporary Jewry, Justin can ascribe to them some of the same negative qualities that the gospels ascribe to the Pharisees.[37] The faults of the Pharisees of Jesus' time remain the faults of the teachers of Justin's, but Justin nowhere labels contemporary teachers as Pharisees. Thus our passage probably should be interpreted as follows, "Do not mock Jesus as the Pharisaic teachers once taught you and as the rulers of the synagogues teach you now." If this is correct, our passage says nothing about the influence of Pharisees on the synagogue of Justin's time. In any case, it is worth noting that Justin clearly distinguishes between Pharisees-teachers and heads of synagogues.

This passage also provides evidence, or might be thought to provide evidence, of another sort for Pharisaic-rabbinic control of synagogues. In a series of passages, Justin accuses the Jews of cursing or anathematizing either Christians (93.4, 123.6) or Christ and Christians together (95.4 [an

---

[33] 51.2, 76.7, 102.5, 103.1, 105.6.
[34] Shaye J. D. Cohen, "The Significance of Yavneh," *HUCA* 55 (1984) 27-53, at 34-35 and 52 n. 70.
[35] Adolf Harnack, *Judentum und Judenchristentum in Justins Dialog mit Trypho* (TU 39; Leipzig: Hinrichs, 1913) 56-57. Διδάσκαλοι are mentioned, aside from 137, in *Dialogue* 9, 38, 43, 48, 62, 68, 71, 83, 94, 102, 103, 110, 112, 114, 117, 120, 134, 140, and 142.
[36] Pharisees and Scribes: 102.5 and 103.1-2 (perhaps inspired by Matthew 15:1-7 // Mark 7:1-6 and Luke 5:17; see next note). Priests: 117.
[37] For example: in 38.2, 48.2, and 140.2 Justin implicitly connects Isaiah 29:13 with the teachers; this polemic comes from Matthew // Mark (see previous note). Teachers want to be called "rabbi, rabbi" (112.5); cf. Matthew 23:7.

"if" clause], 108.3, and 133.6). In three further passages, Justin specifies that the cursing (of Christians) takes place in the synagogues (16.4, 47.4, 96.2).[38] And in our passage he states that the rulers of the synagogues teach the Jews to scoff Christ after the prayer.[39] Many scholars have connected these and various other patristic passages (and, indeed, the passages from the gospel of John just cited) with the *birkat ha-minim*, a prayer reportedly instituted or formulated by Rabban Gamaliel and the sages of Yavneh and directed against "heretics."[40] If this identification is correct, it would provide good evidence for the adoption of a rabbinic liturgical innovation by the Jews in their synagogues, thus for rabbinic influence on the synagogues of late antiquity.[41]

In all likelihood, however, *birkat ha-minim* has no connection either with John or Justin Martyr. The *birkat ha-minim* was a curse against heretics in general; it was not, and was not intended to be, a curse against all Christians, and it certainly was not a curse against Christ. John claims that Jews who believe in Christ will be ejected from the Jewish community; John had any number of reasons for making this claim, whether the claim be true or false. He says nothing about a prayer or a curse. Justin speaks of scoffing after the prayer, which is not the same thing as cursing during the prayer. At some point in its history the *birkat ha-minim* became a curse directed against "Jewish Christians" (Nazoreans), and was (mis)understood by Jerome as a curse against all Christians, but originally it was not so. These passages of John and Justin have nothing to do with the *birkat ha-minim* and offer no evidence concerning rabbinic influence over synagogues.[42]

---

[38] "Synagogues" almost certainly means "places of communal prayer and study"; see 72.3.
[39] Does "after the prayer" modify the verb "teach" (after the prayer the rulers of the synagogues teach the Jews to mock Christ) or the verb "mock" (the rulers of the synagogues teach the Jews: mock Christ after the prayer)? The syntax is ambiguous.
[40] Schrage, "συναγωγή," *TDNT* 7.848-852, s.v. ἀποσυνάγωγος; W. Horbury, "The Benediction of the Minim and Early Jewish-Christian Controversy," *JTS* 33 (1982) 19-61; Oskar Skarsaune, *The Proof from Prophecy* (NTSup 56; Leiden: Brill, 1987) 290-291; and many others.
[41] Thus it would be much better evidence than that provided by the Greek Jewish prayers contained in book 8 of the Apostolic Constitutions, because those prayers may well attest not rabbinic liturgical innovations but the standard Sabbath prayer of pre-rabbinic times.
[42] For studies that deny, or at least question, the relevance of the *birkat ha-minim* to John and Justin see: Peter Schäfer, "Die sogenannte Synode von Jabne. Zur Trennung von Juden und Christen im 1./2. Jh. n. Chr.," *Studien zur Geschichte und Theologie des rabbinischen Judentums* (Leiden: Brill, 1978) 45-64; A. Finkel, "Yavneh's Liturgy and Early Christianity," *Journal of Ecumenical Studies* 18 (1981) 231-250; Reuven Kimelman, "*Birkat ha-minim* and the Lack of Evidence for an

8. Jerome (c. 380 CE) knows the rabbinic *birkat ha-minim*.[43] He also clearly identifies the Pharisees of old with the rabbis (or sages, *sophoi*) of his own time, and sees them as the leaders of the Jews.[44] Some of these sages (*sapientissimi*) are the heads of synagogues (*praepositi synagogis*) who render decisions on questions of Jewish law.[45] Jerome gives us our first unambiguous evidence of rabbinic suzerainty over synagogues in the land of Israel.

In conclusion: I have surveyed eight passages from the New Testament, Josephus, and the church fathers. These passages constitute the major non-rabbinic literary evidence for the view that communal Jewish prayer and Torah study were led by Pharisees before 70 CE and rabbis after 70 CE. The most striking fact to emerge from this survey is the paucity of relevant evidence; of the eight passages, only one, the set of passages from Jerome, is explicit and unambiguous. Perhaps there is other relevant evidence that I have missed, especially in the church fathers, but even with some additional evidence I do not think that the overall picture will change. The widely-held notion that Pharisees and rabbis led communal prayer and study seems to derive ultimately from rabbinic literature, which conceives of the rabbis and their predecessors as *the* leaders of Judaism, indeed as synonymous with Judaism itself. If

---

anti-Christian Jewish Prayer in Late Antiquity," *Jewish and Christian Self-Definition II* (ed. E. P. Sanders et al.; Philadelphia: Fortress, 1981) 226-244; Cohen, "Yavneh"; Johann Maier, *Judische Auseinandersetzung mit dem Christentum in der Antike* (Darmstadt: Wissenschaftliche Buchgesellschaft, 1982) 136-141; T. G. G. Thornton, "Christian Understandings of the *Birkath Ha-Minim* in the Eastern Roman Empire," *JTS* 38 (1987) 419-431; and others.

[43] See Thornton, "Christian Understandings"; the *birkat ha-minim* may also be known to Epiphanius, somewhat before Jerome.

[44] Cohen, "Yavneh," 52-53. A full study of Jerome's knowledge of contemporary Judaism is a desideratum; the fullest study remains that of Samuel Krauss, "The Jews in the Works of the Church Fathers: Jerome," *JQR* 6 (1894) 225-261.

[45] *Epistle* 121.10.19 (CSEL 56:48): quantae traditiones pharisaeorum sint, quas hodie *deuteroseis* vocant, et quam aniles fabulae, revolvere nequeo ... dicam tamen unum in ignominiam gentis inimicae: praepositos habent synagogis sapientissimos quosque foedo operi delegatos, ut sanguinem virginis sive menstruatae mundum vel inmundum, si oculis discernere non potuerint, gustatu probent ("How many are the traditions of the Pharisees, which today they call [in Greek] *deuteroseis,* and how foolish are their stories, I am unable to recount ... Nevertheless, I shall say one of them, in order to shame that hateful people: they have as the heads of their synagogues certain very learned men who are assigned the disgusting task of determining by taste, if they are unable to discern by the eyes (alone), whether the blood of a virgin or a menstruant is pure or impure"). Compare *m. Nid.* 2:6-7. There is no reason to think that *synagoga* in Jerome means anything other than "synagogue," but I have been unable to locate any study of the subject; on συναγωγή in the church fathers, see Schrage, "συναγωγή," *TDNT* 7.838-841.

rabbinic Judaism is Judaism, and if the synagogue is the central institution of Judaism, then surely the rabbis, and their predecessors the Pharisees, will have been the leaders of all that took place in the synagogue! However, both this conception and the conclusion that derives from it are flawed, because neither the Judaism nor the synagogue of antiquity should be conceived in monistic terms. Pharisaic Judaism and rabbinic Judaism are not synonymous with Judaism.

According to Matthew and Josephus, the Pharisees are the most powerful and influential Jewish "school": they control prayers (vows?), sacred rites, sit on the seat of Moses (a metaphor), and sit on seats of honor (not a metaphor) in public assemblies. According to John, Pharisees have the power to exclude from the community whomever they wish. The reliability and purpose of Matthew's and Josephus' assertions of Pharisaic dominance have been much debated,[46] but even if they are largely accurate we should not simplify a complicated situation. Texts of or about the second temple period, including Matthew and Josephus, do not locate Pharisees in or near synagogues (that is, assemblies for the sake of communal prayer and Torah study).[47] Matthew places the Pharisees on the seat of Moses, but does not place the seat of Moses in the synagogue. Matthew (and parallels in Mark and Luke) and John use the word συναγωγή in connection with Pharisaic power, but the word is ambiguous and seems to refer to public "assemblies," whether judicial or communal, rather than "synagogues." Some synagogues, like the Theodotus synagogue of Jerusalem, were controlled not by Pharisees but by priests.[48] The office of ἀρχισυνάγωγος is known from the New Testament, inscriptions, and rabbinic literature (where the office is called ראש הכנסת), but not a single Pharisee or rabbi can be shown to have been an archisynagogue. Justin, as we have seen, distinguishes Pharisees from archisynagogues.[49]

---

[46] David Goodblatt, "The Place of the Pharisees in First Century Judaism," *JSJ* 20 (1989) 12-30; Mason, *Flavius Josephus on the Pharisees*, 372-373 and "Pharisaic Dominance before 70 CE and the Gospels' Hypocrisy Charge (Matt 23:2-3)," *HTR* 83 (1990) 363-381, esp. 371-379.

[47] In Josephus, *Life* 276-303, four delegates from Jerusalem, three of whom are Pharisees, take a prominent role in a series of meetings that take place over a Shabbat-Sunday-Monday in the large synagogue (προσευχή) of Tiberias. But these were exceptional times and events, and hardly indicate anything about Pharisaic power generally in synagogues.

[48] On priests in the synagogue, see E. P. Sanders, *Judaism: Practice and Belief 63 BCE-66 CE* (Philadelphia: Trinity, 1992) 201.

[49] Nicodemus the Pharisee (John 3:1) is an archon, not an archisynagogue. For a discussion of the title and the office see Brooten, *Leaders*, 15-33. For a full survey of synagogue officers in antiquity, see James Burtchaell, *From Synagogue to Church* (Cambridge University, 1992) 228-271.

Since the synagogue has its ultimate origins not in sectarian piety but in the social ethos and political forms of the Hellenistic period, it was predominantly a democratic lay organization, not beholden to a single group or party. There never was a central synagogue organization in antiquity – there was no "United Synagogue," no chief rabbinate, and no pope. There was no office that was empowered to enforce standards (for example, *birkat ha-minim*) in all synagogues, and there was no political mechanism by which standards could have been enforced.[50] There was not a standardized liturgy. These facts are no less true for the period after 70 CE than for the second temple period. Aside from the synagogue of Rehov, with a piece of the Yerushalmi spelled out in mosaic tile on its floor,[51] there is not a single synagogue excavated in the land of Israel that is demonstrably rabbinic. Synagogue inscriptions do not place rabbis in positions of leadership; neither does the Theodosian code (which refers to the patriarch, patriarchs, archisynagogues, and various other officials).[52] How to reconcile the art and architecture of the synagogues that have been discovered with rabbinic law and piety, is a well-known and enduring problem. In Jerome's perspective, Jewish communities and synagogues were led by sages, but this is evidence, at most, only for his time and place (land of Israel, c. 400 CE).

I conclude therefore that these eight passages do not provide sufficient evidence for the view, still held in many circles, that the synagogue was the main institutional base of Pharisaic and rabbinic piety and power. No doubt some, perhaps many, synagogues in antiquity will have been under the religious influence of the Pharisees/rabbis, but many will not have been. As their name indicates, synagogues belonged to the community.[53]

---

[50] Contrast William Horbury, "Extirpation and Excommunication," *VT* 35 (1985) 13-38, who ascribes to Jewish communities a much higher degree of organization and centralization than is warranted by the evidence.
[51] J. Naveh, *On Stone and Mosaic: The Aramaic and Hebrew Inscriptions from Ancient Synagogues* (Jerusalem: Israel Exploration Society, 1978) 79-85.
[52] On the inscriptions see Shaye J. D. Cohen, "Epigraphical Rabbis," *JQR* 72 (1981) 1-17; on the Theodosian code see Cohen, "Pagan and Christian Evidence."
[53] *B. Shabb.* 32a, "bet am."

8

The "Dead Sea Scrolls" or "The Community of the Renewed Covenant?"*

Shemaryahu Talmon

I.

The Scrolls, the Caves, and the Qumran Settlement[1]

The happenstance discovery in the spring of 1946 of seven ancient scrolls in a cave in the Desert of Judah was followed by similar finds in another ten out of some 80 caves that trained scholars investigated during the ensuing decade.[2] All eleven caves are situated near a site known by the modern Arabic name Qumran, which is located some ten miles to the south of Jericho and just over one mile to the west of the shores of the Dead Sea.[3] After a decade of no new discoveries, Yigael

---

* This is a revised version of the author's 1993 Albert T. Bilgray Lecture at the University of Arizona. It is reprinted with the permission of the author and of the Bilgray Lectureship Committee of Temple Emanu-el, Tucson, Arizona.

[1] References to the voluminous literature on Qumran research will be necessarily restricted to a bare minimum. J. A. Fitzmyer, *The Dead Sea Scrolls. Major Publications and Tools for Study* (Atlanta, GA: Scholars Press, 1990) provides an up-to-date roster of basic publications.

[2] For a handy summary of the history of the discovery and its importance, see F. M. Cross, *The Ancient Library of Qumran & Modern Biblical Studies*, rev. ed. (New York: Doubleday, 1961; reprint Grand Rapids, MI: Baker, 1980); G. Vermes, *The Dead Sea Scrolls: Qumran in Perspective* (London: SCM, 1982).

[3] The individual scrolls and fragments are identified by a siglum in which a digit indicates the cave in which the item was found, Q stands for Qumran, and an

Yadin retrieved from the cellars of an antique dealer in Bethlehem the *Temple Scroll* (11QTemple[a]), the largest scroll of all, which originally hails from Cave 11.[4] The geographical proximity of the caves to the Dead Sea resulted in the finds becoming widely known by the misnomer "Dead Sea Scrolls." They should in fact be designated "Judean Desert Scrolls,"[5] or more accurately "Qumran Scrolls," to keep them apart from manuscript discoveries in several other locations in the Desert of Judah, such as Masadah, Wadi Seyyal, Wadi Murabba'at, and Wadi Daliyeh.

The seven scrolls recovered from the first cave had been stored in two large earthenware jars of a type not previously found in excavations in Palestine, covered with lids and made airtight by the application of a layer of bitumen to the gap between the lid and the receptacle. It appears that the vessels had been especially manufactured in two standard sizes to accommodate bundles of 3-4 scrolls of comparable height. In addition, the cave contained sherds of more jars, which were possibly broken in antiquity or else were fractured by the bedouins who made the discovery. In contrast, in the other caves the partial scrolls and fragments were found lying on the floor.

Scholars assume that the Qumran assemblage consisted originally of ca. 800 manuscripts. This assessment often conjures up the misleading picture of a huge Torah-Shrine in which hundreds of rolled-up scrolls were placed one next to the other. This mistaken impression gave rise to nagging questions concerning the slow pace of their publication. But we must keep in mind that only some ten to twenty scrolls are preserved almost completely or to a considerable extent. All others are represented by large or small fragments, often by mere slivers of leather, which was the predominant writing material, or by snippets of papyrus. One arrives

---

abbreviated title or a symbol give a clue to the contents (as far as ascertainable), preceded by a lower case letter which refers to its literary character. If several copies of a work were discovered, each is circumscribed by a raised lower case letter: e.g. 1QIs[b] = Second Isaiah Scroll of Cave 1; 11QPs[a] = First Psalms Scroll of Cave 11; 1QpHab = the actualizing interpretation (pesher) of the book of the biblical prophet Habakkuk from Cave 1. In other instances, a serial number is stated by which an item is registered in the official publication: *e.g.* 6Q22 = unidentified fragment 22 of Cave 6; 4Q325 = item 325 of Cave 4. E. Tov, "The Unpublished Qumran Texts from Caves 4 and 11," *JJS* 43:1 (1992) provides an updated, although not final, inventory of not yet edited fragments.

[4] Y. Yadin, *The Temple Scroll* (Jerusalem: Israel Exploration Society/Hebrew University/Shrine of the Book, Hebrew ed. 1977; English ed. 1983); *The Temple Scroll. A Critical Edition with Extensive Reconstructions* by E. Qimron, *Bibliography* by F. Garcia Martinez (Beer Sheva: Ben Gurion University Press/Jerusalem: Israel Exploration Society, 1996).

[5] The official publication of the finds is properly named *Discoveries in the Judaean Desert* (Oxford: Clarendon Press) and abbreviated DJD.

at the estimated total of 800 scrolls by assigning various quantities of fragments to one manuscript, fitting them together as in a puzzle on the basis of content and vocabulary, script and scribal peculiarities, consistency and color of the material, dovetailing diverse pieces, *etc.*

Classification of the Scrolls

By content and literary genre, the scrolls can be subsumed under four main categories, which stand, however, in need of further subdivision.

1. Copies of books of the Hebrew Bible make up about 30% of the total.[6] With the exception of the book of Esther, all of the books of the Hebrew Scriptures are represented at Qumran.[7] Some, like the book of Psalms, are extant in fragments of scores of copies; others, like Ezra, by only a few snippets of text.[8] We should stress that to date not one indisputable text from the New Testament,[9] or, for that matter, from the known rabbinic literature, has turned up.

2. Hebrew and Aramaic manuscripts of apocryphal books, such as the Testaments of the 12 Patriarchs,[10] Tobit,[11] Jubilees[12] and 1 Enoch

---

[6] The data given derive from statistics assembled by Prof. D. Dimant.
[7] No persuasive explanation has been offered for the absence of Esther from the Qumran finds, nor for the fact that not one certain quotation from the book has been identified in non-biblical writings. It remains to be seen whether J. T. Milik's publication of a presumed Aramaic proto-Esther text will throw some light on this question: "Les Modèles Araméens du Livre d'Esther dans la Grotte 4 de Qumrân," *Mémorial Jean Starcky, RevQ* 59 (1992) 321-99. See now: S. Talmon, "Was the Book of Esther Known at Qumran?," *Dead Sea Discoveries* 2:3 (1995) 249-67.
[8] No part of the book of Nehemiah has as yet been identified. Its presumed presence among the Qumran finds can only be indirectly ascertained by assuming that, as in the massoretic tradition, also at Qumran Nehemiah was combined with Ezra. See S. Talmon, "Ezra and Nehemiah (Books and Men)," *IDB Suppl. Vol.* (ed. K. Crim; Nashville: Abingdon, 1976) 317-28.
[9] The attempted ascription to the Gospel of Mark of a tiny papyrus fragment from Cave 7 has not found acceptance. See C. P. Thiede, *The Earliest Gospel Manuscript? The Qumran Fragment 7Q5 and its Significance for New Testament Studies* (Torquay, Devon: Paternoster Press, 1992).
[10] J. T. Milik, "Écrits prééesséniens de Qumrân: d'Henoch à 'Amram," *Qumrân: Sa piété, sa théologie et son milieu* (ed. M. Delcor; BETL 46; Gembloux: Duculot/Louvain: Leuven University Press, 1978) 91-106; idem, "Le Testament de Lévi en araméen: Fragment de la grotte 4 de Qumran," *RB* 62 (1955) 398-406.
[11] J. T. Milik, "La patrie de Tobie," *RB* 73 (1966) 522-30.
[12] Fragments of 12 or 13 exemplars of Jubilees were discovered at Qumran. See J. C. VanderKam, *Textual and Historical Studies in the Book of Jubilees* (Harvard Semitic Monographs 14; Missoula, MT: Scholars Press, 1977); idem, "Jubilees," *Qumran Cave 4.VIII* (ed. H. Attridge; et al.; *DJD XIII*; Oxford: Clarendon, 1994) 1-185.

have been found.¹³ These works were not handed down in Jewish tradition; but, as is well known, Greek and Ethiopic translations of them were included in the Canon of the Church. We can include in this category copies of hitherto unknown compositions of a similar character, such as the Genesis Apocryphon,¹⁴ the Psalms of Joshua,¹⁵ *etc*. Taken together, manuscripts of works of this category amount to ca. 25% of the total.¹⁶

3. Another 25% of the total are copies of previously unknown compositions: wisdom writings, prayers and prayer compilations, *etc*.¹⁷ These texts are not characterized by any idiosyncratic content or linguistic peculiarities that would tie them to the Covenanters' community and theology. Rather, they presumably derive from what may be considered the common literary heritage of Jewry in the late Second Temple Period.

4. Approximately a fifth of the manuscript assemblage consists of Hebrew compositions of various literary genres, which evidently constitute the particular literature of the "Community of the Renewed Covenant."¹⁸ These works are of special interest since they enlighten us on the Covenanters' conceptual universe and the socio-religious structure of their community.¹⁹ The more reliable means for gauging the Covenanters' world of ideas are the major scrolls that hail from Cave 1, in which are laid down the precepts that govern the proper societal and religious conduct of *yahad*-members. They are best designated "Foundation Documents."

---

[13] J. T. Milik, *The Books of Enoch: Aramaic Fragments of Qumran Cave 4*, with the collaboration of M. Black (Oxford: Clarendon, 1976).

[14] *A Genesis Apocryphon: A Scroll from the Wilderness of Judaea* (ed. N. Avigad and Y. Yadin; Jerusalem: Magnes/Shrine of the Book, 1956).

[15] C. Newsom, "The 'Psalms of Joshua' From Qumran Cave 4," *JJS* 39:1 (1988) 58-61.

[16] In the wake of the publication of new texts, the scholarly literature on this genre is growing by leaps and bounds. See D. Dimant, "New Light From Qumran on the Jewish Pseudepigrapha – 4Q390," *Proceedings of the International Congress on the Dead Sea Scrolls, Madrid 18-21 March 1991* (ed. J. Trebolle and L. Vegas; Leiden: Brill, 1993) 1-44.

[17] See M. Baillet, "Texte liturgiques," *Qumrân Grotte 4* (DJD VII; Oxford: Clarendon, 1982) 73-286; B. Nitzan, *Qumran Prayer and Religious Poetry* (Leiden: Brill, 1994).

[18] I shall yet explain this designation.

[19] D. Dimant gives an excellent overview of the "Qumran Sectarian Literature" in *Jewish Writings of the Second Temple Period. Apocrypha, Pseudepigrapha, Qumran Sectarian Writings, Philo, Josephus* (ed. M. E. Stone; Compendia Rerum Iudaicarum ad Novum Testamentum II; Assen/Philadelphia: Van Gorcum/Fortress, 1984) 483-550.

a. The *Zadokite Document(s)* or the *Damascus Rule* (CD)[20] combines a compressed survey of the history of the yaḥad with a selection of legal materials, in the vein of the biblical book of Deuteronomy. The historical account and the statutes pertain to the entire "Community of the Renewed Covenant," viz., to the majority of members who live with their families in "camps," מחנות, in various locations in Palestine, as well as to the relatively small "Commune," viz., the contingent of male members who reside for a season at Qumran.[21]

b. The *Community Rule* or *Manual of Discipline* (1QS) lists precepts that pertain predominantly, but not exclusively, to the "Qumran Commune," its structure, and public procedures, and prescribes the conduct of its (temporarily) celibate members.[22]

c. The *Messianic Rule* (1QS^a) offers a description of the envisioned "Messianic Banquet," molded on the Covenanters' common meals in historical reality. It further portrays the future "General Assembly" at which "all precepts of the (renewed) covenant" will be publicly read before the entire community – priests, Levites and lay-Israelites, men and women alike, and also children who are mature enough to understand the proceedings and the legal tenets that pertain to them (1QS^a I,1-5). This gathering is, in fact, a replica of Nehemiah's "great convocation" (Neh 8).[23]

d. The *War Rule* (1QM) presents legal and descriptive details of the cataclysmic encounter in which the "Sons of Light", viz., the Covenanters, will finally overcome all "Sons of Darkness." In the ensuing era of universal peace they will reestablish the temple in

---

[20] C. Rabin, *The Zadokite Documents: I. The Admonitions; II. The Laws*, edited with a Translation, (rev. ed; Oxford: Clarendon, 1958). Two medieval partial copies of this work were discovered at the end of the last century in a Genizah attached to the Ezra Synagogue in Old Cairo. They were edited by S. Schechter, who correctly dated the work to the Second Temple Period: *Documents of Jewish Sectaries: Volume 1: Fragments of a Zadokite Work* (Cambridge: University Press, 1910), reprinted with a Prolegomenon by J. A. Fitzmyer (New York: Ktav, 1970). Schechter's identification became a certainty when fragments of several copies of the Zadokite Documents were discovered at Qumran. The fragments are being edited by J. Baumgarten.
[21] I shall yet remark on this characterization of the Qumran contingent.
[22] See below.
[23] See S. Talmon, "Waiting for the Messiah – The Conceptual Universe of the Qumran Covenanters," *Judaisms and Their Messiahs* (ed. J. Neusner, W. S. Green and E. Frerichs; New York/Cambridge: Cambridge University Press, 1988) 111-37 = Talmon, *The World of Qumran From Within* (Jerusalem: Magnes, 1989) 273-300, esp. 287-300.

the "New Jerusalem," the very center of their messianic kingdom, a glorified reflection of Israel's historical commonwealth.

e. The *Temple Scroll* (11QTemple^a) enlarges on matters pertaining to the future body politic and its ritual center, the temple. The work is conceived in the form of a "Deutero-Deuteronomium." It differs from the biblical book in respect to certain legal prescriptions, and above all, in that it presents not Moses, but God himself, as addressing the people of Israel.

f. Pesharim and other works provide information on some aspects of the Covenanters' history through an actualizing interpretation of non-historical portions of the Hebrew Bible that lend themselves more easily to an *ad hoc* extrapolation, such as the prophetic literature and the book of Psalms. The *yahad* authors take the scriptural texts to foreshadow events in the historical experience of their community, especially in reference to the contention of the "Legitimate Teacher," מורה (ה)צדק, their protagonist, with his antagonist, the "Wicked Priest," הכהן הרשע, who leads the opposing faction in contemporary Judaism. The *Pesher Habakkuk* (1QpHab) is a prime example of this literary genre.

g. Supplementary information pertaining to these aspects can be extracted from the *Temple Scroll* and from fragmentary remains of various other documents. In this context, special reference must be made to "An Unpublished Halakhic Letter from Qumran," which its editors entitle *miqsat ma'asē* (or *dibrē*) *tōrāh* (4QMMT).[24]

Languages and Scripts
1. The great majority of the Qumran scrolls are written in Hebrew. Non-biblical texts are written in what may be considered the vernacular of the times, which is marked by a mixture of biblical and

---

[24] See E. Qimron and J. Strugnell, in *Biblical Archaeology Today: Proceedings of the International Congress on Biblical Archaeology, Jerusalem, April 1984* (Jerusalem: Israel Exploration Society, 1985) 400-407, and *Qumran Cave 4. V: Miqsat Ma'ase ha-Torah* (ed. E. Qimron and J. Strugnell; DJD X; Oxford/New York: Clarendon/Oxford University Press, 1994). It appears that too much store is being set upon this comparatively short and fragmentary document. It attracted attention because scholars were appraised of its existence at a time when Qumran studies suffered from acute attrition. The delay of its announced publication enhanced speculations about its contents, and raised over-optimistic expectations as to the light it may shed on the Covenanters' historical identity (see below).

mishnaic or rabbinic linguistic peculiarities.[25] A smaller number are couched in Aramaic.[26] Several items are written in Greek, and naturally also in the Greek alphabet. With a few exceptions, they are remains of Greek translations of biblical books.[27] The linguistic diversity provides added proof that in the late Second Temple Period many Jews were bi- or even trilingual. But it is significant that to date only very few Greek loan-words have turned up in Qumran writings, in contrast to rabbinic literature in which some 3000 such loan-words have been identified.[28]

2. Hebrew and Aramaic manuscripts are commonly penned in the "square" script which was current at the turn of the era and is in use to this day. In rabbinic parlance it is named כתב מיושר / כתב מאושר(ת) / כתב אשורית (m. Yad. 4:5; t. Sanh. 4.7; b. Sanh. 21b-22a; b. Shab. 115b; y. Meg. 1.71b-c, et al.). Like the modern name "square alphabet," these ancient designations derive from the rectangular form of the characters in this script.

Several manuscripts and fragments, mostly copies of biblical books, are written in the palaeo-Hebrew alphabet,[29] which in rabbinic literature is known as כתב עברי, "Hebrew script," or כתב רע"ץ or כתב דע"ץ (b. Sanh. 21b), "broken script," due to the angularity of its letters.[30] Modern publications often refer to it as "Phoenician alphabet."

3. Differences of *ductus*, linguistic peculiarities and vocabulary, plain and defective spelling, *etc.*, prove that the scrolls were penned by a considerable number of scribes. However, the layout and paragraphing, the spacing of letters, words and lines, *etc.*, evidence a common scribal tradition, which in many aspects dovetails with rules recorded in rabbinic literature pertaining to the writing of "holy books," foremost in the tractates *Sefer Torah, Soferim,* and

---

[25] See E. Qimron, *The Hebrew of the Dead Sea Scrolls* (Harvard Semitic Studies 29; Atlanta, GA: Scholars Press, 1986).
[26] See J. A. Fitzmyer, *A Wandering Aramean: Collected Aramaic Essays* (SBLMS 25; Missoula, MT: Scholars Press, 1979); K. Beyer, *Die aramäischen Texte vom Toten Meer* (Göttingen: Vandenhoeck & Ruprecht, 1984).
[27] See P. W. Skehan, E. Ulrich, J. E. Sanderson, with contributions by P. J. Parsons, *Palaeo-Hebrew and Greek Biblical Manuscripts. Qumran Cave 4 IV* (DJD IX; Oxford: Clarendon, 1992).
[28] See S. Lieberman, *Greek in Jewish Palestine* (New York: Jewish Theological Seminary, 1942; reprint, 1965).
[29] See Skehan-Ulrich, *Palaeo-Hebrew*.
[30] Another name כתב ליבונאה, remains unexplained. See S. Kraus, *Talmudische Archäologie* (3 vols.; Leipzig: Fock, 1912) 3.137-38, 142.

Megillah.³¹ But some statistically verifiable differences lead scholars to conclude that these special features possibly evince the existence of a "scribal school," which was intimately connected with the Covenanters' community.³²

Material Aspects

1. With the exception of a small quantity of papyri, the scrolls are made from animal hides of which the hair was shaved off. The lettering is on the porous side. This technique facilitates the penetration of the ink into the leather, and thus makes for better preservation of the writing. At the same time, no inscriptions on hard materials were found at Qumran, comparable to the stone and potsherd inscriptions of the First or the Second Temple period. The one exception is the *Copper Scroll* (3Q15), which consists of several thin copper strips riveted together. It contains a roster of treasure hoards, together with an enumeration of their locations.³³ The nature of this document and its putative connection with the Covenanters' community still remain under scholarly discussion.

2. The employment of hides as writing material is unprecedented in Jewish scribal tradition. The exceedingly large quantity of scrolls that turned up at Qumran suggests that the use of leather for this purpose was already well established at the time. But the practice is not documented for an earlier period. Therefore, we cannot trace the history of the use of leather as a writing surface in Jewish culture.

Date

1. Personal names mentioned in some fragments designate exclusively historical figures of the Hasmonean period: *e.g.*, the high priest הירקנוס, either Hyrcanus I (134-104 B.C.E.) or Hyrcanus II (76-67 B.C.E.); שלמציון, Queen Alexandra Salome (76-67 B.C.E.); אמיליוס, Aemilius Scaurus, the first Roman Governor of Syria (62 B.C.E.); and presumably המלך יונתן, King Jonathan, possibly the Hebrew name of

---

[31] E. L. Sukenik underscored this similarity soon after the initial discovery of the scrolls. See his *Megilloth Genuzot: From an Ancient Genizah Found in the Judaean Desert. A First Report* (Jerusalem: Bialik, 1948) 11-13 (Hebrew).
[32] See E. Tov, "Scribal Practices Reflected in the Documents from the Judean Desert and in the Rabbinic Literature. A Comparative Study." *Text, Temples and Traditions* (ed. M. V. Fox, V. A. Hurowitz, A. Hurvitz, M. L. Klein, B. J. Schwartz and N. Shupak (Winona Lake, IN: Eisenbrauns, 1996) 383-403.
[33] J. T. Milik, "Le Rouleau de Cuivre Provenant de la Grotte 3Q (3Q15)," *Les Petites Grottes de Qumrân* (ed. M. Baillet, J. T. Milik and R. de Vaux; DJD III; Oxford: Clarendon, 1962) 201-302, 314-17.

Alexander Jannaeus (103-76 B.C.E.).[34] Not a single name of a historical personality of a later period has turned up. Most important, all references pertain to figures connected with the history of Judaism in pre-Christian times. Not one name identifies a personality known from early Christian traditions.

2. Palaeographical analyses indicate that the documents were mostly penned in the last two centuries B.C.E., with some stemming from the first century C.E. These findings dovetail to a surprising degree with the results of carbon-14 tests, carried out by an international team of scientists who had not been apprised of the dates proposed by palaeographers.[35]

3. As noted above, the caves are situated close to a nearby site, known by the modern Arabic name Qumran. While no signs of human habitation were discovered in the caves, archaeologists at Qumran excavated the ruins of several impressive buildings. The geographical proximity suggests that in antiquity these buildings were inhabited by the people who deposited the scrolls in the caves. Remains of public structures, intricate installations for water supply, ritual baths, and what appears to be a synagogue *cum* assembly hall, prompt the conclusion that the settlement at Qumran served as a community center. The discovery on the site of a considerable number of earthenware plates, three ink pots, and what seems to be the top of a writing desk, all give credence to this inference. The connection of the caves with the ancient settlement was conclusively proven in the winter of 1992. Exceptionally heavy rainfalls eroded a sand wall on the site and laid bare a completely preserved, albeit empty, earthenware jar of exactly the same make as the intact jar found in Cave 1 that had served as the receptacle of four scrolls.

4. It follows that the Qumran scrolls, and the community whose members deposited them in the caves, must be dated to the turn of the era, approximately to between 200 B.C.E. and 100 C.E.[36] We should, however, bear in mind that by dating the scrolls we have not yet established the time of the composition of the works preserved in them. The manuscripts are not necessarily autographs. Rather, most,

---

[34] E. Eshel, H. Eshel and A. Yardeni, "A Qumran Composition Containing Part of Ps. 154 and a Prayer for the Welfare of King Jonathan and his Kingdom," *IEJ* 42 (1992) 199-229.

[35] See G. Bonani, M. Broshi, I. Carmi, S. Ivy and W. Wölfli, "Radiocarbon Testing Dating of the Dead Sea Scrolls", '*Atiqot* 20 (1994) 27-32. I leave aside some additional considerations that further undergird the above conclusions.

[36] This conclusion would not be seriously put in doubt even if it could be proven that certain items should be dated somewhat later in the early Christian era.

if not all, were copied from earlier prototypes. A case in point is the numerous copies of books of the Hebrew Bible, which were certainly authored before 200 B.C.E. The same may be said of manuscripts of literary works, in part known, in part hitherto unknown, which can be shown to have been written in the early Second Temple period, *viz.*, in the third or even the fourth century B.C.E.

II.

The Importance of the Qumran Finds

1. Prior to the discovery of the Qumran scrolls in the summer of 1947, the centuries immediately preceding the turn of the era were altogether considered a dark age in Judaeo-Christian history. No contemporary sources survive from those times. Scholarly assessments of actual events and ideological developments that shaped the contours of that period were based solely on information derived from secondary reports of Hellenistic, Rabbinic, and Christian authors, who viewed them retrospectively from the vantage point of later generations. In contrast, the Qumran scrolls are the only original contemporary documents at our disposal. They were produced by Jewish writers who flourished in the Hellenistic-Roman era, *viz.*, in the last three centuries B.C.E., and they contain firsthand evidence that relates directly to that crucial period. Their exceeding importance lies in their being firsthand, contemporaneous witnesses of the events that they record.

The momentous difference between information culled from the scrolls and previously available data is illustrated by the following fact which pertains to biblical studies: the oldest extant codices of the major Greek translation of the Hebrew Bible, Codex Alexandrinus, and Codex Sinaiticus of the Septuagint,[37] were penned in the third and fourth century C.E. Of an even later date is the earliest preserved Hebrew Bible manuscript, the Cairo Codex of the Prophets, written in 899 C.E. Further, Hebrew documents and partial copies of diverse literary compositions found in the Cairo Genizah, *e.g.*, the already mentioned Zadokite Documents and the apocryphal Testament of Levi, are dated to the end of the first millennium C.E. or the beginning of the second, and none is prior to the eighth century. By contrast, comparable Qumran materials, *viz.*, the immense quantity of biblical scrolls, fragments of the very same Zadokite Documents, or of the Testament of Levi, hail from the last

---

[37] We do not need to consider remnants of some earlier copies of the Greek Old Testament, such as the John Rylands Library Fragments, which in part stem from pre-Christian times.

centuries B.C.E. Thus they precede the Cairo Genizah finds by approximately one millennium.

2. It is for these reasons that after the initial discovery of the Qumran scrolls, scholars confidently expected that the previously totally unknown documents would illuminate that "dark age" in the history of Judaism and Christianity, the centuries at the turn of the era. However, the great hopes did not materialize. In actual fact, the writings that emanated from the caves throw no direct light on events that affected Judaism at large at the height of the Second Temple Period. The authors turn their attention almost exclusively to matters that pertain specifically to their own community, its genesis and ensuing history, its societal structure, and its particular beliefs and concepts.

3. Even the information on these issues is far from complete. We do not know *inter alia* who the members of the community were, from which strata of society they were recruited, and from which localities in Eretz Israel they came. Nor can we fully fathom the considerations that had moved them to join the *yahad*. The identity of the protagonists of the drama portrayed in the Covenanters' literature still escapes us.[38] Scholars can only offer intelligent guesses in attempting to explain the reasons for storing the scrolls in the caves.

Most vexing is the fact that the Qumran writings do not contain sufficient data for conclusively ascertaining the "historical" identity of the community, to which the authors refer by appellations that often contain the vocable יחד. In the Hebrew Bible, יחד is equivalent to יחד(י)ו and is used as an adverb. But in Qumran literature it is mostly employed as a noun: עצת היחד, [סר]ך היחד, ברית יחד, אנשי היחד, *etc.*,[39] and it evidently connotes "community" or "commune."[40] Designations, such as יחד אל, "Divine Community" (1QH I,11-12; II,22-23, 25-26), give eloquent expression to the members' elite consciousness.[41] Not one of these appellations was known from any extant literary source before the

---

[38] There is no substance to recently offered fanciful hypotheses which identify the leaders of the community and of its opponents with prominent figures of whom the Gospels speak.
[39] I have argued that the rudimentary employment of יחד as a noun can be still traced in some biblical books. See: "The Qumran יחד – a Biblical Noun," *VT* 3 (1953) 133-40, reprinted in Talmon, *World of Qumran*, 53-60.
[40] It appears to be synonymous with Greek κοινονία. See R. Marcus, "Philo, Josephus and the Dead Sea Yahad," *JBL* 71 (1952) 207-9.
[41] Cp. standard phrases like להיחד עם בני קודש, להיחד בעדת, להיחד בעצת אל השמים (1QH I,8,9; III,22; V,20; IX,2; XI,8; frg. II,10).

discovery of the Qumran scrolls, with the exception of the Cairo Genizah Zadokite Fragments.[42]

Who Were the Covenanters?

The Covenanters are known only from the Qumran writings and are never explicitly mentioned in any ancient source. This silence caused surprise. Scholars considered it improbable, nay impossible, that classical authors, who gave attention to the internal diversity of Judaism at the end of the Second Temple period, would have left unrecorded such a seemingly substantial community. As a result, one attempted to identify the *yahad* with practically any known Jewish "sect" of the Second Temple period, and even of later times, such as the medieval Karaites.

A widely accepted hypothesis equates the Covenanters with the Essenes.[43] Flavius Josephus, Philo of Alexandria, and the Roman historian Pliny the Elder describe the Essenes in some detail: they are presented as the third Jewish "philosophy," next to the Pharisees and the Sadducees. Their main settlement is said to have been located on the shores of the Dead Sea near Ein Gedi, some fifteen miles to the south of Qumran. Therefore scholars concluded that thanks to the Qumran finds "for the first time, the hitherto mysterious Essenes stand revealed to us. The story of their spiritual struggle swells out of the past like a mighty hymn."[44]

Frank Cross, the persuasive proponent of the Covenanters = Essenes theory, summarizes the argument as follows:

> The scholar who would "exercise caution" in identifying the sect of Qumran with the Essenes places himself in an astonishing position; he must suggest seriously that two major parties formed communistic religious communities in the same district of the desert of the Dead Sea and lived together in effect for two centuries, holding similar bizarre views, performing similar or rather identical lustrations, ritual meals, and ceremonies. He must suppose that one, carefully described by classical authors, disappeared without leaving building remains or even potsherds behind; the other, systematically ignored by classical authors, left extensive ruins, and

---

[42] The word is spelled there three times with a yod, היחיד (CD XX,1,14,32). In all three instances E. Qimron suggests to read היחד. See his "The Text of CDC," *The Damascus Document Reconsidered* (ed. M. Broshi; Jerusalem: Israel Exploration Society, 1992).
[43] In fact, all other proposals are by now passed over in silence.
[44] A. D. Tushingham, "The Men Who Hid the Dead Sea Scrolls," *National Geographic Magazine* 94.6 (1958) 785-808; quoted by J. H. Charlesworth, "The Dead Scrolls and the Historical Jesus," *Jesus and the Dead Sea Scrolls* (ed. J. H. Charlesworth; New York/London: Doubleday, 1992) 41, n. 3.

indeed a great library. I prefer to be reckless and flatly identify the men of Qumran with their perennial house guests, the Essenes.⁴⁵

Most scholars subscribe to the Qumran–Essenes theory. Warnings sounded by some students of the scrolls against this summary equation were altogether ignored or shrugged off.⁴⁶ Surprisingly, though, the staunch defenders of this hypothesis do not give attention to the astounding circumstance that in contrast to the massive documentation on the Pharisees and the more sketchy information on the Sadducees, the Essenes, like the Covenanters, are never mentioned in the Gospels nor in the early rabbinic literature. In the past, this glaring lacuna had triggered the conclusion that the Essenes, and the Covenanters, should be identified with one of the other two "philosophies," the abundantly documented Pharisees or the lesser known Sadducees.

Little is known of the later phases of the Essenes' fate. The uncertainty prompted the hypothesis that the sect faded from history sometime in the first or second century C.E. and that its erstwhile members were ultimately absorbed into the Christian community. Thus there arose another, rather simplistic equation: Covenanters equal Essenes; Essenes equal nascent Christianity; therefore the *yahad* equals the Jesus movement. More recently, the identification of the Covenanters with the Essenes has encountered new difficulties. The well-publicized open letter or epistle from Qumran Cave 4 (4QMMT), preserved in fragments of six copies,⁴⁷ has led some scholars to put that equation in doubt. It has been argued that the writer of this missive – possibly the מורה הצדק, the "Righteous" or "Legitimate Teacher," the Covenanters' spiritual leader – propagated particular halakhic rulings that rabbinic literature ascribes to the Sadducees, and attempted to win over the addressee – assumedly the "Wicked Priest," הכהן הרשע, the *yahad's* foremost antagonist – who presumably adhered to the pharisaic interpretation of the halakhic issues under debate. Thus one concludes

---

⁴⁵ F. M. Cross, *Canaanite Myth and Hebrew Epic: Essays in the History of the Religion of Israel* (Cambridge, MA: Harvard University Press, 1973) 331-32.
⁴⁶ M. H. Goshen-Gottstein, "Anti-Essene Traits in the Dead Sea Scrolls," *VT* 4 (1954) 141-47; S. Talmon, "The Calendar of the Covenanters of the Judean Desert," *Aspects of the Dead Sea Scrolls. Scripta Hierosolymitana* 4 (ed. C. Rabin and Y. Yadin; Jerusalem: Magnes, 1958) 197-99; reprinted in Talmon, *World of Qumran*, 184-86; C. Roth, "Why the Qumran Sect cannot have been Essenes," *RevQ* 1 (1958-59) 417-22; *idem*, "Were the Qumran Sectaries Essenes? A reexamination of some Evidences," *JTS* 10 (1959) 122-29.
⁴⁷ See above, n. 24.

that the Covenanters are in fact none other than the Sadducees,[48] or else that the Essenes were but a sect[49] that branched off from the Sadducees.[50]

Investigative Methods

From the very inception of Qumran studies, I have sounded a caveat against all attempts to equate the "Community of the Renewed Covenant" with any one socio-religious group or movement in the late Second Temple period mentioned in the classical sources:

1. The community is solely known from the Qumran writings. A proper appreciation of the *yahad*, its theology and societal structure, its historical parameters, and its place in Judaism of the Second Temple period must be based on data that can be elicited from its own writings, foremost from the "Foundation Documents."
2. Considerations of proper methodology require that a new phenomenon, like the *yahad*, should be first and foremost investigated from within, *viz.*, by an analysis of its rich literature, before any attempt is made to compare it, much less equate it, with any other contemporary socio-religious phenomenon.
3. In the application of such comparisons, one should avoid pitting an isolated feature of one phenomenon against its presumed counterpart. Rather, the comparison should be informed by a holistic approach that takes into account the relative importance of a feature or features compared in the overall socio-religious context of the entities under review.[51]
4. It may be considered axiomatic that a comparison of societal and religious phenomena of various groups in Judaism at the end of the Second Temple period will bring to the fore telling similarities, since all belong to one and the same "historical stream" and derive their basic beliefs and concepts from the common biblical tradition. But

---

[48] Solomon Schechter (followed by other scholars) had proposed this hypothesis already at the beginning of the century when he published the Cairo Genizah Fragments of the Zadokite Documents. See above, n. 20.

[49] The technical term "sect" is invoked in Qumran research without the required attention to its socio-religious technical connotation.

[50] See Y. Sussman, "The History of Halakha and the Dead Sea Scrolls – A Preliminary to the Publication of 4QMMT," *Tarbiz* 59:1-2 (1989/90) 17-76 (Hebrew); L. Schiffman, "The Saducean Origin of the Dead Sea Scroll Sect," *Understanding the Dead Sea Scrolls* (ed. H. Shanks; New York: Random House, 1992) 35-49. For a defense of the original Essene hypothesis, see J. C. VanderKam, "The People of the Dead Sea Scrolls: Essenes or Sadducees?" *ibid.*, 50-62.

[51] See my remarks in "The Comparative Method in Biblical Interpretation," *Göttingen Congress Volume 1977* (ed. J. E. Emerton; VTSup 29; Leiden: Brill, 1978) 320-52.

the individual profile of any one faction is ultimately determined by its discordant interpretation of the shared religious traditions and credal values.

5. We must take into account a general sociological principle. Comparable traits in the posture of discrete religious, or, for that matter, political groups are wont to arise from analogous societal conditions and credal tenets that were operative in the initial stages of their formation. The very confrontation with established religious and/or political authorities will sometimes produce surprising similarities of conceptual thought and organization in widely divergent opposition parties, foremost in dissident factions which are in the same "historical stream."

6. The disjunctive comparison of the Covenanters' community, in each case with only one discrete socio-religious entity in the compass of Judaism at the turn of the era – Essenes, Sadducees, Pharisees or primitive Christianity – produces a slanted impression of a special affinity with one or the other and obfuscates the intricate web of overlapping analogies and divergences. What is needed is a synoptic overview that would enable the scholar to define, as accurately as possible, the place that the "Community of the Renewed Covenant" occupied in the composition of the Jewish people at the height of the Second Temple period.

7. When one compares various configurations of Judaism at the turn of the era, and probes the specific profile of this or another group, divergences in the interpretation of the common heritage are decisive, not analogies.[52] A disregard of discrepancies in the search for similarities produces "Parallelomania"[53] and obfuscates the individuality of discrete socio-religious entities. By fusing the *yahad* with any other faction in late Second Temple Judaism, one reduces this assumedly major movement to a mere incident in Jewish history. Viewed as a phenomenon *sui generis*, the "Community of the Renewed Covenant" significantly enriches the multicolored mosaic in which Judaism presents itself to the historian at the turn of the era.

III.

The Community of the Renewed Covenant – באי הברית החדשה בדמשק

Like the overwhelming majority of scholars engaged in Qumran research, I date the community whose members deposited the scrolls in the caves to a period between ca. 200 B.C.E. and 100 C.E. In that span of

---
[52] See *ibid*.
[53] See S. Sandmel, "Parallelomania," *JBL* 81 (1962) 1-13.

time, the Jewish people was involved in a process of internal diversification that climaxed in the consolidation of pharisaic or "normative Judaism"[54] on the one hand, and of Christianity on the other hand. Taking an approach that in many respects differs from a prevalent orientation in scholarly research, I propose to show that the heuristic value of the Qumran finds does not lie in their revealing significant data concerning actual events that shaped the contours of that period. Rather, their importance inheres: (a) in whatever limited light which they throw on the opaque social history and the history of ideas of Judaism in the late Second Temple period; (b) in the information that can be elicited from them pertaining to the conceptual universe of Judaism, in an era in which Christianity progressively emerges as the most powerful force in the ancient world.

I conceive of the "Community of the Renewed Covenant" as standing at a three-point juncture in the history of Judaism and Christianity. Its existence coincides with the last phase of the biblical era, *viz.*, the last two or three centuries B.C.E., when the latest biblical writings were authored or completed, *e.g.*, the book of Daniel. Somewhat later, the collection of authoritative books, known as the "Canon"[55] of Hebrew Scriptures, the "Old" or the "First Testament," came effectively to a close. Concurrently, those days are marked by the onset of the process that at the height of the period culminated in the crystallization of "normative", *lege* pharisaic Judaism, which became the predominant factor in the ensuing history of the Jewish people and in the development of its religion.

The "Community of the Renewed Covenant" straddles two significant stages in Jewish history. It stands, as it were, with one foot in the waning biblical age, and with the other in the incipient era of the sages. It could be said that the Covenanters' spiritual universe was stressed between the Bible and the Mishnah.[56] Close to the apex of the

---

[54] G. F. Moore thus designated mainstream Judaism in *Judaism in the First Century of the Christian Era: The Age of the Tannaim* (2 vols.; Oxford: Clarendon, 1927) 1.3. The term is often mistakenly applied to Judaism in pre-Christian times, in which the consolidation of a "normative" trend cannot be verified on the basis of contemporary evidence.

[55] I use this term with reservation. For my view concerning the progressive emergence of the collection of Hebrew Scriptures see "Heiliges Schrifttum und kanonische Bücher aus jüdischer Sicht: Überlegungen zur Ausbildung der Grösse 'Die Schrift' im Judentum," *Mitte der Schrift? Ein jüdisch-christliches Gespräch: Texte des Berner Symposions vom 6-12 Januar 1985* (ed. M. Klopfenstein, U. Luz, S. Talmon and E. Tov; Judaica et Christiana 11; Bern/New York: Lang, 1987) 45-79= *Israels Gedankenwelt in der Hebräischen Bibel. Gesammelte Aufsätze Band 3* (Neukirchen – Vluyn: Neukirchener Verlag, 1995) 241-71.

[56] See my "Between the Bible and the Mishnah," *World of Qumran*, 11-52.

period, the curtain rose on nascent Christianity. Therefore, those times concomitantly constitute the backdrop before which the history of the primitive Church that is to become Judaism's rival claimant to the biblical heritage unfolds. Viewed against this background, the scrolls hold out promise of throwing some light on the otherwise undocumented transition in the Jewish conceptual universe from the biblical to the rabbinic era, on the one hand, and on the other hand, for partly inscribing the proverbial 'blank page' between the Hebrew Bible and the New Testament.

IV.

It is my thesis that the "Community of the Renewed Covenant" should be viewed as the second or third century B.C.E. crystallization of a major socio-religious movement that arose in early post-exilic Judaism. The movement was prophetically inspired and inclined to apocalypticism. It perpetuated a spiritual trend whose origin can be traced to the great prophets of the First Temple period – Isaiah, Jeremiah, and Ezekiel – and to the post-exilic prophets Haggai and Zechariah.[57] The development of the movement runs parallel to that of the competing "rationalist" stream that surfaces in the book of Ezra, and especially in the book of Nehemiah, and that will ultimately crystallize in rabbinic or "normative Judaism."[58] The roots of the *yahad's* prophetically inspired belief system, as that of the nascent rationalist stream, reach down into the period of the Return from the Babylonian Exile, that is to say into the fifth, possibly even into the sixth century B.C.E. At that time a bifurcation of the Jewish body politic appears to have set in. Led by two rival priestly houses, two major strands emerged, which were divided on a variety of issues pertaining to belief and ritual. In their subsequent development, both movements experienced internal diversifications of their respective interpretations of the biblical tradition. In the course of time, this divisive process generated the formation of new schismatic groups and culminated at the turn of the era in the distinct pluriformity of Judaism, to which the classical sources give witness.

We can differentiate two main phases in the historical development of the prophetic strand: the largely undocumented "primitive" stage of the unstructured "movement," and a second stage at which the "movement" took on the form of the "Community of the Renewed Covenant" reflected in the Qumran literature. I propose to address my

---

[57] The divergent views of Haggai and Zechariah, who were active contemporaneously in the last decades of the 6th century B.C.E., seem to be reflected in successive stages of the *yahad's* redemption hopes. See below.
[58] See above, n. 54.

ensuing remarks to highlighting some significant factors in the confrontation of the prophetically inspired movement with the concomitantly emerging rational brand that is to become rabbinic Judaism.

1. From its inception, the prophetic movement attracted followers in many Palestinian localities on a countrywide scale. In their urban habitations members lived a regular family life, conforming to the emphatically familial stance that biblical society put on a pedestal. We cannot accurately assess the size of the movement's membership. But we may assume that it was substantial, so much so that it could vie with other groups for supremacy in the Jewish body politic, foremost with the emerging rationalist stream that experienced a parallel consolidation.

2. The "movement" crystallized progressively in the fourth and third centuries B.C.E., and emerged in the late third or early second century as the structured "Community of the Renewed Covenant." It follows that in the diverse stages of its development, the life-span of this spiritual-ritual strand in early Judaism extends from some time after the Babylonian conquest of Judah in 586 B.C.E. to the destruction of the Second Temple in 70 C.E. by the Romans.

3. The sector living at Qumran was the spearhead of the "Community." It was constituted as a "Commune" of exclusively male members who resided at Qumran for a specified number of years. They were organized in paramilitary divisions, preparing for the final war of cosmic dimensions, which they expected to erupt at an uncharted future point in time.[59] It was only during this period of service to the wider community that these men refrained from sexual intercourse and family life. Qumran was the site of a permanent settlement with a periodically changing celibate population of not more than 200-250 males at a time.

4. The considerable length of time of the movement's existence stands in the way of fully gauging its essential character. As said, the diversity of contents, of ideas and literary genres, that marks Qumran literature may reflect discrete stages of a spiritual development which was shared by all members. But it may also have resulted from a diversity of opinions on theological and organizational matters that arose synchronously among the members in the span of half a millennium.

---

[59] See below.

5. The "Community of the Renewed Covenant" is a socio-religious phenomenon *sui generis* that should not be identified with any subdivision of Second Temple Judaism of which the classical sources speak. Similarities of the *yahad's* ritual laws with Sadducean *halakhah*, of its communal structure with that of the Essenes, of their legalistic outlook with that of the Samaritans, or of a religious vocabulary that at times overlaps with the credal terminology of primitive Christianity, result from a storehouse of common traditions rooted in the Hebrew Bible, in which all configurations of Judaism at the turn of the era shared.

6. The Covenanters' theology was caught up between a utopian vision of an imminent restoration of biblical Israel's glorified history and the palpably different reality of Jewish life in the Greco-Roman period. In their world of ideas wishful thinking coalesced indiscriminately with historical actuality. No other faction of Judaism at the turn of the era, or for that matter of nascent Christianity, bears upon itself this stamp of fact wedded to fancy, and of a hyper-nomism wedded to a fervent messianism, of which I shall yet speak.

The Conceptual World of the Yahad

The Covenanters view their community as the new link in the historical chain that had snapped when Judah was conquered by the Babylonians in 586 B.C.E., and as the sole legitimate representative of biblical Israel.[60] This self-identification, their *Eigenbegrifflichkeit*,[61] distinguishes them from their rabbinic opponents who conceived of the biblical period as a closed chapter, and of their own times as an intrinsically new phase in the history of Israel. For this reason, the Sages abandoned the use of typical biblical literary *Gattungen* – historiography, psalmody, and the prophetic genre – and initiated or developed altogether new modes, such as *midrash*. Similarly, the legal language of the Mishnah differs perceptibly from biblical Hebrew.

Moreover, the Sages drew a clear line between the biblical books, termed "written law," תורה שבכתב, and their own writings, designated "oral law," תורה שבעל פה. Both collections were held to be "holy" and "authoritative." A third category consisted of "extraneous books," ספרים חיצונים, that were excluded from both the תורה שבכתב and the

---

[60] I developed this point at some length in "Between the Hebrew Bible and the Mishnah," *World of Qumran*, 25-51.
[61] Cp. B. Landsberger, "Die Eigenbegrifflichkeit der babylonischen Welt," *Islamica* 2 (1926) 355-72.

תורה שבעל פה.⁶² These books were not handed down in the rabbinic tradition, but were preserved in the Old Testament canon of the Church in Greek, Latin, and Ethiopic translations. As mentioned, Hebrew and/or Aramaic originals of several such works, as well as of hitherto unknown similar writings, have turned up among the Qumran finds – 1 Enoch, Jubilees, Tobit, the Testaments of the Patriarchs, and the Proverbs of Ben Sira.

The Living Bible
1. We may assume that, like the Sages, the Covenanters' also invested some of their writings with various grades of authority and holiness. I do not know, however, of any explicit statement that gives evidence to a clear-cut differentiation between books of the Hebrew Bible and "extra-biblical" writings, like Jubilees or the "Foundation Documents."

Living conceptually in the world of the Bible, the *yahad*-members did not develop the notion of a "closed biblical canon." Rather, they seem to have viewed the biblical books as constituent parts of an open-ended, expandable collection of sanctified writings. In fact, the application of the very term "canon," and the pursuance of "canon research" in the context of Qumran are anachronisms.

2. Similarly, the textual variability that characterizes the copies of biblical books proves that idea of a fixed text, a *textus receptus*, had not taken root at Qumran. I would suggest that an unalterable wording of Scriptures was established only when the reading of Bible texts became, somewhat later, an integral part of the synagogue service. A close reading of the pertinent sources proves that in the Covenanters' assemblies and convocations only prayers were offered. There is no hint at a concomitant reading of biblical texts.

3. *Yahad* authors and scribes appear to have accepted and preserved with equanimity discrete copies of biblical books that exhibit varying text-traditions. Like the Chronicler had done before them, they injected their personalities into the materials that they transmitted, adapting biblical texts to their own needs, rephrasing, expanding

---

⁶² In addition, we find in rabbinic literature scattered references to sundry works which did not belong to any of these three classes, and seem to have been devoid of a common denominator: translations of biblical books into Aramaic, prayer collections, compositions of a presumably foreign origin, such as the rather nebulous ספרי המירם (*m. Yad.* 4:6), and possibly also writings of a heretical character.

and contracting, obviously within a "legitimate latitude of variation" that, however, still needs to be defined.

4. The *yahad* embraced unreservedly the biblical authors' high appreciation of prophetic teaching and continued to subject the life of the individual and the life of the community to the guidance of personalities who were possessed of the divine spirit, first and foremost to the guidance of the מורה (ה)צדק, the "Legitimate Teacher." Being prophetically inspired, the Teacher's decisions were beyond debate and unconditionally binding. In contrast, the nascent rabbinic faction shelved prophetic inspiration[63] and progressively developed a rationalist stance: "After the demise of the last (biblical) prophets – Haggai, Zechariah and Malachi – the holy spirit (*viz.*, prophetic inspiration) departed from Israel (*t. Sota*, ed. Zuckermandel 318, 21-23; *b. Sotah* 48b; *b. Sanh.* 11a). From now on incline your ear and listen to the instructions of the Sages" (*Seder 'Olam Rabbah* 6 [ed. Ratner, 2]).[64] Majority decisions, arrived at by logical investigation and finely honed interpretation, took the place of prophetically inspired dicta, which are beyond questioning. Rational thought[65] and expert knowledge replaced pronouncements that drew their legitimization from the unfathomable divine spirit.[66]

The Concept of "Covenant"[67]

1. The "Teacher" molded the amorphous prophetic movement into a viable socio-religious order. Under his guidance, the Covenanters established the "Community of those who entered into the Renewed Covenant," באי הברית החדשה (CD VI,19) or אשר באו בברית החדשה (CD

---

[63] See E. E. Urbach, "When did Prophecy Cease?" *Tarbiz* 17 (1945) 1-11 (Hebrew).
[64] משמתו נביאים אחרונים חגי זכריה ומלאכי ניטלה רוח הקדש מישראל מעתה הט אוזנך ושמע דברי חכמים.
[65] M. Weber speaks of a "Rationalisierungsprozess" which unfolded already in the biblical era, differentiating Israelite religion from paganism. I suggest that this process came to full fruition in the world of the rabbinic Sages. See my "The Emergence of Jewish Sectarianism in the Early Second Temple Period," *Ancient Israelite Religion: Essays in Honor of F. M. Cross* (ed. P. D. Miller Jr., P. D. Hanson and S. D. McBride; Philadelphia: Fortress, 1987) 587-616 = Talmon, *King, Cult and Calendar* (Jerusalem: Magnes, 1986) 165-201.
[66] See Talmon, *World of Qumran*, 29-31.
[67] It must suffice to list here only some items from the rich literature in which ברית, "covenant" is discussed: G. Quell and J. Behm, "διαθήκη. AT ברית," *TWNT* 2.106-37; M. Weinfeld, "ברית b^erith," *Theological Dictionary of the Old Testament* (Grand Rapids, MI: Eerdmans, 1972) 253-79; A. Jaubert, *La Notion d'Alliance dans le Judaïsme aux abords de l'ère chrétienne* (Paris: Gabalda, 1963); N. Lohfink, *Der Niemals Gekündigte Bund* (Freiburg: Herder, 1989).

VIII,29),⁶⁸ from which are excluded all opponents and backsliders who betray the "covenant and the compact⁶⁹ they had established in the Land of Damascus,⁷⁰ which is the 'renewed covenant'" (CD VIII,35; cp. 1QpHab II,3).

2. The pregnant term "Renewed Covenant," which the Covenanters apply to themselves in "Foundation Documents,"⁷¹ underscores again the intended self-identification with the world of biblical Israel. The collocation ברית חדשה, "renewed covenant" (Jer 31:31), is a *hapax legomenon*,⁷² which Jeremiah employs in a prophecy set in a series of oracles of comfort (Jer 31:1-14; 23-30; 31-34; 35-40).⁷³ The prophet invokes a divine promise of a future renewal of the ancient covenant that God had established with the Exodus generation (Jer 31:32) and that had been suspended in the wake of the destruction of Jerusalem and the ensuing exile (Jer 31:15-22).

Post-exilic historiographers and prophets had perceived in their return from the Babylonian exile the realization of Jeremiah's oracle of a restoration 70 years after the fall of the Judean kingdom. In contrast, the Covenanters evidently disregarded Jeremiah's prophecy. In its stead, they fastened on a symbolic act performed by the prophet Ezekiel in the face of the Babylonians' siege of Jerusalem (Ezek 4:4-6), invested it with an implied promise of restoration, and claimed this promise for themselves (see below). They view their community as the youngest link in a chain of sequential reaffirmations of the covenant, to which the Bible gives witness (CD II,14-III,20). God had originally established his covenant with Adam. He renewed it after each critical juncture in the history of the world, and of Israel: after the flood, with Noah, the "second Adam"; then with the patriarchs; again with all Israel at Sinai;

---

⁶⁸ R. F. Collins, "The Berith-Notion of the Cairo Damascus Covenant and its Comparison with the New Testament," *ETL* 39 (1963) 555-94; A. S. Kapelrud, "Der Bund in den Qumranschriften," *Bibel und Qumran. Beiträge zur Erforschung der Beziehungen zwischen Bibel- und Qumranwissenschaft* (ed. F. Bardtke; Berlin: Töpelmann, 1968) 137-49; N. Ilg, "Überlegungen zum Verständnis von Berît in den Qumrantexten," *Qumrân: Sa piété, sa théologie et son milieu*, 257-64.

⁶⁹ ומאסו בברית ואמנה אשר קימו בארץ דמשק והיא ברית החדשה. The term אמנה is a virtual *hapax legomenon*, which significantly turns up only in post-exilic biblical literature in one and the same context as a designation of Nehemiah's "compact" with his compatriots (Neh 10:1; 11:23).

⁷⁰ I subscribe to the interpretation of 'Land of Damascus' as a *topos* for the community center at Qumran.

⁷¹ To the best of my knowledge, this title has not turned up in any other, published or unpublished text.

⁷² Like אמנה, "compact." See above.

⁷³ The term is picked up in the New Testament phrase *kainē diathēkē*.

with the priestly house of Aaron; and ensuingly with the royal house of David, after the monarchical system had taken root in Israel. In the present generation, בדור אחרון, "he raised for himself" from among all the evildoers "men called by name, that a remnant be left in the land, and that the earth be filled with their offspring" (CD II,11-12). The thread of Israel's historical past, which snapped when Jerusalem and the temple were destroyed, is retied with the foundation of the *yahad's* "renewed covenant."

3. The intrinsic pertinence of ברית to *community* comes to the fore in the Covenanters' induction rite of novices. At that time, the veterans' membership was also presumably reaffirmed. The annual ritual was evidently molded upon the "Blessing and Curse" ceremony that in a Pentateuchal tradition preceded Israel's settlement in the Land of Canaan (Deut 27-28).[74] That ceremony was reenacted by Joshua so as to give a *de jure* covenantal underpinning to the *de facto* conquest of the land (Jos 8:30-35; cf. 23:1-24:26). The reenactment of the biblical tradition in their induction ritual is viewed by the *yahad* members as a confirmation of their community's claim to be the only legitimate heir to biblical Israel.

4. The *yahad's* understanding of the signification of ברית is totally absent from the rabbinic conceptual universe,[75] pointing up a weighty divergence of the Covenanters' Bible-oriented posture from the "rabbinic" faction's non-biblical stance. As we have said, the rabbis understood their own existential situation as fundamentally different from that of biblical Israel. In contrast to the pointed *communal* thrust of the Covenanters' concept of ברית and ברית חדשה, they did not develop the notion that in their days God renewed his covenant of old with their community. In the rabbinic vocabulary, the noun ברית connotes exclusively the act of circumcision, which proleptically symbolizes the *individual* child's readiness to abide by the divine law, but is devoid of the *community*-centeredness that it has in the Covenanters' world of ideas.

Millenarian Restoration Hopes

1. The author of the Zadokite Documents establishes a direct connection between the beginnings of the *yahad's* history and the termination of Israel's pre-exilic past. Like the writers of other

---

[74] N. Lohfink, "Der Bundesschluss im Lande Moab: Redaktionsgeschichtliches zu Dtn 28,69-32,47," *BZ* 6 (1962) 32-56.
[75] For a different view see A. Segal, "Covenant in Rabbinic Writings," *The Other Judaisms of Late Antiquity* (BJS 127; Atlanta: Scholars Press, 1987) 147-65.

"Foundation Documents," he disregards altogether the "returners from the exile" of whom the post-exilic biblical books speak.[76] The leading figures of that period – Zerubbabel, Joshua the high priest, Ezra, and Nehemiah – are passed over in silence in the Covenanters' literature. The author of the Zadokite Documents presents the founding fathers of the community as the first "returners to the land" after the deportation of the Judeans in the wake of the Babylonian conquest of Jerusalem (CD I, 2-8). Qumran writers show a penchant for biblical "Exile and Return" terminology and imagery, preferring vocables derived from שוב over constructions with עלה.[77] They claim for their community honorific titles, such as זרע ישראל, "Israel's (legitimate) seed," and זרע הקדש, "holy seed" (4QMMT 79-82), by which the prophet Isaiah had designated the remnant, עשריה, that will be saved from the impending debacle (Isa 6:13), and which the returning exiles had applied to themselves (Neh 9:2; Ezra 9:2).

> CD I,2-8: "For when they were unfaithful and forsook him, he (God) hid his face from Israel and his sanctuary and delivered them up to the sword. But remembering the covenant of the forefathers, he left a remnant for Israel and did not deliver them to (utter) destruction (cp. Jer 5:18; 30:11; 46:28; Neh 9:31 *et sim.*). At the preordained point in time[78] he caused the root he had planted to sprout (again) from Israel and Aaron to take possession of his land and enjoy the fruits of its soil (cp. Isa 6:11-13; Hag 2:18-19; Zech 3:10; 8:12)".

Those who returned from the exile in the early Persian period had seen in their return the realization of Jeremiah's prophecy that 70 years after the destruction of the Temple God would restore Israel's fortunes (Jer 25:11-13). Taking the figure of 70 years at face value (Jer. 29:10; Zech 1:12; Ezra 1:1; 2 Chr 36:21-22; cf. Dan. 9:2), they maintained that the period of punishment had not yet run its full course, and that therefore "the time has not yet come for the rebuilding of the house of God" (Hag 1:2).[79] The prophet Haggai rejects this contention. He never tires of proclaiming that from the very day of the temple foundation on the 24th of the ninth month in the reign of Darius I (520 B.C.E.), "from this day

---

[76] In comparison with other biblical writings, the books of Ezra-Nehemiah, Haggai, Zechariah and Malachi are poorly represented in the Qumran find of biblical scrolls.
[77] See Talmon, *World of Qumran*, 39-45.
[78] I suggest to read ובקץ אחרון instead of ובקץ חרון. In the scrolls, קץ connotes mostly "predetermined period" or "juncture in history." See S. Talmon, *TWAT* 7 (1990) 84-92, s.v. קץ qeṣ. אחרון designates the "last," *viz.* the "present" generation.
[79] לא עת בא עת בית יהוה להבנות.

on," מן היום הזה ומעלה, God's blessing will again be on his people (Hag 2:15-23).

As we have said, the Covenanters likewise established an ideational connection between the destruction of the Temple and the founding of their community. Ignoring Jeremiah's prophecy of 70 years, they ascertain the exact date of the hoped-for redemption by attaching a real historical interpretation to Ezekiel's above-mentioned symbolic act (Ezek 4:4-6), which he performed when the Babylonians laid siege on Jerusalem. At divine command, the prophet lay immobile on one side for 390 days, thus to symbolize a period of woe for Israel that would last for 390 years. Then he lay on his other side for 40 days to represent 40 years of Judah's punishment (Ezek 4:4-6). Relying on "millenarian numerology," and reading a message of hope into the prophet's oracle of woe, the *yahad's* founding fathers resolved that exactly 390 years after the fall of Jerusalem, Israel's glorious past would be restored.

2. Confidently awaiting the unfolding of history, immutably established by divine fiat and prophetically revealed, the founding fathers of the *yahad* initially fostered a quietist millenarianism. No human initiative was required to ensure the restitution of Israel's good fortunes at the preordained turning point in history. However, when the "appointed time" passed uneventfully, they were caught in a dire predicament. The author of CD woefully relates that "for twenty years they were like blind men groping their way" (CD I,9-10). His complaint appears to echo the equally mournful question that Haggai's contemporary, the prophet Zechariah, quotes from the mouth of his mediator-angel who confronted God in a similar situation: "for how much longer will you not have mercy with Jerusalem and the cities of Judah, against whom you have turned your anger for seventy years" (Zech 1:12).

3. The Covenanters' despondency was ameliorated when God "raised up for them the (or: a) legitimate teacher, מורה צדק, to guide them in the way of his heart" (CD I,11). The divinely inspired Teacher, together with the previously mentioned "sprout(s) from Aaron and Israel" who represent the priesthood and the royal house of David, form the triad of public figures and institutions that had been the pillars of biblical society: kingship, priesthood, and prophecy. In their combination, the "Sprouts" and the "Teacher" were seen to constitute the prerequisite basis for the re-establishment of the biblical body politic. However, when their reliance on millenarian arithmetic failed them, the Covenanters no longer dared pinpoint the

fervently expected onset of the restoration. It was now transported to an indeterminable future time (see below).

Their incertitude mirrors Zechariah's resignation when the improvement of Israel's fortunes, announced by Haggai (Hag 2:20-23), failed to materialize. Zechariah does not give up hope that there will indeed be a restoration. Rather, he defuses Haggai's excessive confidence, founded on "millenarian numerology," by deferring its realization to an uncharted future time. His guardian-angel comforts him with the divine promise: "I will return to Jerusalem in mercy, my house will be (re)built in her ... and the (builder's) measuring rod will be again upon Jerusalem. Announce *yet*, עוד, thus speaks God: my cities will *yet*, עוד, brim over with (all that is) good ... God will *yet*, עוד, comfort Zion and will *yet*, עוד, elect Jerusalem" (Zech 1:13-17; 8:1-17). In glaring contrast to Haggai's "from this day on," the four times repeated *"yet"* highlights Zechariah's reluctance to set a precise date for the foreseen restitution of Israel's national sovereignty.

From "Restoration Hope" to "Messianic Expectation"

It appears that when the fervent hope of an imminent restoration did not materialize, the Covenanters' world of beliefs underwent significant changes. Searching for the factors that had prevented the realization of the preordained restoration, they found the causes in their own shortcomings, ויבינו בעונם וידעו כי אנשים אשימים הם, and in the sinfulness of their opponents, the "gang of backsliders," עדת בוגדים, who "turn aside from the (rightful) way", הם סרי דרך (CD I,12-13). Now, they see themselves called upon actively to pave the way for the realization of their restoration hopes. Led by the "Teacher," every male member repairs for a season to the desert, there to prepare for the final cosmic battle portrayed in the War Scroll (1QM), in which the Sons of Light will vanquish all the Sons of Darkness. The *yahad's* erstwhile quietism turned into militant millennialism. Concomitantly, their disappointment prompted the infusion of a messianic idea into the Covenanters' theology, which was initially centered on the expectation of an imminent restoration of Israel's body politic in their own days.[80]

The Covenanters' Messianism

The messianic idea emerges in the "Foundation Documents" in a characteristic bifurcation.[81] At the onset of the ideal eon, two figures will arise simultaneously, together with the "Prophet": a (priestly) Anointed (of the House) of Aaron, and an Anointed of Israel, associated with the

---

[80] See the above quoted opening passage of the Zadokite Documents.
[81] See S. Talmon, "Waiting for the Messiah" above, n. 23.

royal house of David.[82] The triad King, Priest, Prophet, the three pillars of biblical society, is foreseen to be reconstituted in the messianic age, as it had been previously expected to be realized in the "Period of Restoration," projected by Ezekiel's symbolic act.

The doctrine of a priestly anointed who presides over Israel's body politic together with the royal messiah is reflected also in some strata of the apocryphal literature. This wider currency proves that it is not the Covenanters' exclusive legacy, but rather was rooted in a common Jewish tradition. However, in no other context does it play the significant role that it is accorded in the Covenanters' theology.[83] Also in this instance, the recurrently stressed conceptual self-identification of the *yahad* with biblical Israel comes to the fore. The vision of "Two Anointed" who together will govern Israel's reconstituted polity is derived from Zechariah's teaching. The post-exilic prophet presented to the returnees a blueprint of the organization of the province of Jahud as a state *in nuce* in the framework of the Persian Empire. The structure that he proposed is quite distinct from the one which obtained in the Judaean body politic of the monarchic period. Then the king was not only in charge of the mundane affairs of the realm, but also wielded controlling power over the religious institutions, foremost over the temple in Jerusalem (2 Kgs 12:7-17 = 2 Chr 24:4-14; 2 Kgs 22-23 = 2 Chr 34-35; 2 Chr 17:7-9; 26:16-19; 29-31; 33:15-16). The high priest was a royal official (2 Sam 8:17 = 1 Chr 18:16; 2 Sam 20:25-26; 1 Kgs 4:2,4,5) whom the king appointed or deposed at will (1 Kgs 2:26-27,35; cp. 2 Chr 24:20, 22). In the face of profoundly changed internal and external political circumstances, Zechariah propagated a system of shared responsibilities (Zech 3): king and priest, the two anointed (4:11-14; 6:9-15), were to complement each other, their cooperation guided by a "counsel of peace" (6:13).

The prophetically-apocalyptically motivated Covenanters embraced Zechariah's plan. They modeled their perception of the future age upon it. Identifying themselves as the returnees from the exile, they accepted the embellished image of that period as the prototype of the future eon. An idealized biblical past was projected into the vision of the blissful age to come.

The Development of the Yahad's Particular Life-style

The indeterminable lapse of time between the historical "now" and the onset of the messianic "then" necessitated the development of a

---

[82] (1QS) ונשפטו במשפטים הרשונים אשר החלו אנשי היחד לתיסר בם עד בוא נביא ומשיחי אהרון וישראל IX,10-11).

[83] See A. S. van der Woude, *Die messianischen Vorstellungen der Gemeinde von Qumran* (Assen: Van Gorcum, 1957).

societal structure and a socio-religious code to forestall the dissolution of the "Community of the Renewed Covenant" and to ensure its continuous semi-independent existence alongside the progressively consolidating rabbinic stream. In this context, the figure of the "Legitimate Teacher," an inspired interpreter and not an innovator of religious precepts nor a "founding-prophet,"[84] played a decisive role. Under the Teacher's guidance, the former anti-establishment millenarians formed an establishment of their own, which was soon to surpass their opponents' institutions in societal rigidity and legalistic exactitude. It would appear that the Teacher inaugurated a canon of norms, of rules and statutes, that gave the "movement" the structural underpinning needed to enable its adherents to bridge successfully the chasm between the disappointing historical present and the fervently awaited messianic age.

I am inclined to date to this early stage in the genesis of the "Community of the Renewed Covenant," the inception of the "Foundation Documents," of additional halakhic-legal texts such as 4QMMT and of diverse fragmentary calendrical documents.

The Yahad's Special Calendar

The Covenanters' adherence to a solar calendar of 364 days,[85] which exceeds the Jewish lunar year of 354 days by 10 days per annum, was a decisive factor in the process of consolidation of the two rival factions in contemporary Judaism. Each side accused the other of following an aberrant time table, and thus of throwing out of kilter the correct, divinely established flow of the hallowed seasons.[86]

1. The harnessing of the cultic seasons to the solar year effectively prevented the Covenanters' participation in the sacrificial service in the temple, which was riveted to the lunar calendar by which the Jerusalem priesthood abided. This resulted in a void in their religious life that they filled by introducing "institutionalized prayer" as a substitute for "animal sacrifice."[87] This innovation preceded the development of synagogal prayer-service in rabbinic

---

[84] In M. Weber's categories.
[85] It is well known that for the authors of 1 Enoch and the Book of Jubilees this ephemeris is the only legitimate calendar.
[86] See S. Talmon, "The Calendar of the Covenanters of the Judean Desert," *World of Qumran*, 147-85. Since the publication of that paper, the number of studies of the Qumran solar calendar has increased in leaps and bounds.
[87] The transition explains the presence of a large amount of standardized prayer texts among the Qumran finds. See Baillet, "Textes liturgiques"; Nitzan, *Qumran Prayer* (above, n. 17). A thorough-going study of the very introduction of standardized prayer as a religious institution is an urgent desideratum.

Judaism after the destruction of the Second Temple in 70 C.E. and in nascent Christianity.[88]

2. The Covenanters' adherence to a different time-table was viewed by the civic and religious leaders in Jerusalem as an act of open defiance of their authority. The calendar-controversy, to which I drew attention from the very inception of Qumran Research,[89] became an essential factor in the final dissension of the "Community of the Renewed Covenant" from the rabbinic mainstream faction.

The Covenanters' Distinctive Legal Literature

1. Passages in the "Foundation Documents" that deal with issues of legal import, as well as fragments of other Qumran legal writings, such as 4QMMT, exhibit a vocabulary and style that again give witness to their authors' intention to place their community in the framework of biblical Israel. In contrast, the rabbis appear to have consciously discarded biblical literary genres and terminology. They availed themselves of a terminology and couched their writings in a style that are patently different from their biblical counterparts, summarizing their attitude in the pithy saying: לשון תורה לעצמהי לשון חכמים לעצמו "the language of Torah (*viz.*, the books of the Bible) is one matter; the language of the (teachings of the) Sages is another matter" (*b. 'Abod. Zar.* 58b; *b. Menah.* 65a).[90]

2. An even more decisive signifier than vocabulary and style is the very makeup of Qumran legal literature. The Covenanters' particular injunctions may be viewed as functionally paralleling rabbinic laws codified in the Mishnah. But these two bodies of legal prescriptions exhibit quite different structures. The Mishnah is presented as the record of deliberations in the academy, which are often formulated in a "question and answer" pattern without a specific "address,"[91] leading up to decisions arrived at on the basis of precedents, traditied

---

[88] See S. Talmon, "The Emergence of Institutionalized Prayer in Israel in Light of Qumran Literature," *Qumrân: Sa piété, sa théologie et son milieu*, 265-84; idem, "The Manual of Benedictions of the Judean Desert Covenanters," *RevQ* 2 (1959-60) 475-500; combined in *World of Qumran*, 200-243; idem, "Extra-Canonical Psalms from Qumran – Psalm 151," *World of Qumran*, 244-72.

[89] "Yom Hakkippurim in the Habakkuk Scroll," *Bib* 32 (1951) 549-63 = *World of Qumran*, 186-99.

[90] See *World of Qumran*, 36-47: idem, "Oral Tradition and Written Transmission, or the Seen and the Heard Word in Judaism of the Second Temple Period," *Jesus and the Gospel Tradition* (ed. H. Wansbrough: JSNTSup 64; Sheffield: Academic Press, 1997) 130-58.

[91] See J. Neusner, *Max Weber Revisited: Religion and Society in Ancient Judaism with Special Reference to the Late First and Second Centuries* (Oxford: Clarendon, 1981).

rulings, or majority vote. Learning and expert knowledge are of paramount importance. Exploration of the traditional lore is subject to an ever-growing fund of hermeneutic rules, מידות שבהן התורה נדרשת, the proper handling of which can be acquired through study.[92]

3. Tradition has it that from its very inception the rabbinic world of discourse revolved around "pairs," זוגות, of conflicting Sages like Hillel and Shammai. The system was perpetuated in later stages when "pairs" like Rabbi Akiba and Rabbi Ishmael, Rabah and Abaye arose. Their respective disciples formed "schools," transmitted their masters' teachings and spun out their debates. In fact, rational debate was and still is the very lifeblood of the rabbinic academy. The aura of "discourse" that pervaded it furthered the "democratization" of learning, which ultimately affected community life as whole.[93]

4. The Covenanters' world is altogether different. Their "Foundation Documents" are addressed to a specific audience. The legal codes contained in them are never debated. Based on inspiration, they are binding and irrevocable. They are "handed down" like biblical ordinances. The *ex cathedra* spirit also pervades the repeatedly mentioned open letter, *miqṣat ma'aśē* (or *dibrē*) *tōrāh* (4QMMT). The writer of the epistle "lays down" one law after the other, without ever mentioning a dissenting opinion, which the addressee entertained or which were advocated by other parties. Experts of *halakhah* conclude that the author of 4QMMT champions Saducean legal rulings and aims at impressing their acceptance on the presumedly pharisaic addressee, who assumably abides by different interpretations of the issues in question. However, due to the opaqueness of the document, scholars are by necessity forced to derive their arguments from rabbinic literature, although it is extraneous to the issue on hand.

Concluding Remarks

The widely entertained expectation that the scrolls, the only contemporary evidence from the turn of the era, would shed new light on historical events that then affected Judaism as a whole, did not materialize. The various attempts to identify the *yahad* with a specific

---

[92] Perseverance and arduous study let the erstwhile lowly shepherd Akiba achieve prominence and become the most revered teacher of his time.
[93] See E. E. Urbach, "Class Status and Leadership in the World of the Palestinian Sage," *Proceedings of the Israel Academy of Sciences* 2 (Jerusalem: Israel Academy of Sciences, 1968) 38-74; D. R. Schwartz, "Law and Truth: On Qumran-Sadducean and Rabbinic Views of Law," *The Dead Sea Scrolls: Forty Years of Research* (ed. D. Dimant and U. Rappaport; Jerusalem/Leiden: Magnes/Brill, 1992) 229-40.

faction in Judaism of that dark age of documentation, previously known from retrospective classical sources, has not produced satisfactory results. A shift of emphasis is needed.

Practically all studies of the Covenanters' community take their departure from the juncture in history at which it emerges as a fully organized socio-religious entity. In contrast, I suggest that in order to achieve a better comprehension of the *yahad's* specificity, we should endeavor to uncover the roots of that "prophetic-apocalyptic movement," and to trace the early stages of its development, before it crystallized in the structured "Community of the Renewed Covenant" whose members deposited the scrolls in the Qumran caves. Future efforts at elucidating the socio-religious profile of the "Community" should aim at extracting pertinent information from the Covenanters' own literature, first and foremost from their "Foundation Documents." Instead of pursuing the disappointing search for a historical "equation" of the *yahad*, and of the main antagonists in the drama of which the scrolls speak, with groups and figures known from ancient sources, scholars would be well advised to concentrate their efforts on the attempt to gauge the essence of that community's socio-religious "identity." The more transparent this identity will become, the better we shall be able to define its place in the panorama of diverse socio-religious entities in Judaism on the threshold of the Christian era.

9

Hebrews 11:37 and the Death of the Prophet Ezekiel

J. Edward Wright

One of the benefits of my appointment to the Committee on Judaic Studies at the University of Arizona is the privilege I have had of sharing an office with Lou Silberman during the spring semesters. Our conversations have ranged from the ancient Israelites to the Crypto-Jews of the American Southwest. Every conversation was a continuation of my education. When it came to biblical and Judaic Studies, it seemed as if Lou personally knew, studied with, or taught almost all of this century's leading figures. Lou has a deep interest in Jewish-Christian dialogue and especially the relationships between early Judaism and nascent Christianity. It is with this in mind that I offer this essay on Hebrews 11:37. In fact, this essay benefits from Lou's input during a conversation in our office over two years ago.

Hebrews 11 details the triumphs and tragedies of many biblical figures.[1] The first half of the chapter highlights the accomplishments of several notables (Enoch, Noah, Abraham, Moses, etc.). Following this, the author provides only a catalogue of activities without identifying the

---

[1] The modern history of Hebrews scholarship is succinctly surveyed by Craig R. Koester, "The Epistle to the Hebrews in Recent Study," *Currents in Research: Biblical Studies* 2 (1994) 123-45. See also George Wesley Buchanan, "The Present State of Scholarship on Hebrews," *Christianity, Judaism and Other Greco-Roman Cults: Studies for Morton Smith at Sixty* (ed. Jacob Neusner; Part 1: New Testament; Leiden: Brill, 1975) 299-330.

people by name.[2] It is in this latter half of the chapter that we encounter Hebrews 11:37a: "they were stoned, they were sawn in two, they were put to death by the sword." A survey of the commentators on this verse reveals that many are able to identify the people alluded to by the statements "they were stoned, they were sawn in two." These are typically identified as referring to Jeremiah and Isaiah, since the traditions about their deaths are well-known. The other statement, however, has eluded certain identification. Only one person to my knowledge has correctly identified the person alluded to by the words "they were put to death by the sword," and that is Erwin R. Goodenough. Goodenough makes the connection between this statement and the prophet Ezekiel in his discussion of the last section of the Ezekiel Panel in the Dura-Europos synagogue.[3] Although Goodenough was correct to link Hebrews 11:37 with the traditions about the deaths of the three great prophets, his explanation of the traditions about the prophet Ezekiel's death was incomplete. This essay attempts to fill in the picture.

Jeremiah
"they were stoned"

The depiction of the prophet Jeremiah continues to develop in early Jewish and Christian tradition. The Bible has no account of the prophet's demise, and perhaps because of this there arose a great deal of speculation about what happened to him. There are several traditions about the fate of Jeremiah. The biblical account describes how he was taken unwillingly to Egypt (Jer 43:4-7).[4] *2 Baruch* 10:1-3 and *Paraleipomena Jeremiou* (3:15; 4:6; 5:17-19; 6:11, 19, 24; 7:5-37; 8:1-3) report that Jeremiah went to Babylon. Rashi (commenting on Jer 44:14) reports that Jeremiah returned to Jerusalem when Nebuchadnezzar conquered Egypt. Josephus,[5] *Seder Olam* 26 (ed. Ratner, 120), and *Midrash Eser Galuyot*[6] recount that although Jeremiah went initially to Egypt, Nebuchadnezzar

---

[2] Michael Cosby, "The Rhetorical Composition of Hebrews 11," *JBL* 107:2 (1988) 257-73, provides a insightful analysis of the literary features of this chapter.
[3] *Jewish Symbols of the Greco-roman Period* (13 vols.; New York: Bollingen Foundation, 1964) 10.188.
[4] Jerome follows this tradition in his commentary on Isaiah 30:7 (Minge, *PL*, 24.353), as does the Vita of Jeremiah in the *Vitae Prophetarum* (see D. R. A. Hare, "The Lives of the Prophets," *The Old Testament Pseudepigrapha* (2 vols.; ed. James H. Charlesworth; Garden City, NY: Doubleday, 1983 and 1985) 2.387, and *Seder Olam* 26 (ed. Ratner, 119). See also K. H. Kuhn, "A Coptic Jeremiah Apocryphon," *Le Muséon* 83:1-2 (1970) 305, 320.
[5] *Ant.* 10.9.5.
[6] *Bet HaMidrash* (6 vols.; ed. Adolph Jellinek; Jerusalem: Wahrmann, 1967) 4.135.

eventually conquered Egypt and then took Jeremiah and other Jews from Egypt to Babylon.

Regarding his death, the most complete tradition is found in *Paraleipomena Jeremiou*. According to this text Jeremiah was stoned to death by the people of Jerusalem who opposed his messages after he returned from exile in Babylon (*Par. Jer.* 9:21-32). This tradition appears also in several other texts.[7] The *Lives of the Prophets*, a Byzantine Christian collection of hagiographical traditions, recounts that Jeremiah was stoned to death in Egypt.[8] So, whether it was in Jerusalem or Egypt, tradition is clear that Jeremiah was stoned to death.[9]

Isaiah
"they were sawn in two"

The prophet Isaiah's death is also recounted in early Jewish and Christian apocryphal and hagiographical literature. Jewish tradition recounts that Isaiah died at the hands of king Manasseh, a wicked king known for "shedding much blood" (2 Kgs 21:16).[10] The clearest and fullest account of Isaiah's demise is in the *Martyrdom and Ascension of Isaiah*.[11] Here we learn that Isaiah was sawn in two by Manasseh because

---

[7] See Vision of Paul §49 (H. Duensing, "Apocalypse of Paul," *New Testament Apocrypha* [ed. Edgar Hennecke and W. Schneemelcher; trans. R. McL. Wilson; London: Lutterworth, 1965] 2.792); Hippolytus, *Concerning Christ and Antichrist* 31 (Minge, *PG* 10.652); Jerome, *Against Jovinian* 2:37 (Minge, *PL* 23.350); Tertullian, *On Scorpions* 8 (*CCSL* 2.1082-83); *The Uncanonical Writings of the Old Testament Found in the Armenian Mss. of the Library of St. Lazarus* (trans. J. Issaverdens; 2d ed.; Venice: Monastery of St. Lazarus, 1934) 232. Cf. F. Halkin, "Le prophete 'saint' Jeremie dans le menologe imperial byzantin," *Bib* 65 (1984) 111-16.
[8] Hare, "Lives," 386; *Prophetarum vitae fabulosae: indices apostolorum discipulorumque Domini Dorotheo, Epiphanio, Hippolyto aliisque vindicata* (ed. T. Schermann; Leipzig: Teubner, 1907) 81, 84. This tradition is preserved also in Syriac Christian sources, see *The Book of the Bee* (ed. E. A. Wallis Budge; Anecdota Oxoniensia I:2; Oxford: Clarendon, 1886) 72.
[9] This tradition appears also in medieval Christian iconography; see Wilhelm Neuss, *Die katalanische Bibelillustration um die Wende des ersten Jahrtausends und die altspanische Buchmalerei* (Bonn and Leipzig: Kurt Schroeder, 1922) 86-87, plate 29, fig. 92.
[10] *b. Yebam.* 49b; *b. Sanh.* 103b; *j. Sanh.* 10:2 (ed. M. Schwab, vol. 11, p. 49); *Pesiq. R.* 4:3 (Friedmann, 14a; Braude, 1.88-89); Rashi (on Isa 1:1); Acts of Philip in M.R. James, *The Apocryphal New Testament* (Oxford: Clarendon Press, 1955) 452; cf. Josephus, *Ant.* 3.1, and note Louis H. Feldman, "Josephus' Portrait of Manasseh," *JSP* 9 (1991) 3-20. See also the gloss added to the last chapter of a targum to Isaiah discussed in P. Grelot, "Deux tosephtas tarqoumiques inédites sur Isaïe LXVI," *RB* 79 (1972) 515-18.
[11] See M. A. Knibb, "Martyrdom and Ascension of Isaiah," *Old Testament Pseudepigrapha*, 2.163-64.

he decried Manasseh's wickedness.¹² This tradition is also widely attested in Christian texts. The *Vision of Paul* §49 knows a slightly variant tradition when it states that Manasseh cut Isaiah's head off with a wooden saw.¹³ The tradition that Isaiah was killed by a saw wielded by Manasseh was well-known, and it seems clear that Hebrews 11:37 is alluding to it at this point.¹⁴

Ezekiel
"they were put to death by the sword"

Hebrews 11:37 has already alluded to the deaths of Jeremiah and Isaiah, but the allusion here to the death of Ezekiel seems to have escaped the notice of all but Goodenough.¹⁵ Other referents for the phrase "they were put to death by the sword" have been suggested, the most common of which are: the prophets of Yahweh (1 Kgs 19:10);¹⁶

---

¹² See M. Gaster and B. Heller, "Beiträge zur vergleichenden Sagen- und Märchenkunde: 7. Der Prophet Jesajah und der Baum," *Monatschrift für Geschichte und Wissenschaft des Judentums* 80:1 (1936) 32-52.

¹³ Duensing, "Apocalypse of Paul," 792. Also see Justinian, *Dialogue with Trypho* 120.5 (Minge, *PG* 6.756); Tertullian, *De Patientia* 14 (*SC* 310.107), *On Scorpions* 8 (*CCSL* 2.1082-83). Clearly, this results from a misunderstanding of the "saw of wood" as a saw made of wood. This same confusion appears in a Greek fragment of the *Martyrdom of Isaiah* 3:16 (for text see Albert-Marie Denis, *Fragmenta pseudepigraphorum que supersunt graeca* [PVTG 3; Leiden: Brill, 1970] 113) and in "The Book of the Bee" (Budge, "Book of the Bee," 69). See also note 42 below.

¹⁴ This is also how Origen, *Epistle to Africanus* 9 (Minge, *PG* 11.65), and Jerome, *Commentary on Isaiah* (Minge, *PL* 24.568), interpreted this verse. See also *Die Apokryphen und Pseudepigraphen des Alten Testaments* (2 vols.; ed. Emil Kautzsch; Tübingen: J. C. B. Mohr [Paul Siebeck], 1900) 2.122-23. The tradition appears also in medieval iconography; see Neuss, *Die katalanische Bibelillustration*, 84-86, plate 28, fig. 90.

¹⁵ *Jewish Symbols*, 10.188. Note that the verbs here are all third person plural ("they"). While one may argue that the author intends to allude to more than one person, this seems unlikely especially in the case of Isaiah for surely few people were sawn in two. I take it, therefore, that the verbs in this verse, though plural, allude to specific incidents.

¹⁶ See for example Hans Joakim Schoeps, *Aus Frühchristlichen Zeit* (Tübingen: Mohr, 1950) 142; F. F. Bruce, *The Epistle to the Hebrews* (NICNT; Grand Rapids: Eerdmans, 1990) 238; Claus-Peter März, *Hebräerbrief* (Würburg: Echter Verlag, 1989) 74; R. McL. Wilson, *Hebrews* (NCB; Grand Rapids: Eerdmans, 1987) 217; James Moffatt, *A Critical and Exegetical Commentary on the Epistle to the Hebrews* (ICC; Edinburgh: T. & T. Clark, 1924) 188; William L. Lane, *Hebrews* (2 vols.; WBC 47a-b; Dallas: Word Books, 1991) 2.391; Otto Michel, *Der Brief an die Hebräer* (Kritisch-exegetischer Kommentar über das Neue Testament, vol. 11; Göttingen: Vandenhoeck & Ruprecht, 1960) 281; J. H. Davies, *A Letter to Hebrews* (CBC; Cambridge: Cambridge University Press, 1967) 117; Frederick W. Danker, *Invitation to the New Testament Epistles, IV* (Garden City, NY: Image Books/Doubleday, 1980) 74; Stanislaw Lach, *List Do Hebrajczyków* (Pismo Swiete

Uriah the prophet (Jer 26:23);[17] or the martyrs of the Maccabean period.[18] Because of the vagueness of this statement, commentators either offer speculations, provide a list of possible options, or simply state that since so many prophets suffered this fate through the years, it is impossible to be specific.[19] Although many martyrs have indeed died "by the sword," given the clear allusions to Jeremiah and Isaiah in the preceding two verbs, and the literary structure and rhythm of this section, which together serve to unite the sequence,[20] I agree with Goodenough that the phrase ἐν φόνῳ μαχαίρης ἀπέθανον (they were put to death by the sword) refers to Ezekiel. I suggest, however, that the traditions about Ezekiel's demise are not as uniform as Goodenough claims.

Goodenough cites the Ezekiel Panel in the frescoes of the third century C.E. Dura-Europos synagogue to support his claim that this phrase in Hebrews 11:37 is referring to the demise of the prophet Ezekiel. The Ezekiel Panel is on the north wall of the synagogue and is divided

---

Nowego Testamentu 12; Poznan: Pallottinum, 1959) 267; Franz Delitzsch, *Commentary on the Epistle to the Hebrews* (trans. Thomas L. Kingsbury; Grand Rapids: Eerdmans, 1952) 287-88; C. Spicq, *L'Épitre aux Hébreux* (2 vols.; Etudes Bibliques; Paris: J. Gabalda, 1952) 366; and Harald Hegermann, *Der Brief an die Hebräer* (THKNT 16; Berlin: Evangelische Verlagsanstalt, 1988) 241.
[17] Schoeps, *Aus Frühchristlichen Zeit*, 142; Bruce, *Hebrews*, 328; Søren Ruager, *Hebräerbrief* (Bibel-Kommentars zum Neuen Testament; Neuhausen-Stuttgart: Hänssler, 1987) 242; Wilson, *Hebrews*, 217; Moffatt, *Epistle to the Hebrews*, 188; Lane, *Hebrews*, 2.391; Michel, *Brief an die Hebräer*, 281; Davies, *Letter to Hebrews*, 117; Danker, *Invitation*, 74; Delitzsch, *Epistle to the Hebrews*, 287; and Hegermann, *Brief an die Hebräer*, 241.
[18] John Calvin, *Commentaries on the Epistle of Paul the Apostle to the Hebrews* (Calvin's Commentaries 22, trans. John Owen; Edinburgh: Calvin Translation Society, n.d.; reprinted, Grand Rapids, MI: Baker Book House, 1984) 306; and Marcus Dods, *The Epistle to the Hebrews* (The Expositor's Greek Testament, vol. 4; New York: Dodd, Mead and Co., 1910) 364.
[19] For other specific identifications see Bruce, *Hebrews*, 329. For a list of options see Herbert Braun, *An die Hebräer* (HNT 14; Tübingen: J. C. B. Mohr/Paul Siebeck, 1984) 398. Those not attempting to identify any specific allusions include Harold W. Attridge, *The Epistle to the Hebrews* (Hermeneia; Philadelphia: Fortress, 1989) 350; George Wesley Buchanan, *To the Hebrews* (AB 36; Garden City, NY: Doubleday, 1972) 204; Hans-Fredrich Weiss, *Der Brief an die Hebräer* (Kritisch-exegetischer Kommentar über das Neue Testament, vol. 13; Göttingen: Vandenhoeck & Ruprecht, 1991) 622; Philip E. Hughes, *A Commentary on the Epistle to the Hebrews* (Grand Rapids: Eerdmans, 1977) 515; Samuel Benetreau, *L'Epitre aux Hebreux* (2 vols.; Vaux-sur-Seine: Éditions de la Faculté Libre de Théologie Évangélique, 1990) 2.164; Leon Morris, *Hebrews* (Expositor's Bible Commentary, vol. 12; Grand Rapids: Zondervan, 1981) 131; C. Spicq, *L'Epitre aux Hebreux* (SB; Paris: J. Gabalda, 1977) 198; and Theodore H. Robinson, *The Epistle to the Hebrews* (New York: Harper and Brothers, 1934) 175.
[20] See Cosby, "Rhetorical Composition," and Albert Vanhoye, *La Structure Littéraire de l'Epitre aux Hébreux* (Paris: Descleé de Brouwer, 1963) 192-93.

into three separate scenes. The first two scenes depict Ezekiel 37, the vision of the "Valley of Dry bones." They show Ezekiel praying over the bones and the bones joining together to become revived people. This fresco signifies that God will bring Israel back from the dead, that is, back from the exile in Babylon, and resettle them in their land. Although the final section of this panel has prompted much debate, the explanation that accounts most fully for the unity within the panel is that the final section is depicting the execution of the prophet Ezekiel. Originally suggested by du Mesnil du Buisson,[21] this interpretation was championed by Goodenough.[22] This interpretation best explains both the imagery of this individual section and its relation to the rest of the panel.

According to Goodenough, the soldier holding the sword over the prophet's head in the third section of the Ezekiel panel represents the leader of the exiles mentioned in the *Vitae Prophetarum*, the leader who killed Ezekiel after the prophet rebuked him for his idolatry.[23] Goodenough has made a significant contribution to the understanding of this section. C. Kraeling objected to du Mesnil du Buisson's initial suggestion that this was the execution of Ezekiel by noting that no such tradition exists.[24] Goodenough's marshaling of the pertinent textual and iconographic evidence proves the opposite. Though his overall mystical interpretation of the panel is the product of his idiosyncratic reading of the material, his interpretation of the particulars is most illuminating, yet it needs to be slightly refined.[25]

In identifying the figures in the third section of the panel with those mentioned in the account of the death of Ezekiel in the *Vitae Prophetarum*, Goodenough has been less than complete in his treatment of that text. He

---

[21] "Les peintures de la synagogue de Doura-Europos," *RB* 43 (1934) 118. He later expressed some reservations about this explanation in "Les nouvelles découvertes de la synagogue de Doura-Europos," *RB* 43 (1934) 560, and eventually connected it instead with Joab in *Les peintures de la synagogue de Doura-Europos, 245-256 apres Jesus-Christ* (Rome: Institut Biblique Pontifical, 1939) 100-103.

[22] *Jewish Symbols*, 10.185-91; Gabrielle Sed-Kajna, *L'Art Juif-Orient et Occident* (Paris: Arts et Metiers Graphiques, 1975) 76-80, follows Goodenough explicitly.

[23] *Jewish Symbols*, 10.189-90.

[24] See M. I. Rostovtzeff, et al., *The Excavations at Dura Europos: Preliminary Report of the Sixth Season of Work, October 1932-March 1933* (New Haven: Yale University Press, 1936) 359.

[25] For comprehensive critiques of Goodenough's work see Elias J. Bickerman, "Symbolism in the Dura Synagogue: A Review Article," *HTR* 58:1 (1965) 127-51; Bickerman, "Sur la theologie de l'art figuratif: A propos de l'ouvrage de E.R. Goodenough," *Syria* 44 (1967) 131-62; Morton Smith, "Goodenough's Jewish Symbols in Retrospect," *JBL* 86:1 (1967) 53-68; and Jacob Neusner, "Studying Ancient Judaism through the Art of the Synagogue," *Art as Religious Studies* (ed. Doug Adams and D. Apostolos-Cappadona; New York: Crossroad, 1987) 29-57.

says that the following sentence from the Vita of Ezekiel explains the Dura painting: "The governor of the people of Israel there killed him, being rebuked by him for worshipping idols." Actually, this is only one of two traditions regarding Ezekiel's demise contained in the Vita of Ezekiel. The second reads, "And the one who murdered him was from among them (i.e., the tribes of Dan and Gad), for they opposed him all the days of his life." So this work, which likely originated in a fourth century Palestinian Christian context,[26] incorporates more than one tradition about who killed Ezekiel. The various traditions about Ezekiel's death appear in several texts and *objets d'art*.

Vita of Ezekiel in the Vita Prophetarum (4th Century)

> The governor of the people of Israel there killed him, being rebuked by him for worshipping idols.
>
> And the one who murdered him was from among them (i.e., the tribes of Dan and Gad), for they opposed him all the days of his life.[27]

Apocalypse of Paul (4th-5th Century)

> "I am Ezekiel whom the children of Israel dragged by the feet over the rocks on the mountain until they dashed out my brains."[28]

Syriac Version of the Acts of Philip (5th Century)

> ". . . Ezekiel and ye dragged him by his feet until his brains were dashed out."[29]

---

[26] So David Satran, "Daniel: Seer, Philosopher, Holy Man," *Ideal Figures in Ancient Judaism* (ed. G. W. E. Nickelsburg and J. J. Collins; Chicago: Scholars Press, 1980) 47, n. 18, and Satran, "Biblical Prophets and Christian Legend: The Lives of the Prophets Reconsidered," *Messiah and Christos: Studies in the Jewish Origins of Christianity Presented to David Flusser on the Occasion of his Seventy-fifth Birthday* (ed. I. Gruenwald, S. Shaked and G. Stroumsa; Texte und Studien zum Antiken Judentum 32; Tübingen: Mohr [Paul Siebeck], 1992) 143-49. Others have claimed that this text was written originally in Hebrew by a Jew in the first century. Compare Hare, "Lives of the Prophets," 380-81; James H. Charlesworth, *The Old Testament Pseudepigrapha and the New Testament* (Cambridge: Cambridge University Press, 1985) 42; and D. S. Russell, *Old Testament Pseudepigrapha* (Philadelphia: Fortress Press, 1987) 113.

[27] Schermann, *Prophetarum vitae fabulosae*, 47, 63; cf. E. Nestle, *Marginalien und Materialien* (Tübingen: J. J. Heckenhauer, 1893) 11, 74.

[28] Duensing, "Apocalypse of Paul," 792.

[29] James, *Apocryphal New Testament*, 452. Cf. "The History of Philip the Apostle and Evangelist," *Apocryphal Acts of the Apostles* (2 vols; ed. W. Wright; London: Williams and Northgate, 1871) 2.83.

The Book of the Bee (7th century)

> "The chief of the Jews who was in the land of the Chaldeans slew him, because he rebuked him for worshipping idols."[30]

Isidore of Seville, De Ortu et Obitu Patrum (7th Century)

> A leader of the people of Israel killed him there because he was rebuked by him with sternness and pontifical authority on account of the impiety of sacrilege.[31]

Synaxaria of the Greek Church (10th Century)

> The tribe of Gad killed the prophet because he prohibited it from worshipping idols.[32]

Roda Bible, San Piedro, Spain (10th Century)

> This illustrated Bible manuscript pictures Ezekiel as he is about to be beheaded.[33]

Hebrew Version of the Life of Ezekiel (12th Century)

> Because he reproved them (tribes of Dan and Gad) for transgression, they tied him to the tails of horses and dragged him upon the thorns and briars and he died.[34]

Peter Comestor, Historia Scholastica (12th Century)

> Angered at him because of this (sending serpents to eat their children and cattle and predicting that they would not return to their own land) they (the tribes of Dan and Gad) pulled him apart with horses through foundations of rocks and they debrained him,...[35]

Latin Bible, Palermo, Spain (13th-14th Century)[36]

> This illustrated Bible manuscript pictures Ezekiel being dragged while tied by his heels to the tail of a horse.

---

[30] Budge, *Book of the Bee*, 72.
[31] Minge, *PL* 83.129-56.
[32] From Atanase Negoita, "La vie des prophetes selon le synaxaire de l'eglise grecque," *Studia Semitica Ioanni Bakos Dicata* (ed. Stanislav Segert; Bratislava: Vydavatelstvo Slovenskej Vidc., 1965) 183.
[33] Roda Bible III, fol. 45v in Neuss, *Die katalanische Bibelillustration*, 87-89, plate 31, fig. 96. See also Goodenough, *Jewish Symbols*, 10.188, plates 307-9.
[34] MS Paris Bibl. Nat. Heb. 326, fol. 158r, cited in *Sepher Josippon* (2 vols.; ed. David Flusser; Jerusalem: Bialik Institute, 1978 and 1980) 2.153, n. 448 (Hebrew).
[35] Minge, *PL* 198.1441-46. Prof. Theodore Bergren of the University of Richmond alerted me to the passages in Isidore of Seville and Peter Comestor.
[36] Lib. Bibl. Naz., I.f.6-f.7, Bible, II. fol. 242r.

Latin Bible, Oxford (13th-14th Century)[37]

> This illustrated Bible manuscript shows Ezekiel bent over with a soldier holding a sword about to behead him.

The Names, Works and Deaths of the Holy Prophets (18th Century)

> "And (because) of envy of Ganim, the Jew, he was dragged from the tail of a horse over snows and hard rocks until he was broken in all his limbs."[38]

The study of later Christian and Islamic iconographic traditions has proven invaluable in retrieving early traditions otherwise not preserved in Jewish texts.[39] Goodenough led the way in bringing later texts and *objets d'art* to bear on the interpretation of this panel.[40] It is clear, however, that there were at least two traditions regarding the mode of Ezekiel's execution: (1) he was put to death by the sword; and (2) he was dragged by his feet until dead. Hebrews 11:37a clearly depends upon then current traditions regarding the deaths of Jeremiah and Isaiah: "They were stoned; they were sawn in two." As noted above, according to the traditions preserved in both Jewish and Christian circles, Isaiah was sawn in two by Manasseh and Jeremiah was stoned to death. The third major prophet is Ezekiel, and it is to him that Hebrews is referring when it says of some, "they were killed by the sword." Three later iconographic representations cited above depict Ezekiel being beheaded. Hebrews 11:37, however, refers simply to death by a sword, omitting whether the fatal blow was struck to the neck or elsewhere. The beheading tradition appears fully and clearly in the third century Ezekiel Panel at Dura-Europos, the drawing from the tenth century Roda Bible, and a 13th-14th century Oxford Latin manuscript. These later iconographic representations, however, may not be independent witnesses to an early beheading tradition, representing instead an exegetical tradition or expansion based on Hebrews 11:37.

---

[37] Oxford Bodl. Laud. Misc. 752, fol. 186r. The portraits in the Palermo and Oxford illustrated Bibles were brought to my attention by Prof. Michael Stone of the Hebrew University.

[38] Michael E. Stone, *Armenian Apocrypha Relating to the Patriarchs and Prophets* (Jerusalem: Israel Academy of Sciences and Humanities, 1982) 165.

[39] See Joseph Gutmann, "The Illustrated Midrash in the Dura Synagogue Paintings: A New Dimension for the Study of Judaism," *American Academy for Jewish Research Proceedings* 50 (1983) 91-104.

[40] For further information on Ezekiel in Christian art, see the articles on Ezekiel in Louis Reau, *Iconographie de l'Art Chrétien* (3 vols. in 6 pts.; Paris: Presses Universitaires de France, 1956) 2.373-78; Fernand Cabrol and Henri Leclercq, *Dictionnaire d'Archéologie Chrétienne et de Liturgie* (15 vols. in 30 pts.; Paris: Libraire Letouzey et Ane, 1922) 5.1050-51; and Engelbert Kirschbaum, *Lexikon der Christlichen Ikonographie* (8 vols.; Rome: Herder, 1968) 1.716-18.

The other tradition described the mode of Ezekiel's execution as being dragged by the feet until dead. There is, however, some variety among the various witnesses to this tradition. In one form the Israelites, or perhaps more specifically the tribes of Dan and Gad, dragged him over the ground until his brains were dashed out.[41] The earliest witness to this form of the tradition is the fourth century *Apocalypse of Paul* which, like the passage in the book of Hebrews, presents the death accounts of the three great prophets in succession. Here the apostle Paul is being introduced to the saints in paradise when he meets Isaiah, Jeremiah, and Ezekiel.

> I am Isaiah whose head Manasseh cut off with a wooden saw[42]...
> I am Jeremiah who was stoned by the children of Israel and killed...
> I am Ezekiel whom the children of Israel dragged by the feet over the rocks on the mountain until they dashed my brains.[43]

The Syriac "History of Philip the Apostle and Evangelist," which is later than but related to the Acts of Philip,[44] also cites the death traditions of the three great prophets together:

> There arose Isaiah the prophet, and ye sawed him with a saw of boxwood. There arose Ezekiel the prophet, and ye dragged him by his feet until his brains were dashed out. There arose Jeremiah the prophet, and ye cast him into a pit of mire.[45]

The authors of the book of Hebrews, the Apocalypse of Paul, and the "History of Philip the Apostle and Evangelist" all utilized these traditions about the deaths of the three major prophets for their own homiletical purposes. The author of Hebrews had access to and used,

---

[41] Apoc. Paul; Acts Philip; Hebrew *Vita*; Peter Comestor; and, possibly, the Palermo illustrated manuscript.

[42] In his discussion of the original language of the Martyrdom of Isaiah, M. A. Knibb, "Martyrdom and Ascension of Isaiah," *Old Testament Pseudepigrapha*, 2.146-47, makes the following observation: "Finally, in 5:1, 11 the Ethiopic states that Isaiah was sawed in half with 'a wood saw' (i.e. a saw to cut wood). But the Ethiopic expression is ambiguous and could be translated 'a wooden saw' (a saw made out of wood), and the corresponding passage in the Greek Legend (3:16) actually has this. The context and sense obviously require the meaning 'a wood saw,' but the evidence of the Greek Legend suggests that in the original a Hebrew construct-relationship was used, for which the translation 'a wood saw' and 'a wooden saw' would both be possible, and the Hebrew was incorrectly translated into Greek as the latter."

[43] Duensing, "Apocalypse of Paul," 2.792.

[44] Cf. James, *Apocryphal New Testament*, 439, and W. Schneemelcher and A. de Santos, "Later Acts of Apostles," *New Testament Apocrypha*, 2.577.

[45] Wright, *Apocryphal Acts*, 2.83. In the Syriac Acts of Philip, the death accounts of Isaiah and Ezekiel are followed by that of Habakkuk, Jeremiah's death account being omitted; see M. R. James, *Apocryphal New Testament*, 452.

however, a different tradition regarding the mode of Ezekiel's execution. In most cases, when Ezekiel dies by being dragged over the ground, the responsible party is either a group of Israelites or, more specifically, the tribes of Dan and Gad. Only in the 18th century Armenian text is an individual identified as the one who had Ezekiel dragged over the ground until dead. This Armenian text is further unique in that it specifies the name of the person who had Ezekiel killed, Ganim.[46]

The other form of the tradition identifies the murderer as a leader of the people, but it does not indicate how the prophet was killed. This appears to depend upon one of the death accounts in the *Vita Prophetarum*: "The governor of the people of Israel there killed him, being rebuked by him for worshipping idols."[47] It may be that when an individual kills Ezekiel, the mode of death is by the sword. The only exception, however, is the late Armenian work that has the individual named "Ganim" responsible for Ezekiel's being dragged behind a horse.

Goodenough's suggestion that the scene in the Ezekiel Panel is illustrating Ezekiel's demise fits with one of the two known traditions regarding the mode of the prophet's death, but the strict identification with one of the two death accounts in the *Vitae Prophetarum* is shortsighted. That the tradition was multifarious is clear. It seems that by the first century C.E. there was a widespread belief that the prophets suffered martyrdom at the hands of infidels.[48] Such a martyrdom is mentioned in the Deuteronomistic History in relation to Jezebel's putting the prophets of YHWH to death by the sword (1 Kgs 18:4; 19:10). In an act of poetic and deuteronomistic justice, Elijah later struck down with the sword the prophets of Baal whom Jezebel supported (1 Kgs 18:40; 19:1). Amidst his prayer of communal confession, Ezra admits that despite having always enjoyed God's favor, the Israelites disobeyed the Torah and "killed the prophets" (Neh 9:26). Hebrews 11 recounts the triumphs and tragedies experienced by several biblical figures, and in this recitation the author alludes to how the three major prophets of the Bible died: Jeremiah was stoned, Isaiah was cut in two, and Ezekiel was put to death by the sword.

As many of Lou Silberman's publications have shown, a knowledge of early Jewish and Christian traditions is indispensable in explaining enigmatic passages in either Jewish or Christian texts. I offer this attempt

---

[46] See Stone, *Armenian Apocrypha*, 164.
[47] Book of the Bee; Isidore of Seville.
[48] Matt 23:30-35; Luke 11:47-51; Acts 7:51-52; Rom 11:3; Apocalypse of Paul §44. See also Kuhn, "A Coptic Jeremiah Apocryphon," 115; H. A. Fischel, "Martyr and Prophet," *JQR* 37 (1946-47) 265-80; Otto Steck, *Israel und das gewaltsame Geschick der Propheten* (WMANT 23; Neukirchen-Vluyn: Neukirchener, 1967); and Schoeps, *Aus Frühchristlicher Zeit*, 126-43.

at explaining the referents of Hebrews 11:37 by tracing the widespread traditions on the deaths of Isaiah, Jeremiah and Ezekiel in honor of the man whose expertise at unraveling mysteries has been evident since his earliest publications on the Qumran Pesharim.

10

Identity, Apocalyptic, and Dialogue

James A. Sanders

Among the most delightful and gratifying teaching experiences I have ever had took place in the spring of 1992 and of 1994 at Ghost Ranch in northern New Mexico. Lou Silberman and I team-taught seminars on intertextuality in Jewish and Christian Scripture. The focus was on intertextuality in the Dead Sea Scrolls, Tannaitic midrashim, and the Second Christian Testament. On the first day of class Lou and I made it quite clear that while we both participate fully in Western Enlightenment culture and both read the literature under study with all the critical tools developed in scholarship since the Enlightenment, each of us had quite distinct faith identities that neither of us would set aside during the two weeks of the seminar.

Silberman and I share more in common than most inter-faith dialogue partners in that we are both graduates of the Hebrew Union College. Many of Lou's professors were still teaching at the College some fifteen years later when I was there. Our ties run even deeper. Lou Silberman taught for twenty-eight years at Vanderbilt University, succeeding Sam Sandmel who had left the Hillel professorship at Vanderbilt University, my own alma mater, to join the faculty of the Hebrew Union College. Lou became a colleague at Vanderbilt of my first mentor in biblical studies, James Philip Hyatt, who was the one who advised me to study for a year at the College to get Jewish backgrounds to New Testament study, the formal track I was on at the time. But I never got to Yale, where Hyatt and Sandmel both had studied, and where I was going to study New Testament with Paul Schubert. Sam Sandmel at the College became my advisor and first reader for my dissertation on suffering as divine discipline in the Tanach and Early Judaism.

Silberman and I wanted the students in the University of New Mexico seminar to know where our backgrounds were similar but also where our faith identities differed. It was a fulfillment of a dream for me. I had long dreamt of reading biblical and other religious texts with Jewish colleagues, as an aspect of inter-faith dialogue, on just such an intensive and sustained basis. The course was on intertextuality in early Jewish and Christian literature – in two senses of the word "intertextuality". That is, we not only probed the function of earlier Scripture in later Scripture and Jewish religious literature, but we did so quite conscious of the fact that we were texts ourselves encountering each other as well as encountering the written texts we were reading together. It was exhilarating.

Tannaim

Because Silberman and I had shared rabbinic training in reading the Tanach, we both had therefore read the entire Hebrew Bible, not only critically in terms of the history of its formation, but also as the very ground of all our other study. Lou at one point explained to the students at Ghost Ranch that a *Tanna* was a computer with stored memory of every phrase of Hebrew Scripture, so that all one had to do was press the right keys and Scripture would pour out.

I had a moving experience of the sort only four years earlier in 1988 when, at commencement ceremonies at the Hebrew Union College where I had been invited to speak, I heard something in the service that prompted me to say quietly, but aloud from where I was sitting with the faculty, the first (Hebrew) words of Habakkuk 3:17. Spontaneously, and I am sure without thinking consciously about it, a few of the older professors around me automatically completed recitation of the whole verse, and then went right on with what they had been doing.[1] I had pressed the right buttons, and my own former *Tannaim* recited Scripture from memory. I had not consciously intended to trigger any such reaction, nor, I am sure, did they consciously do anything but continue the recitation, simply because a *pasuq* was there in the air to be completed. I had a very hard time restraining tears of joy just for being in such company. One of those who completed the passage that day was my closest friend and classmate at Hebrew Union College, Jakob Josef

---

[1] Habakkuk 5:17-18: "Though the fig tree do not blossom, and no fruit be on the vines; though the produce of the olive fail and the fields yield no food; though the flock be cut off from the fold and there be no herd in the stalls, yet will I exult in the Lord, I will rejoice in the God of my salvation."

Petuchowski, who three years later passed away unexpectedly, in November 1991.

Scripture for a Jew is the ground of being, or as Michael Fishbane says, Torah is God incarnate.[2] It is that out of which everything else flows; it is truly the ספר חיים (the book of life), indeed the ספר שכול בו (the book that contains it all). Or as Sam Sandmel often said, Torah is Judaism, and Judaism is Torah, in *sensu lato*, of course. At Ghost Ranch, I had weeks of again being in the presence of such a *Tanna*, an experience totally unavailable in *goyische* biblical scholarship, but abundantly so, with grace, in the company of Lou Silberman.

Dialogue and Identity

Jewish Christian dialogue at the moment is caught up in a much larger debate. A colleague at Claremont, Prof. Burton Mack, recently gave a paper titled "Caretakers and Critics: The Social Role of Scholars in Biblical Study."[3] In the paper Mack argues that biblical scholars, whether in the university department of religion or in the seminary, are called on to be critics only. He proposes a game in which whenever a scholar seems to care about the role of scripture in current communities of faith, the others would cry out, "Gotcha!" He even disparages the value of ethnic or liberation hermeneutics in Scripture study. For him the Bible scholar should be critic only and not "caretaker," as he puts it.[4]

By contrast Jon Levenson and James Kugel, both at Harvard, in a conference at Notre Dame in 1989, both denied that there can be an effective or meaningful Jewish/Christian dialogue, precisely because the dialogue would be based on the superficial common ground of narrowly conceived, western, cultural, critical study of the texts and not on the genuine identities of Jews and Christians, the very sort of study Mack claims is the only truthful stance from which to study Scripture.

For Levenson and Kugel, critical study will in the end always give way to our true social locations as either Jew or Christian; they denied explicitly the possibility of what Mack calls for. Mack would counter that his own social location, as one who is distancing himself from his charismatic, evangelical roots, overrides his identity as a Christian. And Levenson and Kugel would respond finally that whatever that may

---

[2] In *Garments of Torah* (Bloomington: Indiana University Press, 1989) 42, 125-29.
[3] Unpublished paper presented in 1989 at Wesleyan University and in 1993 at the School of Theology at Claremont.
[4] Other faculty responses indicated that very few academics or intellectuals have a singular identity but have hyphenated identities, even multiple ones.

mean in Mack's own work as a scholar, it is not a basis for Jewish/Christian dialogue.[5]

My response to my colleague Mack was that, while I fully support and defend his right to his position, even on a theological seminary faculty, my concern is his assumption, that only his position, a kind of academic fundamentalism, is a valid one for the critic, with his zeal as evangelist of his new position perhaps equaling his earlier evangelical role. I do not consider myself a caretaker of tradition, but a latter day critical tradent or traditionist, on the order of a Silberman or a Petuchowski.

Criticism and Identity

A late twentieth century traditionist, or tradent, who would engage in dialogue must read the Bible both critically and faithfully, that is, as a western cultural reader (critic) *and* as a member, or at least heir, of a faith community. To put it another way, I believe the Enlightenment was a gift of God in due season, just as I believe that a vital, agile, ever-adapting faith is a gift of God. While we are learning from the southern and eastern hemispheres of the planet that the western, cultural forms of criticism are as limited in perspective as others, I must personally affirm the excitement that a combined critical and faithful reading of these texts renders. And it is on that dual basis that I believe the Jewish/Christian conversation can be fruitful for both parties. On the first day of the New Mexico seminar, Silberman and I stressed for the students our common critical training as well as our different faith identities, his at the foot of a mountain and mine at the foot of a cross.

Why stress both, why combine the two in interfaith dialogue? Simply put, the world needs the model of taking seriously both past and present, the Jewish past and the Christian past, as well as the newer gifts of the Enlightenment. To seek one's identity in only a present, western, cultural, critical reading of these texts is to deny any value to the thinking and experience of those who wrote, shaped, and passed them on. But to seek one's identity in only the traditioning process of one's faith identity is to continue to engage in denominational falsehood.

---

[5] See *Hebrew Bible or Old Testament? Studying the Bible in Judaism and Christianity* (Notre Dame: University of Notre Dame Press, 1990) 109-45 and 167-90. See also Levenson's "Why Jews Are Not Interested in Biblical Theology," *Judaic Perspectives on Ancient Israel* (ed. J. Neusner et al.; Philadelphia: Fortress, 1987) 281-307, as well as Levenson's *The Hebrew Bible, The Old Testament, and Historical Criticism: Jews and Christians in Biblical Studies* (Louisville: Westminster/John Knox, 1993).

Oberammergau

A case in point is the Oberammergau Passion Play. In the years 1632-1633 the Black Death raged throughout Bavaria and adjoining parts of Austria and Germany. The village of Oberammergau was largely spared, in comparison to towns in the lower Ammer Valley. In deep piety and faith, the folk of the village made a solemn vow to God to perform a play of the passion and death of Jesus Christ, in thanksgiving for God's grace toward them, and to perform it every ten years in perpetuity. As the *Offizieller Bildband* published in 1980 states: "Their pledge to enact the Passion culminates in their historic consciousness, which maintains its continuance throughout all hindrances, difficulties and dissensions. In this may be seen and recognized a moral pledge, a sense of being bound to norms and values, an unbreakable bond with custom and usage. The community of Oberammergau freely bound itself by a solemn oath: the people made a lasting vow, a sworn promise to God."[6] One cannot imagine a testimony by any community to greater piety and faith, except (need I say it?) Jewish communities in Europe, which through centuries of Christian cultural dominance continued to recite Torah in all its phases.

But by the end of the Second World War, the post-Holocaust, outside world had begun to listen in. What they found in and through all the faithfulness and piety was a play that in effect sponsored anti-semitism and anti-Jewishness. In the English version of "The Official Text" for 1960 the Abbot of Ettal wrote, "What was once a pious custom, understood by all, often became in later years an offense to adherents of other creeds and to the cynical, even well-wishers were disquieted by the many unpleasant concomitants of increasing fame."

The abbot, however, goes on to defend the play. "Be that as it may; for those whose vision is still clear enough to penetrate through all changes and accidental blemishes, for those who are still sufficiently pure in heart to accept and absorb what they see and hear at this Play, it will remain what it has always been, and still is, in its deepest sense: the *Memoria Passionis Domini*, the remembrance of the sufferings of Our Lord ... the remembrance of the suffering and death which Christ took upon Himself 'for the life of the world', the mystery of the Cross, which for some is a vexation of the spirit, for others mere tomfoolery, but for believers a sign of the power, the wisdom and the love of God."[7] The text

---

[6] *Passion Oberammergau: Offizieller Bildband* (Munich: Eigenverlag, 1980), the fourth (unnumbered) page in the German written by Professor Johannes Goldner, with translations into English and French.
[7] *The Passion Play at Oberammergau* (Oberammergau: Gemeinde Oberammergau, 1960), foreword by Johannes Maria Hoeck, Abbot of Ettal, 11.

of the play, despite much editing and modification, is basically taken from the four Gospels.

But, as the good abbot wrote; "adherents of other creeds" began to listen in. And here is my point. Piety and good works generated and sponsored solely within one tradition may be seen to be dehumanizing and evil from the viewpoint of a different, equally pious tradition. Learning to review one's own traditions only from a western, cultural, critical stance still may not reveal what listening to those traditions through the eyes and ears of a different tradition cherished by a different identity group may reveal.

One God

Belief that there is but One God, and belief that Jews and Christians, and Muslims as well, worship that same God through differing traditioning processes, requires and mandates dialogue. As Jacob Neusner has recently said, it requires sharing of stories that are meaningful to each tradition so that we can at least try to understand what Israel means to Judaism and what Christ means to Christianity.[8] From a distance, each looks like sheer idolatry to the other. In dialogue it may be possible for each to confess its own idolatry rather than just silently accuse the other of embracing idolatry at the heart of its faith.[9]

The sharing of stories should begin with common readings of Scripture, that compendium of stories that surpasses all others. That would be an exercise in intertextuality in a mode beyond what has yet been seriously attempted. But Levenson and Kugel are right that it cannot be a sharing of western-cultural, critical readings of biblical passages only. It must be a sharing of readings also through both Jewish and Christian traditioning processes. And that is what Silberman and I tried to do for our students at Ghost Ranch. Using the vehicle of the Dead Sea Scrolls and its massive amounts of intertextuality as a catalyst, we probed the function of Scripture in Tannaitic midrashim and in the Second Testament.

I hope Lou will not object to my saying that by the final session on the last Friday morning, there was little left for us to do but embrace and pass the peace; and there was, I dare say, not a dry eye in the room. It

---

[8] In *Jewish Spectator* (Winter 1991-92) 36. Anthropologist Michael Taussig, speaking at the University of Florida in 1988, quoted Columbian Indians' explanation for imperialism's success: "The others won because their stories were better than ours" (quoted by my colleague Prof. Jack Coogan in an unpublished paper "The Moving Image and Theological Education").
[9] See the writer's review of Fishbane's *Garments* in *Theology Today* 47:4 (1991) 433-35.

was moving. One had the feeling of the joy that comes with recognizing what John Calvin called God's *opus alienum*, the work of God elsewhere than in one's own tradition.

Silberman and Apocalyptic

I would like to highlight the relevance of Silberman's work on apocalyptic, in Early Judaism generally and in early Tannaitic literature, to the question of the relation of synagogue and church in the sixty-year period between the two Jewish Revolts of 66 to 75 and of 132 to 155 CE. I am thinking especially of his contribution to the James Philip Hyatt memorial volume; his work on Albert Schweitzer's understanding of eschatology and apocalyptic; and his more recent work on Rabbis Tarphon and Akiba. In these Lou has drawn a map of the terrain out of which apocalyptic rose.

Loss of identity through absence of community, as in prison or exile, gives rise to despair. Despair then gives rise to torpor, out of which one gives in to a death wish or turns to eschatological thinking in an apocalyptic mode, which is in actuality a rallying cry for a return to history.[10] "Apocalyptic serves as a means of signifying that hoped for future (return to history) in a particular context."[11] In contrast to the common wisdom that apocalyptic was occultated (marginalized) by the Pharisees soon after the first revolt, Lou has convincingly shown that apocalyptic, as in IV Ezra and II Baruch, was still alive and well in Pharisaic, emerging rabbinic Judaism during the period up to the Bar Kochba revolt.[12]

In study of a dictum from the period of Rabbi Tarphon, Silberman writes: "...the events of the Second Revolt (132 CE) suggest to me that apocalyptic thought was still active, indeed, was able to ignite the flames of revolt under the leadership of Bar Kosiba (=Bar Kokhba) abetted by Rabbi Akiba. Thus it was only after the failure of that uprising and the subsequent persecutions under Hadrian that the apocalyptic fires faded into embers, not extinguished, but smouldering under the ashes of a failed hope."[13] "The situation of the Jewish community in the years between 70 C.E. and 132 C.E. ... was one in which ... eschatological/messianic expectations had not faded but motivated

---

[10] Silberman, "The Human Deed in a Time of Despair: The Ethics of Apocalyptic," *Essays in Old Testament Ethics: J. Philip Hyatt, In Memoriam* (ed. James L. Crenshaw and John T. Willis; New York: KTAV, 1974) 191-202.
[11] Silberman, "Apocalyptic Revisited: Reflections on the Thought of Albert Schweitzer," *JAAR* 44 (1976) 498.
[12] Silberman, "From Apocalyptic Proclamation to Moral Prescript: Abot 2, 15-16," *JJS* 40:1 (1989) 55-60.
[13] *Ibid.*, 54.

many sections of the community, so that within two generations of the fall of Jerusalem and the destruction of the Temple a second revolt against the Roman *imperium* flared up."[14] "With the failure of the Second Revolt and its tragic outcome for the community, all such conjecture ... came ... to an end and Judaism turned its back on the apocalyptic literature it had created."[15]

I would suggest that what Lou has done with regard to rabbinic Judaism's continued engagement with apocalyptic until the middle of the second quarter of the second century C.E. has implications for the status of Christian Judaism within the larger picture of numerous Judaisms in the first century. Whereas it has become almost commonplace to think of a complete break between synagogue and church after 70,[16] it now is more responsible to view the break as occurring gradually between the two revolts. The historian's principle of the complexity of reality would indicate that the break was not a clean one at a specific moment in history but that, since Early Judaism was highly multifarious, some Christian Jewish synagogues, or churches, were more hellenized than others, and some Pharisaic/rabbinic synagogues were more tolerant toward Christian synagogues than others. The Second Testament itself indicates this kind of complexity within Pharisaic/rabbinic Judaism and within the various forms of Christian Judaism.[17]

---

[14] *Ibid.*, 56.

[15] *Ibid.*, 60. Silberman goes on to say that even after 135 C.E. apocalyptic simply went underground to emerge in various ways in Jewish literature through the middle ages.

[16] See in *Christianity and Rabbinic Judaism: A Parallel History of Their Origins and Early Development* (ed. Hershel Shanks; Washington: Biblical Archaeology Society, 1992), the introduction by Geza Vermes, xvii-xxii. In the same volume, Howard Kee (85-124), moves in the opposite direction, claiming that Christianity was distinct from "official Judaism" almost from the beginning. Such a position fails to take account of the immense shift in thinking about the older designations of "normative and heterodox Judaism" in the period; instead it is becoming almost commonplace to speak of the Judaisms, some forms more hellenized than others, of the period without real certainty about Jewish normativeness. The study by Harold Attridge, "Christianity from the Destruction of Jerusalem to Constantine's Adoption of the New Religion: 70-312 C.E." in the same volume (151-94, esp. 151-74) is, by contrast, a judiciously nuanced study of the varieties of Christianity and their relations to other forms of Judaism in the crucial sixty-year period from 70 to 135 C.E.

[17] Lee I. A. Levine's "Judaism from the Destruction of Jerusalem to the End of the Second Jewish Revolt: 70-135 C.E.," in *op. cit.* (above, n. 16) 125-49, reflects well the sources read by the principle of the complexity of reality, with the exception of his passing remark on p. 129 supporting the simplistic view that Christianity separated after 70. He rightly agrees with Silberman's position that apocalyptic played a continuing role in Judaism in the sixty-year period 70-135 C.E., but

Συναγωγή and Ἐκκλησία

The passages that indicate enmity between συναγωγή and ἐκκλησία must now be seen on a larger scale of variation and diversity within Judaism until the end of the Bar Kochba Revolt when the break indeed became complete. One should even allow for the possibility that perhaps a few Christian synagogues (Jacobean/Petrine?) became disillusioned over the apparent failure of the *parousia*, or Second Coming of Christ, and became a part of continuing halachic or rabbinic Judaism. As Silberman points out, a great deal of the literature that can be read one way can also be resignified as pertinent to the new non-apocalyptic situation. And, as he also notes, the disillusionment over the failure of either a First or a Second Coming of messiah, according to which קהל or ἐκκλησία one adhered to, came about also because such expectations caused neglect of obligations and duties.

Some time ago, following a paper of Abraham Heschel's published posthumously, I suggested that Torah, in all its senses, was made up of both *haggadah* and *halachah*, that is, theocentric narrative, or "gospel" (God's story), and law (God's will).[18] While Christian and other forms of eschatological Judaism fell heir to the former, rabbinic Judaism fell heir to the latter – an emphasis on prescripts for believers, rather than on speculations about what God was going to do next. The apocrypha and pseudepigrapha, which exhibit considerable apocalyptic thought, were then preserved in translations by the early churches, but sluffed off by the surviving rabbinic synagogues.

According to Silberman's work, and I agree with it, the sluffing off would have been complete by the middle of the second century C.E., but not as early as has been generally thought. The complexity of reality principle of the historian would lead to the hypothesis that some synagogues, in the sixty-year period between the two revolts, were clearer in their views than others, just as some would have been clearer about their opposition to the Christian Jewish sect than others.

The cataclysm of the Second Revolt would have caused the necessity of cleaning up the mess left not only by violence but also by neglect of work due to the high eschatological expectations, hence the move from apocalyptic proclamation to moral prescript in both forms of surviving Judaism. But after 135 C.E. those two forms of survival were so distinct, with a preponderance of converts to the emerging very distinct

---

when he speaks of Judaism in that period he means only the Johanan ben Zakkai to Akiba/Gamliel II Judaism. His view of the canonical process in the period is also limited (139-40).

[18] "Torah and Christ," *Interpretation* 29 (1975) 352-90. See also the writer's *God Has a Story Too* (Philadelphia: Fortress, 1979).

Christianity being Gentile and causing the ἐκκλησία to energize (Philippians 2:12-13) or work out their understandings of salvation in ways that were less and less rabbinic Jewish at all.

In other words, when both groupings found themselves turning more toward obedience in specifically recognized forms, away from eschatological expectation, those forms of service and work made the distinctions between the two very clear, considerably more clear than when the emphasis was on expectations of what God was going to do next. When one focuses on God's grace rather than on how humans should respond to that grace, the differences between Judaism and Christianity, as we now know them, are minimal and can be summed up in large measure by Reinhold Niebuhr's two questions. The world is so evil, why doesn't the Messiah come? Or, the messiah has come, why is the world still so evil? Neither question can be satisfactorily answered by either party. But when it comes to focusing on how humans should respond to stories of the grace of God, already established in a community as identity-giving stories, those responses take on distinct forms that separate and divide.

Dialogue Today

Implications arising out of Silberman's work in this regard are important for the Jewish/Christian dialogue today. We have learned since the discovery of the Dead Sea Scrolls to speak of Judaisms in the Second Temple Period. We must now learn to extend that observation through to the period of the Second Revolt. This would mean that the whole of the Second Testament was written by Jews for Jews, or by Christian Jews for Christian Jews, with the number of Gentile converts to Christian Judaism differing according to the synagogue or ἐκκλησία, and its location. It would mean that the term οἱ Ἰουδαῖοι would have to be translated in differentiated ways, as has been attempted in the new *Contemporary English Version*.[19]

But it would also mean hermeneutically that Christians in reading the Second Testament would have to give up their centuries-long habit of reading the Second Testament as a non-Jewish or even anti-Jewish

---

[19] The context of each occurrence would determine the appropriate English word or phrase selected. The important point is to sponsor translations that reflect the multifarious forms of Judaism in the first century, the Christian form as one of them, albeit near the margin in the view of some, especially Pharisaic/rabbinic Judaism. Examples would be: "fellow Jews," "people," "Judaeans" (if they really were), "authorities," etc. "Scribes and Pharisees" could well be translated as "religious experts." The fact that the Gospels in the terms used often reflect the late situation is clearly seen in the strange statement in Matthew 13:54, "He came to *his* hometown and began to teach them in *their* synagogue ..." (emphasis mine).

document. The New Testament is Jewish literature. It is as Jewish as the Dead Sea Scrolls, apocrypha, or pseudepigrapha. The conflicts in it were *intra muros judaeos*, keeping in mind the highly diverse forms of Judaism of the period up to the Second Revolt. The criticisms of and challenges to the Jewish leadership of the first century must be seen, in their canonical context, as of the same order as the very similar criticisms and challenges of the Iron Age prophets to the leadership of their day, or historically as of an order similar to the anti-Pharisaic and anti-Hasmonean, and generally anti-Jerusalem polemics in the Qumran Scrolls. The Bible is a remarkable corpus of literature in that it enshrines an immense amount of self-criticism, and the Second Testament should be read in the same light.

It is basically a question of the hermeneutics brought to reading the Second Testament. One could call Isaiah or Jeremiah anti-semitic if read out of canonical context. It means for Christians, keeping the Second Testament in the Bible – as the churches, soon after the Second Revolt in response to Marcion, have traditionally always insisted.

The whole Bible is Jewish, with the understanding that in every period of its formation, the Bronze Age, Iron Age, the Persian, Hellenistic and Roman periods, elements of many cultures, as well as of converts and adherents originating in those cultures find expression in its pages. The Second Testament is just not all that different, in terms of how Scripture functioned in it and helped shape it, from other Hellenistic Jewish literature of the period; it is part of a larger corpus of Jewish literature, with its own particular foci and contours.[20]

Jews and Jews

During the Ghost Ranch seminars one of the texts studied was the parable of the so-called good Samaritan. In retelling the story, in the light of 2 Chronicles 28:8-15, the story of the good Samarians, the victim who had been mugged was described as a Jew who was going down from Jerusalem to Jericho. Silberman remarked during the discussion that it was the first time he had ever heard the victim called a Jew. It was a sad remark, but true for myself as well. One should assume that he was a Jew, but most Christians hardly think of him at all in their focus on the

---

[20] See Shemaryahu Talmon, "Oral Tradition and Written Transmission, or the Heard and the Seen Word in Judaism of the Second Temple Period," *Jesus and the Oral Gospel Tradition* (ed. Henry Wansbrough; JSNT Supplement Series 64; Sheffield: Sheffield University Press, 1991) 121-58; esp. 127-32, where Talmon effectively compares and contrasts the Qumran community and Early Christianity as two forms of Judaism within the larger pluriform Judaism of the first century.

Samaritan and the good deed he performed. What he did, he did for a Jew; and therein lies the power of the story in terms of the alienation of the time between the two Torah observing groups.

But Silberman's point has deeper implications; everyone in the Gospel accounts should be assumed to have been Jewish unless otherwise designated. Jesus has with good reason been called a marginal Jew;[21] but that again assumes that there was a normative Judaism at the time, and that assumption has been effectively challenged. The Christians of the first century can all be called marginal Jews in that even Gentile Christians understood themselves to have converted to a form of Judaism, even if from the standpoint of a Rabbi Akiba they would have been very marginal.

Lou's work on the influence of apocalyptic thought in surviving Pharisaic/rabbinic Judaism between the two revolts converges with other work on the Judaisms of the period to indicate a mandate on the part of Christians today to cease and desist anti-semitic and anti-Jewish readings of the Second Testament. As Silberman rightly says, "metaphoric language permits new ideas to be poured into old vessels."[22] Christians have for two thousand years read their own supersessionist anti-semitism into the metaphoric language of the Gospels and Epistles.

It is time now to eliminate the evil that the church has sponsored in its misreading of these texts. Reading it both critically and faithfully, and teaching the faithful how to do so, can offer both church and synagogue the καιρός, or opportunity, to proclaim to all who would listen that God is not a Jew, God is not a Christian, God is not a Muslim; God is God, *revelatus* and *absconditus*, the Integrity of Reality. And that Reality is far bigger and more complex than any single religion is capable of comprehending, much less expressing.

We need each other. We need to hear each other's understandings, in dialogue, of shared and unshared stories. Only in that way can we hope to enter the twenty-first century with hope that these two distinct identity groups can appreciate and even celebrate what each holds dear. And if, please God, that should happen, Lou Silberman's work and witness will have been an important factor contributing to the hope we all so desperately need to hear.

---

[21] John P. Meier, *A Marginal Jew: Rethinking the Historical Jesus* (New York: Doubleday, 1991). See also Geza Vermes, *Jesus the Jew: A Historian's Reading of the Gospels* (New York, 1974), with a response to his critics in *Jesus' Jewishness* (ed. James H. Charlesworth; New York: Crossword, 1991) 108-22.
[22] See "From Apocalyptic Proclamation to Moral Prescript," 60.

11

The Literary Structure of the Amidah and the Rhetoric of Redemption*

Reuven Kimelman

Abstract

The nineteen blessings of the Amidah constitute an argument for redemption. In the opening triad of blessings (1-3), the first presents the argument for a redeemer, the second makes the case for resurrection, and the third brings about the acclamation of God's kingship on earth. All three affirm divine sovereignty. Understanding God as Lord over history, Lord over nature and death, and Lord over heaven and earth in a single continuum sustains the hope of redemption.

The first half of the intermediate blessings (4-9) presents three accessible dimensions of redemption: personal salvation (4-7); physical recovery (8); and agricultural revival (9). Together they enhance the plausibility of the not yet available national redemption of the upcoming blessings (10-15). The second half (10-15) delineates the order of national redemption. It commences with the great shofar's blast of freedom, announcing the ingathering of the exiles, and culminates in the rebuilding of Jerusalem. Since the motifs are all biblical, the contribution

---

* This article is a revision of my "The Daily 'Amidah and the Rhetoric of Redemption," *JQR* 74 (1988/89) 165-97. It takes into consideration literature published since then, especially that of Ezra Fleischer, "The Shemone Esre – Its Character, Internal Order, Content and Goals," *Tarbiz* 62 (1993) 179-223 (Hebrew), and Yechezkel Luger, *Weekday 'Amidah Based on the Genizah* (2 vols.; Ph.D. diss., Bar Ilan University, 1992) who was kind enough to send me a copy of his helpful dissertation.

of the liturgy lies in the particular linguistic formulation, in the sequence, and in the uncompromising emphasis on divine involvement. All three converge to make the point that God alone is the redeemer.

Blessings 17 and 18 also advance the drama of redemption by focusing on God's return to Zion and His universal recognition. Thus the Amidah advances from personal (4-7) through national (10-15) to universal redemption (18), each stage involving the progressive realization of divine sovereignty. With blessing 19, the Amidah ends on a note of peace.

When the Amidah, with its theme of future redemption, was welded to the service of the Shema, whose final motif is past redemption, the memory of past redemption became the liturgical basis for future redemption.

Prolegomenon

Most liturgical studies follow either a historical or a literary orientation.[1] The historical orientation is primarily concerned with the liturgy as a document of its time from which it derives information about the past. It seeks to understand the liturgy as a response to internal needs or as a reaction to external events. The analysis centers on the different stages of the composition of the text rather than on its finished product. Such an approach is inclined to decompose the texts and analyze them through their different stages in order to reconstruct their development through history. This is referred to as its diachronic history. In contrast, the literary orientation is primarily concerned with the liturgy as a finished product. It seeks to understand the liturgy in the light of its purpose and intention. For it, the significating framework is found within the text itself. The analysis centers on the integration of the various elements to create a compositional whole. Such an approach is inclined to construct the meaning of the whole, what is called its synthetic meaning. Much of classical and modern scholarship has adopted the historical approach with its focus on philology, semantics, allusions to biblical and rabbinic literature, and the diachronic development of the liturgy. There is precious little work on the synthetic meaning of liturgical units as integrated pieces of literature. Even less extant are literary treatments of liturgical units and their overall

---

[1] For a critical analysis of the historical-philological and form-critical approaches; see R. Sarason, "On the Use of Method in the Modern Study of Jewish Liturgy," *Approaches to Ancient Judaism: Theory and Practice* (ed. W. S. Green; Missoula, MT: Scholars Press, 1978) 97-172. For a survey of recent literature with emphasis on the Qumran connections; see J. Maier, "Zu Kult und Liturgie der Qumrangemeinde," *RevQ* 14 (1990) 543-86.

framework that incorporate the findings of the historical school and that of the classical commentaries.² My study, in contrast, focuses on the liturgy as an ideational and literary composition within a historical context. My concern with the diachronic development is only as a means of constructing its synthetic meaning. Through such an integration of historical and literary approaches, I aim to show how the liturgy functions as an expression of the ideology of its composers as well as an expression of worship.

In order to present the ideology of the liturgy, I will focus on how it functions as persuasive literature.³ The literary method concerned with the persuasive techniques of literature is rhetorical criticism. Rhetorical criticism focuses on the art of persuasive discourse as opposed to just the analysis of discourse of general literary criticism. Its application to the liturgy is based on the assumption that liturgy is involved in persuasion. It seeks to persuade the worshiper of something, thereby bringing about a change in feeling and/or thinking. My analysis thus focuses on the persuasive strategies and rhetorical techniques used to enhance the worshiper's receptivity to the argument or perspective of the liturgy – in other words, how the liturgy makes its case.⁴

---

² Notable exceptions are M. Kadushin, *Worship and Ethics: A Study in Rabbinic Judaism* (Evanston, IL: Northwestern University Press, 1964) who moved in his own way in this direction; L. Hoffman, *Beyond the Text: A Holistic Approach to Liturgy* (Bloomington, IN: Indiania University Press, 1987), who also integrated previous modes of liturgical study in his own approach; and E. Levy, *Torat Ha-Tefillah* (Tel Aviv: Abraham Zioni, 1967), in contrast to his earlier *Yesodot Ha-Tefillah* (Tel Aviv: Abraham Zioni, 1955). The pioneer of the literary study of the liturgy is Eleazar b. Judah of Worms, *Siddur Ha-Tefillah La-Roqeah* (2 vols.; ed. M. and Y. Hershler; Jerusalem: Machon Harav Hershler, 1992); see J. Dan, "The Emergence of Mystical Prayer," *Studies in Jewish Mysticism* (ed. J. Dan and F. Talmadge; Cambridge, MA: Association for Jewish Studies, 1982) 87-93.

³ As explicated by C. Rabin, "The Linguistic Investigation of the Language of Jewish Prayer," *Studies in Aggadah, Targum and Jewish Liturgy in Memory of Joseph Heinemann* (ed. J. Petuchowski and E. Fleischer; Jerusalem: Magnes, 1981) 169.

⁴ For a survey of the literature and the implications of rhetorical criticism, see W. Wüllner, "Where Is Rhetorical Criticism Taking Us," *CBQ* 49 (1987) 448-63. For the difference in emphasis between literary and rhetorical criticism, see C. Koelb, *Inventions of Reading: Rhetoric and the Literary Imagination* (Ithaca: Cornell University Press, 1988) 254. For Rabbinic knowledge of Greco-Roman rhetoric, see the studies by S. Lieberman, D. Daube, and H. Fischel cited in E. Schürer, *The History of the Jewish People in the Age of Jesus Christ* (175 B.C.-A.D. 135 (3 vols.; ed. G. Vermes, et al.; Edinburgh: T. & T. Clark, 1973-1987) 2.78, n. 265; and R. Kimelman, "Rabbi Yohanan and the Professionalization of the Rabbinate," *Shenaton Ha-Mishpat Ha-Ivri*, vols. 9-10 (ed. M. Elon and M. Rabello; Jerusalem: Institute for Research in Jewish Law, 1982-83) 336-39. Rabbinic knowledge of rhetoric seems to have gone hand in hand with a legal education as was the case in Rome; see S. F. Bonner, *Education in Ancient Rome* (Berkeley: University of

In liturgy, the argument is more than its logic; it also involves attention to the structure of the argument, the texture of the language, the recontextualization of images, and the concatenation of themes. Recontextualization is concerned with the difference in meaning between the original context and the present context. Since meaning is a function of context, total meaning must take into consideration both present and past context. Concatenation is concerned with the sequence of the parts of the liturgy. It assumes that order and location are also parts of meaning. All these together constitute the literary context of the prayer. All are essential to meaning.

Specifically, much of the liturgy derives from biblical and midrashic sources. The meaning of these images and allusions is a combination both of their original and new contexts. What the biblical and midrashic elements come to mean in the liturgy is their recontextualized significance. It is also important to note the impact of sequence in the structure of the liturgy. The impact of ideas is a factor of their order of appearance. Previous ideas influence how a reader understands those that follow. An idea that precedes another becomes part of the consciousness of the reader when encountering the next idea.[5]

The subtext that is implicit in a text is its intertext. The intertexts of the liturgy are often from the Bible and the Midrash. By designating a source as a liturgical intertext, I refer to a textual allusion that unlocks a dimension of the meaning of the liturgy. In other words, the intertext is the background allusion that accounts for a meaning of the text. It is the convergence of language and image, sequence and context that orchestrates the interplay, sometimes very subtle, between statement and subtext that creates liturgical meaning.

These rhetorical operations provide the key for how the liturgy is supposed to function in the mind of the worshiper. They pave the way for understanding how the liturgy brings about a change in the perspective of the worshiper. By tracing the transformation of the worshiper's perspective, the text is shown to be what it really is – liturgy. In applying this approach to the Amidah, we should be able to present its total meaning as a literary composition.

California Press, 1977) 250-327. The arguments for rhetorical techniques having informed the religious assertions of both Jewish and Christian literature in the first centuries are assembled by J. L. Kinneavy, *Greek Rhetorical Origins of Christian Faith: An Inquiry* (Oxford: Oxford University Press, 1987) 26-100.

[5] Based on W. Iser, *The Act of Reading: A Theory of Aesthetic Response* (Baltimore: Johns Hopkins University Press, 1978) 148-49.

Prologue

The Amidah appears more often in the cycle of the liturgy than any other prayer. There is no communal or statutory service without some form of it. As the first communal statutory service, it was called *ha-tefillah*, "the prayer." There are different variations for special occasions.[6] The Sabbath and Festival versions each contain seven blessings, while the Rosh Hashanah *Musaf* comprises nine. The weekday version now consists of nineteen blessings. While still composed of only eighteen, it became known as the *Shemoneh Esreh*,[7] the Hebrew for "eighteen," a misnomer that has remained in use down to our day. Since the Amidah now comprises nineteen blessings, and it is recited while standing, the name *Amidah*, which means "standing," has rightfully gained in usage.[8]

The Amidah was not created out of nothing. It is a composite prayer. Elements of it were once part of the Temple service while semblances of other parts have shown up in other ancient Jewish sources.[9] In something like its present form, it became the first communal statutory prayer to emerge in post-Temple times.[10] According to the Talmud, the number of blessings and their order became known as the Yavnean order since they were fixed under the auspices of Rabban Gamaliel of Yavneh.[11] Whether or not the pre-history of the Amidah reflects various historical events or an extended liturgical process, the Yavnean order is not a random selection of liturgical materials or a serendipitous reflection of historical events. A specific order implies a purposeful montage of units with an overall structure. Its structure as well as its organizing principle(s) is reflected in the sequencing of material and the attendant meaning of each blessing. Indeed, the most common way of formalizing

---

[6] See J. Heinemann, s.v., "Berakhah," *Encyclopedia Judaica*, 2.837-45.
[7] On the change see *ibid.*, 841; and R. Kimelman, "Birkat Ha-Minim and the Lack of Evidence for an Anti-Christian Jewish Prayer in Late Antiquity," *Jewish and Christian Self-Definition* (ed. E. P. Sanders; Philadelphia: Fortress, 1981) 226-44, 391-403.
[8] The term first appears in *Massekhet Soferim* 16:9; see M. Maher, "The Meturgamanim and Prayer," *JJS* 51 (1990) 235-36. The term may be a twist on the phrase אין עמידה אלא תפילה (*b. Ber.* 6b, *y. Ber.* 4:1, 7a, *Gen. Rab.* 68:9).
[9] Semblances of twelve to thirteen of the blessings have appeared elsewhere, including *hekhalot* literature; see M. Bar-Ilan, *The Mysteries of Jewish Prayer and Hekhalot* (Ramat Gan: BarIlan University Press, 1987) 120-52, esp. 124 and 152; and J. Heinemann, *Prayer in the Period of the Tanna'im and the Amora'im* (Jerusalem: Magnes, 1964) 139-41 (Hebrew).
[10] On the possibility of fixed communal prayer in Second Temple times, see E. G. Chazon, "Prayers from Qumran and Their Historical Implications," *Dead Sea Discoveries* 1 (1994) 279-84.
[11] *b. Ber.* 28b; *b. Meg.* 17b, and *y. Ber.* 2:4, 4d. See N. G. Cohen, "The Nature of Shim'on Hapekuli's Act," *Tarbiz* 52 (1983) 547-56.

material as liturgy is by mandating a fixed sequence. Examples of such mandatory sequence are the Hallel, the lectionary reading of the Megillah, and the Shema.[12]

Many past attempts to uncover the underlying structure of the Amidah are predicated on the significance of the number 18 in the "Eighteen Blessings." These attempts include the drawing of correlations between the eighteen blessings and the eighteen vertebrae of the spine, or eighteen matters of the Sanctuary, or eighteen pivotal events in Jewish history, or eighteen select biblical texts.[13] R. Saadya Gaon provided no less than twelve reasons for this number of blessings.[14]

None of these correlations explain the literary structure of the Amidah. Indeed, the focus on the number eighteen as cipher of the Amidah diverts attention from the literary structure by presuming that the project of understanding the Amidah is like that of deciphering a code. The task of the literary understanding of the Amidah, however, is not to figure it out by reference to some external code, but rather to grasp the Amidah as a composition with its own internal agendum. Although the findings of philology along with historical and form-critical approaches are helpful in understanding individual blessing, they contribute little to the task of constructing the overall meaning of the Amidah. The overall meaning involves an additional concern with the interplay of ideas and rhetorical techniques.

The initial attempts to understand the literary structure of the Amidah were made by the first generation of talmudic rabbis known as amoraim. In the mid-third century, R. Joshua b. Levi argued that the structure of the Amidah consists of a beginning and ending triad of blessings of praise with a middle section constituting requests.[15] His contemporary, R. Hanina nuanced this scheme, saying:

> "The first [blessings] are like a slave who organizes his praise before his master; the middle are like a slave who requests his allotment from his master; and the latter are like a slave who received his allotment from his master and takes his leave."[16]

---

[12] *t. Ber.* 2:3-4, and *t. Meg.* 2:1-3.
[13] All of which are analyzed by L. Ginzberg, *A Commentary on the Palestinian Talmud* (4 vols.; New York: The Jewish Theological Seminary, 1941-1961) 3.238-62 (Hebrew).
[14] *Siddur Rav Saadya Gaon* (ed. I. Davidson, et al.; reprint, Jerusalem: Reuben Mass, 1970) 2, n. 14.
[15] *y. Ber.* 2:4, 4d. The characterization of the eighteen blessings in *Sifre Deut.* 343 (ed. Finkelstein, 394-395 = *Midrash Ha-Gadol* [ed. Fish, 650]), is similar and since anonymous probably contemporaneous.
[16] *b. Ber.* 34a. See Dan 6:11.

Although R. Hanina shares R. Joshua's characterization of the first two units, he sees the last unit as an implicit expression of gratitude in the context of making closing remarks. Some six hundred years later, R. Saadya Gaon, in contrast, argued that the first triad consists of gratitude for the past, the middle part consists of request for the future, whereas the last triad consists of acknowledgment of divine power.[17] Two centuries later in the 1100s, Maimonides refined R. Hanina's analysis by stating explicitly that the third part constitutes gratitude. His scheme states: "The first three blessings consists of praises of God, the last three of thanksgiving to Him, whereas the middle blessings are petitions."[18] Most subsequent discussions of the Amidah have taken their cue from Maimonides with his emphasis on the thanksgiving theme for the final triad.[19]

All of these schemes are based on the tripartite division of the Amidah and the assumption of a common modality of prayer for each unit such as praise or petition. The tripartite division creates an impression of symmetry. It divides the Amidah into two units of three and one of twelve. The emphasis on three conforms with that of other liturgical units created in the tannaitic period such as the Grace after Meals, the Shema and its blessings, and the three middle blessings of the High Holiday liturgy.[20]

The division based on the distinction between praise/thanksgiving and petition, however, is questionable. Unlike the number three, it does not account for other tannaitic liturgical units. It does not even account totally for the Amidah. According to it, the first triad should be exclusively praise, but, as we shall see, it contains oblique petitions for redemption and resurrection. The description of the last triad as only thanksgiving is also misleading. Blessing 18 begins with "May our eyes behold Your merciful return to Zion" while blessing 19 begins with "Grant peace." Clearly, this triad is as much petition as thanksgiving. In fact, there is a medieval tradition of characterizing the two triads as

---

[17] *Siddur Rav Saadya Gaon*, 3.
[18] Maimonides, *Mishneh Torah, Book of Love*, Laws of Prayer 1:4. In *ibid*. 1:2, proper prayer is composed of (1) praise, (2) petition, (3) praise and thanksgiving.
[19] Including *Midrash Ha-Gadol: Genesis* (ed. M. Margulies, 312; see Ginzberg, *Commentary* 3.241. An exception is the *Tur Orah Hayyim* 112 who repeats R. Hanina's formulation with the insertion שמשבחו ("for he had praised Him") before "and takes his leave."
[20] For the Grace after meals, see S. Lieberman, *Tosefta Ki-fshutah* (10 vols.; New York; The Jewish Theological Seminary, 1955-1988) 1.101; for the Shema' and its blessings, see R. Kimelman "The Shema' and Its Rhetoric: The Case for the Shema' Being More than Creation, Revelation, and Redemption," *Jewish Thought and Philosophy* 2 (1992) 111-32; for the High Holiday liturgy, see J. Heinemann, *Studies in Jewish Liturgy* (Jerusalem: Magnes, 1981) 54-55 (Hebrew).

petionary[21] as well as the whole Amidah.[22] Even if it were true that the opening triad were mostly praise, the last triad mostly thanksgiving, and the middle mostly petition, the formula praise-petition-thanksgiving would be too schematized for understanding the Amidah as presently constituted.[23]

In order to salvage the three-fold classification, it has been suggested that the requests in the opening and closing triad are collective as opposed to personal, as if to say that collective requests can be subsumed under the category of praise.[24] Salvaging the relevance of the traditional rubrics of praise and petition by categorizing collective petition under praise is problematic. The request for agricultural prosperity of blessing 9, for example, is no less collective than the request of God to return to Zion of blessing 18, or the request to grant peace of blessing 19. In fact, a major intertext of the Amidah, Psalm 103, mixes freely individual and collective concerns. As such, there is little reason to believe that the Amidah was originally constructed on the basis of a distinction between praise and petition. This is not to deny the fact that there are prayers that are total doxologies or praise,[25] but once petition is introduced the distinction becomes blurred. Praise, thanksgiving, and petition too often presume and entail each other.[26] The Bible is full of cases where "address, petition, motivation ... are all expressed via declarations of

---

[21] See *Sefer Ha-Manhig* (2 vols.; ed. Y. Rafael; Jerusalem: Mossad Harav Kook, 1978) 1.93 and n. 48; and L. Ginzberg, *Genizah Studies* (2 vols.; New York: Hermon, 1969) 2.512 (Hebrew).

[22] See *Siddur Rav Saadya Gaon*, 9 with Abramson, *Inyyanot Be-Sifrut Ha-Geonim* (Jerusalem: Mossad Harav Kook, 1974) 49, n. 17; and *Mishnat Rabbi Eliezer* (ed. H. G. Enelow, 232). See also Rashi, *b. Ber.* 4b. s.v., *zeh ha-somekah* = D. Abudarham, *Abudarham Ha-Shalem* (Jerusalem: Usha, 1963) 90, second paragraph.

[23] The mischaracterization of the Amidah as praise-petition-thanksgiving has been duly noted in the history of research. For the classical commentators, see *Sefer RAVYaH* (4 vols.; ed. A. Aptowitzer; Hevrat Mekize Nir-damim; reprint, Brooklyn, 1983) 1.72, n. 1. For the moderns, see *inter alios*, I. Elbogen, *Jewish Liturgy: A Comprehensive History* (ed. R. Scheindlin; Philadelphia: Jewish Publication Society, 1993) 49-50 (= *Ha-Tefillah Be-Yisrael Be-Hitpathut Ha-Historit* [ed. J. Heinemann, *et al.*; Tel Aviv: Dvir, 1972] 43), M. Liber, "Structure and History of the *Tefillah*," *JQR* 40 (1949) 334-35; Z. Yawitz, *Siddur Avodat Ha-Levavot and Sefer Maqor Ha-Berakot* (Jerusalem: Qiryah Ne'emanah, 1966) part 2, 66; and Heinemann, *Prayer*, 150-51.

[24] First noted by R. Hananel, *Oṣar Ha-Ge'onim* (ed. B. Lewin, 1.42 [*nispahim*]). For later comments, see *Tur Oraḥ Ḥayyim* 112 with commentaries; and *Shibolei Ha-Leqet Ha-Shalem* (ed. S. Mirsky; New York: Sura, 1966) 215.

[25] Such as the Sabbath liturgy of Qumran; see E. Chazon, "On the Special Character of Sabbath Prayer," 1-21.

[26] See E. Berkovits, "Prayer," *Studies in Torah Judaism* (ed. L. Stitskin; New York: KTAV, 1969) 127-28.

praise."²⁷ Frequently, what thanksgiving and praise are to the past, petition is to the future. Since they are so often intertwined in petitionary prayer, it is wiser to predicate the meaning of the clustering of blessing on content rather than on the nature of the formulation. Classifying by subject rather than by praise or petition allows for the possibility that even the blessings of the first triad could be formulated as petition, as indeed they are in some versions of the Genizah.²⁸

The Intermediate Blessings

Since the opening and closing triads of blessings are found in all versions of the Amidah and may have preceded the composition of the nineteen-blessing Amidah,²⁹ let us begin the literary analysis of the Amidah with its distinctive intermediate blessings.

These thirteen blessings consists of prayers for:

4. knowledge
5. return to God (= repentance)
6. forgiveness
7. deliverance
8. healing
9. year of (agricultural) prosperity
10. ingathering of the exiles
11. restoration of proper judges/leaders
12. destruction of the wicked
13. support of the righteous
14. rebuilding of Jerusalem
15. restoration of the Davidic line (the Palestinian ritual combines 14 and 15)
16. acceptance of prayer

The issue for the literary understanding of the liturgy is whether such an ostensibly disparate list of requests exhibits a pattern possessing

---

²⁷ Miller, They *Cried to the Lord: the Form and Function of Biblical Prayer* (Minneapolis: Fortress, 1994) 66.
²⁸ See J. Mann, "Genizah Fragments of the Palestinian Order of Service," *HUCA* 2 (1925) 310; and *Seder Ḥibbur Berakhot*, in A. I. Schechter, *Studies in Jewish Liturgy* (Philadelphia: Jewish Publication Society, 1930) 97-98.
²⁹ So L. Zunz, *Ha-Derashot Be-Yisrael* (ed. H. Albeck; Jerusalem: Mossad Bialik, 1947) 178; see Mirsky, *Ha-Piyyut*, 18-19.

a coherent conceptual framework. As noted above, the prerequisite for literary coherence is the establishment of a mandatory sequence. Once established, even the intermediate blessings became a single unit.[30] Building upon the efforts of late third century amoraim, the Talmud accounts for the sequence through a combination of logical linkages and biblical correspondences.[31] This oscillation between logical connections and verse correspondences provides a basis for the linear sequencing of each blessing of the intermediate blessings without providing for any single pattern or explanation of the petitions as a whole. The Amidah is treated just as the Mishnah. In both cases, the *amoraim* supply the verses that link the Mishnah to Scripture without supplying an overall scheme for its structure. The concern is rather with establishing the tannaitic text as derivative of Scripture.[32]

The medieval and modern periods produced several theories of the overall scheme of the Amidah. These theories explicate the Amidah in terms of its own internal agendum and not just in line with its biblical antecedents. In the tenth century, Saadya Gaon sees the petitions as examples of the full gamut of human needs, each one paradigmatic of a category.[33] In the twelfth century, Judah Halevi explains the linkage between blessings 4-7 and contends that the petitions are "about the needs of all Israel and about the needs of the individual contained within them."[34] Later in the century, Maimonides integrates these two positions, saying: "The intermediate blessings contain the request of all things, for they are archetypes of the desires of each person and the needs of the community."[35]

In the thirteenth century, Rabbenu Bahya b. Asher understood the first six as reflecting human needs and the second as reflecting the six stages of Israel's restoration to its former glory.[36] His contemporary, R.

---

[30] See Lieberman, *Tosefta Ki-fshutah*, 1:15, line 5; *Hidushei Ha-RaShBA, Megillah* (ed. H. Dimitrovsky, 100); and E. Levy, *Yesodot Ha-Tefillah* (Tel Aviv: Abraham Zioni, 1955) 153.

[31] See *y. Ber.* 2:4, 4d; *b. Meg.* 17b; and J. Mann, "Some Midrashic Genizah Fragments," *HUCA* 14 (1939) 322; along with Ginzberg, *Commentary*, 1.333; and Halivni, *Sources and Tradition: Seder Moed from Yoma to Hagiga* (Jerusalem: The Jewish Theological Seminary, 1975) 488-89. The lack of consistency is noted by the commentaries to *Tur Orah Hayyim* 113-119, especially *Derisha* to *siman* 115.

[32] See J. Neusner, *Judaism in Society: The Evidence of the Yerushalmi* (Chicago: University of Chicago Press, 1983) 79.

[33] *Siddur Rav Saadya Gaon*, 6.

[34] *Kuzari* 3.17-19.

[35] Maimonides, *Mishneh Torah*, Laws of Prayer 1.4. See *Sefer Hasidim*, ed. J. Wistinetaki, p. 393.

[36] Rabbenu Bahye, *ad* Deut 11:13; and *idem*, *Kad Ha-Qemah*, s.v., "tefillah," *Kitvei Rabbenu Bahye* (ed. Chavel) 435.

Jacob (or Yehiel) b. Asher, allocates the first set of six (4-9) to individual needs and the last set of six (10-15) to collective needs. He adds the idea that both sets are structured sequentially. The first set represents a sequence of developments in the life of the individual; the second in the life of the nation. He also sees an artful symmetrical arrangement between 4-9 and 10-15 that reveals a causal relationship. Thus blessing 4 does not only precede blessing 5, but is linked to blessing 10. Similarly, blessing 5 does not only precede blessing 6, but is linked to blessing 11 and so on up to 9 and 15.[37]

Although this theory of the relationship between the two sets did not strike roots in subsequent scholarship, the division into two sets of six has become the basis of much of the modern discussion.[38] The theory of an internal sequence within each set also has much to say for it and will be developed later on. The division into two sets of six was further divided by Eliezer Levi, over a generation ago, into two triads each, the first comprising spiritual (4-6) and physical (7-9) needs, whereas the second comprising the prerequisites of national rebuilding (10-12) and the elements of their realization (13-15).[39] The symmetry of dividing twelve blessings into sets of six that in turn are divided into units of three is most impressive.

Other comprehensive theories for the intermediate blessings include seeing them as replicating the rite of expiation of the blood offering on the altar,[40] or as reflecting the future collective needs of the messianic era,[41] or as modeled on Greek civic prayers,[42] or as reflecting the kabbalistic sefirotic system.[43] Not dealing with the Amidah as a literary unit with its own internal agenda, these theories need not detain us. A recent ambitious comprehensive theory that grasps the Amidah in literary terms is that of Ezra Fleischer. He describes the intermediate blessings as:

---

[37] Cited in *Abudarham*, 107-108.
[38] See Zunz, *Ha-Derashot Be-Yisrael*, 179; and Elbogen, *Jewish Liturgy*, 28 (Hebrew, 24).
[39] E. Levy, *Torat Ha-Tefillah*,' 103, 110.
[40] See S. R. Hirsch, *Siddur Tefillot Yisrael* (Jerusalem: Mossad Harav Kook, 1992) 74-75; and E. Munk, *The World of Prayer* (2 vols.; New York: Feldheim, 1961) 1.123.
[41] L. Liebreich, "The Intermediate Benedictions of the Amidah," *JQR* 42 (1951/52) 423-26. Also Kadushin argues that blessings 7, 10, 11, 15, and 17 are "future events ... subsumed under the concept of the days of Messiah or of the world to come" (*Worship and Ethics*, 113).
[42] So Y. Baer, *Yisrael Be-Amim* (Jerusalem: Mossad Bialik, 1955) 32; and E. J. Bickerman, "The Civic Prayer for Jerusalem" *HTR* 55 (1962) 163-85.
[43] A comprehensive example of this genre is R. Meir Ibn Gabbai, *Avodat Ha-Qodesh* (Jerusalem: Levine-Epstein, 1953/1954 [5714]) 30c-32d.

a chronologically organized plan, in logical sequence, for the rebuilding of the nation from its post-destruction historical reality to its spiritual and political restoration in the ideal future .... Thus they pray that God grant them the knowledge to understand their situation ("He who grants knowledge" [blessing 4]), to know why their world fell apart, and their temple was destroyed, and their independence taken from them. Were they granted the knowledge – they would realize that their iniquities caused their punishment and they would repent ("He who desires repentance" [blessing 5]); by the merit of their repentance God would make atonement for their iniquities and forgive them ("He who multiplies repentance" [blessing 6]). The pardoning of their iniquities would open the gate to the repair of their condition. God would redeem them (in the present) from every trouble, adversary, and tribulation ("He who redeems Israel" [blessing 7]), and heal their sick ("He who heals His people Israel" [blessing 8]), and give them sustenance to endure their subjugation until the end time ("He who blesses the years"). Up to here, the repair of the national condition in the present, which is temporary, necessary but not sufficient for the true repair of the nation is not in the present but the future, in which, at the end of a gradual and slow process, she shall return to her former state and merit again her independence. This eschatological process has the following stages," [i.e., the next cluster of blessings].[44]

The advantage of this reading of blessings 4-9 is that it consists of a single story line somewhat parallel to blessings 10-15. The result is the appearance of the middle section being divided into two symmetrical halves. Indeed, Fleischer goes on to say that the first half is really an introductory blessing plus five, whereas the second part consists of five blessings plus a concluding one. What begins as a set of 1+5 ends as set of 5+1. The resultant symmetry is as impressive as that of Levi's above. The disadvantage lies not in its literary structure, but in the anchoring of its meaning in historical events. The cogency of the analysis is too dependent upon the Amidah being composed in the immediate wake of the destruction of the Temple in 70 C.E. and as a reaction to it. Predicating literary analysis on too close an adherence to a historical happening is always fraught with danger. Modern literary analysis has repeatedly shown the gap between historical happenings and their literary formulation. Too often, a single literary formulation fits too many different historical backgrounds. A blessing for knowledge, for example, is far too common to be limited to a specific historical moment in time. As such, it is a staple of Qumran, Christian, and Jewish prayer without any connection to any specific event in history.[45] In this regard,

---

[44] Fleischer, "The Shemone Esre," 198.
[45] See M. Weinfeld, "The Prayers for Knowledge, Repentance, and Forgiveness in the Eighteen Benedictions," *Tarbiz* 48 (1979) 194-95 (Hebrew); and *The Thanksgiving Scroll* (ed. Licht) 42-43.

Fleischer reverts to the discredited classic critical-historical method that reduces liturgical formulations to reflexes of historical events.[46]

An added difficulty of the analysis is the reliance on the peroration (ḥitum/ḥatimah) of the blessings without due consideration of their content. Although any analysis of the blessing must be based on the peroration as the key to its meaning as well as its most stable part, it may not disregard the body of the blessing whatever its variations. Only by such disregard of the body of the fourth blessing could Fleischer possibly consider the knowledge therein to be of their political plight and the theological explanation thereof. On the contrary, the Amidah makes no explicit reference to the destruction nor to any explanation. At most, the destruction and exile only become implicit in blessings ten to fifteen which deal with the restoration. Since they do not even enter the consciousness of the worshiper till after the first six intermediate blessings, they cannot be used to explain any of them, surely not the first. Without reference to such knowledge or its explanation elsewhere in the Amidah, no reader could be expected to grasp the point of the blessing. By comparing the theme of the daily Amidah with the "Because of our sins we were exiled from our land," motif of the *Musaf* pilgrimage holiday liturgy, Fleischer mistakenly reads the former through the prism of the latter. In actuality, the absence of any direct reference to the destruction and exile is one of the remarkable characteristics of the Amidah. Whatever the importance of parallels, analysis must not lose sight of the distinctiveness of each composition.

Fleischer is right, however, to emphasize how much the meaning of a blessing is derivative of sequence. He repeatedly underscores the meaning of a blessing in the light of its location in the Amidah. In the case of 4 and 5, however, the divinely granted knowledge of the former is not to be applied to their social and religious reality, but to the Torah of the latter.[47]

---

[46] For critiques of this approach, see Sarason's discussion of "Historical-Philological Studies" in his "On the Use of Method in the Modern Study of Jewish Liturgy," esp. 116; and Kimelman, "Liturgical Studies in the 90's," *Jewish Book Annual* 52 (1994-1995/5755) 61-67. A recent effort at the "historicizing" of the Amidah is that of Flusser, "Some of the Precepts of the Torah from Qumran (4QMMT) and the Benediction Against the Heretics," *Tarbiz* 61 (1992) 366-74 (Hebrew), with regard to blessings 11-13.

[47] As noted by Halevy, *Kuzari* 3:19 (ed. Even-Shmuel, 116, bottom) and made explicit in the beginning of the interpolation in the Amidah at the conclusion of Sabbaths and festivals, אתה חוננתנו למדע תורתך according to the Ashkenazic version (see Sirkes, ב"ח to *Tur Oraḥ Ḥayyim*, 294), and Genizah versions such as: חננו אבינו דעה מאתך / ובינה והשכל מתורתך (*JQR* 10 [1898] 657, lines 1-2); תורתך אבינו הבינו דעה לתלמוד (S. Assaf, "Me-Seder Ha-Tefillah Be-Eretz Yisrael," *Sefer Dinaburg* [ed. I. Baer; Jerusalem, 1949] 117); דעה ותבונה תתן בלבינו / הבינינו לשמור פקודיך.

His contention that blessings 7-9 constitute a remedy of the national condition is also difficult. Whereas all agree that the meaning of blessing 7 is problematic (see *infra*), it is hard to imagine that blessings of healing and of agricultural prosperity would become symptomatic of the national condition in the wake of the destruction. Blessings on healing and agricultural prosperity are far too general and universal to be locked into any specific historical condition. Indeed, they are probably not even specific to Israel. Although the Babylonian version of blessing 8 does conclude with "He who heals the sick of His people Israel," the Palestinian version has only "He who heals the sick."[48] Similarly, the prosperity of blessing 9 is brought about by proper rainfall for the world in general and not just for the Land of Israel.[49] Indeed were these the two salient deficiencies of post-Temple Israel, their cure would have been prominent in the upcoming eschatological blessings. Instead there is no mention of them at all. There is thus insufficient reason to limit blessings 8-9 to any specific historical context.

Fleischer's theory in general assumes that the Babylonian version is closer to the original. Babylon, for him, was more conservative and more meticulous with regard to halakhic obligation while free from the liturgical ferment spawned by the religious poetry that was constantly tampering with liturgical texts in Palestine.[50] He argues against their being a fluid text, asserting that it would be an impossible demand of the people to have to utter eighteen blessings in a fixed sequence daily without a fixed text. In my opinion, the differences between what passes as the Babylonian and Palestinian rescensions are too great to permit the

---

(Fleischer, *Eretz-Israel Prayers and Prayer Rituals as Portrayed in the Genizah Documents* [Jerusalem: Magnes, 1988] 71 [Hebrew]); and חנינו דיעה מאתך / ולמדנו בינה מתורתך (N. Wieder, "The Old Palestinian Ritual – New Sources," *JJS* 4 [1953] 36); see also Y. Luger, *Weekday 'Amidah Based on the Genizah*, 1.84-85.

[48] For the Babylonian, see *b. Shabb* 12a. For the Palestinian, see *j. Ber.* 2:4, 5a; *Sifre Deut.* 343 (ed. Finkelstein, 395, lines 5-6). Even *b. 'Abod. Zar.* 8a, dubs the blessing ברכת החולים ("the blessing of the sick").

[49] Thus the emphasis on "earth" as opposed to "land," as noted by Ginzberg, *Commentary*, 1.323, bottom, and as evidenced by the versions of *Siddur Rav Saadya Gaon*, 21; *Seder Rav Amram Gaon* (ed. D. Goldschmidt; Jerusalem: Mossad Harav Kook, 1871) 25, lines 29-30; and Maimonides, *Liturgy*, in D. Goldschmidt, *On Jewish Liturgy* (Jerusalem: Magnes, 1980) 199, line 15 (Hebrew); and *Minhag Benei Roma*, (Goldschmidt, *Liturgy*, 158) which all contain a version of the following: ושבע את העולם כולו מברכות טובך ורוה פני תבל מעושר מתנות ידיך ("and satiate the whole world from the blessings of Your goodness and fill the face of the earth from the wealth of the gifts of Your hand" [*Siddur Rav Saadya Gaon*, 21]). On whether the liturgical text is actually that of R. Saadya, see N. Cohen, "For the Original Character of the Siddur of Rav Saadya Gaon," *Sinai* 95 (1984) 249-68 (Hebrew).

[50] Fleischer, "On the Beginnings of Obligatory Jewish Prayer," *Tarbiz* 59 (1990) 440.

assumption of a single fixed text.[51] Still, the argument that the common person could not be expected to pray daily such a long prayer without a fixed text makes sense. The problem lies with our ignorance of when the Amidah moved from the academy to the synagogue. To argue, as Fleischer does, from Rabban's Gamaliel's ruling about the daily praying of eighteen blessings to a pervasive, yea universal, practice in the late first century is far too facile. Fleischer's picture of Rabban Gamaliel's authority in particular and of the rabbis in general is based on realities that were emerging in the third century, not the first.[52] And even when the Amidah became a synagogue norm, it may not yet have become a widely practiced individual obligation beyond the academy. As the practice spread there arose the need for a more fixed formulation of the Yavnean order. One of the formulations achieved hegemony in Palestine, the other in Babylon, though an absolute division of the two is unwarranted by the evidence.[53] It is thus quite possible that the two rescensions in their basic formulation are coeval, neither being the sole original text. My analysis of the redemption theme is primarily based on the Babylonian rescension with an eye to the Palestinian.

Nonetheless, I agree with Fleischer's effort at clustering the blessings into units in order to discern a coherent conceptual framework. The more common way of dividing the first section, however, is to subsume the first half (4-6) under the rubric of spiritual/moral needs and the second half (7-9) under the rubric of material/physical needs, as if to confirm Seneca's counsel: "Pray for a sound mind and for good health, first of the soul and then of the body."[54]

The problem with this division is the subsuming of blessing 7 under material needs. The difficulty with most theories of coherence lies in determining the meaning of the deliverance in blessing 7 and in deciding whether it should be aligned with the preceding blessings (4-6) or with the succeeding ones (8-9). An alternative, which supports the latter division, holds that blessing 7 is linked with what follows, since the deliverance here connotes the future resurrection that will be

---

[51] See the comprehensive discussion of Luger, *Weekday 'Amidah Based on the Genizah*, 1.2-7.

[52] On the Gamalielian Patriarchate, see D. Goodblatt, *The Monarchic Principle: Studies in Jewish Self-Government in Antiquity* (Tübingen: J. C. B. Mohr, 1994) 131-75. On the growth of rabbinic authority from the second to the third century, compare the chapter "Rabbinic Authority in Galilee," in M. Goodman, *State and Society in roman Galilee A.D. 132-212* (Totowa, NJ: Rowman & Allanheld, 1983) 93-118 with Kimelman, "Rabbi Yohanan and the Professionalization of the Rabbinate."

[53] See Luger, *Weekday 'Amidah Based on the Genizah*, 1.7-14.

[54] Seneca, *Epistulae Morales*, 10.4, cited by Kaminka, *Meḥqarim Ba-Talmud* (Tel Aviv, 1951) 62.

accompanied by a healing of persons as well as of the land.[55] Others, however, find it hard to conceive of it as national or universal in scope, or linked to resurrection, since it follows three blessings that deal with the individual situation, and since it may once have served as a blessing of gratitude for release from tribulation, prison, or captivity.[56] Such a background bespeaks its individual orientation.

Preceded by a blessing on forgiveness and succeeded by one on healing, the deliverance theme denotes a personal spiritual deliverance, a deliverance experienced as a healing of the soul.[57] This understanding of deliverance as personal salvation is seconded by a midrash that correlates the eighteen benedictions and the prayer of Hannah (1 Sam 2:1-10). By correlating "I rejoice in Your salvation" (1 Sam 2:1) with blessing 6 on forgiveness, the midrash underscores the role of forgiveness in the scenario of personal redemption.[58]

There is much to be said for understanding this deliverance as individual. First, the biblical roots of the blessing reinforce the individual dimension of the deliverance theme. According to Ps 103:3-4, the reasons for "blessing the Lord for all His benefits" include His forgiving iniquity, healing diseases, and redeeming life from the pit. These themes correspond respectively to blessings 6, 8, and 7.[59] According to the Talmud, this would have been the order were it not for the verse, "His heart will understand, repent, and be healed" (Isa 6:10), implying that in the wake of understanding (blessing 4) and repentance (blessing 5) comes healing – the healing of forgiveness.[60] It is this healing which generates the sense of redemption that is incorporated in blessing 7.[61]

---

[55] Ginzberg, *Commentary*, 1.323; see Luger, *Weekday 'Amidah Based on the Genizah*, 1.122.
[56] See Elbogen, *Jewish Liturgy*, 31 (Hebrew, 27); and E. Urbach, *The Sages: The World and Wisdom of the Rabbis of the Talmud* (Cambridge, MA: Harvard University Press, 1987) 654-55, translation of *The Sages: Their Concepts and Beliefs* (Jerusalem: Magnes, 1969) 590-91 (Hebrew). Note that *Siddur Rav Saadya Gaon*, 7, describes blessing 7 as "redemption and liberation."
[57] *Abudarham*, 107.
[58] *Yalqut Shim'oni* 2:80.
[59] Following Mirsky, "The Origin of the Eighteen Benediction of the Daily Prayer," *Ha-Piyyut*, 18-29. *b. Yoma* 86a records several passages that make explicit the connections among repentance, redemption, and recovery.
[60] רפואה דסליחה *b. Meg.* 17b and *y. Ber.* 2:4, 4d. The word for forgiveness, סליח, comes from the Akkadian word for "asperse," salahu, which is also a common term for healing; see J. Milgrom, *Numbers: The JPS Torah Commentary* (Philadelphia: Jewish Publication Society, 1990) 396. In fact, *Siddur Rav Saadya Gaon*, 7, line 5 explains ורפא לו by יסלח לו.
[61] The subsequent explanation there (*b. Meg.* 17b and *y. Ber.* 2:4, 4d) that redemption marks the seventh blessing because redemption will come in the seventh (year?) supports the collective understanding of redemption. The

The initial step in this process is shared by the psalmist: "O Lord, have mercy on me, heal my soul, for I have sinned against You" (Ps 41:5). The next step is spelled out in *The Prayer of Manasseh:* "You, O Lord .... In the multitude of Your mercies appointed repentance as the salvation for sinners."[62]

Second, the link between redemption and forgiveness is tightened in a Genizah version of blessing 6. This version juxtaposes a verse on redemption (Ps 34:23) with a reworked one on forgiveness (1 Kings 8:34-36). The first two strophes state: "The Lord redeems the soul of his servants / and forgives the sin of his beloved."[63]

Finally, and most conclusively, the talmudic abridgment of the Amidah, the *Havinenu*, also tightens the link between forgiveness and deliverance from sin by condensing blessings 6 and 7 into the single phrase "forgive us in order that we may be delivered."[64] The fact that blessings 6 and 7 are conflated into one,[65] whereas every other blessing has its own phrase, further underscores the link between forgiveness and redemption. This abridgment, which serves as the earliest commentary on the Amidah, makes clear that rather than starting a new unit, blessing 7 caps blessing 6 by pointing to the redemption, which is spawned by forgiveness, in the belief that God "will redeem Israel from all their iniquities" (Ps 130:8). This linkage between personal salvation and

---

difficulty is that it reverts to the code modality of explanation whereas the individual understanding is based on the literary structure of the Amidah. The juxtaposition of the two explanations indicates that the debate over its orientation is talmudic. Both orientations have textual support. The collective orientation emphasizes that the subject is גאולה שלימה "complete redemption" as opposed to the individual orientation; see Luger, *Weekday 'Amidah Based on the Genizah*, 1.191-92. Although, as Heinemann, *Prayer*, 141, notes, the blessing on its own can be read both ways, it is the literary structure and context that argues for its individual orientation.

[62] *The Old Testament Pseudepigrapha* (2 vols.; ed. James H. Charlesworth; Garden City, NY: Doubleday, 1983, 1985) 2.636. See Bickerman, "The Civic Prayer for Jerusalem," 172-73.

[63]
1. פודה ה' נפש עבדיו
2. וסולח לחטאת ידידיו
3. בא"י המרבה לסלח

See A. Marmorstein, "Mitteilungen zur Geschichte und Literatur aus der Geniza," *MGWJ* 68 (1924) 38-39; and idem, "The Attitude of the Jews Towards Early Christianity," *The Expositor* 49 (1923) 386. The synonymy of פקדה and סולח is apparent in two parallel midrashic texts where one reads ואושיעם ואפדם מעונות (*Midrash Tanhuma*, end of vayera') and the other ואני סולח לעונותיהם (*Midrash Tanhuma* (ed. S. Buber, end of *vayera'*).

[64] תסלח לנו להיות גאולים, as in *b. Ber.* 29a, or סלח לנו גואלינו, as in *y. Ber.* 4:3, 8a.

[65] This holds throughout the many textual variants; see J. Hadani, "Havinenu: Tefillah Qesarah Me'en Shemoneh Esreh," *Sinai* 100 (1987) 305; and Abramson, "Le-Toledot Ha-Siddur," *Sinai* 81 (1977) 202.

forgiveness is tied tight in the midrash that understands, "The Lord is ... my salvation" (Ps 27:1), to refer to "the Day of Atonement when He saves us and forgives us all our sins."[66]

The sequence of blessings 6 and 7 finds its biblical parallel, according to one source, in a verse that is also central to the High Holiday liturgy: "I wiped away your sins like a cloud, your transgression like mist. Return to Me, for I redeem you" (Isa 44:22).[67] Such is the redemption/salvation that ensues from the removal of sins and the return to God. The location of blessing 5 makes the case for the centrality of Torah and service/prayer in this process of personal redemption:

	a	b	c
1.	Bring us back	our Father	to Your Torah.
2.	Draw us near	our King	to Your service.
3.	Lead us back	in complete repentance	before You.

The rhetoric of the blessing is a rhetoric of return. Its first strophe is based on the parallel drawn by Nehemiah between "returning ... to You" (Neh 9:26) and "returning ... to Your Torah" (Neh 9:29), the point being that the return to God is through the Torah. The persuasiveness of this point is enhanced by associating the two elements of Torah and return with the addressee "our Father." Through both – "bring us back," and "our Father" – the case is made that one need not start over to repent, only to recommit to what was once one's own. The idea that repentance entails the recovery of lost ground smoothes the path for such a return. The argument is strengthened through the use of the same term *teshuvah* for both return and repentance.[68]

The second strophe is so rich with associations that it defies any single construction.[69] Biblically, it could mean "grant us access to the Temple/cult service," since "to draw near" is the technical term for access to the Temple, whereas "service" (*'avodah*) is the technical term for

---

[66] *Midrash Ps.* 27:4. Compare the contemporaneous explanation of the apothegm of Epicurus, "The knowledge of sin is the beginning of salvation," by Seneca: "For he who does not know that he has sinned does not desire correction" (*Epistulae Morales* 28.9).

[67] So Mann, "Some Midrashic Genizah Fragments," 322, n. 128.

[68] The same rhetoric of return appears in the description of the Torah as an "inheritance" (Deut 33:4); see *Sifre Deut.* 345.

[69] J. Yaqar, *Perush Ha-Tefillot Ve-Ha-Berakhot* (2 vols.; Jerusalem: Meorei Yisrael, 1968) 1.45, shows the links of *'avodah* with Torah, *mitsvot,* and prayer. See Ramban to Deut 6:13.

the cult.[70] The meaning of drawing near is retained in its Qumran and rabbinic use in the sense of gaining admission.[71] In the pilgrimage holiday liturgy, however, it refers to the Sinaitic revelation.[72] There as here, God is addressed as "our king."[73] A similar expression appears at the end of the second blessing before the Shema.[74] As a post-Temple formulation, however, the connotation of "service" points more to the general service of God, as it appears in the *Haggadah*,[75] or to prayer as the service of the heart, as it appears elsewhere in rabbinic literature.[76] There is also the association with *m. Avot* 1:2 where "the world/age stands on three things: Torah, *'avodah*, and acts of piety." This tripartite statement parallels significantly the three in our blessing: Torah, *'avodah*, and repentance. In both cases, the term *'avodah* bears a similar range of associations.[77] Even if the rabbinic meanings are foregrounded here, the appropriation of biblical cultic terminology for communal prayer keeps the cultic connotation close to consciousness.[78] As such, the use of *'avodah* for worship reinforces the policy of replacing the daily Tamid-sacrifice by fixed communal prayer[79] along with making the point that God is now as accessible through communal prayer as He once was through the cult.

The equation of the value of prayer and the cult is made in blessing 17 where the word for "prayer" (*tefillah*) is interpolated into an ancient

---

[70] See Milgrom, *Studies in Levitical Terminology* (Berkeley: University of California Press, 1970) 37, 87.
[71] See Lieberman, "The Discipline in the So-Called Dead Sea Manual of Discipline," *JBL* 71 (1952) 202, n. 36. Cf. Hillel, *m. Avot* 1:12.
[72] וקרבתנו מלכנו לעבודתך; see *Maḥzor Sukkot Shemini Aseret Ve-Simhat Torah* (ed. D. Goldschmidt; Jerusalem: Koren, 1981) 9-11.
[73] For the use of "King" in this blessing and the next, see M. Friedman, "Notes by a Disciple in Maimonides' Academy Pertaining to Beliefs and Concepts and Halakha," *Tarbiz* 62 (1993) 547-50 (Hebrew).
[74] וקרבתנו לשמך הגדול (*Seder Rav Amram Gaon*, 14, line 29).
[75] מתחילה עובדי עבודה זרה היו אבותינו ועכשיו קרבנו המקום לעבודתו ("Initially our fathers were idol-worshipers, but now God has brought us close to His service"); see E. D. Goldschmidt, *The Passover Haggadah: Its Sources and History* (Jerusalem: Bialik, 1960) 13-14 (Hebrew).
[76] *Sifre Deut.* 41 (ed. Finkelstein, 86.)
[77] See Goldin, "The Three Pillars of Simeon the Righteous," *PAAJR* 17 (1958) 43-58.
[78] The double entendre is caught by *Sifre Deut.* 85, in glossing Deut 13:5 ואותו תעבודו ("And you shall serve Him") by עבדו בתורתו עבדו במקדש ("Serve Him through His Torah; serve Him through His Temple"). On this use of polysemy, see Kimelman, "The Seduction of Eve and the Exegetical Politics of Gender," *Biblical Interpretation* 4 (1996) 33, n. 75.
[79] *b. Ber.* 26b. On the subject of fixed prayer in Rabbinic Judaism and in Qumran, see B. Nitzan, *Qumran Prayer and Religious Poetry* (Leiden: Brill, 1994) Part I.

blessing on the Temple service (*'avodah*) twice.⁸⁰ The result is an *a b a b* structure that alternates between "prayer" and "service":

1. Be pleased, Lord our God, with Your people Israel and with their *tefillah*
2. Return the *'avodah* to the Temple precincts
3. Accept willingly and with love the offerings of Israel and their *tefillah*
4. May the Tamid offering of the *'avodah* of Israel, Your people, be acceptable to You ....⁸¹

By alternating *tefillah* and *'avodah*, the blessing creates an equivalency between them. It also intersperses forms of the technical term for the acceptance of a sacrifice (*le-raṣon*) three times.⁸² They are rendered above as "be pleased," "accept willingly," and "be acceptable."⁸³ The location of this blessing at the head of the last triad of the Amidah guarantees that the Amidah is the prayer being referred to by the term *tefillah*, as it was then called.

Returning to blessing 5: Note that whereas strophes 1 and 2 are parallel, adhering to a pattern of *a b c*, strophe 3 reverses the order of *b* and *c*. The reversal makes the blessing conclude with "before You." The result is that the return to Torah and the drawing near to the service of God become the means for the complete repentance that is epitomized by being brought "before You."⁸⁴

The significance of the location of this blessing on Torah in the redemptive scheme is seen through a comparison of blessing 7 with the biblical mint whence it was coined:

---

⁸⁰ For versions of the blessing that make no mention of *tefillah*, see *Lev. Rab.* (ed. Margulies, 1:151, 5:89); Fleischer, *Eretz-Yisrael Prayer*, 72, line 16; and Rashi *b. Yoma* 68b, s.v., *ve-'al ha-'avodah*.

⁸¹
1. רצה ה' אלהינו בעמך ישראל ובתפילתם
2. והשב את העבודה לדביר ביתך
3. ואישי ישראל ותפילתם באהבה תקבל ברצון
4. ותהי לרצון תמיד עבודת ישראל עמך

⁸² Lev 1:4, 19:7; Isa 57:7.
⁸³ The analysis follows Hoffman, *Beyond the Text*, 109.
⁸⁴ This emphasis on Torah distinguishes it from the parallel sentiments in the Qumran Thanksgiving Scroll (ed. Licht, 7, lines 26-27) and Psalm 51. Psalm 25 does have the whole scenario in embryo, albeit dispersed, as pointed out by Weinfeld, "The Prayers for Knowledge, Repentance, and Forgiveness in the Eighteen Benedictions," 186-200.

Ps 119:153-54	Blessing
A. See my affliction and rescue me,	A. See our affliction
B. for I have not neglected Your Torah.	
C. Champion my cause and redeem me.	C. Champion our cause and redeem us.

Besides the standard change from Bible to liturgy and of singular to plural, both Psalm and blessing assume that redemption is grounded in Torah. What the former has to state, the latter, by virtue of its strategic position in the order of the Amidah, can presume.

In sum, the individual deliverance motif of blessing 7 extends the personal redemptive scenario to four blessings: the understanding graciously granted by God in blessing 4 is pressed into the return to Torah, etc., of blessing 5, which in turn sparks the awareness of sin that leads to the seeking of forgiveness of blessing 6, which in turn paves the way for the atonement of personal redemption[85] of blessing 7.[86]

---

[85] Parallel to the פדוח נפשו that precedes the second cup of the Passover *Haggadah*. Similarly, a prayer of the Qumran *Thanksgiving Scroll* (6:3-6) begins: ואתה אלי פדיתה נפש עבדך בחסדיכה ... ("And You my God have redeemed the soul of Your servant in Your kindness ...") and then goes on to spell out the redemption of the soul: וחזקתני מעוון וטהרתני מאשמה / ואדעה כי יש מקוה לשבי פשע ("And You will cleanse me of iniquity and purify me of guilt / and I will know that there is hope for those who repent of sin").

[86] Also Marmorstein says: "The prayers for knowledge, return to God, forgiveness of sin, and redemption belong formally and logically together. Wisdom and learning lead to repentance, repentance to the step leading to forgiveness of sin. Atonement causes redemption. These are preparatory means of the eschatological benedictions X-XVI" ("A Misunderstood Question in the Yerushalmi," *JQR* 20 [1929/30] 319). I differ only with regard to the relationship between the sections. For me, the experience of personal redemption, restoration of health, and agricultural revival function more as grist for belief in the eschatological blessings than as "preparatory means" for the latter. Otherwise, physical and agrarian recovery would also have to be considered "preparatory means" for the eschaton, a reading that both of us reject. For my objections, see the discussion of Fleischer above. Bickerman sees "benedictions 4-7 form[ing] a group centered on the idea of sin" ("The Civic Prayer for Jerusalem," 172). For him, blessing 7 is also about personal redemption and not national (see Mann, "Genizah Fragments," 296, 310) or extrication from daily tribulations (see Halevy, *Kuzari* 3:19; Rashi to *b. Meg.* 17b, s.v., *athalta*; and apparently *Mishnat Rabbi Eliezer*, 230). B. Bokser argues that the idea of personal redemption was introduced into the Passover celebration by the Palestinian Talmud, by presenting a "personalized dimension of redemption which addresses each individual" ("Changing Views of Passover and the Meaning of Redemption according to the Palestinian Talmud," *AJS Review* 10 [1985] 18). Thus, Rav (*y. Pesaḥ.* 10:4, 37d) applies the mishnaic ruling to start the recitation from the Bible with the disgrace and end it with the glory to the transition from idolatry to true worship. For him, this is evidence that the Palestinian Talmud "defines redemption as the release from the false ideology of idolatry" (15).

After the four blessing unit delineating the process of personal redemption come blessings 8 and 9. Some think they are juxtaposed because after praying for "the redemption of his soul and health for his body, one prays for sustenance to preserve the life of body and soul."[87] This fails to do justice to the specifics of blessings 8 and 9, which focus not only on the substance of health and sustenance but also on the restoration of bodily vigor along with the maintenance and revival of agricultural prosperity. Both are presented as divine involvements in the natural process, comparable to redemption. As the midrash says, "As the sick looks to relief, so Israel looks to redemption."[88] For the worshiper, they evidence in the natural realm the same reversal of destiny or saving grace that is available in the human realm through personal redemption. Indeed, the themes of seasonal revival and healing the sick are also associated with resurrection in blessing 2, as we shall see, as well as in those versions of the blessing for the new month that pray for "timely rains, complete recovery, and speedy redemption."

The rhetoric of these blessings flows through the furrows plowed by the biblical rhetoric of redemption. As there so here, physical and natural transformations are deemed indicative of historical transformations. If the desert can bloom, can the flowering of Israel's redemption be far off, asks Isaiah who goes on to predict (Isa 35:6,10):

> The lame shall leap like deer ...
> Waters shall burst forth in the desert ....
> And the ransomed of the Lord shall return, and come with shouting to Zion.

In all, the first two units of the intermediate blessings (4-9) present three accessible dimensions of redemption in order to sustain the hope

---

[87] *Abudarham*, 107.
[88] *Midrash Zutta*, (ed. Buber, 12b, *ad* Song 2:4). For the parallel structure or homology between healing and redeeming, see, Jer 8:22, 30:17. For the comparison between the wondrous nature of sustenance and that of redemption, see *Gen. Rab.* 20:9 (ed. Theodor-Albeck), 192 with notes.

for the not yet available national redemption.[89] By locating the former (4-9) before the latter (10-15), the plausibility of the latter is enhanced.[90]

The necessity of enhancing the plausibility of the upcoming unit of blessings (10-15) is due to the absence of any correlate in available experience. Being eschatological, the unit delineates the order of national redemption. It commences with the great shofar's blast of freedom, announcing the ingathering of the exiles, and culminates in the return of God to Jerusalem. Since the motifs are all biblical,[91] the liturgical contribution lies in their linguistic formulation, in their sequencing of events, and in their emphasis on divine involvement. All three converge to make the point that God alone is the redeemer.

Linguistically, these blessings weave threads of verses from Isaiah, Micah, Zephaniah, Jeremiah, Ezekiel, Joel, Malachi, and Psalms into a liturgical tapestry. There is hardly a word not pronounced by the prophets.[92] By reformulating their prophecies into requests, "It is as if the Deity were reminded of his promise and asked to fulfill it."[93]

The eschatological sequence of the Amidah does not match any antecedent or contemporary scenario.[94] It is not dictated by any single biblical text[95] nor paralleled by any other post-biblical scenario[96] or, for that matter, any other rabbinic liturgical formulation of eschatology.[97]

---

[89] Indeed, blessing 9 (ברכת השנים) was constantly tampered with, especially in allegedly Palestinian texts, by insertions of pleas for future redemption; see Marmorstein, "A Misunderstood Question in the Yerushalmi," 319. For opposition to such insertions, see *Siddur Rav Saadya Gaon*, 22; and Heinemann, *Studies in Jewish Liturgy*, 112, 114. Such insertions resulted in an association between agricultural prosperity and redemption as in the following Genizah version: "Bless for us O Lord our God this year for good with all types of produce and bring nigh quickly the end [?] year of our redemption;" see Luger, *Weekday 'Amidah Based on the Genizah*, 1.122.
[90] In this sense personal redemption does have a messianic meaning; cf. G. Scholem, *The Messianic Idea in Judaism* (New York: Schocken, 1971) 194.
[91] For the biblical and extrabiblical models, see Weinfeld, "Mesopotamian Eschatological Prophecies," *Shenaton* 3 (1978) 263-76 (Hebrew).
[92] See Yawitz, *Siddur*, part 2, 75-77; and Levy, *Torat Ha-Tefillah*, 115-122. b. *Meg*. 17b-18a and *y*. *Ber*. 2:4, 4d understand the sequencing of the Amidah as a function of verses from Isaiah, Ezekiel, Hosea, and Psalms.
[93] Finkelstein, "The Development of the Amidah," *Contributions to the Scientific Study of Jewish Liturgy* (ed. J. Petuchowski; New York: KTAV, 1970; reprinted from *JQR* 16 [1925/26] 1-43, 127-70) 104.
[94] Which is not totally surprising since post-biblical literature as a whole lacks "any quotations of the synagogal prayers transmitted by rabbinic traditions" (D. Flusser, "Psalms, Hymns, and Prayer," *Jewish Writings of the Second Temple Period* [ed. M. E. Stone; Philadelphia: Fortress, 1984] 576).
[95] The use of Ezek. 20:34ff. by Elbogen, *Jewish Liturgy*, 30, (Hebrew, 26) to account for the sequence of blessings 10, 11, and 13 fails to correlate their sequences adequately. A similar failure obtains in the effort of Wachholder, *Messianism and*

Its distinctive sequence of national redemption is refracted through a comparison of the alternatives. Such a comparison highlights what is said as well as what is not said. The absence of so many staples of ancient redemptive scenarios is noteworthy. Unlike so many other post-biblical eschatological scenarios, it is free of apocalyptic elements, whether utopian or catastrophic, symptomatic of which is the absence of any reference to the Book of Daniel. Its sobriety verges on the Maimonidean.[98] But even Maimonides had to reverse the order of the Amidah in order to come up with a Messiah who can "restore the kingdom of David ..., rebuild the Temple, and gather the dispersed of Israel."[99]

In contrast, not only does the Amidah lack the term "Messiah,"[100] but the role of the "Sprout of David," is downplayed despite its pregnant

---

Mishnah: Time and Place in the Early Halakhah (Cincinnati: Hebrew Union College Press, 1978) 27-28.

[96] Be it that of *Ben Sira, Jubilees, Enoch, 4 Ezra, 2 Baruch, Psalms of Solomon, Tobith,* the Jewish Sibyllines, or the Dead Sea Scrolls; see the comprehensive survey in the second volume of Schürer, *The History of the Jewish People,* chapter 29. The Hebrew *Ben Sira* 51:12ff. is inadequate to account for the sequence, limited, as it is, to blessings 7, 10, 14, and 15. Moreover, its absence from the Greek and Syriac versions casts doubt on whether the Hebrew version is prior to the Amidah; see Marmorstein, "Jesus Sirach 51:12ff.," *ZAW* 29 (1909) 287-93; and Zeitlin, "The Tefillah, the Shemoneh Esreh: A Historical Study of the First Canonization of the Hebrew Liturgy," *JQR* 54 (1963/64) 241. More important is the fact that no dependency can be established, since too many of the expressions that parallel the Amidah are also paralleled in the Bible; see P. Skehan and A. Di Lella, *The Wisdom of Ben Sira* (AB 39; Garden City, NY: Doubleday, 1986) 570.

[97] See Heinemann, *Studies in Jewish Liturgy,* 68-73.

[98] See I. Twersky, *Introduction to the Code of Maimonides (Mishneh Torah)* (New Haven: Yale University Press, 1980) 451, n. 231; and D. Hartman, *Crisis and Leadership: Epistles of Maimonides* (Philadelphia: Jewish Publication Society, 1985) 171-86.

[99] *Mishneh Torah,* Laws of Kings and Wars 11.1; see J. L. Kramer, "On Maimonides' Messianic Posture," *Studies in Medieval Jewish History and Literature* (2 vols.; ed. I. Twersky; Cambridge, MA: Harvard University Press, 1984) 2.124-26.

[100] Although *Menorat Ha-Maor* (4 vols.; ed. H. G. Enelow; New York: Block, 1930) 2.133, does refer to blessing 15 as ביאת המשיח, Ginzberg, *Commentary,* 3.244, has argued for its post-talmudic provenance. For the infrequency of the term משיח, see D. Flusser, "The Reflection of Jewish Messianic Beliefs in Early Christianity," *Messianism and Eschatology* (ed. Z. Baras; Jerusalem: Mercaz Salman Shazar, 1983) 113-14. It is also absent in a Genizah version of the *Ya'aleh Ve-Yavo (Fleischer, Eretz-Israel Prayer,* 96), though it does in the *Kaddish* (ibid., 245) as well as in blessing 14 of the Genizah version in the expression מלכות בית דוד משיח צדקך. Doubt, however, has been raised about the latter referring to a messianic belief; see J. H. Charlesworth, "From Jewish Messianology to Christian Christology: Some Caveats and Perspectives," *Judaisms and Their Messiahs at the Turn of the Christian*

biblical antecedents.[101] Of these antecedents, the closest is that of Zech 3:8, which employs both the term "sprout" (צמח) and the term "servant." Zechariah (6:12), however, prophesies that the "sprout" will rebuild the Temple. Even Jeremiah has the "sprout" reigning and executing justice in the land,[102] a function which is in line with its use as a royal title.[103] Fragment 5 of the Qumran manuscript entitled 4Q285 equates the sprout of David with the Prince of the community and the "just anointed one" to whom is given the royal covenant.[104] In the Qumran 4QFlorlegium, he is associated with the expounder of Torah.[105] Although there is some controversy over the messianic overtones of these texts, there is no disagreement on the prominence of the epithet "sprout of David."[106]

As for the Amidah, "the sprout of David Your servant," appears without any reference to name or to ruling function.[107] He neither teaches nor determines pedigrees, conducts wars, resurrects the dead, judges, or marks an age of travail. Appearing only after God has reassembled the dispersed (blessing 10),[108] restored His rule through

---

Era (ed. J. Neusner, W. S. Green, and E. Frerichs; New York: Cambridge University Press, 1987) 250. Similar doubts mark its presence in the *Haftarah* blessing and in the second blessing of the Grace after meals, independent of their interpolation in their present context; see Finkelstein, "The Development of the Amidah," 135-36.

[101] See Yawitz, *Siddur*, part 2, 77; Levy, *Torat Ha-Tefillah*, 122; J. Baldwin, "Ṣemaḥ as a Technical Term in the Prophets," *VT* 14 (1964) 93-97; and D. Flusser, *Judaism and the Origins of Christianity* (Jerusalem: Magnes, 1981) 149.

[102] Jer 23:5-6; 33:14-16.

[103] See M. Fishbane, *Biblical Interpretation in Ancient Israel* (Oxford: Oxford University Press, 1985) 472, n. 36; and M. Weinfeld, *Justice and Righteousness in Israel and the Nations* (Jerusalem: Magnes, 1985) 35, n. 9 (Hebrew).

[104] See M. G. Abegg, "Messianic Hope and 4Q285: A Reassessment," *JBL* 113 (1994) 86; and Kenneth E. Pomykala, *The Davidic Dynasty Tradition in Early Judaism* (Atlanta: Scholars Press, 1995) 171-216.

[105] 4Q174 1:11-12.

[106] See J. J. Collins, *The Scepter and the Star: The Messiahs of the Dead Sea Scrolls and Other Ancient Literature* (New York: Doubleday, 1995) 56-68; and Reuven Kimelman, "The Messiah of the Amidah," *JBL* (forthcoming).

[107] Even if "servant" serves as a royal designation, it would still underscore the subsidiary role of this scion of David. In any case, the term is missing from so many of the early versions that little can be made of its presence; see Finkelstein, "The Development of the Amidah," 165; and Luger, *Weekday 'Amidah Based on the Genizah*, 1.184.

[108] Contrast *Gen. Rab.* 98:9: "Why does the messianic king come? And what does he come to do? It is to gather together the exiles of Israel." On the other hand, another midrash, as the Amidah, has the ingathering of the dispersed prior to the appearance of the messiah; see *Seder Eliahu Zuta* (ed. Friedmann, 38, n. 21). For the general theme of the gathering of the dispersed, see Schürer, *The History of the Jewish People*, 2.530.

righteous leaders (blessing 11),[109] meted out the appropriate deserts to the righteous and the wicked (blessing 12 and 13), and rebuilt Jerusalem (blessing 14),[110] the messiah marks the culmination of the process.

By highlighting near the beginning God's exclusive rule (blessing 11), the appearance of the Davidic scion (blessing 15) at the end turns out to be more a manifestation of divine power than an expression of acute messianism. It is less a messianic liturgy[111] than a divinely orchestrated redemptive drama on the order of the Exodus.

The Amidah fits into the tendency of downplaying the significance of Davidic rule.[112] According to *t. Ber.* 3:25, the blessing of David is to be denied separate status by being incorporated into the blessing on the building of Jerusalem. As such, the Palestinian rescension of the Amidah lacked, at one time, a separate blessing on David,[113] whereas one of its version of the *Havinenu* abridgment makes no mention of David at all whether in conjunction with the rebuilding of Jerusalem or with the restoration of the Temple.[114] Indeed, a Palestinian *amora* says explicitly that the Temple will be rebuilt before the appearance of the Davidic monarchy,[115] while the explanation for the sequence between blessing 14

---

[109] The precise meaning or reference of this blessing is unclear; see Elbogen, *Jewish Liturgy*, 29-30 (Hebrew, 25-26); Ginzberg, *Commentary*, 1.185-86, 3.325-27; Flusser "Some of the Precepts of the Torah from Qumran (4QMMT) and the Benediction Against the Heretics," 367-68 and literature in notes; and the comprehensive treatment of Luger, *Weekday 'Amidah Based on the Genizah*, 1.135-48.

[110] For these themes in general, see Schürer, *The History of the Jewish People*, 2.526-29.

[111] Cf. S. S. Schwarzchild, "The Messianic Doctrine in Contemporary Jewish Thought," *Great Jewish Ideas* (ed. A. Millgram; Washington, DC: B'nai B'rith, 1964) 246-47; idem , "On Jewish Eschatology," *The Human Condition in the Jewish and Christian Traditions* (ed. F. Greenspahn; Hoboken, NJ: KTAV, 1986) 197, n. 7; and I. Elbogen, "Die Messianische Idee in den alten jüdischen Gebeten," *Festschrift zu Herman Cohens siebzigsten Geburtstage* (Berlin, 1912) 669-79.

[112] Compare the alternative treatments in Schürer, *The History of the Jewish People*, 2.517-25. In the light of the minor role assigned to the scion of David, the absence of the term משיח is likely ideological, unless the Amidah is simply hewing to the idiom of the Bible with its lacks of any eschatological meaning thereof; see Franz Hesse, "χριω," *Theological Dictionary of the New Testament* (10 vols.; ed. G. Kittle, G. W. Bromiley, and G. Friedrich; Grand Rapids, MI: W. B. Eerdmans, 1964-1976) 9.501-5; and J. Liver, "משיח," *Enṣiqlopediyah Miqrait*, 5.508ff. The term itself is also absent in most of the Apocrypha, in Philo, and in Josephus.

[113] See Abramson, *Inyyanot Be-Sifrut Ha-Geonim*, 150-55; Flusser, "Some of the Precepts of the Torah from Qumran (4QMMT) and the Benediction Against the Heretics," 369, n. 144; and Luger, *Weekday 'Amidah Based on the Genizah*, 1.182-84.

[114] *y. Ta'an.* 2:4, 75c.

[115] R. Aha, *y. Ma'aser S.* 5:2, 56a.

and 15 simply says: "Once Jerusalem is built, David comes."[116] None of these sources grant the Davidic house any role in precipitating the redemption.[117]

The key player, indeed virtually the only player, is God. The motif of God as redeemer as opposed to a human redeemer is emphasized elsewhere to underscore the permanence of divine redemption as opposed to the temporary nature of human redemption.[118] Thus God says with regard to Jerusalem: "In the future, I will rebuild her and not destroy her forever (le'olam)."[119] Similarly, blessing 14 states that the rebuilding of Jerusalem will be forever ('olam).[120] In short, God alone is the redeemer and the restorer of Israel's fortunes. In the same vein, R. Hillel's statement: "Israel has no Messiah," was taken by Rashi to mean: "The Holy One, blessed be He, will reign by Himself and redeem them on His own."[121] In this emphasis upon exclusive divine redemption the vision of the Amidah harks back to that of the prophets Nahum, Zephaniah, Habakkuk, Joel, Malachi, and Daniel as well as approaching the restorative vision of the Mishnah.[122]

The eschatological scenario of blessings (10-15) is followed by a blessing on the acceptance of prayer. Such a prayer is so much in order that it need not fit any redemptive scheme. Nonetheless, the epitome of blessing 16 in the *Havinenu* rings with a redemptive resonance. It appears in the form of the following verse: "Before we call, You will answer; while they are still speaking, I will respond" (Isa 65:24).[123] This verse of

---

[116] *b. Meg.* 17b.
[117] The overreading of the Davidic role in the Amidah by G. W. E. Nickelsburg and M. E. Stone is thus surprising: "Hope for the restoration of Jerusalem is here tied to the hope that the Davidic dynasty will be revived. The messianic king will rule from the capital of the renewed Israel; he will bring salvation to his people by delivering them from their enemies, their Roman overlords" (*Faith and Piety in Early Judaism: Texts and Documents* [Philadelphia: Fortress, 1983] 197).
[118] See *Pesiq. Rab Kah.* 21.3 (ed. Mandelbaum, 320 and parallels), along with *Mekhilta*, Be-Shalaḥ, Shir[a]ta 1 (ed. Horovitz-Rabin, 118).
[119] *Midr. Tan.*, Noah 11; *Ibid.*, (ed. Buber, 17). See Jer 17:25.
[120] As opposed to the absence of that motif elsewhere; see Heinemann, *Prayer*, 48-51. The use of 'olam in Isa 35:10 is taken the same way; see *Pesiq. Rab.* 37 (ed. Friedmann, 164); and *Pesiq. Rab Kah.* (ed. Mandelbaum, 2.470). Note Dan 7:27.
[121] *b. Sanh.* 99a. According to Ginzberg, *Commentary*, 4.183, it is precisely this emphasis on God as redeemer that explains the absence of the expression "brings a redeemer" in strophe 9 of blessing 1 (see *infra*) in the Palestinian rescension.
[122] See L. H. Schiffman, "Neusner's Messiah in Context," *JQR* 77 (1987) 240-43.
[123] *y. Ber.* 4:3, 8c = *Ta'anit* 2:2, 65c. See J. Mann and I. Sonne, *The Bible as Read and Preached in the Old Synagogue* (New York: KTAV, 1971) 2.112 (Hebrew). On whether a verse should constitute a blessing, see Ginzberg, *Commentary*, 1.200-201, 4.68-70; Heinemann, *Prayer*, 60, n. 22; and N. Wieder, "On an Obscure Passage in the Palestinian Talmud," *Tarbiz* 43 (1974) 47, n. 8 (Hebrew).

Isaiah marks the advent of redemption. The last part of that chapter presents Isaiah's vision of the *eschaton* or end. It begins, "Behold I am creating a new heaven and a new earth" and ends with "the wolf and the lamb shall graze together." The citation of such a verse on the acceptance of prayer at the end of an eschatological scenario has the capacity of turning a standard request for prayer to be answered into the finale of the redemptive program of the intermediate blessings. In fact, *The Persian Jewish Prayer Book* (p. 86) alludes to Isaiah 65:24, saying "Before we call, You will answer us," and then goes on to cite a hallmark of eschatological hopes, Ps 65:3, that states: "To you all flesh shall come."

This understanding of the intermediate blessings as a grammar of redemption is grounded in an ancient midrash. The midrash claims that the Eighteen Benedictions are predicated on biblical models of prayers which open with praise of God before turning to the needs of Israel. It states:

> A   Thus it begins: "Blessed are You, O Lord our God and God of our fathers, God of Abraham, God of Isaac, and God of Jacob."
> B.   And for the second, it says: "Resurrection of the dead."
> C.   And for the third, it says: "Sanctification of the Name."
> D.   Afterwards it says: " Redeem us, O Lord our God, a complete redemption from (before) You.
> E.   And at the end, it says: "And now we worship (*modim*) You."[124]

Since A, B, C, and E correspond to blessings 1, 2, 3, and 18, respectively, of the Amidah (see *infra*), the request for redemption in D serves to sum up the intermediate set from blessing 4 to 16. Had only one of those blessings been intended, its number would have been mentioned as in the case of the first three, rather than just saying "afterwards." As it is, the "needs of Israel," as the intermediate blessings are called, are epitomized in the request for redemption. The reference to "eighteen benedictions" precludes this epitome from functioning as a single blessing such as the middle blessing of the seven-blessing, Sabbath Amidah.[125] According to this epitome of the Amidah, the central motif is redemption.

In sum, grasping the intermediate blessings as a redemptive scenario leads to grouping them in three units, namely, blessings 4-7, blessings 8-9, and blessings 10-15/16. This sequence of ideas, or clustering of motifs,

---

[124] *Midrash Tanna'im* (ed. Hoffman, 209 = *Midrash Ha-Gadol* [ed. Fish, 750]).
[125] There is thus no need to postulate "an original, germinal Amidah," as does Finkelstein (*New Light from the Prophets* [New York: Basic Books, 1969] 47), or to specify a specific blessing, as does Urbach (*The Sages*, 655 [Hebrew, 590-91]), or to identify it with the comparable, but not similar, comment in *Sifre Deut.* 343 (ed. Finkelstein, 395, lines 5-6).

has a partial parallel in a selection that appears in almost every nondaily version of the Amidah.[126] It reads as follows:

> A. Sanctify us by Your commandments,
> B. and grant our portion in Your Torah;
> C. satisfy us with Your goodness,
> D. and cause us to rejoice in Your salvation,
> E. and purify our hearts to serve You in truth.

A and B correspond to the first unit (4-7),[127] C corresponds to the second (8-9),[128] and D to the third (10-15/16).[129] While less clear, E apparently refers to blessing 16, or leads into blessing 17 with its theme of worship/service.[130] This epitome, reflecting a spiritualization of the daily requests in a manner befitting the holy days of the calendar, clearly takes the whole middle section as a unit.

The First Three Blessings

Once the ear is attuned to the theme of redemption, it becomes possible to hear its reverberation in the first and the last triad of blessings as well. Many of these echo out of biblical materials. As we have seen repeatedly, biblical elements are constantly being rearranged into new mosaics with all the richness of their allusions pressed into liturgical service. For the biblically tone-deaf the redemptive notes will surely fall flat.

The opening blessing of the Amidah contains its share of biblical redemptive tones.

1. Blessed are You, Lord our God
2. and God of our fathers (Deut 26:7; Ezra 7:27; 2 Chron 20:6),
3. God of Abraham, God of Isaac, and God of Jacob (Exod 3:6,15,16),

---

[126] The exception is the Yom Kippur liturgy; see *Mahzor La-Yamim Ha-Nora'im* (ed. Goldschmidt, 2.9, n. 3 of Introduction).

[127] Following E. Eliner, "Perush Meluqat Le-Tefillot Shel Yamim Nora'im," *Ma'ayanot 9, Yamim Nora'im* (2 vols.; ed. H. Hamiel; Jerusalem: World Zionist Organization, 1968) 2.645. Strophe A is mentioned in *b. Pesah.* 117b.

[128] שבענו מטובך epitomizes blessing 9; see Schiffman, *The Halakhah at Qumran*, 87-90. The change to שבענו מטובה is likely due to the kabbalistic insertion of the tetragrammaton in the final letters of פְּנֵי הָאֲדָמָה וְשַׂבְּעֵנוּ מִטּוּבָהּ .

[129] שמחנו בישועתך. Maimonides' *Liturgy* (205, line 31) reverses C and D, and reads for C ושמח נפשנו בישועתך. As such it probably refers to blessing 7. According to *Siddur Rav Saadya Gaon*, 12, C matches that of Maimonides, but D שמחנו בישועתך is excluded altogether.

[130] לעבדך, originally blessing 17 concluded with some form of the expression שאותך ביראה נעבוד; see the *baraita* cited in *y. Yoma* 7:1, 44b.

4. the God (called) great, mighty, and awesome (Deut 10:17, Neh 9:32),[131]
5. exalted God (Ps 78:35),
6. who bestowing loving kindness (alludes to Isa 63:7)
7. is creator of all (alludes to Gen 14:19),
8. who mindful of the piety of the patriarchs (based on Lev 26:45/Ps 106:45),
9. brings a redeemer to their children's children in love
10. for the sake of His name (alludes to Isa 63:16/Ezek 20:9).
11. King (Isa 33:22), Helper (Ps 30:11/54:6), Savior (Jer 14:8), and Shield (Deut 33:29).
12. Blessed are You, O Lord,
13. Shield of Abraham (Gen 15:1).

Although the parenthetic sources are not exhaustive, they do indicate the redemptive overtones that hover over the blessing. The most important of these is the opening three strophes and the closing one (13). In the opening, God is addressed as "Lord our God, God of your fathers, God of Abraham, God of Isaac, and God of Jacob." This usage is unique in the standard liturgy,[132] and it appears in the Bible only in the burning bush scene of Exodus three. There God identifies Himself to Moses as "Lord, the God of your Fathers, the God of Abraham, the God of Isaac, and the God of Jacob" (Exod 3:15). Afterwards God announces the imminent redemption of the people Israel from Egypt. Identifying the intertext shows how the Amidah sets the tone for the theme of

---

[131] On translating the divine epithets as vocatives, see J. Faur, "Delocutive Expressions in the Hebrew Liturgy," *JANES (Ancient Studies in Memory of Elias Bickerman)* 16/17 (1984/85) 52, who translates the beginning of strophes 1 and 12 as "Blessed You, the Lord" (50).

[132] Though it does introduce R. Simeon b. Yohai's prayer for redemption (*Midreshe Ge'ulah*, 270) and two mystical prayers (M. S. Cohen, *The Shi'ur Qomah: Liturgy and Theurgy in Pre-Kabbalistic Jewish Mysticism* (Lanham, MD: University Press of America, 1983) 187; and *Merkavah Shelemah* (ed. Mossayef, 34a), as noted by Bar-Ilan, *Mysteries*, 126-27. The formula, "O Lord, God of our fathers, God of Abraham, Isaac, and of Jacob," also begins the *Prayer of Manasseh* (*Old Testament Pseudepigrapha*, 2.635), whereas "God of our ... fathers ... God of Abraham, Isaac, and of Jacob" appears near the beginning of the second prayer of book 7 of the *Apostolic Constitutions (ibid.,* 677). This last prayer is all the more striking a parallel for having as its Greek peroration: "O Defender" (*hupermachos*), which is like Symmachus' translation of מגן in Gen 15:1), "of the offspring of Abraham, blessed are You forever" (D. A. Fiensy, *Prayers Alleged to be Jewish: An Examination of the Constitutiones Apostolorum* [Chico, CA: Scholars Press, 1985] 59, 132, where Symmachus is cited). See below, n. 135.

redemption.[133] For the Amidah, the God of the Patriarchs is the redeeming God. By saying "blessed" is such a God, the worshiper is calling upon the God who once redeemed to redeem again. This formulation was so integral to the Amidah that it withstood all efforts to make it conform to the subsequent standard benedictory formula.[134]

The closing strophe 13 may have once read: "shield of the fathers," a non-biblical expression albeit found in *Ben Sira* 36. The change adds to the redemptive echo of the blessing by evoking God's reassurance to Abraham that He would remain His "shield" (Gen 15:1), while continuing to maintain the verbal association with the only other Pentateuchal attestation of "shield" (מגן), "A people delivered by the Lord, Your protecting shield " (Deut 33:29).[135] Strophe 9 spells out the redemptive plea of the blessing but lacks a direct scriptural correlate. It flows from the Biblical association of remembering the patriarchs, the idea of the covenant, and the promise of redemption as they appear in

---

[133] As does *Mekhilta*, Pisḥa 16 (ed. Horovitz-Rabin, 60; ed. Lauterbach, 1.136). The *Mekhilta* as well as other sources quoted below, is cited by Liber, "Structure and History of the Tefillah," 331-57. His thesis with regard to the redemptive theme of the first triad of blessings has been refined and extended to the rest of the Amidah.

[134] This intertext obviates explanations about the absence or implied presence of the later (probably third century) requirement of mentioning "kingship" in blessings; cf. *Sefer Ha-Eshkol* 99 (ed. A. Albeck; Jerusalem: Wagsel, 1984) with notes; *Sefer Ha-Manhig* 1.87 with notes; and Fleisher, "The Shemoneh Esre," 191, n. 44.

[135] See *Abudarham*, 95. *Mekhilta*, Be-Shallah 4 (ed. Horovitz-Rabin, 102; ed. Lauterbach, 1.227) associates Gen 15:1 אנכי מגן לך שכרך הרבה מאד with ישעי וקרן מגיני (Ps 18:3 = 2 Sam 22:3). Following this lead, *Midrash Psalms*, 18.25, comments on the former Psalm verse: "I am His shield even as He is a shield to all them that take refuge in Him; and thus on the morrow His children will bless in the *Tefillah* [*viz.* the Amidah], "Blessed are You, O, Lord, Shield of Abraham." Similarly, *Midrash Psalms*, 119.46, associates Gen 15:1 with "You have given me Your shield of salvation," (Ps 18:36= 2 Sam 22:36) adding, "and not only to me, but to every man that trusts in You." As Scripture says, "He is a shield to all that trust in Him" (Ps 18:31 = 2 Sam 22:31). Such associations likely induced R. Simeon b. Laqish – the colleague of the very same R. Yohanan (see *infra*) who underscored the need of always juxtaposing the blessing of redemption with the Amidah – to promote "the shield of Abraham" as the peroration of the first blessing (*b. Pesah.* 117b; *Num. Rab.* 11.2). Apparently, heretofore there had been two alternative perorations: "the shield of Abraham" and "the shield of the patriarchs" (*pace* Heinemann, *Studies in Jewish Liturgy*, 41). On the issue of standardized alternatives, see Ginzberg, *Commentary*, 4.182; E. Fleisher, "Between Occasional and Standardized in Public Prayer in Early Eretz-Yisrael," *Studies in Memory of the Rishon Le-Zion R. Yitzhak Nissim* (ed. M. Benayahu; Jerusalem: Yad Harav Nissim, 5785) 9, 13, n. 12; Hadani, "Havinenu," 305; and Y. Brody, "Sifrut Ha-Geonim Ve-Ha-Teqst Ha-Talmudi," *Mehqerei Talmud* (ed. D. Rosenthal; Jerusalem: Magnes, 1990) 244, n. 38 and 278, n. 169.

Lev 26:42 and Exod 6:5. Strophes 6-10 makes the case for God redeeming Israel. Both in expression and motif, they recall Isaiah 63 verses 7-9 and 16. There as here, the recital of God's former mercies is not a mere expression of gratitude, but a warranty for the future. Here, the argument takes the form of a *quid pro quo* – as a bestower of kindness, God is entreated to reciprocate the kindness shown by the patriarchs by redeeming their descendants. The worshiper, by being told of the kindness or merit, to use rabbinic parlance, of the patriarchs, is apprised of his warrant for maintaining hope in redemption, as Isaiah 63:16 states: "From of old, Your name is 'Our Redeemer'".[136]

The second blessing makes the case for resurrection, mentioning it no less than six times:

1. You, are mighty forever, O Lord,
2. *Reviver of the dead* are You, of great saving power.
3. (causing the wind to blow and the rain to fall).
4. You sustain the living with kindness, *reviving the dead* with manifold mercies,
5. [You] support the fallen, heal the sick, free the fettered.
6. *And maintains His faithfulness with those asleep in the dust.*
7. Who is like You, O Powerful One, who can compare with You?
8. The King who *brings death and life*
9. and causes salvation to sprout,
10. Faithful are You *to revive the dead,*
11. Blessed are You, O Lord, *reviver of the dead.*

The arguments rests on culling the intimations of resurrection that punctuate the course of life. By methodically amplifying "the wonders which daily attend us," the blessing enables the worshiper to perceive the divine workings behind the natural course of events.

Strophes 1-2 make the point that even death cannot forestall a divine power that is forever and salvific.[137] Strophe 3, as does strophe 9 with its

---

[136] A Genizah epitome of this blessing (Mann, "Genizah Fragments," 309) proclaims: אשרי עם מצפים לישועתך בא"י מגן אברהם ("Fortunate are the people who look forward to Your redemption ... Blessed are You O Lord shield of Abraham"). *Maḥzor Romania* and *Minhag Benei Roma* contain גואל ("Redeemer") before the peroration (E. D. Goldschmidt, *On Jewish Liturgy* [Jerusalem: Magnes, 1980] 129, 158 [Hebrew]).

[137] For its possible biblical allusions, see Ginzberg *Commentary*, 4.191. The argument for resurrection from the omnipotence of God is frequently appealed to

symbolic use of the agricultural metaphor "sprout,"[138] associates resurrection with rain and seasonal change. If the "Bringer of rain" can wondrously awaken to life the seed that slumbers in the soil, so can He awaken the dead to new life.[139] It is possible that behind this image lies the comparison of human life with a seed.[140] Such a comparison would allow death, burial, and decomposition to be seen as preparatory stages in the process of rebirth and germination as the paradigm for resurrection.

An alternative version of strophe 3, for the summer, reads: "Who brings dew."[141] Similarly, here or in blessing 9, the phrase "King who revives all with rain" was changed in the summer to "King who revives all with dew."[142] Its location here would evoke Isaiah's association of dew with resurrection: "Your dead shall live, their corpses shall rise. O dwellers in the dust, awake and sing for joy? For your dew is a radiant dew and the earth will give birth to those long dead" (26:19 – NRSV).

Strophe 4 draws the connection between the miracle of sustaining life in the present and reviving it in the future. The choice of liturgical terminology creates a continuum between the miracle of the future and that of the present. True, rebirth does require "manifold mercies," but life itself requires the sustaining power of "divine grace."[143] Viewing resurrection as but an extra dose of divine mercy serves to enhance its

---

by Church Fathers; see H. Chadwick, "Origen, Celsus and the Resurrection of the Body," *HTR* 41 (1948) 84-86.

[138] The word מצמיח, "causes to sprout," is, as would be expected, also associated with blessings for food from the ground; see *t. Ber.* 4:4. For the agricultural metaphor for resurrection, see *b. Ketub.* 111b.

[139] The probatory nature of the argument from the spring agricultural revival is emphasized by R. Yom Tov b. Abraham Ishbili, *Ḥiddushe Ha-RITBA, Massekhet Ta'anit* (ed. Lichtenstein, *ad b. Ta'an* 2a). The tannaitic mandate (*m. Ber.* 5:2; *t. Ber.* 3:9) for associating the power to bring rain with resurrection is explained in amoraic literature by their comparability (*b. Ber.* 33b), namely, both "bring life to the world" (*Gen. Rab.* 13.6 [ed. Theodor-Albeck, 116 and parallels).

[140] This is how an early third-century Church Father, Marcus Minucius Felix, takes it: "Seeds must rot in order to sprout into new growth. As trees are in winter, so are our bodies in this world ... We must await the springtime – the springtime of the body" (*Octavius* 34.11-12 [Ancient Christian Writers 39; ed. G. W. Clarke; New York: Newman, 1974] 116); see also Justin, *Apology* 1:19.

[141] *Seder Rav Amram Gaon*, 24, n. 9 (ms M); Maimonides, *Liturgy*, 199, n. 2 and subsequent versions.

[142] *Siddur Saadya Gaon*, 22.

[143] See *Sefer Ha-Iqqarim* 4:35 (J. Albo, *Sefer Ha-Iqqarim* [Israel: Maḥberet Le-Sifrut, n.d.] 805). As Albo notes, the first blessing of the Grace after meals also underscores the idea that providing food for all entails special divine grace and kindness, an idea attested in Job 10:11 and in *b. Pesaḥ.* 118a, citing Ps 136:25. The probatory nature of the argument is underscored by Yaqar, *Perush Ha-Tefillot Ve-Ha-Berakhot*, 2.81.

plausibility. The other assumption is that rebirth is not so much more miraculous than birth.[144] As the Talmud argues: "If what was not can be, all the more so what was can be."[145] Or: "Just as the womb receives and returns, so the grave receives and returns" (*b. Sanh.* 92a). The link behind strophes 3 and 4 is reflected in the rabbinic insistence that the keys to life-giving rain, to birth, and to resurrection are exclusively in the hands of God.[146] By harking back to a biblical image of viewing the quickening of nature as life-producing, the strophe is able to compare the awakening of a dormant nature with the process of birth.[147]

Strophe 5 consists of adaptations of expressions from the Book of Psalms,[148] the first two of which have been slightly altered to conform to the liturgically apt third. They appear together only here.[149] They deal with the fallen, the sick, and the imprisoned. If left to languish, all have in common a proximity to death. They may be in a descending order toward death, reflecting in reverse an ascending order toward resurrection. The Bible also compares the taking of life and its restoration with wounding and healing on the one hand, and with bringing down and raising up on the other.[150] In any case, their own reversals represent

---

[144] See Rashi, *b. Pesah.* 68a, s.v., *ketiv*. The homology between birth and rebirth is already noted by Sencea, *Epistulae Morales* 102:23.

[145] *b. Sanh.* 91a. See 2 Maccabees 2:23 with J. Goldstein, *II Maccabees* (AB 41A; Garden City, NY: Doubleday, 1983) 311. The identical argument is made by Minucius Felix: "It is, therefore equally possible for him to be restored from nothing as it was for him to be born from nothing. Besides, it is a much more difficult task to begin something that does not exist than to repeat something that once existed" (*Octavius* 34:9 (ed. G. W. Clarke, 116).

[146] *b. Ta'an.* 2a and *Gen. Rab.* 73.4 (ed. Theodor-Albeck, 848 with parallels).

[147] See Isa 26:17-19, 66:7-9.

[148] Pss 145:14, 103:3, 146:7.

[149] For similar and alternative listings, see Bar-Ilan, *Mysteries*, 88; and 4Q521 2:8, 12. The order of the triad is constant across most of the versions. The exceptions include a Genizah fragment Or. 5557Q (Wieder, "On an Obscure Passage in the Palestinian Talmud," 51), and Maimonides along with the Yemenite version both of which reverse the order of the first two. Also *Siddur Rav Saadya Gaon*, 18, reads ומשען לאביונים instead of סומך נופלים. ומשען לאביונים is added to the triad in *The Siddur of Rabbenu Shelomoh b. R. Natan* (Neubauer MS) on p. 34 but not on p. 37, and appears in *Mahzor Romania* (see Goldschmidt, *On Jewish Liturgy*, 129). For the other variants, see N. Weider, "Fourteen New Genizah-Fragments of Saadya's Siddur Together with a Reproduction of a Missing Part," *Saadya Studies* (ed. E. S. Rosenthal; Manchester, 1943) 264. *The Persian Jewish Prayer Book*, 12, and n. 15 thereto, appears to be a composite of the standard triad and the version of *Siddur Rav Saadya Gaon* with one addition.

[150] Deut 32:39 and 1 Sam 2:6; see L. J. Greenspoon, "The Origin of the Idea of Resurrection," *Traditions in Transformation: Turning Points in biblical Faith* (ed. B. Halperin and J. Levinson; Winona Lake, IN: Eisenbrauns, 1981) 310, 315, along with the discussion in *b. Pesah.* 68a.

The Literary Structure of the Amidah

miniature, if not preliminary, resurrections. A dead person may have fallen prostrate, been overcome by terminal disease, or been entombed forever.[151] Moves toward death anticipate death as moves toward life anticipate resurrection. The assumption is that God's capacity to cure prefigures His capacity to resurrect, recoveries and revivals being on the same rescue continuum.[152] Once the continuum is established, and rescue from sickness is deemed as wondrous as rescue from death,[153] then only one more step is needed to believe that God can accomplish that greatest of all rescue operations – release from death.

Some see a reference to national restoration in this strophe.[154] If national restoration were then available as evidence of a reversal of fortunes, an allusion to Ezekiel 37 would have been in order. In actuality, national restoration is, as the Amidah demonstrates, as much in need of reinforcement as resurrection. Only the individual condition can account for the resurrection-like character of the whole triad.

Strophes 3-5 cluster a variety of ideas and images that rework the uses of the causative of the biblical חיה ('live') with all its associations pressed into liturgical service. The *Piel* form can mean "allow to live," *i.e.* to continue living as in Exod 1:7. The *Hiphil* form can mean "restore to health" as in 2 Kings 5:7. With regard to vegetation, the verb can mean "cause to grow," or "produce" as in Hos 14:8. It can also mean "revive the heart and spirit" as in Isa 57:15 and, of course, "restore to life" as in 2 Kings 8:1.[155]

Strophe 6 is modeled after Dan 12:2: "those that sleep in the dust of the earth will awake." The sleep metaphor allows resurrection to be described as a great awakening and death to be imagined as an

---

[151] So *Abudarham*, 96-97, apparently following R. Meir of Rothenburg (*She'elot U-Teshuvot MaHaRaM b. R. Barukh* [Budapest, 1895] 150b) who noted that the triad is comprised of diminutives of resurrection. Recuperation and release from prison are also linked by a blessing of gratitude (*b. Ber.* 54b; *Midr. Ps.* 107.5), whereas God is praised for resurrecting the dead, raising the fallen, and releasing the imprisoned in a *hekhalot* blessing (באיהמ"ה אלהי הרוחות מחייה המתים סומך נופלים מתיר אסורים ...), as cited in Bar-Ilan, *Mysteries*, 88, n. 11).

[152] A similar association of recovery with redemption is created by the juxtaposition of בורא רפואות with מצמיח ישועות in the אל ברוך unit of the first blessing of the morning Shema. The argument for resurrection from recovery was also made by the late second-century church father Theophilus of Antioch in his *To Autolycus* 1.13.

[153] See *b. Ned.* 41a.

[154] *b. Ber.* 4b, takes סומך נופלים of Psalm 145 as reflecting the condition of the nation as, apparently, does R. Meir of Rothenburg (*She'elot U-Teshuvot*, #1018, p. 150b).

[155] See J. Barr, *The Garden of Eden and the Hope of Immortality* (Minneapolis: Fortress, 1992) 34-35.

intensification of sleep.[156] If God can be trusted to return the spirit after sleep, why would He not be considered reliable enough to do so after death? Indeed, the standard prayer upon awakening thanks God for returning the soul to "dead tired" or "lifeless" bodies. The more waking is experienced as an expression of divine renewal, the more a great future renewal becomes believable.[157] It is not surprising then to find that upon awakening one is urged to praise God for restoring life to the dead.[158] Such is the liturgical response to the intimations of immortality, or presentiments of rebirth. Finally, note that the resurrection is unqualified, unlike 1 Sam 2:6 and many interpretations of Daniel that limit the resurrection to the righteous. As such, it takes its cue from the aforecited verse from Isaiah as do the aforementioned phrases that God "revives all with rain/dew." Predicating the argument for resurrection on that of nature makes it so inclusive that exceptions on moral grounds are eliminated.

Strophe 8 refers to God as "King," as does blessing 1. There only the sovereign over history could assure redemption; here only the sovereign over death can assure resurrection. Neither the future nor the grave are barriers to God's providential care. In fact, God is first called "King of the universe" in a prayer on resurrection.[159]

Strophe 10 refers to God as "faithful" as do some versions of blessing 8 on recuperation.[160] Both allude to its biblical use where God is called "faithful" when maintaining the covenant and when effectuating redemption.[161]

In all, the blessing succeeds in condensing the gamut of rabbinic arguments for resurrection to about fifty words. The aim is to increase the plausibility of the not yet available resurrection by grounding it in

---

[156] The argument is repeated by the late second-century Church Father Athenagoras, *On the Resurrection of Corpses*.

[157] So *Gen . Rab.* 78.1 (ed. Theodor-Albeck, 915 and parallels, esp. *Midr. Ps.* 25.2. Yaqar, *Perush Ha-Tefillot Ve-Ha-Berakhot*, 1.38-39 makes the nature of the argument explicit.

[158] See *y. Ber.* 4:2, 7d; *Pesiq. Rab.* 40 (ed. Friedmann, 168 and parallels); *Sefer Halakhot Gedolot* (ed. Hildesheimer, 1.151); and Mann, "Genizah Fragments," 278. Cf. J. Petuchowski, "Modern Misunderstandings of an Ancient Benediction," *Studies in Aggadah, Targum and Jewish Liturgy in Memory of Joseph Heinemann* (ed. J. Petuchowski and E. Fleischer; Jerusalem: Magnes, 1981) 45-54. The liturgical association of resurrection with awakening is attested by a version that contains the words ומחיר נשמות לפגרים מתים after לישני עפר (see Finkelstein, "The Development of the Amidah," 146) and the replacement of the peroration, בא"י מעורר ברחמים יצורים with בא"י מחיה המתים (see Lieberman, *Tosefta Ki-shutah*, 1.51).

[159] 2 Maccabees 7:9.

[160] *Mahzor Romania*, 130; *Minhag Benei Roma*, 158; and a Genizah text (Luger, *Weekday 'Amidah Based on the Genizah*, 1.110).

[161] Deut 7:9; Isa 49:7.

experiences that are available, such as seasonal revival, birth, life, raising the fallen, healing the sick, freeing the fettered, and awakening, all of which can be conceived of as diminutives of resurrection.[162] Still, as strophe 7 notes, resurrection remains an incomparable event performable only by an incomparably powerful God.[163]

The third blessing is concerned with the establishment of God's kingship on earth just as it is in heaven. It contains the Qedushah (*sanctus*) which opens by citing both Isaiah (6:3) and Ezekiel (3:12), who describe the angels acclaiming the divine sovereignty above, and concludes with Israel proclaiming God's kingship below, saying: "The Lord shall reign forever, your God, O Zion, through all generations. Halleluiah" (Ps 146:10). The blessing creates such a convergence between terrestrial and celestial liturgies that it remains unclear whether angels, Israel, or both are meant by the phrase, "the holy ones praise You daily."[164] It is of course possible that the ambiguity is meant to convey the idea of the simultaneous realization of divine kingship in both earthly and heavenly realms. The blessing continues:

1. You are *holy* and Your name is *holy*,
2. the *holy* ones praise You daily,
3. [for (God), king, great and *holy* are You].[165]
4. Blessed are You, O Lord, *holy* God.

---

[162] This blessing of God's wonders and salvations integrates the resurrection motif so completely that it appears indigenous; see Ginzberg, *Commentary*, 4.167, 189; and Bar-Ilan, *Mysteries*, 131.

[163] As the liturgical midrash of the first blessing of the Shema in the Sabbath morning prayer service states: ואין דומה לך מושיענו – לתחיית המתים ("And there is no one comparable to You, our Savior, – for the resurrection of the dead"). The wondrous nature of the content of the blessing is indicated by the term גבורות, which, as Ginzberg (*Commentary*, 4.155, 196) and Bar-Ilan (*Mysteries*, 128-35) have shown, is synonymous with miracles (ניסים). Thus the parallel between פועל גבורות and אדון הנפלאות in the first blessing of the Shema service. Indeed, a *hekhalot* blessing concludes בא"י אדון ניסים וגבורות (cited by Bar-Ilan, *Mysteries*, 131, from *Ma'aseh Merkabah*); see also *The Book of Biblical Antiquities*, 26:6. Thus the expression of 4Q403 1.i.2-3, ישבח לאלוהי גבורות, should be translated as "and he will praise the God of wonders," and not as "the God of power."

[164] The ambiguity has been frequently noticed; see Weinfeld, "The Prayers for Knowledge, Repentance, and Forgiveness in the Eighteen Benedictions," 191, n. 30; Ginzberg, *Commentary*, 4.206; and P. Schäfer, *Rivalität zwischen Engeln und Menschen: Untersuchungen zur rabbinischen Engelvorstellung* (Studia Judaica 8; Berlin/New York: Walter de Gruyter, 1975) 36-37.

[165] This strophe is missing in Genizah versions; see Luger, *Weekday 'Amidah Based on the Genizah*, 1.76. Abudarham, 97, noting its presence in "Gaonic Siddurim" (see *Seder Rav Amram Gaon*, 24, line 16), argued for its inclusion. It appears in *Minhag Benei Roma* (p. 158); *Maḥzor Vitry MS Reggio* (p. 69); and *Maḥzor Romania* (p. 129).

This blessing resounds with notes of the holiness of God. The aforementioned prophets, Isaiah and Ezekiel, emphasize the holiness of both God and His name. Isaiah who refers to God's name as "holy" (57:15) uses the divine epithet, "the Holy One of Israel," as a designator of God as redeemer.[166] For Ezekiel, God's name, albeit for other reasons, becomes holy through the redemption of Israel.[167] The use of "great and holy" in the third strophe recalls Ezek 38:23: "Thus will I manifest My greatness and My holiness, and make Myself known in the sight of many nations, and they shall know that I am the Lord." The same verse informs the opening of the Qaddish: "May God's name become great and holy." In each, the theme is redemption. For both Isaiah and Ezekiel, the holy god is the redeeming god.

Even in the alternative version of the Qedushah, where God's name is called "awesome,"[168] a redemptive note is intoned, as it says: "He sent redemption to His people ... His name is 'Holy' and 'Awesome'" (Ps 111:9). Nonetheless, the peals of redemption rings more loudly by formulating the first strophe as *"You are holy and Your name is holy"* in a manner paralleling the strophe *"You are one and Your name is one"* of the Sabbath afternoon service. In both cases, there is an allusion to universal

---

[166] Isa 41:14; 43:3, 14; 47:4; 48:17; 49:7; 54:6; see E. Berkovitz, *Man and God: Studies in Biblical Theology* (Detroit: Wayne State University Press, 1969) 153-55.
[167] Ezek 20:41, 36:23-24, 39:25ff.
[168] קדוש אתה ונורא שמך, attested already in *Sifre Deut.* 343 (ed. Finkelstein, 395), likely represents the Palestinian version whereas the other the Babylonian (see Schechter, *Studies in Jewish Liturgy*, 58). Both versions appear among the Genizah fragments (Mann, "Genizah Fragments," 306) with one containing both, representing a conflation of the two (see N. Wieder, "Five Topics in the Field of Liturgy," *Areshet* 6 (1981) 86-87 [Hebrew]). The more widely accepted version אתה קדוש ושמך קדוש – "You are holy and Your name is holy" (see Finkelstein, "The Development of the Amidah," 151; and N. Wieder, "Le-Heqer Minhag Bavel Qadmon," *Tarbiz* 37 (1968) 258-59), which according to Ginzberg (*Commentary*, 4.172) is the original, echoes that of the biblical formulation of divine incomparability שמך נדול אתה וגדול (Jer 10:6 – for the order of the terms, see Mirsky, *Ha-Piyyut*, 29, n. 34). The formula "You are x and your name is x" reappears in אתה שלום ושמך שלום (*b. Ber.* 55b) of the conclusion of the expanded priestly benediction in the *Musaf* service and forms the basis of an entire Qedushah hymn in the *hekhalot* corpus (see Bar-Ilan, *Mysteries*, 71). Reformulated in the third person as "He is x and His name is x," it appears as well in the morning prayer of redemption, הוא קיים ושמו קיים as well as in the version of the *Aleynu* prayer of *Ma'aseh Merkabah*: ה' אלהינו ה' אחד / הוא אחד ושמו אחד (G. Scholem, *Jewish Gnosticism, Merkabah Mysticism, and Talmudic Tradition* [New York: Jewish Theological Seminary of America, 1965] 105). On the composition of the blessing itself and whether the variations reflect daily versus holiday versions, see the literature cited by E. D. Goldschmidt, *Mahzor Le-Yamim Ha-Nora'im* (2 vols.; Jerusalem, 1970) 1.20, n. 16.

redemption, as its says, "When the Lord shall be king over all the earth, on that day *the Lord shall be one and His name one*" (Zech 14:9).[169]

In sum, the opening triad of blessings (1-3) presents a tripartite thesis: it argues for God bringing a redeemer, followed by the case for resurrection, and ends with Israel's acclamation of the kingship of God on earth. All three contain the affirmation that God is King.[170] Perceiving of God as Lord over history, Lord over nature and death, and Lord over all, heightens our expectation that He will redeem us. The expectation of redemption triggered by divine kingship is articulated by Isaiah: "Since... the Lord is our King, He will deliver us" (33:22).

The Last Three Blessings

Blessings 17 and 18 also advance the drama of redemption, the former through God's return to Zion and the latter through His universal acceptance. Blessing 17 concludes: "May our eyes behold Your merciful return to Zion. Blessed are You, O Lord, who restores His presence to Zion."[171] It is followed by blessing 18's theme of God's universal acceptance. Together they conform to a motif that reverberates throughout the Prophets and the liturgy, especially on the High

---

[169] The link between the liturgical formula and this verse was duly noted by *Abudarham*, 148; *Maḥzor Vitry*, 155; *Siddur of R. Solomon b. Samson of Garmaise* (ed. M. Hershler: Jerusalem: Hemed, 1971) 182; Yaqar, *Perush Ha-Tefillot Ve-Ha-Berakhot*, 1.115; and alluded to by *Menorat Ha-Ma'or*, 2.190, strophe 15. The verse itself probably appears in a talmudic version of the Qedushah; see E. S. Rosenthal, "Two Comments," *Tarbiz* 41 (1971) 450. Professor M. Bialik Lerner alerted me to the pertinence of this study.

[170] In each – blessing 1, strophe 11; blessing 2, strophe 8; and blessing 3, strophe 3 – this immediately precedes the peroration. In some versions of the third blessing the designation of God as King appears only in the Sabbath, Festival, or High Holiday versions. The High Holiday versions conclude blessing 3 with המלך הקדוש ("the holy King"). These versions make explicit the correlation between the extension of God's holiness and the extension of divine kingship; see Heinemann, *Studies in Jewish Liturgy*, 15, n. 11; and M. Weinfeld, "The Day of the Lord: Aspirations for the Kingdom of God in the Bible and Jewish Liturgy," *Scripta Hierosolymitana* 31 (1986) 366-68. The sovereignty motif is highlighted by an epitome of the blessing in a *qerovah* from the Genizah: גדולה וגבורה אתה תלבש על כל מעשיך מהרה תמלך ("Greatness and power You will wear; over all Your creatures You will quickly rule" [Fleischer, *Eretz-Israel Prayers*, 71]).

[171] This combination of Mic 4:11, Zech 1:15, and the Qumran version of Isa 52:8 is absent in the Palestinian versions, see Elbogen, *Jewish Liturgy*, 50-51 (Hebrew, 44). Fleischer suggests: "Many Palestinian communities abroad changed their version to the Babylonian one ("who restores His presence to Zion") out of yearnings for the Land of Israel" (*Eretz-Israel Prayer*, 311, n. 71).

Holidays, namely, that the precursor of the universal recognition of divine sovereignty is God's return to Zion.[172]

The argument of blessing 18 for God's universal recognition deserves special attention. It begins: "We worship [*modim*][173] You," followed by a listing of examples of divine beneficence that elicit thrice daily praise. The central part of the blessing goes as follows:

1. We will thank You
2. and tell of Your praise
3. for our lives which are in Your hand
4. and for our souls which are entrusted to You
5. and for Your miracles which are daily with us
6. and for Your wonders and kindnesses at all times.

Strophes 1 and 2 state what we shall do; strophes 3-6 state why. The whys are divided into two categories: strophes 3 and 4 express gratitude to God for our lives and souls; strophes 5 and 6 enunciate praise for God's miracles and wonders. Thus 1 is to 3-4 as 2 is to 5-6, making for an *a b a b* structure. Simply stated, it says: We will thank You for our lives that are in Your hand and for our souls that are entrusted to You. And tell of Your praise for Your miracles that are daily with us and for Your wonders and kindnesses at all times.

The blessing concludes, saying: "For all of these [strophes 3-6] may Your name be blessed, exalted, and extolled, O our King, continually and forever," followed by the expectation that "all the living shall worship You". The envelope structure of the blessing has the ending echo the beginning. What began as "we worship/acknowledge You" culminates in "all the living shall worship/acknowledge You."[174] The bridge

---

[172] See L. Liebreich, "Aspects of the New Year Liturgy," *HUCA* 34 (1963) 151-52; and M. Weinfeld, "The Expectation of the Kingship of God in the Bible and its Reflection in Jewish Liturgy," *Messianism and Eschatology* (ed. Z. Baras; Jerusalem: Mercaz Zalman Shazar, 1983) 81-83, 92ff.; and *idem*, "The Day of the Lord," 349-55.

[173] In biblical idiom *modim* denotes primarily "praise," and in rabbinic idiom primarily "acknowledge." It can also denote an attendant prostration; see Lieberman, *Tosefta Ki-fshutah*, 4.696, n. 58. In the context of worship, such as here, these meanings converge; see M. Kadushin, *The Rabbinic Mind* (New York: The Jewish Theological Seminary of America, 1952) 344-46. According to Saadya Gaon, Gen 49:8 already used the term to denote the acceptance of authority; see M. Zucker, *Rav Saadya Gaon's Translation of the Torah* (New York: Feldheim, 1959) 302 (Hebrew), as does the third blessing of the Shema; see *Seder Rav Amram Gaon*, 20, lines 14 and 18.

[174] See A. Süsskind, *Yesod Ve-Shoresh Ha-Avodah* (Brooklyn, 1984) 135. This formulation וכל החיים יודוך parallels the biblical usage of Ps 145:10 יודוך ה' כל מעשיך

between the two is the recognition of how the divine margin permeates human life continually [*i.e.*, every moment of the day] and forever. God is exalted at all times, for all time, and by all.[175] As a bridge between the particular and the universal, the blessing purposely lacks any reference to anything peculiarly Jewish as grounds for thanks and praise of the divine. It seeks to invite all to share in recognizing the divine margin of human life.

Nonetheless, rather than understanding "all the living" to refer to all humanity, some extend the "all" forward in time to include the resurrected;[176] while others extend the "all" vertically in space to include the heavenly beings.[177] The extension of the "all" horizontally to all humanity makes the Amidah conform to the common liturgical conclusion of the universal acknowledgment of divine sovereignty. The perorations thus translate as "Your name [alone] is Good,[178] and You [alone] are fitting to acknowledge."[179] The version of *The Persian Jewish Prayer Book* reinforces this emphasis on divine singularity by leading into the peroration with the words: "You O Living alone are good".[180] *Siddur Rav Saadya Gaon* underscores the exclusivity of divine worship by doing

---

("all Your creatures will praise/acknowledge You, O Lord"); see Kimelman, "Psalm 145, Theme, Structure and Impact" *JBL* 113 (1994) 44, n. 35; and the refrain of Psalm 67, יודוך עמים כולם ("All the peoples shall praise/acknowledge You"). In the liturgy, it parallels the opening *piyyut* of the Sabbath version of the first blessing of the Shema, הכל יודוך ("All will acknowledge You"). A *qerovah* of R. Pinchas epitomizes this blessing with these words: פלא יודוך / ויבואו עדיך / בא"י הטב לך להודות (cited in A. Marmorstein, "Nispahim Le-Ma'amare Qiddush Yerahim De-Rabbe Pinhas," *Ha-Sofe Le-Hokhmat Yisrael* 6 (1922) 56, a statement whose middle part alludes to Ps 65:3 with its hope that עדיך יבואו כל בשר ("all flesh will come to You"). The blessing is also associated with *todah*, a term that doubles for both sacrifice and acknowledgment (so *Siddur Rav Saadya Gaon*, 8). The acknowledgment denotation as in God's universal acknowledgment appears in the following pertinent midrash: "A Psalm of *Todah* (Ps. 100:1) – Let all the nations of the earth acknowledge Me, and I shall receive them, as is said: 'Look to Me, and be saved, all the ends of the earth; for I am God, and there is none else ... unto Me every knee shall bow, every tongue shall swear (Isa 45:22-23) – that is, "When every knee bows to Me and every tongue swears, I will receive them" (*Midr. Ps.* 100.1).
[175] For these three motifs of ancient prayer, see Miller, *They Cried to the Lord*, 19.
[176] Such as Yaqar, *Perush Ha-Tefillot Ve-Ha-Berakhot*, 1.64, who takes his cue from Isa 38:19.
[177] Such as Eleazar b. Judah of Worms, *Siddur Ha-Tefillah La-Roqeah*, 1.353.
[178] הטוב שמך (see *Midr. Ps.* 29:2; and 2 Chr 30:18).
[179] Also the Palestinian peroration הטוב לך להודות / אל ההודאות (see Heinemann, *Studies in Jewish Liturgy*, 36, n. 2) indicates that God alone who is to be acknowledged and/or to Whom all praise is due.
[180] ואתה חי לבדך הטוב (p. 16, line 6). See Mark 10:18 = Luke 18:19 = Matthew 19:17: "No one is good but God alone."

the same with the words: "for You are the One and there is none other than You."[181] The idea that God is the One and the idea of His universal recognition go hand in hand, as it says, "When idolatry will be eradicated ... God will be One in the world[182] and His kingship established forever."[183]

As noted, the shift from our acknowledgment of God to His universal recognition frames much of the eschatological core of the rest of the liturgy. The best-known example is the *Aleynu* prayer, which like the *Modim*[184] begins with Israel alone bowing in worship (*modim*) and concludes with all humanity, upon realizing divine sovereignty, doing likewise.[185] This shift is also reflected in the rabbinic gloss of the Shema verse: "'the Lord is our God,' – for us; 'the Lord is One,' – for all humanity. 'The Lord is our God' – in the present; 'the Lord is one' – in the future, as its says, 'And the Lord shall be king over all the earth, on that day the Lord shall be one and His name One.'"[186]

In sum, the latter sections of the Amidah advance from personal (4-7) through national (10-15) to universal redemption (18), each stage involving the progressive realization of divine sovereignty from self to nation to humanity. The three stage development from self to nation or community to humanity is a liturgical staple that characterizes Psalm 145, the Shema, and the benedictory formulary.[187]

The Amidah concludes with a prayer on peace. It begins: "Grant Peace," taking its cue from the last strophe of the priestly benediction in Num 6:24-26: "May He grant you peace." The remainder continues to flesh out the benediction. The three strophes of each loosely correlate,

---

[181] כי יחיד אתה ואין זולתך (p. 19, line 7); see also Wieder, "Fourteen New Genizah Fragments," 265.
[182] יחידי בעולם
[183] *Mekhilta, Be-Shallah, amaleq* 2 (ed. Horovitz-Rabin, 186; ed. Lauterbach 2.159).
[184] The אלוהי כל בשר and יוצר בראשית of the *modim de-rabbanan*, as well as the reworking of Isa 45:23 of Bar Qappara's version לך תכרע כל ברך תשבע כל לשון ("to You will bend every knee; every tongue swear) [*y. Ber.* 1:8, 3d] all evoke '*Aleynu* terminology. The linkage between the two is further evidenced by the following Genizah version: וימלך על כל העולם ... וישתחוו לו כל בריותיו וכיון שהכל מודים לשמו ("And He will rule over all the world ... and all His creatures shall prostrate before Him for all acknowledge/praise His name"); see L. Ginzberg, *Genizah Studies* (2 vols.; New York: Hermon, 1969) 2.165 (Hebrew).
[185] For other well-known examples, see the second blessing of the Grace after meals as well as in the concluding blessing for the Sabbath *haftarah*. Present: יתברך שמך בפי כל חי לעולם ועד ;ועל הכל אנחנו מודים לך ומברכים אותך. *Seder Ḥibbur Berakhot*, 92, has in the aforementioned second blessing תתברך שמך בפי כל חי, followed up by כל החיים יודוך.
[186] *Sifre Deut.* 31 (ed. Finkelstein, 54).
[187] See Kimelman, "Psalm 145," 58.

both having the recurring terms "peace," "light," "countenance," and "blessing".[188] This prayer of peace confirms the priestly benediction.

At one time, blessing 18, with its climax of the universal acknowledgment of God, may have marked the end of the Amidah. Subsequently, the priestly benediction was appended to increase the correspondence between Temple and synagogue worship.[189] Thus we have the many tannaitic treatments of the Amidah that end with either *Modim* or the priestly benediction,[190] and the tradition of a seventeen-blessing Amidah,[191] as opposed to what rapidly became the accepted eighteen. Tannaitic literature already mandates the marking of blessing 1 and *Modim* (our 18) with a double genuflection at beginning and end,[192] possibly on the model of royal entrance and exit etiquette.[193] Even if the final double genuflection harks back to Temple practice, where, after the sacrifice, the people prostrated themselves as the priests sounded the trumpets, and again as the priests pronounced their blessing,[194] it would still designate the end. In any case, it is incongruous to have an added blessing, even one for peace, after the concluding genuflection.[195]

---

[188] The correlations have been drawn by commentators from the thirteenth to the twentieth century; see Yaqar, *Perush Ha-Tefillot Ve-Ha-Berakhot*, 1.67, *Abudarham*, 203, Moses Przemysl, *Matteh Mosheh* (ed. M. Knoblowicz; Jerusalem: Osar Haposqim, 1978) #175; I. S. Baer, *'Avodat Yisra'el* (Rödelheim, 1868) *ad loc.*; A. Gordon, *Siddur Oṣar Ha-Tefillot* (Jerusalem, 1960) 370-71; A. Landau, *Siddur Ṣeluta De-Avraham* (2 vols.; ed. Y. Werdiger; Tel Aviv, 1958) 1.321; Z. Karl, *Meḥqarim Be-Toledot Ha-Tefillah* (Tel Aviv: , 1950) 77; I. Jacobson, *Netiv Binah* (5 vols.; Tel Aviv: Sinai, 1964-1978) 1.340; and M. Fishbane, "Form and Reformulation of the Biblical Priestly Blessing," *JAOS* 83 (1983) 115-21.
[189] See Elbogen, *Jewish Liturgy*, 62-63 (Hebrew, 54-55); and S. Safrai, "The Temple and the Synagogue," *Synagogues in Antiquity* (ed. A. Kasher, A. Oppenheimer, and U. Rappaport; Jerusalem: Yad Izhak Ben Zvi, 1987) 35 (Hebrew).
[190] See *m. Roš. Haš.* 4:5; *Sifra*, Emor 11 (ed. Weiss, 101d), and Lieberman, *Tosefta Ki-fshutah*, 4.801; along with *m. Tam.* 5:1 and *m. Soṭ.* 7:7; as well as the summary of the Amidah cited above from *Midrash Tanna'im*. Note also the order of מצלא ומדא of Dan 6:11.
[191] See *y. Ber.* 4:3, 8a; and *Num. Rab.* 18.21; along with Elbogen, *Jewish Liturgy*, 34 (Hebrew, 30); and Heinemann, *Prayer*, 142, n. 20.
[192] *t. Ber.* 1:8 and parallels.
[193] So "Rashi" to *Gen. Rab.* 39.12 (Vilna edition, 81a); and Maimonides, *Laws of Prayer* 1:11.
[194] See Ben Sira 50:17,21; 2 Chr 29:28-29; and *Sefer Ben-Sira Ha-Shalem* (ed. Segal, 347). Blessing 17, which introduces the *Modim*, has the following Genizah variant (Mann, "Genizah Fragments," 306-307): רצה יי' אלהינו ושכון בציון כמאז מהרה יעבדוך עבדיך ובירושלים משחוה לך בא"י ש[אותך] ב[יראה] נעבוד ("Be pleased O Lord our God and dwell in Zion as in former times quickly Your servants will serve You and in Jerusalem we will prostrate to You. Blessed are You, O Lord, w[hom] in [awe] we shall serve"). For other such texts, see Luger, *Weekday 'Amidah Based on the Genizah*, 1.205-6.
[195] So *Siddur of R. Solomon of Garmaise*, 102.

The wide variety of versions of blessing 19, including its peroration,[196] also indicate both lateness and a lack of any standardized formulation.[197] Its presence simply reflects the mandate of concluding prayer with a hope for peace.[198] Its formulation is secondary to the mandate itself. Since the motif is not universal peace,[199] its presence is not a function of the Amidah, but a function of the priestly benediction in particular and of conclusions of prayer in general. As it says: "When God sought to bless His people, He found no vessel that would contain all the blessings with which to bless them except peace, as it is said, 'The Lord blesses His people with peace'" (Ps 29:11).[200]

Epilogue

The Amidah turns out to be a remarkable orchestration of redemptive motifs. The absence of the major liturgical indicator of redemption, the Exodus, is thus all the more noticeable. As the major staple in liturgies of redemption, its absence can best be explained by the assumption that the Amidah was composed with the awareness that the Shema, with its conclusion of the redemption from Egypt, will have already been said even if not as part of the same service. The Exodus so complements the Amidah's theme of redemption that it was only a matter of time before the third blessing of the Shema in the morning service – celebrating as it does the redemption from Egypt in such a manner as to quicken the hope for future redemption – was juxtaposed with the Amidah.[201] Once the two were welded together, the Amidah came to be seen as the functional equivalent of the song of salvation intoned during the Exodus. In other words, as the faith-producing salvation at the Re[e]d Sea was followed by the singing of the Song of the Sea (Exod 15:1-19), so should mention of the Exodus be followed by the recital of the Amidah.[202] Similarly, there were efforts to correlate the Amidah and the Song of the Sea.[203] Thus the Amidah came to be the liturgical song of redemption.

---

[196] For some of them, see Finkelstein, "The Development of the Amidah," 173-76.
[197] See Fleischer, "The Shemone Esre," 210.
[198] See *Lev. Rab.* 9.9 (ed. Margulies, 194); and *Massechet Derekh Eretz Zuta*, Pereq Ha-Shalom³ (ed. Sperber, 229 with parallels). The prayer of 3 Maccabees 2:2-20 also ends on a request for peace, but otherwise does not resemble the Amidah (cf. *The Old Testament Pseudepigrapha*, 2.518, note b).
[199] *Pace, Siddur Rav Saadya Gaon*, 19, line 11.
[200] *Sifre Num., Naso* 42, (p. 47, with parallels in notes and elsewhere).
[201] See Kimelman, "The Shema' and Its Rhetoric," 128-30.
[202] *Exod. Rab.* 22.3; see Ginzberg, *Commentary*, 3.239-44.
[203] See *Batei Midrashot* (ed. Wertheimer, 2.72, n. 50; and *Midrash Ha-Gadol, Exodus* (ed. Margulies, 312).

Upon the conjoining of the Shema liturgy with the Amidah, the theme of past redemption was relegated to the third blessing of the Shema, leaving future redemption to the Amidah.²⁰⁴ Once joined for the morning service, they were not to be rent asunder even for the evening service. Keeping them so linked, according to R. Yohanan, rendered one worthy of the future world.²⁰⁵ His senior colleague, R. Joshua b. Levi,

---

²⁰⁴ As Rava said (*B. Pesah.* 117b) קריאת שמע והלל -- גאל ישראל דצלותא -- גואל ישראל. By such standardization of the two perorations, Rava sought to limit the participial form גואל to the Amidah, where, as RaShBaM comments, "we are praying about the future;" see Buber's note in *Midrash Psalms* 107.3 (p. 462, n. 7); *Oṣar Ha-Gaonim* (ed. B. Lewin, 1:34 [responsa]); and S. Sharvit, "The Tense System of Mishnaic Hebrew," *Studies in Hebrew and Semitic Languages Dedicated to the Memory of Professor Eduard Yechezkel Kutscher* (ed. G. Sarfatti, et al.; Ramat Gan: Bar Ilan University Press, 1980) 113. Before the blessing became a prolegomenon to the Amidah, it had concluded with גאל ישראל in the participial form as the other two blessings, יוצר המאורות and הבוחר ב/אוהב עמו ישראל, as attested in a Genizah text (*Kiryat Sefer* 29 [1953/1954] 172. The idea was retained in the Palestinian peroration בא"י צור ישראל וגואלו (*y. Ber.* 1:9, 3d [R. Joshua b. Levi]; and Mann, "Genizah Fragments," 305, frag. #6; 307, frag. #7; 308, frag. #8; 320, frag. #11; and 323, frag. #12) which appears to be a conflation of גאל ישראל and צור ישראל as noted by Goldschmidt, *The Passover Haggada*, 58, n. 29; and Wieder, "Peraqim Be-Toledot Ha-Tefillah Ve-Ha-Berakhot," *Sinai* 77 (1975) 119. Not surprisingly, many of the texts that retain that peroration include petitions for redemption. The Gaonim sought to exclude such petitions by denouncing them as later insertions; see Hoffman, *The Canonization of the Synagogue Service*, 43-46. Since similar petitions appear in the second blessing, for which there is no opposition (see L. Ginzberg, *Geonica* (2 vols.; New York: Hermon, 1968) 1.128), they both must be pre-gaonic. The result of gaonic objections to the widespread practice of petitions for redemption was, as so often is the case, an internally contradictory composite text such as:

1. בגלל אבות הושעת בנים
2. ותביא גאולה לבני בניהם
3. בא"י גאל ישראל

as cited in *Siddur Rav Saadya Gaon*, 110. Even if the הושעת of strophe one is changed to הושיע (as *Seder Rav Amram Gaon*, 20, line 21), the peroration גאל ישראל is inconsistent with the request for redemption; see Heinemann, *Studies in Jewish Liturgy*, 131, n. 8, and 186. Once the Amidah and the third blessing were linked, there arose a need for a clear division of labor, as noted by Rava above. What followed was the effort to expunge from the third blessing petitions for redemption, as R. Saadya Gaon makes explicit; see Heinemann, *Studies in Jewish Liturgy*, 113. Such petitions must be old since the practice of inserting hopes for redemption in commemorations of redemption harks back at least to R. Akiba (see *m. Pesaḥ.* 10:6 with Bokser, *The Origins of the Seder*, 73; and Heinemann, *Prayer*, 130) if not as far back as Isa 63:7-19; see M. Fishbane, *Text and Texture: Close Readings of Select Biblical Texts* (New York: Schocken, 1979) 138-40. See also 1 Macc 7:41-47; 2 Macc 15:22; and 3 Macc 2:4-8, 6:4-8.

²⁰⁵ *b. Ber.* 4b, 9b, see *y. Ber.* 1:1, 2d. Since the idea of the juxtaposition of the prayer of redemption with the Amidah does not appear in any tannaitic document and is only attributed to a *tanna* in some versions of *b. Ber.* 30a, albeit absent in others

however, held that the Amidah should precede the Shema in the evening as it succeeds it in the morning, making the day begin and end with the Shema. His position that the Shema should be the first thing in the morning and the last at night can be backed up by the Shema itself, as it says: "You shall speak of them ... when you lie down and when you get up." The fact that R. Yohanan's position still won out,[206] indicates how powerful the links between the two redemptions were becoming. According to R. Yohanan, since the Shema service always precedes the Amidah, the hope for redemption never becomes disjoined from its living memory.

R. Yohanan's focus on the redemptive theme of the Amidah was sharpened by his appending of the verse, "May the words of my mouth and the meditations of my heart be acceptable to You, my Rock and my Redeemer " (Ps 19:15).[207] This redemptive thrust may explain as well his choice for the preamble to the Amidah: "O Lord, open my lips, and my mouth will proclaim Your praise" (Ps. 51:17),[208] which was deemed by many to be an extension of the theme of redemption.[209]

(see MS Munich 1:286; and *Sefer Ha-Eshkol* (ed. Albeck, 25, n. 8), it owes its acceptance if not its existence to the amoraic period. The innovation is probably that of R. Yohanan, as noted by M. Friedmann in his edition of *Pesiqta Rabbati*, 168a (cf. Lieberman, *Tosefta Ki-fshutah*, 1.31, line 26). Those who sought to locate the practice in the tannaitic period limited R. Yohanan's innovation to the evening service. Apparently his ruling was based on the dawn practice of the "holy community of Jerusalem," which he adopted for all and extended to the evening service. He also introduced the positive reward of redemption for the linkage as opposed to their apotropaic understanding of it as "warding off harm all day long" (*b. Ber.* 9b). On the other hand, the explanation that the juxtaposition follows Ps 20:2 is, as Ginzberg noted (*Commentary*, 1.72), homiletical and not etiological.

[206] Still, it took generations, if not centuries, before R. Yohanan's ruling became universal. In *Midr. Ps.* 19.7, the ruling of R. Joshua b. Levi's remained the evening norm, and medieval authorities were still arguing over whether the blessing of redemption must precede the Amidah in the evening; see J. Katz, *Halakhah and Kabbalah* (Jerusalem: Magnes, 1984) 177-79.

[207] *b. Ber.* 4b and 9b; *y. Ber.* 4:3, 8a. Indeed, the requirement of juxtaposing (the prayer of past) redemption with the Amidah came to supersede the injunction to rise for the Amidah; see *Tosafot*, *b. Ber.* 30a, s.v., *mismakh*, and text thereto. On the appropriateness of Ps 19:15 concluding a petition-prayer, see the apt observation of Fishbane, *Text and Texture*, 90.

[208] *b. Ber.* 9b.

[209] גאולה אריכתא דמי, see Abramson, "Le-Toledot Ha-Sidddur," 208; *idem*, *Inyyanot Be-Sifrut Ha-Ge'onim*, 225; R. Hananel, *Oṣar Ha-Ge'onim, Berakhot*, part 3 (p. 8) as well as apparently Jacob b. Judah Hazan of London, *'Eṣ Ḥayyim* (ed. Brodie, 1.40); Eliezer b. Judah of Worms, *Sefer Ha-Roqeaḥ Ha-Gadol* (ed. Schneersohn, 213); *Sefer RAVYaH* (4 vols.; ed. A. Aptowitzer; Hevrat Mekizie Nir-damim; reprint, Brooklyn, 1983), 1:6 and 16; *Menorat Ha-Maor* (ed. Enelow) 2:176; Rabbenu Yonah *ad* RIF *Berakhot* 4b; Meiri to *b. Ber.* 11b (ed. Dikman) 29, along with his

Others saw Ps 51:17 as proleptic to the Amidah.[210] It serves as an apt lead in to the Amidah because of its intrinsic pertinence to prayer and because of its location before the verses: "You do not want me to bring sacrifices, You do not desire burnt offerings. True sacrifice to God is a contrite spirit" (Ps 51:18f.). By recontextualizing the verse before the Amidah, it makes the point that since statutory communal prayer is either compensatory for, or equivalent to, the sacrifice, the Amidah dispenses with the sacrifice.[211]

The former view that the verse extends the redemption theme may be based on the preceding Psalm verse: "God my Redeemer, that I may sing forth Your beneficence" (Ps 51:16). Psalm 51:17 would then well up out of gratitude to God for being "my Redeemer." Indeed, there was a practice to recite both Ps 51:17 and 19:15 prior to the Amidah.[212] The result has Psalm 51:17, "O Lord, open my lips, and my mouth will proclaim Your praise," serving as a bridge between "Redeemer of Israel" of the blessing and "My Rock and my Redeemer" of Psalm 19:15.

The redemptive thrust is continued in a later midrash that sees a correspondence between the Eighteen Benedictions and the eighteen spiritual blessings for the future.[213] Supplementary requests to the Amidah added to this thrust,[214] along with the verse – "That Your beloved may be delivered, save for Your right hand's sake, and answer me," (Ps 60:7), which was taken as an allusion to the redemption.[215] More recently, a reworking of the question posed on the Day of Judgment: "Did you look forward to redemption?"[216] has found its way in from the margins to some versions of blessing 15 next to "For we have hoped for Your deliverance each and every day."[217]

---

contemporary David b. Samuel of Eatoile, *Sefer Ha-Batim, Bet Ha-Tefillah* (ed. Hershler, 3.1267), who explicitly refers to the verse as מענין הגאולה; and Jacob b. Asher, *Tur Oraḥ Ḥayyim*, section 111 (*pace* Joseph Caro, *Bet Yosef, ad loc.*, s.v., אבל), and so cited in Yechiel Michal Epstein, *Arukh Ha-Shulkhan, Oraḥ Ḥayyim*, 1.111.2.

[210] כתפילה אריכתא דמי (*b. Ber.* 9b).
[211] So *Abudarham*, 94.
[212] *y. Ber.* 4:3, 8a (R. Yudan). Such a practice appears in the Genizah; see Mirsky, *Ha-Piyyut*, 15-16.
[213] Cited in *Sefer Ha-Manhig* 1:109.
[214] See *Seder Rav Amram Gaon*, 28; and Elbogen, *Jewish Liturgy*, 54 (Hebrew, 46-47).
[215] See *Pesiq. Rav Kah.* 17.5 (ed. Mandelbaum, 1.287; and *Midr. Ps.* 137.7.
[216] ציפית לישועה *b. Shab.* 31a), which, according to Albo, "refers to the salvation of the whole nation" (*Iqqarim* 4:48, p. 887).
[217] See M. Weinstock, *Siddur Ha-Ge'onim Ve-Ha-Mequballim Ve-Ha-Ḥasidim* (Jerusalem, 1971) 3.609-610.

In the light of these latter attestations of the redemptive trajectory of the Amidah,[218] and of the liturgical achievement of the orchestration of the full complement of redemptive motifs in order to sustain the hope of redemption, it is no wonder that one ancient version went so far as to complement each of the Amidah's blessings with the request, "Save us,"[219] whereas a late midrash, summarizing communal prayer, notes: "When Israel enters synagogues and academies, they say to the Holy One, blessed be He: 'Redeem us.'"[220]

---

[218] For the messianic speculation of the day; see S. W. Baron, *A Social and Religious History of the Jews* (18 vols.; New York: Columbia University Press, 1952-1983) 5.138-208.

[219] והושיענו (Abramson, "Le-Toledot Ha-Siddur," 189-190; and Schechter, *Studies in Jewish Liturgy*, 98).

[220] גאל אותנו (*Midr. Ps.* 31.1). A similar statement has Israel entering synagogues and academies to acclaim God's kingship (*ibid.*, 5.6). Together they show a synagogue service comprised of an acclamation of divine sovereignty and a prayer of redemption, i.e., the Shema and the Amidah, a combination noted in *Yalqut Shim'oni* 2:1055, p. 1058a (= *Midrash Panim Aḥerim* B, p. 34b) and 2:986, p. 1069b, line 24.

12

Justification through Living – Martin Buber's Third Alternative

Michael Fishbane

For Lou H. Silberman, Scholar and Theologian – In Admiration and Friendship

A Talmud teaching found in *b. Sanhedrin* 119b strikingly conveys Martin Buber's challenge to contemporary religious consciousness. It reads as follows:

> Whoever answers *'amen* with all his strength, for him the gates of paradise are opened. As is said (Isaiah 26:2), "Open ye the gates that the righteous nation, who preserves faithfulness (שׁמר אמנים, *šōmēr 'emunîm*), may enter." Do not recite *šōmēr 'emunîm* (as written) but rather: *še'omrîm 'amen* (שׁאמרים אמן), (those) who say *'amen*!

In this midrash, Resh Lakish has deftly re-cited Isaiah's use of a liturgy of Temple entrance in order to make a new theological point: that righteousness is characterized by the vocal affirmation of communal prayers, and that just this is the gate of paradise. In the process, the prophetic lemma first spoken to the nation is readdressed to individuals; and the ancient "act" of faithfulness is reconstituted as a linguistic performance – as a "speech-act," in fact.

Buber would agree, I think, for he, too, considered "faith," or *'emunā*, to be a life-act realized through the logos of affirmation; that is, through the ever-new response of the individual to the divine Logos of reality – to the fullness of his or her strength in the moment. The chorus of these "dialogical deeds" is the colloquy of faithful living since such "yea-saying" renews one's stance in the world. Religious reality is thus present in the concrete immanence of everyday life, in the on-going saying of *'amen*. In Buber's view, just this act of verification, expressed with all one's strength, opens the gates of paradise – now and forever.

It should thus be clear that in his great teaching of divine immanence, Martin Buber has provided a radical reconfiguration of revelation and religious action. For him, revelation is no unique event, once and past, *in illo tempore*; it is rather a moment *hic et nunc*, here and recurrently present. Or as he put it in *I and Thou*: "(t)hat before which we live, that in which we live, that out of which and into which we live, the mystery (*das Geheimnis*) ... has become present for us (*[e]s ist uns gegenwärtig geworden*)."[1] Following Buber, one may even say that this *Es* (or "it"), this unsayable mystery, becomes personally present to us in the actuality of our life: it becomes "presence as strength" (*eine Gegenwart als Kraft*).[2] Significantly, no fixed content is received here; no solution to a riddle, and "no ... unveiling of being." Rather, Buber adds, "we can only go," each time in a new way and according to the demands of the moment, "and put (this presence as strength) to the proof in action (*bewähren*)."[3] However – and this is a great "however" – even this putting to the proof in action (this "*Bewährung*")

> cannot be handed on (*tradiert*) as a valid ought; it is not prescribed, not inscribed on a table (*Tafel*) that could be put up over everybody's head. The meaning we receive can be put to the proof in action (*bewähren*) only by each person in the uniqueness of his being and the uniqueness of his life. No prescription can lead us to the encounter, and none leads from it. Only the acceptance of the presence (*Gegenwart*) is required to come to it or, in a new sense, to go from it. As we have nothing but a You (*Du*) on our lips when we enter the encounter, it is with this on our lips that we are released from it into the world.[4]

On closer inspection, it is clear that this instruction is a hermeneutical restatement of an earlier one. Buber not only remarks that revelations in the "*Jetzt und Hier*" cannot be transmitted as an impersonal content to others; he also says that it is no "table" that can be "pre-scribed" or "in-scribed" for another. In this formulation, one may surely hear an outright rejection of the לוחות, or tablets of the Sinaitic covenant, upon which were written, or inscribed, prescriptions for all the people. Instead, revelation is for him a direct encounter with the divine presence

---

[1] Here and below the English translation follows *I and Thou* (trans. W. Kaufman; New York: Charles Scribner's Sons, 1970) 159. The German is cited from the edition *Ich und Du* (Leipzig: Inselverlag, 1923) 128.
[2] *I and Thou*, English, 158; German, 127.
[3] *Ibid.*, English, 160; German, 128.
[4] *Ibid.*, English, 159; German, 128.

in and through the living logos of reality.⁵ One can only greet the moment with a verbalization of the presentness that addresses the self. This *"Du"* or "thou-saying," is thus a primal acceptance of the personal presence that reveals itself in the moment. Its more neutral variant is "Amen," just as the communal form of this testimony is Israel's ancient word at Sinai: נעשה ונשמע, "we shall do and hear" (Exod 24:7). That is, we shall hear through doing the demands of the hour.

In a telling passage in *I and Thou*, Buber elaborates the point:

> The life-structure of the pure relation, the "lonesomeness" of the I before the You ... [can] in truth be built up into spatio-temporal continuity only by becoming embodied in the whole stuff of life. It cannot be preserved (*bewahrt*) but only put to the proof in action (*bewährt*)... Man can do justice to the relation to God that has been given to him only by actualizing God in the world in accordance with his ability (*Kraft*) and the measure of each day, daily. This is the only genuine guarantee of continuity.⁶

The task, then, is to renew Sinai in every moment; to overcome the "trials" (*Proben*) and "unavoidable failures" (*Versagen*) of living by a determined "ascent to prove" oneself, a determined *"Aufsteig zur Bewährung."*⁷

Now this *Leitwort "Bewährung,"* as well as the theme of proving oneself in action (*bewähren*), were in Buber's mind long before the final version of *I and Thou*. In fact, virtually all the preceding citations appear in much the same form in Buber's Lehrhaus lectures for 5 March 1922, and the week following, on 12 March 1922.⁸ But the notion already appears in 1919, in the course of an influential lecture delivered to the *"Jung Juda"* group in Prague (entitled-*Cherut*). In this piece, Buber articulated some thoughts on Jewish spiritual renewal and, in particular, criticized those who presented religious truth (*Wahrheit*) as a conceptual abstraction. By contrast, he put forth the view that this truth is a vital

---

⁵ Cf. Buber's treatment of this theme in *Moses, The Revelation and the Covenant* (1946; reprint, Atlantic Highlands, N J: Humanities Press, 1988) 119-40 ('The Words of the Tablets'). For Buber's biblical method and his book *Moses*, see my "Introduction" in the above reprint, pp. 4-12.
⁶ *I and Thou*, English, 162-163; German, 131-32 (I have added the word "can" to link the citations).
⁷ Ibid., English, 152; German, 120.
⁸ Cf. the lectures entitled "Religion als Gegenwart," in R. Horwitz, *Buber's Way to "I and Thou." The Development of Martin Buber's Thought and His "Religion as Presence" Lectures* (Philadelphia: The Jewish Publication Society, 1988) 110, 115 (lectures seven and eight). For the German edition, see idem., *Buber's Way to "I and Thou": An Historical Analysis and the First Publication of Martin Buber's Lectures "Religion als Gegenwart"* (Heidelberg: L. Schneider, 1978). The passages are reformulated in *I and Thou*, 158-59 and 161-63 (cf. German, 128, 132).

force, realized in and through the actions of individuals and communities who put their lives to the proof: *"im Leben des religiösen bewährenden Menschen, im Leben der religiösen bewährenden Menschengemeinschaft."*[9] Many years later Buber returned to this theme of spiritual rebirth in an essay called "Biblical Humanism." He there stated that this "Humanism" depends, in part, on a renewal of the "normative primal forces" latent in the Hebrew Bible – for in this text the voice of God may still be heard – and in this hearing a person who "wills to do and hear what the mouth of the Unconditioned commands" may be renewed.[10] Thus, he said,

> Humanism moves from the mystery of language to the mystery of the human person. The reality of language must become operative in a man's spirit. The truth (*Wahrheit*) of language must prove itself (*soll sich ... bewähren*) in a person's existence. That was the intent of humanistic education, so long as it was alive.[11]

These heroic words were spoken in 1933.[12]

II

I shall return to Buber's remarks on "Biblical Humanism" below. But now, having considered several instances in which the *Leitwort* "*Bewährung-bewähren*" articulates important aspects of his thought, it may be instinctive to note just how the term is used in Buber's translation of the Hebrew Bible – which he rendered into a radically voiced and nuanced German with his great friend, Franz Rosenzweig.

An examination of the one hundred-plus instances of the stem צדק in the Hebrew text – especially the full nominal distribution of such terms as צדק, צדיק, צדקה, צדקות or צדיקות, terms which are commonly rendered by "justice," "just person," "righteousness," "acts of justice/righteousness" and the "just/victorious acts of God," respectively – shows that Buber and Rosenzweig consistently utilized variants of the verb "*bewähren*" or the noun "*Bewährung*" in their Bible translation (though also by such

---

[9] *Cheruth: Eine Rede über Jugend und Religion* (Berlin: Löwit, 1919) 18. The German original uses the verb *bewährenden*, which conveys the living quality of putting life "to the proof." The English edition of "Herut: On Youth and Religion," *On Judaism* (New York: Schocken Books, 1967) 161, gives a misimpression by using the more static phrase "religious actualization" and putting *Bewährung* in a parenthesis.
[10] *On the Bible* (New York: Schocken Books, 1968) 212. Note the allusion to Exod 24:7 here.
[11] *Ibid.*, 213. For the German, see Buber's *Werke* (3 vols.; Munich & Heidelberg: KöselVerlag u. Verlag L. Schneider, 1963) 2.1089.
[12] In *Der Morgen*, Jg. 9 H. 4. Otober 1933. Reprinted in *Die Stunde und die Erkenntnis* (2 vols.; Berlin: Schocken, 1936).

Justification through Living

punning and instructive variants as *"Wahrheit," "Wahrhaftigkeit"* and *"Wahrspruch"*). The intentional precision of this distribution is confirmed by an almost off-hand remark made by the translators in their essay *"Über die Wortwahl,"* published in *Die Schrift und Ihre Verdeutschung* (1936). There, in a comment on *"wurtzelverschiedene Wörter"* (that is, biblical words with stemmatic variations), Buber and Rosenzweig remark that whereas צדק indicates the *"Wahrspruch"* of a case, that is, literally, its "verdict" or external truth telling, the word צדקה points to the interiorization of a certain truth in the course of personal living.[13] This is the phenomenon of *"Bewährung,"* which I rendered earlier as "proving true through action," but which might equally be translated (in light of the stem צדק and its veridical denotation) as "verification" or even "justification." For the authors, then, the relationship between צדק and צדקה, is that between an objective dictum and its human actualization – in a word: its verification in life.

But despite this posture of philological precision, the remarkable fact remains that Buber and Rosenzweig radically transform those passages where צדקה is translated by *"Bewährung."* Two instances can witness the case. The first comes from Deuteronomy 6:25, וצדקה תהיה לנו כי־נשמר לעשות את־כל־המצוה הזאת לפני יהוה אלהינו. This is rendered as follows: *"Und Bewährung wird uns sein, wenn wir hüten, all dieses Gebot zu tun, von Seinem unseres Gottes Antlitz"*; that is, literally, "And a proving true (or justification) will be ours, if we observe to do all this commandment, before the face of our God." Now as any Bible scholar knows, this verse is notoriously difficult – both with respect to the precise force of the noun צדקה, which may arguably have the sense of "victory" or "success" as the promised *quid pro quo* for observance of the Law, according to Deuteronomistic theological pragmatism; and also with respect to the particular poignancy of doing "all" the mitzvah, or commandment "before God." By and large, the rabbinic tradition cut the hermeneutical knot here, as elsewhere, by taking צדקה in the sense of an earned merit which God will credit those who justly perform His service.[14] In their own striking version, however, Buber and Rosenzweig depart from any sense of a substantive, external benefit accredited the observant person. Indeed, by means of the term *"Bewährung"* they present the significantly different theological perspective that a life lived in immediate response to God's presence will prove or verify the

---

[13] See in *Die Stunde und die Erkentnis*, 2.1124.
[14] On this passage, Targum Onqelos gives the Aramaic word זכותא ("merit"). R. Abraham ibn Ezra cites this interpretation as an anonymous tradition. For his own opinion, however, Ibn Ezra suggests that the phrase means that the gentiles will see that the performance of the commandments makes one "righteous."

objective truth of that meeting through the full subjectivity of that life. That is, one's living not only justifies the encounter with divine mystery, insofar as one is able, but in and through this living one's life is also justified.

A second example of this existential hermeneutic can be adduced from Isaiah 1:27: ציון במשפט תפדה ושביה בצדקה. Buber and Rosenzweig translate: "*Zion wird durch Recht abgegelten, seine Umkehrenden durch Bewährung*"; that is, in a literalizing English, "Zion shall be redeemed through justice and its repentant ones through proving themselves (in action)." Once again, a complicated passage and its exegetical history have been decisively reconfigured. Read straightforwardly, one may note that the toponymn ציון (Zion) is balanced by the noun שביה (her residents), and that the juridical noun משפט (*Recht*) is complemented by the term צדקה (*Bewährung*). That is to say, two objective references to a site (Zion; her) are complemented by two objective terms for justice – the words משפט and צדקה which routinely occur as a hendiadys. Linking the two hemistichs is the one verb תפדה – so that the second verset (ושביה בצדקה) can arguably convey the sense that the residents of Zion will (also) be redeemed by acts of צדק – that is, correct justice. The prophecy thus closes with the *quid pro quo* that will reverse the doom brought about by injustice – so fully detailed at the beginning of the chapter.

By contrast with this construal, rabbinic tradition had long since offered the possibility that the noun שביה could refer to "(Zion's) repentant ones," not "her residents";[15] and just this reading provided the translators with a new theological option. For, once the word שביה was transformed from a noun to a verb, צדקה could legitimately be rendered as the verbal noun "prove true" – that is as "*Bewährung*." Inevitably, the original ballast of the sentence – especially that between the terms משפט and צדקה, "justice" and "righteousness" – was upset, with the result that the sentence now moves cumulatively from the objective acts of "*Recht*," viz. משפט, to their personal realization or verification in lived life, viz. "*Bewährung*." The new verb, ושביה, is now crucial to the sense of the whole, and no mere parallel to the toponymn "Zion." The new meaning is that Zion will be redeemed by acts of משפט, and that those who "turn" or "repent" will be redeemed through proving themselves, or realizing this justice, in action. Thus in addition to the human turning towards God's presence, which is, according to Buber, the worldly side of redemption, there is a salvation in this very encounter with the living presence of God. Indeed, in a remarkable pun in *I and Thou*, Buber observes that this presence is "known to us as salvation (*Erlösung*),"

---

[15] Cf. the influential commentary of Rashi.

though it is no objective "solution (*Lösung*)" to life's mystery.[16] Buber then concludes with the words: "(w)e can only go and put (this encounter) to the proof in action (*bewähren*)."[17] Thus the one who responds justly to the demands of the hour, who wholeheartedly turns to them, verifies himself and the divine truth which has addressed him. The hermeneutical translation of Isaiah 1:27 confirms this new theology of justification.

III

At this point we are required to ask: What is the context for this notion of verification or justification? In posing the question, I do not mean to inquire into the possible roots of the term "*Bewährung*" in the philosophical lexicon, but rather into its place in theological discourse. A look at one more verse will make the point. That verse – of enormous importance to Western religious consciousness – is Genesis 15:6. In it the narrator refers to Abram's confidence in God's promise as follows: והאמן ביהוה ויחשבה לו צדקה. "He (Abram) believed (or: trusted) the Lord, and He (the Lord) reckoned it for him (viz., for Abram) as/for צדקה." As in Deuteronomy 6:25, a theological *quid pro quo* is spelled out here; though now it is precisely an act of faith or trust in a divine promise that results in צדקה for the individual.

But what is צדקה? Characteristically, the Buber-Rosenzweig translation bypasses the ancient Targumic and medieval Jewish tradition, in which צדקה indicates some form of theological credit reckoned to Abram's heavenly account.[18] For this would mean that faith is some "thing," some datum with a discernible – even impersonal – content. But as we have seen, Buber thoroughly rejects this onto-theology of fixed faith, fixed dogmas, and fixed idea of God. For him, faith (אמונה) is a faithfulness (or being true) to a moment of encounter with the divine mystery.[19] Accordingly, the Buber-Rosenzweig translation also disregards Luther's influential use of "*Glaube*" to indicate Abram's faith

---

[16] *I and Thou*, English, 160; German, 128.
[17] *I and Thou*, "*Wir können nur gelten und bewähren.*"
[18] The Aramaic Term is זכו ("merit"). This interpretation is followed by Rashi (who glosses צדקה with זכות) and Seforno. Ibn Ezra refers to Deuteronomy 6:25, and to the legal hendiadys צדק ומשפט. Ramban contradicts Rashi's interpretation, not believing that Abram could be a man of such little faith as to need a reward. He therefore interprets the remark as indicating Abram's faith in God's power to fulfill His promise through "His righteousness." Cf. R. David Kimhi and Hizkuni.
[19] For an extended discussion of Buber's conception of God, see now P. Mendes-Flohr, *Divided Passions, Jewish Intellectuals and the Experience of Modernity* (Detroit: Wayne State University Press, 1991), chapter 10.

as well as his use of *"rechnen"* and *"Gerechtigkeit"* to render the verb חשב and the noun צדקה, respectively. Instead, the following exegetical version is produced: *"Er aber vertraute Ihm; das achtete er ihm als Bewährung"*; that is, "(Abram) however, continued to trust (God); so that (God) deemed this as the proving true of him." The unique point here is that whereas אמונה is normally manifested in צדקה, viz. as *"Bewährung,"* now, in this case, Abram's subjective stance of continuous trust is deemed by God to be an objective act of his proving himself true – for, in fact, this was the only "act" to be done.

Against this background, the theological innovation in Buber's use of *"Bewährung"* to render צדקה is certain. It is not simply a term that emphasizes an ongoing existential verification of God's truth in the world, or one that marks a strong stand against onto-theology and the idea of a fixed "Revelation" in the past with a "Truth" for all believers. It is this and more. Indeed, once we recall that Genesis 15:6 was repeatedly used by Paul in his Epistle to the Romans to support his doctrine of "justification" by faith – that is, of a "righteousness through faith"; or, as he says in Romans 3:21, of a "righteousness from God apart from the law" (χωρὶς νόμου δικαιοσύνη θεοῦ) – and that this teaching is a replacement of righteous works (referred to in Philipians 3:5-6 as κατὰ δικαιοσύνην τὴν ἐν νόμῳ) by a "righteousness through faith," then Buber's theological alternative is clear. Over against any sense of a religious accounting or justification before God through (fixed) righteous deeds, on the one side, or through faith (in a specific "thing") on the other, Buber's use of *"Bewährung"* teaches the challenge of a living אמונה in the course of life – such that one's faithfulness to the address of God's presence is proved only through concrete acts in this world. Righteousness – be it צדקה or δικαιοσύνη – is thus neither observance of the Torah of Moses nor belief in the atoning sacrifice of Jesus Christ, but *"Bewährung"*: a proving true through life of God's living presence. Not works or faith, then – but justification through a faithful realization of the divine truth of the hour. This is Martin Buber's third alternative.

This said, I hasten to stress that such a theological construction is not so much a new reconciliation of classical Judaism and Christianity, or even some post-modernist turn towards an immanentist theology. It is all this and more; and this more is Buber's pronounced return to a radical biblical perspective. In his late monograph *Two Types of Faith* (completed in 1950), Buber is quite explicit on this point. He there refers to ancient Israel as a primordial manifestation of authentic religious trust, in which persons stand firm in their relationship with God during all the trials of life. The great model in this "persistence in trust" is Abraham. According to Buber, his way initiated a genealogy of trust that marks the religiosity of prophets from Moses to Jesus. Paul, however, is excluded from this chain; for in Buber's construction, this man of Tarsus marks the manifestation of the second type of faith. Hereby, "belief" and not "trust" is the keyword; and a person is "converted" as an isolated individual, rather than "finding" or maintaining "himself" in community and relationship.

As a prototype of "immovable steadfastness," Abraham "continued to trust" God (*weiter vertraute*); and "God receives" this "attitude of faith" as a "proving him true," a "*Bewährung.*"[20] Thus does Buber place Genesis 15:6 at the core of *Two Types of Faith*; and so, too, does he further clarify the spiritual modality of *Bewährung* when he remarks: "(Z)edaka is the manifestation of the conformity (*Übereinstimmung*) between what is done and meant in the personal conduct of life, the proving true (which idea is then transferred to God as confirmation of his benevolence)." But "(W)hich action in the past has the character of a proving true (*Bewährung*) can in the nature of the case be decided neither by the individual nor the community, but by God alone, through His 'deeming,' in which everything human becomes openly what it is."[21]

These remarks have an eschatological ring insofar as the true value or verity of earthly actions are deemed clear only within the full perspective of God – and not the thickness of earthly life, where we can only give proof to our share in the reality revealed to us at any one moment. A similar tone reverberates throughout the luminous finale of Rosenzweig's *Star of Redemption*. There, too, we hear that the full truth (*Wahrheit*) is fulfilled only in the ultimate realization of eternity, the great "all-day" of light. Before that divine illumination and confirmation of "All" there is only "*das Bewähren der Wahrheit,*" "the verification of verity."[22] The proving true of that part of Truth as imparted to us in the here and now.

For the Christian this translates theologically into a "*Gestalt der Bewährung*" or "Shape of Verification"[23] which extends eschatologically into the world, forever filling time and space with the rays of Truth's fire, forever parsing this Truth in the languages of the nations. By contrast, says Rosenzweig, the Jew heeds "*Das Gesetz der Bewährung,*" the "Law of Verification"[24] – for he maintains an enduring witness to God's Truth through a faithful commitment to the center of the fire, and a refusal to compromise this flame to the end of time. Indeed, in this theology, the

---

[20] M. Buber, *Zweiglaubensweisen*, in *Werke*, 1.681.
[21] *Werke*, 1.682; *Two Types of Faith* (New York: Harper & Row, 1961) 45.
[22] *Der Stern Der Erlösung* (3 vols.; 2d ed.; Frankfurt am Main: J. Kaufmann, 1930) 3.153; and *The Star of Redemption* (trans. William Hallo; New York: Holt, Reinhart and Winston, 1970) 379.
[23] *Ibid.*, German, 177; English, 398.
[24] *Ibid.*, German, 197; English, 413.

מצות (commandments) are the ever-renewed realization of the eschatological seal stamped upon the heart of Israel at Sinai; and it is to the dialogical truth of that great moment that one remains faithful in all the "Sinaitic" renewals of life. For Rosenzweig, Jewish life is authentic because it is a waiting in trust – not an awakening of love before its time.

There are thus "two types" of Bewährung in the Star of Redemption: two theologies in eternal difference – though each, for its part, remains a valid realization of God's whole Truth. Buber thought otherwise; for though he spoke of "two types" of faith, he acknowledged only one type of Bewährung – this being the living actualization of God's eternal revelation, verified by the way of Abraham. For him, this patriarch is the prototype of true faith; the path of Paul leads elsewhere.

IV

These threads of thought may serve to introduce a final musing on Buber's teaching of "justification" – one in which the issue of "perseverance" is absolutely central. I mention this issue here because it has often and cavalierly been asserted that Buber's "I-Thou" theology offers cheap grace, in the sense that God's presence is supposedly easily available to the fully alert or attentive person. Correlatively, it is also asserted that Buber's writings reveal no tense or intense involvement with evil (however radical, however real). The foregoing consideration of Bewährung suggests otherwise. It rather proves that the whole weight of Buber's teaching was to instruct modern man to stand firm amid the trials of life: to endure the absence of God and the reign of "It" by steadfast allegiance to the truths of God's presence made manifest in rare moments of real hearing – be these when persons speak as persons; when events bespeak their hourly demands; or when the Bible is renewed as an instructing "voice." Such אמונה is spiritual integrity *de profundis*.

Buber gave expression to this ideal of remaining steadfast to the truths of dialogue during the dark nights of history in his 1933 essay on "Biblical Humanism." I remarked earlier how Buber vaunted the Hebrew Bible as one of the means to restore immediacy with the world precisely because biblical language "preserves (*bewahrt*) the dialogical character of living reality"; precisely because it is "an event in mutuality."[25] For Buber, in fact, the biblical "word is fulfilled, by way of individual man and the people, not in a perfected form (*Gebild*), but in a proof of self (*Bewährung*)." The speech of God is thus brought to completion by the one who lives it. The high task of biblical humanism,

---

[25] *art. cit.* (nn. 10-11); English, 216; German, 1092.

Justification through Living

then, is to "train" one to remain "steadfast" in the words of Scripture; "to prove himself in them."

This heroic way does not avoid evil, but resists it with a spiritual determination to remain present to the possibilities of the moment – whatever moment. Indeed, if one listens carefully to the stirring finale of the essay, one may hear (with dramatic irony and eeriness) the overtones of the Sinai theophony behind the satanic sounds of Nazi strife. "This stormy night," says Buber, "these shafts of lightning flashing down, this threat of destruction – do not escape from them into a world of logos, of perfected form! Stand fast, hear the word in the thunder, obey, respond! This terrifying world is the world of God. It lays claim upon you. Prove yourself (*Bewähre dich*) in it as a man of God!"[26]

And this Buber did. For him, the catastrophic crisis of hope in that era of evil became an occasion to exhort fellow Jews to stand firm. Exemplary is his monumental anthology entitled *Aus Tiefen Rufe Ich Dich*.[27] Twenty-three biblical psalms make up this work of spiritual resistance, a number that is certainly a symbolic indicator of the ideal of trust expressed in Psalm 23. But there is more. For this anthology is also marked by the spiritual ideal of *Bewährung*. As a call from the textual depths, the lonely person in history is encouraged to stand firm in the faith that evil will pass, and that truthfulness is a way supported by God. "For you are not a God who desires evil," says the speaker of Psalm 5, (therefore) "scoffers will not stand fast before you." The צדיק (*den Bewährten*), is transfigured by this אמונה, and thus, so to speak, is protected by God's grace (כצנה רצון תעטרנו).[28] Humans are thus justified by their courage to remain faithful to the living presence of God in our world, and this proving true is a way of sorrows and trial.

***

Let me conclude by recalling the patriarch Abraham and a Hasidic teaching about his great trial. It was reported by Buber as a dialogical instruction; not, to be sure, an instruction in specifics, but rather an exhortation to make the dialogical way primary. More paradoxically, it is an instruction in and through the abyss of crisis. Let us hear:

> *Question:* Why is the sacrifice of Isaac considered so glorious? (Surely) [A]t that time, our Father Abraham had already reached a high rung of holiness, and so it was no wonder that he immediately did as God asked him!

---

[26] Ibid.
[27] (Berlin: Schocken, 1936).
[28] *Aus Tiefen Rufe Ich Dich*, 22-25.

Answer: When man is tried, all the rungs and all holiness are taken from him. Stripped of everything he has obtained, he stands face to face with God *who is putting him to the test.*[29]

Nisayon is thus the banner of faith: it is life as *Bewährung,* where the individual stands with ethical and spiritual resolve before the demanding, mysterious face of God. For Buber, this is Torah. All the rest is commentary.

---

[29] Martin Buber, *Ten Rungs: Hasidic Sayings* (New York: Schocken Books, 1947; repr. 1962), 72; emphasis added. The teaching plays on the verb נסה (*nissah*), "to test," in Genesis 22:1. In his translation, Buber renders "God tested" by "*Gottprüfte.*"

Addendum to the Bibliography of Lou H. Silberman in *The Divine Helmsman*

ed. James L. Crenshaw and Samuel Sandmel, New York: KTAV, 1980

Edited Volumes

Aichele, George Jr. *The Limits of Story*. Semeia Studies, ed. Lou H. Silberman. Philadelphia/Atlanta: Fortress/Scholars Press, 1985.

Lategan, Bernard C. and Willem S. Vorster. *Text and Reality: Aspects of Reference in Biblical Texts*. Semeia Studies, ed. Lou H. Silberman. Philadelphia/Atlanta: Fortress/Scholars Press, 1985.

Magness, J. Lee. *Sense and Absence: Structure and Suspension in the Ending of Mark*. Semeia Studies, ed. Lou H. Silberman. Atlanta: Scholars Press, 1986.

Orality, Aurality and Biblical Narrative, ed. Lou H. Silberman. Semeia Studies 39. Decatur, GA: Society of Biblical Literature/Scholars Press, 1987.

Articles and Reviews

1943

"God Requires the Heart," *The Jewish Layman* 18:1 (October 1943) 22-23.

1957

Review of *The Living Talmud: The Wisdom of the Fathers and its Classical Commentaries* by Judah Goldin. *Journal of Biblical Literature* 70:2 (1957) 270.

1958

Review of *Where Judaism Differed* by Abba Hillel Silver. *Studies in Bibliography and Booklore* 3:3-4 (December 1958) 134-36.

Review of *The Religions of Man,* by Houston Smith. *Studies in Bibliography and Booklore* 3:3-4 (December 1958) 173.

1963

Review of *Book of Asseverations (Code of Maimonides),* by B. D. Klien. *Journal of Biblical Literature* 76:2 (1963) 237.

1964

"God and Man" in *Great Jewish Ideas,* ed. Abraham E. Milgram. B'nai B'rith Great Books Series, Vol. 5. Clinton, MA: Colonial Press, 1964, pp. 151-63.

1979

"Whence *Siglum* Q: A Conjecture," *Journal of Biblical Literature* 98:2 (1979) 287-88.

"The Transmigration of a Tale (With an apology to Y. L. Peretz)," *Journal of Reform Judaism* (Fall 1979), 77-79.

1980

"On the Perversity of Historians," *Sh'ma: A Journal of Jewish Responsibility* 10:199 (October 17, 1980) 150-51.

"Not a Mirror but a Window: A Comment on the Study of Rabbinic Literature," in *Go and Study: Essays and Studies in Honor of Alfred Jospe,* ed. Raphael Jospe. Washington, DC: B'nai B'rith Hillel Foundation, 1980, pp. 143-46.

Review of *Visions of the Void: Theological Reflections on the Work of Elie Wiesel,* by Michael Berenbaum. *Religion in Life* XLIX:1 (Spring, 1990) 122-23.

1981

"Prophets/Angels: LXX and Qumran Psalm 151 and the Epistle to the Hebrews," in *Standing Before God: Studies in Prayer in Scripture and Tradition with Essays in Honor of John Oesterreicher*, ed. Asher Finkel and Lawrence Frizzell. New York: KTAV, 1981, pp. 91-101.

"A Theological Treatise on Forgiveness: Chapter Twenty-Three of Pesiqta DeRab Kahana," in *Studies in Aggadah Targum and Jewish Liturgy in Memory of Joseph Heinemann*, ed. by Jakob Petuchowski and Ezra Fleischer. Jerusalem/Cincinnati: Magnes/Hebrew Union College, 1981, pp. 95-107.

1982

Review of *Unfinished Business: An Autobiography*, by W. Gunther Plaut. *Sciences Religieuses/Studies in Religion* 11:3 (1982) 336-37.

"Toward a Rhetoric of Midrash: A Preliminary Account," in *The Biblical Mosaic: Changing Perspectives*, ed. Robert M. Polzin and Eugene Rothman. Philadelphia/Chico, CA: Fortress/Scholars Press, 1982, pp. 15-26.

"Geistesgeschichtliche Aspecte des Verhaltnisses Utopie und Hoffnung," *Christliche Glaube in Moderner Gesellschaft* (Freiburg i.Br, 1982) vol. 23, 57-71, 84-86.

"Das Falkenberg'che Gebetbuch: A Bibliographic Adventure," in *Through the Sound of Many Voices: Writings Contributed on the Occasion of the 70th Birthday of W. Gunther Plaut*, ed. Jonathan V. Plaut. Toronto: Lester & Orpen Dennys, 1982, pp. 209-19.

1983

"Wellhausen and Judaism," in *Wellhausen and His Prolegomenon to the History of Israel*, ed. Douglas A. Knight. Semeia 25. Chico, CA: Scholars Press, 1983, pp. 75-82.

"Listening to the Text. The Presidential Address to The Society of Biblical Literature, 1982," *Journal of Biblical Literature* 102:1 (1983) 3-36.

"Schoolboys and Storytellers: Some Comments on Aphorisms and Chriae," in *Kingdom and Children: Aphorism, Chriae, Structure*, ed. Daniel Patte. Semeia 29. Chico, CA: Society of Biblical Literature/Scholars Press, 1983, pp. 109-15.

Review of *Rabban Gamaliel II: The Legal Tradition*, by Shammai Kanter. *The Second Century: A Journal of Early Christian Studies* 3:2 (Summer, 1983) 124-26.

Review of *Archaeology, the Rabbis, and Early Christianity: The Social and Historical Setting of Palestinian Judaism and Christianity*, by Eric M. Meyers and James F. Strange. *Biblical Archaeologist* 46:2 (Spring 1983) 125-26.

1985

"Response to Douglas Knight: But How Does it Happen? A Note on 'Predecessor and Successors,'" in *Biblical Hermeneutics in Jewish Moral Discourse*, ed. Peter J. Haas. Semeia 34. Decatur, GA: Scholars Press, 1985, pp. 25-27.

1986

"Questing for Justice: Reflections on Deuteronomy and Job." *Founders Day Addresses*. Cincinnati: Hebrew Union College, 1986, pp. 18-27.

"Challenge and Response: Pesiqta deRab Kahana, Chapter 23, as an Oblique Reply to Christian Claims," in *Christians Among Jews and Gentiles: Essays in Honor of Krister Stendahl on his 65th Birthday*, ed. George W. E. Nicklesburg with George MacRae. Philadelphia: Fortress, 1986, pp. 247-53.

"Scholem to Eisler: On the Publication of Das Buch Bahir," in *Studies in Bibliography and Booklore* 16 (1986) 5-7.

"'What's the Matter with Warsaw?' A Comment," *American Jewish Archives* XXXVIII (Nov. 1986) 185-86.

1987

"*Aggadah* and *Halakhah*: Ethos and Ethics in Rabbinic Judaism," in *The Life of the Covenant: The Challenge of Contemporary Judaism: Essays in Honor of Herman Schaalman*, ed. J. A. Edelheit. Chicago: Spertus College of Jewish Studies, 1987, pp. 223-33.

"The Question of Job's Generation. *She'elat Doro Shel Doro Shel 'Iyob*: Buber's Job," in *Judaic Perspectives on Ancient Israel*, ed. Jacob Neusner, Baruch Levine and Ernest Frerichs. Philadelphia: Fortress, 1987, pp. 261-69.

Review of *Biblical Interpretation in Ancient Israel*, by Michael Fishbane, *Hebrew Studies* 26 (1987) 173-76.

"Reflections on Orality, Aurality and Perhaps More," in *Orality, Aurality and Biblical Narrative*, ed. Lou H. Silberman. Semeia 39. Atlanta: Scholars Press, 1987, pp. 1-6.

1988

Review of *The Old Testament Pseudepigrapha. Volume 1: Apocalyptic Literature and Testaments*, ed. James H. Charlesworth. Garden City, NY: Doubleday, 1981, and *Volume 2: Expansions of the "Old Testament" and Legends Wisdom and Philosophical Literature. Prayers Psalms and Odes Fragments of Lost Judeo-Hellenistic Works*, ed. James H. Charlesworth. Garden City, NY: Doubleday, 1985; and James H. Charlesworth, *The Old Testament Pseudepigrapha and the New Testament*. Society for New Testament Studies Monograph Series. Cambridge: Cambridge University Press, 1986. *Biblical Archaeologist* 51:1 (1988) 57-58.

1989

"From Apocalyptic Proclamation to Moral Prescript: Abot 2,15-16," *Journal of Jewish Studies* XL:1 (Spring 1989) 53-60.

"Conflict for the Sake of Heaven," in *Justice and the Holy: Essays in Honor of Walter J. Harrelson*, ed. Douglas A. Knight and Peter J. Paris. Atlanta: Scholars Press, 1989, pp. 187-201.

1990

"Paul's Midrash: Reflections on Romans 4," in *Faith and History: Essays in Honor of Paul W. Meyer*, ed. John T. Carroll, Charles H Cosgrove, E. Elizabeth Johnson. Atlanta: Scholars Press, 1990, pp. 99-104.

"Dionysian Reveller?" *Hebrew Studies* XXXI (1990) 41-45.

1991

Review of *Das Kontrastgleichnis in der rabbinschen Literatur*, by Talia Thorion-Vardi. *Hebrew Studies* XXXII (1991) 176-77.

1992

"My Two Caring Communities," *Sh'ma: A Journal of Jewish Responsibility* 22 (January 1992) 33-34.

1993

"Understanding a Midrash Text: The Case of the Inhabitants of Nineveh," in *Bits of Honey: Essays for Samson H. Levey*, ed. Stanley F.

Chyet and David H. Ellenson. South Florida Studies in the History of Judaism 74. Atlanta: Scholars Press, 1993, pp. 121-30.

1994

Review of *Jew and Gentile in the Ancient World*, by L. H. Feldman, *Shofar* 13:1 (1994) 159-62.

"Whither Are We Going? A Response to David Polish," in *Israel and Diaspora: A New Agenda?* New York: Institute on American-Israeli Relations/The American Jewish Committee, 1994, pp. 10-13.

"Model for the Lucan Infancy Narrative?" *Journal of Biblical Literature* 113:3 (Fall 1994) 491-93.

Review of *From Text to Tradition: A History of Second Temple and Rabbinic Judaism*, by Lawrence H. Schiffman. *Hebrew Studies* XXXV (1994) 207-9.

1995

"Boldness in the Service of Justice," in *Preaching Biblical Texts*, ed. Fredrick L. Holmgren and Herman E. Schaalman. Grand Rapids: Eerdmans, 1995, pp. 29-35.

1996

"Once Again the Use of Rabbinic Material," *New Testament Studies* 42:1 (1996) 153-55.

Sermons and Miscellanea

1986

A Note in *biz hundert un tavantsik: A Tribute Volume for Dr. Jacob Rader Marcus on the Occasion of his 90th Birthday*, edited by Abraham J. Peck and Jonathan D. Sarna. Cincinnati: Hebrew Union College-Jewish Institute of Religion, 1986, p. 71.

Forthcoming

"Paul's Viper," *Forum* 8:3-4

"'You Cannot See My Face': Seeking to Understand Divine Justice," in *The Darkened Face of God in the Old Testament (Crenshaw Festschrift)*, ed. David Penchansky.

Index

Authors

Abegg, M. G. 195
Abusch, Z. 71
Ahlstrom, G. 18, 19
Albeck, A. 201, 216
Albright, W. F. 4, 10
Allison, D. 102
Alt, A. 61
Alter, R. 12, 20
Amusin, I. D. 52
Anderson, B. W. 29, 31
Anderson, G. 80
Ap-Thomas, D. R. 62
Arnaud, D. 59
Assaf, S. 183
Attridge, H. W. 151, 166
Avigad, N. 118
Aviram, J. 13
Bacher, W. 104
Baer, Y. 181, 213
Baillet, M. 18
Baldwin, J. 195
Bar-Ephrat, S. 28
Bar-Ilan, M. . . 104, 175, 200, 204, 207
Bar-Yosef, O. 8
Baron, S. W. 218
Barr, J. 20, 205
Bauer, J. B. 84
Bealieu, P.-A. 56
Beare, F. W. 104
Beentijes, P. C. 84
Ben-Barak, S. 68, 71, 73
Beck, P. 44
Becker, H.-J. 104
Behm, J. 135
Benetreu, S. 151
Benz, F. 103
Berkovits, E. 178
Beyer, K. 121
Bickerman, E. J. 86, 97, 152,
181, 187, 191
Binford, L. R. 16
Biram, A. 13
Blenkinsopp, J. 38, 39, 41, 65
Bokser, B. 191, 215
Bonani, G. 123
Bonner, S. F. 173
Borger, R. 58, 59
Braun, H. 151
Brock, S. P. 67
Brody, Y. 201
Brooten, B. 106, 113
Bronznick, N. M. 44, 45
Broshi, M. 14, 123
Bruce, F. F. 150
Brueggeman, W. 34, 36
Bryan, D. T. 26
Buber, M. 220, 228
Buchanan, G. W. 147, 151
Budge, E. A. W. 149, 152
Buhl, F. 54

237

Buisson, Le Compte du
    Mesnil du 152
Burney, C. F. 72
Burtchall, J. 113
Buss, M. J. 10
Cabrol, F. 155
Calvin, J. 151
Carmi, I. 123
Charlesworth, J. H. 67, 126,
            148, 152, 187, 194
Chazon, E. G. 175, 177
Childs, B. S. 10, 20, 26
Clarcke, G. W. 203, 204
Clements, R. 85-87, 92
Clines, D. J. A. 26, 28
Coats, G. W. 31, 36
Cohen, M. S. 200
Cohen, N. G. 175, 184
Cohen, S. J. D. 31, 110, 112, 114
Cohn, R. L. 29, 30, 37, 38, 41
Conkey, M. W. 16, 18
Collins, J. J. 68, 75, 195
Collins, R. F. 136
Coogin, M. D. 22, 71, 75
Coote, R. B. 10, 22
Cornelius, I. 47
Cosby, M. 148, 151
Cowgill, G. L. 18
Crenshaw, J. L. .... vii-x, 82, 85, 87,
            88, 92
Cross, F. M. 52, 115, 127
Culley, R. C. 10, 14, 15, 29
Damrosch, D. 26, 31, 33, 37, 39
Dan, J. 173
Danker, F. W. 150, 151
Daube, D. 173
Davidson, J. 176
Davies, J. H. 150, 151
Davies, P. R. 20
Davies, W. D. 102
Day, P. L. 11, 14, 20, 89
Delcor, M. 52
Delitzsch, F. 151

Demarest, A. A. 16
Denis, A. M. 150
Dentan, R. C. 87
Dever, W. G. ..... ix, x, 4, 7-10, 13, 14,
            15, 19-23
Dhorme, P. 54
Diakanoff, Z. M. 52
Dietrich, W. 22, 49
DiLella, A. 96, 194
Dimant, D. 118
Dods, M. 151
Dommershausen, W. 57
Dougherty, P. R. 56
Dozeman, T. B. 87
Drinkard, J. F. 11
Duensing, H. 149, 150, 153, 155
Dupont-Sommer, A. 52, 53
Edelman, D. V. 18, 20
Eissfeldt, O. 62
Elbogen, I. 178, 196, 213
Eliner, E. 199
Elon, M. 69
Eshel, E. 123
Eshel, H. 123
Exxum, C. 22
Fauer, J. 200
Feldman, L. H. 149
Feldman, Y. 55
Feliks, Z. 69
Fichtner, J. 85
Fiensy, D. A. 200
Finkel, A. 111
Finkelstein, I. 20, 44
Finkelstein, J. J. 193, 195, 198, 214
Fischel, H. 173
Fischer, G. 14
Fish, M. 213, 215
Fishbane, M. .... x, 26, 29, 31, 80, 87,
            100, 101, 164, 195, 221
Fitzmeyer, J. A. 115, 121
Fleischner, E. 171, 182, 184, 190,
            209, 214
Fohrer, G. 52, 57

Index

Fokkelman, J.P. 28, 29
Fontaine, C. R. 82
Franklin, P. 88
Fraser, G. 8
Freedman, D. N. 10, 40, 52, 104
Frei, H. 20
Frerichs, E. S. 63
Freymer-Kensty, T. 40, 48
Friedman, M. 189, 191, 206, 216
Frick, E. S. 63
Frisch, A. 48
Gadd, C. J. 56, 58
Galling, K. 62
Garbini, G. 20, 22
Garcia, F. 52
Garelli, P. 50
Garland, D. 103
Garrett, S. R. 68
Gaster, M. 150
Geertz, C. 15
Geveryahu, M. I. 52
Germann, H. 84
Gerstenberger, E. 84
Gilman, A. 16
Ginzberg, L. 176-178, 180, 184, 186, 196, 197, 201, 202, 207, 212
Gnuse, R. 35
Goldin, J. 86, 189
Goldschmidt, E. D. 189, 204, 208, 215
Goldstein, J. 204
Goodblatt, D. 113, 185
Goodenough, E. R. 148, 152, 154
Goodman, M. 185
Goshen-Gottstein, M. 127
Gottwald, N. K. 10, 14, 23
Grabbe, L. 100
Graham, W. C. 7
Gray, J. 61
Greenspoon, L. J. 204
Grelot, P. 149
Gunkel, H. 5
Gunn, D. 28

Gunneweg, A. H. J. 89
Gutmann, J. 155
Haberman, A. H. 53
Hachlili, R. 105
Hadani, J. 187, 201
Halkin, F. 149
Halpern, B. 20, 63
Haran, M. 37, 56, 57, 84
Hare, D. R. A. 102, 148, 149, 152
Harnack, A. 107
Harris, W. V. 85
Hartman, D. 194
Hartman, L. 55
Hasel, G. 8
Haspecker, J. L. 92
Hauser, A. J. 28
Hawkes, C. 17
Hayes, J. H. 20
Hegermann, H. 150, 151
Heinemann, J. 96, 175, 177, 187, 193, 194, 197
Heiler, F. 84
Heller, B. 150
Hengel, M. 87
Hershler, M. 173, 209
Hershler, Y. 173
Hess, R. S. 26
Hesse, F. 196
Hestrin, R. 47
Hezser, C. 99
Hinke, W. J. 59
Hirsch, S. R. 181
Hodder, I. 8, 13, 16-18, 23
Hoenig, S. B. 101
Hoffman, L. 173, 180, 215
Holladay, W. L. 44, 50
Hommel, F. 54
Hopf, L. 20
Horbury, M. 111, 114
Horst, P. W. van der 68, 79
Horwitz, R. 221
Huehnergard, J. 71
Hughes, P. E. 151

Hulse, E. V. 55
Ilg, N. 136
Iser, W. 174
Ivry, S. 123
Jackson, J. 29
Jacobsen, T. 86
Jacobson, I. 213
James, M. R. 68, 149, 153, 155
Jansen, T. L. 92
Jaubert, A. 135
Jobling, D. 11, 14, 20, 28, 40
Johnson, M. D. 26
Kadushin, M. 173, 210
Kapelrud, A. S. 136
Karl, Z. 213
Kaufmann, Y. 63
Kautzsch, E. 150
Kee, H. C. 10, 102, 166
Keel, O. 44
Keester, C. R. 147
Kenyon, K. M. 6
Khazanov, A. 8
Kikawada, I. 29, 36
Kimmelman, R. .111, 171, 173, 175, 177, 183, 185, 189, 195, 211, 214
King, L. W. 54
Kinneavy, J. L. 174
Kinnier-Wilson, J. V. 60
Kirschenbaum, E. 155
Klopfenstein, M. 22
Knapp, A. B. 22
Knauf, E. A. 19, 21, 22
Knibb, M. A. 68, 149, 156
Knierim, R. 5, 15, 20
Knight, D. A. 20, 41
Knowles, M. P. 46
Koelb, C. 173
Kraft, R. A. 67
Kramer, C. 8
Kramer, J. L. 194
Kramer, S. N. 58
Kraeling, C. 152
Kraus, F.-J. 84

Kraus, S. 121
Kugel, J. 162
Kuhn, K. H. 148, 157
Kuntz, K. K. 31
LaBianca, O. 11
Lamberg-Karlovsky, C. C. 3, 16, 18
Lambert, W. A. 56, 58
Lambert, W. G. 83, 84
Landau, A. 213
Landsberger, B. 133
Lane, W. L. 150
Langdon, S. 57
Lapide, P. 103
Leclercq, H. 155
Lee, T. R. 92
LeFerre, P. 83
Lemche, N. P. 10, 22
LeRoi-Gourhan, A. 17, 18
Levenson, J. 31, 32, 37, 41, 162
Levine, B. 63
Levine, L. 105, 166
Levy, E. 173, 180, 181, 195, 212
Levy, J. 56
Levy, T. E. 10
Liber, M. 178, 201
Liberman, S. 121, 173, 177, 180, 189, 216
Lichtheim, M. 83, 90
Lidzbarski, M. 52
Liebreich, J. 181, 210
Liver, J. 196
Lohfink, N. 135, 137
Lohse, E. 104
Long, B. O. 31
Loretz, O. 49
Lovin, R. W. 41
Luger, Y. 171, 184-186, 196, 207, 213
Machinist, P. B. ix
Mack, B. M. 93, 161
Maher, N. 175
Maier, J. 172
Mallowan, M. E. L. 60

Index

Mann, J. 179, 180, 188, 197, 202, 206, 208, 213, 215
Mansoor, M. 100
Marböck, H. 84, 93, 96
Marcus, G. 14
Marcus, J. 125
Margalit, J. 47
Margoulies, M. 177, 214
Marmonstein, A. 187, 191, 193, 194, 211
Mason, S. 99, 107, 113
Mattingly, G. L. 11, 22
McGhee, M. C. 31
McKane, W. 82
McKenzie, J. L. 55
McNamara, M. 53
Meier, J. P. 170
Mendes-Flohr, P. 225
Meyer, R. 52
Meyers, C. 14, 23
Meyers, E. 23
Michel, O. 150, 151
Middendorp, T. 94
Milgrom, J. 69, 77, 186, 189
Milik, J. T. 51-53, 117, 118, 122
Miller, J. M. 11, 18, 20-22
Miller, P. D. 179, 211
Mirsky, S. 178, 179
Moffatt, J. 150, 151
Moore, G. F. 72
Moore, R. D. 88
Moran, W. L. 50, 57
Morris, L. 115
Mowinckel, S. 84
Na'aman, N. 44
Naveh, J. 114
Neeman, P. 69
Negoita, A. 154
Nestle, E. 155
Neusner, J. 63, 143, 152, 154, 164, 180
Neuss, W. 149, 150
Newsom, C. 89

Nickelsburg, G. W. E. 197
Nitzan, B. 189
Noth, M. 18, 74
Nougayrol, J. 58, 59
O'Connor, M. P. 40
Oden, R. A. 20, 31, 62
Oesterley, W. O. E. 94
Olbrechts-Tyteca, L. 38
Olyan, S. M. 47, 62, 93, 99
Oppenheim, A. L. 58
Oster, R. 101
Peake, A. S. 62
Perdue, L. G. 58
Perelman, C. 38
Petries, W. M. F. 4
Petuchowski, J. 206
Philonekko, M. 67, 68
Pinski, V. 14
Pognan, H. 56
Pomykala, E. 195
Pope, M. 69
Prewitt, T. J. 26
Preucel, R. W. 14
Qimron, E. 116, 120, 121, 125
Quell, G. 135
Quinn, A. 29, 36
Rabin, C. 119, 173
Rachmani, L. Y. 105
Rad, G. von 20
Radday, Y. T. 30, 35
Rafael, Y. 178
Rathje, W. J. 17, 18
Ratner, R. 45
Rawlings, H. C. 54
Reau, L. 155
Rendsburg, G. A. 26
Rendtorff, R. 15, 18, 20
Renner, J. T. E. 32
Rennaud, B. 26
Renov, I. 103, 104, 105
Riessler, D. 54
Ricouer, P. 12
Robinson, E. 3

Robinson, H. W. 151
Rofe, A. 46
Rogerson, J. W. 10
Rollsten, C. A. 93
Rosenthal, E. S. 209
Rostovtzeff, M. I. 152
Roth, C. 127
Rowley, H. H. 62
Russell, D. S. 152
Safrai, S. 213
Saldarini, A. 103
Sanders, E. P. 113
Sanders, J. A. .... x, 14, 164, 167
Sanders, J. E. 121
Sandmel, S. .... ix, 129
Santos, A. de 156
Sarason, R. 172, 183
Sarna, N. M. 75
Satran, D. 153
Sauer, G. 88, 89
Schäfer, P. 111, 207
Schaller, B. 67, 69, 75, 79
Schechter, A. J. 179
Schechter, S. 119, 128
Schermann, T. 152
Schiel, V. 57
Schiffer, M. B. 6
Schiffman, L. H. 128, 197
Schneemacher, W. 156
Schoeps, H. J. 150, 151, 157
Scholem, G. 193
Schrader, E. 55
Schürer, E. 101, 173, 194, 195
Schwartz, D. R. 144
Schwartzchild, S. S. 196
Scult, A. 31
Sed-Kajna, G. 152
Segal, A. 137
Seters, J. van 20, 26, 35, 36
Shanks, H. 14
Sharvit, S. 215
Shay, T. 23
Sheppard, G. T. 11, 14, 20
Shinnon, A. 104
Shore, H. 30
Silberman, L. H. .. ix, x, 1, 25, 26, 43,
     51, 69, 165, 166, 170
Skarsaune, O. 111
Shenhan, P. W. 96, 121, 194
Smith, M. S. 49
Smith, W. R. 7
Soden, W. von 54
Soggin, J. A. 18
Sonne, I. 197
Sperber, D. 104
Spick, C. 150, 151
Spittler, R. P. 67, 68
Stager, L. E. 22, 23
Steck, O. 157
Steinberg, N. 26-29, 36
Steinkeller, P. 71, 79
Steirt, F.-J. 82
Stone, M. E. 155, 157, 197
Strugnell, J. 120
Studer, G. L. 72
Sukenik, E. L. 105, 122
Susskind, A. 210
Sussman, Y. 128
Tadmor, H. 56, 57
Tanberg, K. A. 48
Talmon, S. ... 117, 119, 125, 127, 128,
     130, 133, 135, 138, 140, 142, 143,
     169
Tengström, S. 27
Terrien, S. 88
Thiele, C. P. 117
Thompson, L. 30, 36
Thompson, R. C. 60
Thompson, T. L.5, 19-22, 26, 32, 33,
     35, 36, 39, 40
Thornton, T. G. G. 112
Tigay, J. 60
Tilley, C. 14
Trigger, B. G. 3
Tribble, P. 28, 31
Tushingham, A. D. 126

Twersky, I. 194
Ulrich, E. 121, 186, 198
Urbach, E. E. 69, 135, 144
Urman, D. 102
Vanderkam, C. 117, 128
Vanhoye, A. 151
Vaux, R. de 62
Vermes, G. 115
Vogt, E. 52
Wachholder, B. Z. 193
Wagner, S. 52
Wallace, H. N. 28
Walsh, J. T. 28
Waskow, A. 33
Watson, W. G. E. 44
Webb, B. G. 39
Weinfeld, M. 61, 135, 182, 190,
                          193, 195, 209, 216
Weinstock, M. 217
Weiss, H.-F. 151
Wellhausen, J. 48
Wendel, A. 84
Wenham, G. 28, 29, 35
Westermann, C. 26, 32, 33, 36, 37
Whitelam, K. W. 10, 22
Wieder, N. 197, 204, 208, 212
Wilson, R. McL. 149, 156
Wilson, R. R. 10, 26
Wiseman, D. J. 58
Wölfin, W. 123
Wöllner, W. 173
Woude, A. S. van der 52, 141
Wright, G. E. 10, 20
Wuellner, W. 38
Wylie, A. 14
Yadin, Y. 116, 118
Yaqar, J. 188, 203, 206, 211, 213
Yardeni, A. 123
Yaron, R. 77
Yawitz, Z. 178, 195
Zeit, S. 194
Zevit, Z. 45, 48, 49
Zias, J. 55

Zucker, M. 210
Zünz, L. 179, 181

Places

Assyria 58
Babylon 53, 58
Chicago 7
Gezer 6
Jericho 6
Jerusalem 13
Judah 6
Kh. el-Oôm 47
Kuntillet, Ajrud 47, 49
Lachish 47
Larsa 57
Massada 7
Megiddo 7
Qumran 115-145
Shechem 6
Teima 57
Ur 54, 57, 58

**Biblical Books
(with the Apocrypha)**

Genesis
1-12 .... 25-26, 38, 39, 40, 41
1:1-2:3 31
1:22 31
1:28 31
1:29 32
2:1-3 31
2:4-3:24 .... 28, 32, 34
2:5 40
2:7 32
2:8 32
2:9 33
3:1-7 28
3:6 33
3:21 32
3:22-23 33
4:1-16 40
4:2 28

Reference	Page
4:3-7	28
4:4-5	33, 40
4:6-7	33
4:8-15	28
4:9	33
4:11	33
5:3	35
5:4	40
5:24	35
5:32	29
6:1-4	29
6:5-7	34
6:18	34
6:19	34
6:19-20	78
7:2-3	78
8:1	29, 34
8:21	34
9:1	34
9:2	34
9:4-6	34
9:8-17	34
9:20-27	29
9:20-23	34
9:25-27	34
9:28-29	29
11:1-9	29
11:11	40
11:27	35, 36
11:29	36
11:30	36
11:31	37
12-50	30
12:2-3	37
12:10-13:1	37
14:19	200
15:1	200, 201
15:6	225, 226, 227
23:6	77
25:6	77
40:20	77
49:24	46

Exodus

Reference	Page
1:7	205
3:6	199
3:15-16	199, 200
6:5	202
7:19	45
15:1-19	214
24:7	221
33:19	33
34:6-7	87

Leviticus

Reference	Page
1:4	190
13:18-23	54
19:7	190
20:22-26	40
26:42	202
26:45	200

Numbers

Reference	Page
6:24-26	212
24:17	96
26:33	70
26:53	72
27:1-11	70
27:2	74
27:3-4	76
27:4	71
27:7	71, 73
34:2	72
36	70

Deuteronomy

Reference	Page
4:28	45
6:25	223, 225
7:9	206
10:17	200
11:13	180
21:15-17	70
26:7	199
28:36	45
28:64	45
28:69-32:47	137
32:3	46

Index

32:4-5 46
32:31 46
32:30 46
32:6 87
32:37 46
33:29 .... 200, 201

Joshua
2:17, 20 43
8:30-35 137
13:6 72
17:3-4 .... 70, 71
17:4 74
18:1 72
19:1, 9 70
19:49 72
23:1-24:36 137
23:4 72

1 Samuel
2:1-10 186
2:6 206

2 Samuel
7:14 .... 50, 87
22:3 201
22:31 201
22:36 201
8:17 141
20:25-26 141

1 Kings
4:2-5 141
8:34-36 187
12:7 48
17:1 61
18:1-16, 41-46 ...... 61, 63, 64, 65
18:1 .... 72, 73
18:2-6 61
18:4 157
18:39 61
18:40 .... 61, 157
18:41 61
18:44 61
18:45 61
19:1 .... 64, 157
19:2 64
19:10 .... 150, 157

2 Kings
5:7 205
8:1 205
19:18 45
20:1-11 54
21:16 149
22 141
23 .... 22, 141

Isaiah
1:3 45
1:27 .... 224, 225
6:3 207
6:10 186
6:13 138
26:2 219
26:4 46
26:17-19 204
26:19 203
29:3 44
30:7 148
33:22 .... 200, 209
35:6 192
35:10 .... 192, 197
38:1-22 54
38:19 211
41:14 208
43:3 208
43:14 208
44:6-20 65
44:22 188
45:22-23 .... 65, 211
45:23 212
47:4 208
48:17 208
49:7 .... 206, 208
52:8 209
54:6 208
57:7 190
57:15 .... 205, 208

63:7 200
63:7-9 202
63:7-19 215
63:16 .... 87, 200, 202
64:8 87
65:3 198
65:24 .... 197, 198
66:7-9 204

Jeremiah
2:8 47
2:23 47
2:26-27 .... 43, 44, 45, 47, 47, 50
2:28 47
3:4 87
3:19 87
7:9 47
7:16 91
8:22 192
9:13 47
10:6 208
12:16 47
14:8 200
17:25 197
25:11-13 138
26:23 151
29:10 138
30:17 192
31 136
37 152
43:4-7 148
44:14 148

Ezekiel
3:12 207
4:4-6 .... 136, 139
20:9 200
20:32 45
37 .... 152, 205
38:23 208
45:1 72
47:22-23 72
47:22 73

Hosea
14:8 205
14:9 .... 47, 48, 49, 50

Amos
6:11 44

Micah
4:11 209

Habakkuk
3:17 160
5:17-18 160

Haggai
1:2 138
2:15-23 139
2:20-23 140

Zechariah
1:12 .... 138, 139
1:13-17 140
1:15 209
3 141
3:8 195
4:11-14 141
6:9-15 141
6:12 195
8:1-17 140
14:9 208

Malachi
1:6 87
2:10 87

Psalms
2:7 .... 49, 50
5 229
18:3 46
18:31 201
18:36 201
19:15 .... 216, 217
20:2 216
23 229
27:1 188
28:1 46

29:11	214
30:11	200
31:3	46
34:23	187
41:5	187
50:14	90
51:16	217
51:17	216, 217
51:18f.	217
54:6	200
60:7	217
65:3	211
67	211
68:5	87
78:35	200
89:27	50, 87
92:3	44
95:1	46
100:1	211
103	178, 186
103:3	204
106:45	200
111:9	208
119:153-54	191
130:8	187
136:25	203
144:1	46
145	212
145:10	209
145:14	204
146:7	204
146:10	207

Job

2:7-8	54
13:20-21	88
15:4	91
22:27	91
33:26	91
38:3	79
40:7	79
42-53	68
42:8	91
42:10	91
42:13-15	69, 71
42:15	70, 73, 75
42:16	73

Proverbs

1-9	89
7:14	90
8:22-31	88
15:8	90
15:29	90
16:16-17	91
17:1	90
17:2	72, 74
21:3	90
21:15	91
21:27	90
28:9	90
30:1-14	83, 88, 89
30:7-9	89

Song of Songs/Canticles

5:9	43

Qohelet/Ecclesiastes

5:1	92

Daniel

3:31-4:34	53, 54, 55, 61, 64
4:33	54
4:34	54
5	65
5:2	54
5:11	554
5:13	54
5:18-23	54
5:4	53
5:23	53
6:11	176
7:27	197
9:2	138
12:2	205

Ezra

1:1	138

7:27 199
9:2 138

Nehemiah
9:2 138
9:26 157
9:29 188
9:32 200

1 Chronicles
18:16 141

2 Chronicles
17:1-9 141
20:6 199
21:3 77
24:4-14 141
24:20 141
24:22 141
26:16-19 141
28:8-15 169
29-31 141
29:28-29 213
30:18 211
33:15-16 141
34-35 141
36:21-22 138

1 Maccabees
7:41-47 215

2 Maccabees
2:23 204
7:9 206
15:22 215

3 Maccabees
2:2-20 214
2:4-8 215
6:4-8 215

Sirach
4:6 92
7:10 93
15:9-10 93
17:25-26 93

18:15 94
18:30-31 94
21:1 93
21:5 92
22:27-23:6 .... 84, 93, 94
23:1, 4 .... 87, 94
23:7-15 95
23:19 95
23:27 .... 94, 95
28:2-4 93
33:20-24 77
34:26 93
34:24-26 93
35:13-18 92
36 201
36:1-22 95-96
37:15 93
38:9 92
38:14 93
38:15 93
39:1-6 93
42:15-43:33 93
44:1-50:24 93
50:17 213
50:21 213
51:12ff 194

Tobit
13:4 87

Matthew
4:23 102
6:2 106
6:5 .... 106, 107
9:35 102
10:17 .... 102, 107
11:1 102
12:2 102
12:9-14 102
13:54 102
15:1-7 110
19:17 211
23:2 .... 103, 105
23:6-7 .... 105, 106, 110

Index

23:16-22 108
23:34 .... 102, 107

Mark

1:23 103
1:39 .... 103, 107
7:1-6 110
10:18 211
12:38-39 .... 105, 106

Luke

5:17 110
6:6 102
7:5 101
11:43 .... 105, 106
11:49 107
12:11 107
18:19 211
20:46 .... 105, 106
21:12 107

John

1:19 109
1:24 109
3:1 .... 109, 113
7:32 109
7:35 109
7:48 109
9:13-17 109
9:22 109
12:42 .... 102, 108, 109
16:2 109

Acts

21:23-26 108

Romans

3:21 226

Philippians

2:12-13 168
3:5-6 226

Hebrews

11:37 .... 147, 150, 155, 158

Apocryphal and Pseudepigraphical Texts

Ahiqar

14-15 94

2 Baruch

10:1-3 148

4 Baruch (Paraleipomena Jeremiou)

3:15 148
4:6 148
5:17-19 148
6:11 148
6:19 148
6:24 148
7:5-37 148
8:1-3 148
9:21-32 149

Testament of Job

45:1-46:2 75
46:1-2 .... 76, 78
46:3 76
46:5 76
46:8 76
47:5-6 76
47:7-10 76
48:1-52:6 78
52:1-2 78

Dead Sea Scrolls

CD

I,2-8 138
I,9-10 139
I,11 139
I,12-13 140
II,11-12 137
II,14-III,20 136
VIII,29 136
VII,35 136
XX,1 126
XX,14 126

XX,32 126
1QH
   I,8-9 125
   I,11-12 125
   II,22-23 125
   II,25-26 125
   III,22 125
   V,20 125
   VI,3-6 191
   IX,2 125
   XI,8 125
1QpHab 120
   II,3 136
1QM 119
1QS 119
1QS^a
   I,1-5 119
3Q15 122
4QFlor 195
4QMMT 120, 127, 138, 142,
                        143, 144, 196
4QPrNab 52ff, 60ff
4Q285 195
4Q403, 1.i.2-3 207
4Q521, II,8 204
11QTemple^a 116, 120

www.ingramcontent.com/pod-product-compliance
Lightning Source LLC
Chambersburg PA
CBHW032021230426
43671CB00005B/156